PASSAGES FROM THE DIARIES OF MRS. PHILIP LYBBE POWYS
OF HARDWICK HOUSE, OXON.

A.D. 1756 TO 1808

EDITED BY

EMILY J. CLIMENSON

" To Nature in my earliest youth,
I vowed my constancy and truth ;
Wherein lie HARDWICK'S much loved shade,
Enamoured of her charms I strayed,
And as I roved the woods among,
Her praise in lisping numbers sung."

DEAN POWYS.

WITH A PORTRAIT

1899

To

My dear friends, the Elder Branch of the
Lybbe Powys, of Hardwick,

I dedicate this effort of pleasing toil in collating
and noting, the interesting Diaries of their
clever and charming ancestress.

EMILY J. CLIMENSON.

SHIPLAKE VICARAGE,
March 1899.

INTRODUCTION

The following extracts from the diaries and travelling journals of Mrs. Philip Lybbe Powys, *née* Caroline Girle, ranging from A.D. 1756 to 1808, present such an accurate picture of life, manners, and customs of the upper class of that period, that though my work of collating, noting, and linking together the many, some twenty books, lent to me by various members of the family, was chiefly undertaken on their account, I feel that they cannot fail to interest the general reader, containing as they do such interesting anecdotes of royalty, and other notable people, descriptions of country seats, places, towns, manufactures, amusements, and general habits of the period which now form history, and that, comparatively little studied; for the immediate century beyond our own days, I fancy, is more often ignored, and less understood, than the more distant periods of time, at whatever period we live. My heroine was the daughter of John Girle, Esq., described of Lincoln's-Inn-Fields,[1] M.D. He

---

[1] Mr. Girle built this house. His daughter states, "We went into the house my father built in Lincoln's-Inn-Fields, September 14, 1754."

owned estates at Beenham, Bucklebury, Padworth,
and Ufton, in Berkshire. He married in 1734
Barbara, third daughter, and co-heiress, of John
Slaney, Esq., of Yardley and Lulsley, Worcestershire; their only child, Caroline, was born on December 27, St. John's Day, 1738, *old style*, but in
new style, January 7, 1739. Her father, Mr. Girle,
had two sisters: Jane, married to Benjamin Bagley,
Esq.; the other, Elizabeth, in 1745, to William Mount,
Esq., of Wasing Place, Berks, as his second wife.
Mrs. Girle had also two sisters: one, Sarah, married
William Goldborough, Esq.; the other, Mary, married
to — Hussey, Esq.

The arms of Girle quartered with Slaney are:
Girle, crest, a gerbe or sheaf of wheat; arms, gules,
on a cross engraved or, a pellet; Slaney, gules, a bend
or between three martlets. The present head of the
Slaney family is Colonel William St. Kenyon Slaney,
of Hatton Grange, Shifnal, Salop. The Slaneys are
of a very ancient family; Adolphus de Slainie or
Slane, is supposed to have come to England from
Bohemia in the Empress Maud's train. The Slaney
motto is " Deo duce comite industria."

Of Caroline Girle's early youth I can find out little,
but that her parents must have been most sedulous in
cultivating her bright mind, in fostering her powers

of memory, observation, and general intelligence, will
be obvious from the following pages.

In Beenham Church, Berks, in the belfry, is a tablet
to the memory of John Girle, which tells us all that
can now be found out about him :—

"This monument was erected by Mrs. Girle in
memory of her deceased husband, John Girle, Esquire,
late of Lincoln's-Inn-Fields, London, Surgeon, who
having early in life acquired an ample fortune, the just
reward of superior eminence, and unremitting diligence
in his profession, indulged himself in the pleasing prospect of dedicating the remainder of his days to the
noblest purpose of humanity, the relief of the distresses,
and infirmities, of his indigent fellow-creatures, an office
which the goodness of his heart made him ever under-
take with readiness, and which the skill of his hand
enabled him generally to execute with success.   But
this pious purpose was broken off by his death, which
happened July 5th, 1761, in the 59th year of his age.
He married the daughter of John Slaney, of Worcestershire, by whom he left an only daughter, married to
Philip Lybbe Powys, Esquire, of Hardwick, Oxon."

In the burial register it states :—

"John Girle, Esq., of Lincoln's-Inn-Fields, Middle-
sex, buried July 13, 1761."   "Affidavit made according
to Act Woollen."

This was an Act of Charles II., to promote the

wool industry, which ordered that every corpse should be buried entirely in woollen material, even the coffin lined with same. This Act became gradually less and less enforced, but was not actually repealed till 1815 !

"On January 14th, 1801, Barbara, widow of John Girle, aged 86, from Henley, Oxon." His widow, therefore, survived him forty years.

The following journal of Caroline Girle, kept by desire of her father, is the first MSS. of our heroine. The spelling and wording is very old fashioned, but I have adhered to the actual text, which, as time goes on, the reader will perceive gradually forms into a more modern style.

PASSAGES

FROM THE DIARIES OF

MRS. PHILIP LYBBE POWYS

NORFOLK JOURNAL

1756

WHEN we went with Mr. Jackson's family into Nor- 1756
folk, my father, not being of our party, desired me
to write him an account of our tour, and to be particular in my description of places or things that
might give me entertainment. From those letters
I collected the following concise journal; if any one
chuses to peruse it, I've only to call their friendship
to my aid, which, like affection in a parent, ever
draws a veil over errors unintended.

Mr. Jackson having been ill the former part of
this summer, we did not set out till the 1st of September, but the weather being delightful, and that, a
peculiar pleasure in travelling, we regretted not that
the autumn was now approaching; a happy chear-
fulness reigned uninterrupted in our little society,
consisting of Mr. and Miss Jackson, my mother, and
self, in one coach, young Mr Jackson on horseback.
and their other coach follow'd with servants. We

1756 breakfasted at Epping, and then I believe had almost got clear of that smoaky fogg which for some miles intails itself on the Metropolis. Mr. Jackson being still an invalid, we went no further that night than Hockerill, a bad town in the county of Hertfordshire, which itself is woody and pretty. We passed Thorley Hall, formerly a seat of Mr. Raper's,[1] whose woods, cut into fine walks, are greatly admired. I remember thinking it a charming place, but one is naturally partial to the spots where one has passed our child-hood, and I used to be there every summer. The next day we breakfasted at Chesterford and dined at Newmarket, famous, I believe, for nothing but the races twice a year near it. From leaving this town the face of the country is quite changed ; before, our views were excessively limited, now quite un-confined, though far from pleasing, as for twenty miles you go over the heath of Newmarket. Lay at Barton Mills, and when we set out the follow-ing morning, having lost sight of the village, we came on those well-known dismal Brand Sands, in the county of Suffolk, where for thirteen miles you have not literally one tree, no verdure, nothing animate or inanimate, to divert your eye from the barren soil. It is indeed a dismal spot in its present state. I was just reading an account where 'tis said it was once a fine fertile country, but, by an amazing high wind, these horrid sands were blown over from the fens of Lincolnshire. A marvellous event, no doubt, and were I unfortunate enough to reside near there, I should certainly pray for a contrary, just of

---

[1] Who left it to his nephew, Sir John Grant of Rothiemurchus, who sold it to Lord Ellenborough in 1807. Rapers, an old Buckinghamshire family, of Norman descent.

equal velocity, to convey them back to their original 1756
home. From this account it will easily be believed
the sight of the town of Brand was a most pleasing
one ; not but we had books, a pack of cards, to amuse
the old gentleman when he liked it, and I think two
or three rubbers of whist was played in these thirteen
dull miles. At Brand we breakfasted, and regained
the life and spirits we seemed to have lost from our
former slow motion, for to make the road still more
intolerable, one's animals were obliged to a creeping
pace for the whole way, but in a few miles of our
evening's journey we had an agreeable contrast, and,
to express myself in a style as much elevated as
ourselves, we once more beheld the several beauties
of the vegetable world, and were again saluted by
the winged songsters ; in short, every object appeared
a wonderful phenomenon. We dined at Swaffham,
in Norfolk, nine miles only from Mr. Jackson's. We
staid there some hours, and got to Wesenham Hall
early in the evening, not too dark but that I could
see the situation was pleasing. The house modern
and elegant, with every convenience to give it the
title of a good one (for, tho' you[1] are not unacquainted
with it, my journal would be deficient if without this
description). It stands in a pretty park, beyond that
a heath, which they have planted promiscuously with
clumps of firs. Beyond that the country rises to the
view. On one side lay the grove and gardens, and
behind the village, than which nothing can be in a
more rural taste. According to annual custom, the
Vicar, and his wife, and near tenants, were at the
hall ready to receive us. You know, my dear sir, the
hospitable manner Mr. Jackson always lives in, and

[1] Meaning Mr. Girle, her father.

1756 will not wonder at the joy expressed on his arrival. Never did landlord seem more beloved, or indeed deserve to be so, for he is a most worthy man, and in however high a stile a man lives in in town, which he certainly does, real benevolence is more distinguishable in a family at their country-seat, and none do more good than that where we now are. Then everything here is regularity itself, but the master's method is, I take it, now become the method of the servants by *use* as well as choice. Nothing but death ever makes a servant leave them. The old housekeeper has now been there one-and-fifty years ; the butler two- or three-and-thirty ; poor Mrs. Jackson's maid, now Miss Jackson's, twenty-four, having been married to one of the footmen (their daughter is grown up, and is one of the housemaids). Mrs. Bridges, (*née* Jackson), when she married, took her servant with her, but 'tis really a pleasure to see them all so happy. I was surprised to see them all, except on Sundays, in green stuff gowns, and on my inquiring of Miss Jackson how they all happened to fix so on one particular colour, she told me a green camblet for a gown used for many years to be an annual present of her mother's to those servants who behaved well, and had been so many years in her family, and that now indeed, as they all behaved well, and had lived there much longer than the limited term, this was constantly their old master's New Year gift. I thought this in Mr. Jackson a pretty compliment to his lady's memory, as well as testimony of the domestics still deserving of his good opinion. They seem to have a vast deal of company, but my mother says not half they used to have in Mrs. Jackson's lifetime, when the Orford, Leicester, and Townsend

families and theirs, used to meet almost every week
at each other's houses, but then indeed there was
young people at each, which generally makes a lively
neighbourhood.

Lord Townsend is not now down at Rainham,[1]
which is very near here, nor are the Leicesters at
Holkham. Lord Orford was here the other day,
and yesterday we had Mr. and Mrs. Lee Warner of
Walsingham,[2] and their three sons to dinner, a Mr.
Spilman too, whose new odd house we are soon to go
and see. On Sundays the tenants dine here in turn,
and always the clergyman and his wife, a good kind
of ordinary couple. The church is indeed superior
to the preaching; but Norfolk is remarkable for fine
churches. This at Weasenham has two aisles, and
really one is amazed at its appearance,—has been built
about seven hundred years. The Vicarage-house I
cannot say is answerable, for in my life I never saw
one so very despicable; 'tis literally a poor cottage,
and even thatched. We have now a Captain Hambleton,[3] and a Mr. Host here, and Mr. and Mrs. Carr
and family dine with us to-morrow. Mr. Jackson's
friends are so kind to come to him, though he tells
them his health won't permit him to return their visits
this summer. You know how he loves company at
home, especially when he can have so good a plea as
at present for not having the fuss of dining out, as he
styles it. If twenty people came in as we were sitting
down to table, his dinners are so good they would

---

[1] Rainham Hall, erected by Inigo Jones, 1630; enlarged by Viscount
Townsend, Secretary of State to George I. and II.

[2] Walsingham Priory, once famous for its shrine of the Virgin; an
object of pilgrimage.

[3] Probably Hamilton, as through the Memoirs Hamilton is constantly
so spelled.

1756 need no alteration; but the larder is really quite a
sight, and different from any I ever saw. 'Tis a
large good room they had built on purpose, in an
open green court, by the kitchen-garden, with every
possible convenience; and I believe always full of
everything in season, and the old gentleman often
makes us walk there after breakfast that we may all,
as he says, have what we like for dinner. The venison
and game now in it is astonishing. The Norfolk
mutton, too, you know, is famous; but theirs particularly so. They kill all their own, and never eat it in the
parlour under three weeks, but in their larder it might
keep six, they say. We went the other day to see
Houghton Hall,[1] the seat of Lord Orford, about seven
miles from hence; the building is stone, and stands in
a park of a thousand acres. Its outside has rather too
heavy an appearance, on the in, the fitting up and
furniture very superb; and the cornishes and mould-
ings of all the apartments being gilt, it makes the
whole what I call magnificently glaringly, more
especially as the rooms are, instead of white, painted
dark green olive; but this most likely will be soon
altered. The body of the house consists of sixteen
rooms on a floor, besides two large wings, the one
offices, the other, the famed picture gallery, seventy-
five feet in length. 'Tis impossible to conceive how
strikingly fine this gallery of paintings[2] is, far indeed
beyond my describing, for I can't even describe one
quarter of the pleasure I had in viewing them; but

[1] Houghton Hall, built by Sir Robert Walpole between 1722-38,
from designs by Colin Campbell. Belongs now to Marquis of Cholmon-
deley by inheritance.
[2] This famous gallery, sold by George, third Earl Orford, in 1779, to
the Empress Catherine of Russia, to the annoyance of his family and the
loss of the nation.

yet I am sure you can guess, knowing what an en- thusiastic daughter yours is when pictures are the subject; but this Lord's is, I believe, esteemed the best collection we have in England. I shall bring you home a catalogue, as I've taken the pains to copy a written one the late Lord gave to Mr. Jackson; every room indeed is adorn'd by them, so that altogether Houghton is exceedingly well worth seeing.

Since my last letter we have had company every day to dinner, as Sir William Turner and gentlemen that were with him; another day Sir Harry and Lady Lestrange, Captain Wilson, &c. ; a third, the Croft family. One morning we went to pay a droll visit to see an odd house, of a still odder Mr. Spilman I before mentioned, a most strange old bachelor of vast fortune, but indeed I'll not fall in love with him. We were introduced to him in the library, where he seemed deep in study (for they say he is really clever), sitting in a jockey-cap and white stiff dog's gloves. I think I never shall forget his figure at that instant; but I must, in order to give you that of his house, equally out of the common style as himself, but to see the man one no longer wonders at the oddity of the edifice he has just finished. 'Tis in a large park, its form the half H. You ascend a flight of twenty-one steps, which, as they don't spread out as usual towards the bottom, seems as if you were mounting a perpendicular staircase; you enter a hall, striking from its strange dimensions, being five cubes of eighteen feet, so it's ninety feet long by eighteen! and might rather be termed a gallery. Besides this (as 'tis only one floor and no staircase), there is a saloon, library, two parlours, and three bed-chambers, all the offices and

1756 servants' rooms are underground. The chimney-
pieces, tables, &c., are of green marble from Sweden;
all the doors solid walnut-tree, off the estate, and
every room paved with Ketton stone. This, as we
ventured to tell him, we thought too cool, but his
reply was, "I never catch colds"; indeed, we might
suppose from his looks that he was not like other
mortals; in short 'tis impossible to innumerate each
oddity throughout the place, so that I shall not
attempt it. . . . We have had Dr. and Mrs.
Hammond here; he is one of the Prebends of
Norwich, and a nephew of Lord Orford's, she a
niece of Lord Walpole's. I had heard young Jackson, who, you know, is particularly clever himself,
talk much of the understanding, and ready wit of
this lady. She is indeed amazingly sensible, and
many lively conversations have pass'd between those
two, to our very high entertainment. We have had
Sir Wm. Harbord here for some days. Sir William,
and all the families I've mentioned as visiting here,
most obligingly insisted on seeing us at each of their
houses, but as we could not at this season go and
return at night to the more distant ones, and could
not go to some without returning all, we declined
at once all these obliging invitations; indeed, as we
came down now merely to keep the old gentleman
company, it would have been cruel to have left him
so many days by himself; he would make us go
one morning tho' to see Lord Leicester's; to this
we consented, tho' eighteen miles off; as we had
heard so much of this place we could not quit Norfolk, which we now talked of, in a few days without
going there; so last Friday we set out very early
in the morning, ordering dinner later than usual.

The name of the magnificent seat is Holkham ;[1] two 1756
miles before you come to the house is a grand
triumphal arch,[2] the rusticated ornaments of which
are very fine ; from this you have the new plantations, which when grown will have a noble effect,
on each side for two miles, in front a grand obelisk,[3]
a church,[4] the numerous buildings in the grounds,
and the whole terminated by the sea, tho' that is
distant ; at the end of this avenue are two lodges.
And now entering the park, you have a view of a
stone building, esteemed the most elegant of its
kind in England. It has already been thirty years
begun, and is not yet completed ; but when that
era arrives it will be magnificent indeed ! It extends 380 feet in front, the grand hall is the height
of the house, which is fifty feet ; round it is a colo-
nade of alabaster pillars which give it a noble appearance. . . . Fronting you is three steps along a vast
way into the hall, which they call the Tribune. This
rise has a pretty effect ; from this you come into a
fine saloon, hung with crimson velvet, the cornishes
richly gilt, many capital pictures standing there to
be put up. On one side of the saloon is a dressing-
room, bed-chamber, and inner apartment, called the
Duke of Cumberland's, all to be hung with and
furnished as the saloon ; on the other side are the
same rooms, called the Duke of Bedford's, hung
and furnished with crimson damask. A gallery 120
feet long is of its kind the most superbly elegant

---

[1] Holkham, built by first Viscount Coke, afterwards Earl of Leicester ;
house built about 1744 ; architect, Kent.

[2] Arch designed by Wyattville.

[3] Obelisk eighty feet high ; first work erected in 1729.

[4] Of the fourteenth century with additions in fifteenth and sixteenth ;
dedicated to St. Withburga ; restored 1868, at cost of £10,000.

1756 I ever saw, but the whole house deserves that distinction. The gallery is painted a dead white, with
ornaments of gilding; at each end is an octagon,
the one fitted up as a library, the other with busts,
bronzes, and curiosities too numerous to mention.
This is the centre of the house, besides are four
wings; one contains all the offices in general, all
answerable to the rest; such an amazing large and
good kitchen I never saw, everything in it so nice
and clever; but I've heard Mr. Jackson talk of Lady
Leicester's great notability; they are there often, you
know, for a week together; she never misses going
round this wing every morning, and one day he
was walking by the windows, and saw her ladyship
in her kitchen at six o'clock (A.M.), thinking all her
guests safe in bed, I suppose. Her dairy is the
neatest place you can imagine, the whole marble;
in Norfolk they never skim their cream off, as in
other places, but let the milk run from it; these
things here are all too of marble, so that it all looks
so delicate, and the butter made into such pretty
patts hardly larger than a sixpence. The second
wing is called the Chapel wing, tho' that is not yet
built. The third is now finishing with grand sets
of apartments for the company they may have with
them; and in the fourth wing is the eating-room,
drawing-room, library, bed-chambers, dressing-rooms,
constantly used by Lord and Lady Leicester [1] themselves, and in a closet here of her ladyship's we
saw the miniature pictures of the family for a series
of years past, done by the best hands. In this little
cabinet, too, are a thousand curiosities of various

---

[1] Was Lady Mary Tufton, fourth daughter; co-heir of Thomas,
sixth Earl of Thanet.

kinds, among the pictures was their daughter-in- 1756
law, the beautiful Lady Mary Coke[1] and their son[2]
Lord Coke, who they had lately lost, to their inexpressible grief, being their only child. He and his
lady I think were far from being happy. The situation of Holkham I don't say much of; the grounds
indeed are laid out with taste, and everything done
that can be to strike the eye, but still it must boast
more of art than Nature's charms, and to me the
reverse is so much more pleasing; but indeed I do not
admire Norfolk's country; 'tis dreary, 'tis unpleasing;
in short, I wished a house like Lord Leicester's in
a spot more delightful, more answerable to itself.
We had a breakfast at Holkham in the genteelest
taste, with all kinds of cakes and fruit, placed un-
desired in an apartment we were to go through,
which, as the family were from home, I thought was
very clever in the housekeeper, for one is so often
asked by people whether one *chuses* chocolate, which
forbidding word puts (as intended), a negative on
the question. The roads being not very good, we
had made poor Mr. Jackson wait dinner some hours;
but as we expressed ourselves so pleased with our
morning's excursion he was happy. We found Captain
Hambleton with him. The next day Sir Harry and
Lady Lestrange came to dinner, and the following
ones we staid many came to take their leave of this
family before their return to town, as Dr. and Mrs.
Hammond, Mr. Host, Mrs. Langley, the Crofts, Mrs.
Rinks, and others. On Tuesday young Jackson is
to go to pay a visit to Sir Thomas Hare's[3] family,

[1] Lady Mary Campbell, daughter and co-heir of John, Duke of
Argyll and Greenwich.
[2] Edward, Viscount Coke, died S.P. 1753.
[3] Stowe Hall, near Downham.

1756 and meet us on Friday on the road at Hockerill. Saturday morning we are all to pay a visit to Mr. Jackson at Theobalds, and shall be in town to dinner about five, where we shall be most happy in seeing you after so long an absence, and I'm desired by the family not to forget that they insist on seeing you at their house at the time of our arrival. And now, my dear sir, I've given, as you desired, a sort of journal of our tour. You must pardon my many *mistakes*, as I think I may plead you are the author of them *all!* However, as apologies only would innumerate them, I shall say nothing more than that six weeks cannot be spent more agreeably than at Weasenham Hall, though the description might have been more entertaining from an abler pen than that of your ever obliged and dutiful,

CAROLINE GIRLE.

The counties went through were Essex, Hertford-shire, Cambridgeshire, Suffolk, Norfolk.

Towns we stopped at.	Distance from London.
Epping .	17 miles.
Hockerill	30 ,,
Chesterford .	45 ,,
Newmarket .	61 ,,
Brand .	79 ,,
Swaffham	95 ,,
Wesenham Hall	104 ,,

On our return through Chesterford in October, it was most exceedingly pretty to see all the fields covered with saffron, which, being in itself a beautiful purple and white flower like a crocus, it has a very pleasing effect. Mr. Jackson did tell me what the clergymen's tythe of saffron only came to in this parish, but I thought it, I remember, quite incredible.

Between the tour in Norfolk and the next journal 1757 of travel, the following extracts are taken from Miss Girle's dairy :—

March 14th, 1757.—Admiral Byng shot on board the *Monarque* at twelve at noon. From his walking out of the cabin to his being taken back dead, exceeded not two minutes. Happy that a scene so shocking could be so soon closed.

April 30th, 1757. — Went to see the Earl of Chesterfield's new house in South Audley Street. The whole very magnificent.

JOURNAL OF A TOUR INTO YORKSHIRE AND DERBYSHIRE

1757

In one of those delightful morns when Nature is decked in every pleasing ornament we quitted the tumultuous scene, left all the pomp and grandeur of the great Metropolis for prospects more serenely gay, blended with every elegant simplicity of rural charms. The variegated objects that now presented themselves to view were, as Milton finely expresses it—

> " Hill, dale, and shady woods, and sunny plains,
> And liquid copse of murmuring streams ; by these
> Creatures that liv'd, and woo'd, and walk'd, or flew,
> Birds on the branches warbling, all things smil'd
> With fragrance, and with joy my heart o'erflowed."

I've so great a partiality for the country that I could not help inserting here the above five lines of this celebrated author, in which he gives one so strong an idea of its several beauties, but I digress no longer, and resume the subject of our journey. In

1757 the county of Hertford, about twenty-four miles
from London, is a town called Hatfield. Our route
being before fixed, this was the place we proposed
to breakfast at. While there, travellers being generally desirous to view each object that is deemed
curious, we went to see a monument in the church
in memory of the first Earl of Salisbury, which we
were told was worth seeing. It was so, being of
statuary marble and kept extremely neat. Formerly
a royal palace added lustre to this town, at which
Edward VI. was brought up and educated. We that
day dined at Baldock,[1] drank tea at Eton[2] in Bed-
fordshire, and by eight in the evening got to Bug-
den[3] in Huntingdonshire; in the time necessary for
preparing supper we went to take an outside view of
an old palace now belonging to the Bishop of Lincoln.
It appears to have been a fine building, and place of
great security, by the height of its surrounding walls,
with a moat and drawbridge, to prevent at pleasure
any one's approach. After our walk we again returned
to our inn. The next morn we breakfasted at Stilton,[4]
and proposed taking Burleigh Hall in our way to
Stamford, tho' we feared obtaining a sight of it, the
present Lord having not long been in possession.
The whole was then repairing, and we had been told
he was not fond of strangers seeing it while it bore
so ruinous an appearance. However, we were more
fortunate than we expected, for as we were walking in

---

[1] A market-town fifteen miles north-west from Hertford.

[2] Eaton-Socon.

[3] Buckden, once a favourite residence of the Bishops of Lincoln ;
granted to them by Abbot of Ely, temp. Henry I.

[4] Stilton gave its name to the famous cheese, first made by Mrs.
Paulet of Wymondham, Leicestershire, who sold it to Cooper Thornhill
of the Bell Inn there : now made in Leicestershire.

the gardens, standing still on a nearer approach to 1757
the house (which seems almost of itself a little town),
Lord Exeter[1] happened to be overlooking his workmen, and reading, as I suppose, curiosity in our
countenances, politely asked if the ladies chose to
see it, our reply being in the affirmative, he himself
informed us where was the most easy entrance. The
rooms are spacious and lofty, the staircase grand,
which with many apartments, the late Earl's closet,
the ceilings, hall, chapel, &c., are all painted by Vario,[2]
whom his Lordship kept twelve years in his family,
wholly employ'd in them (allowing him a coach,
horses, servants, a table, and considerable pension).
The front towards the garden is the most ancient and
noble structure that can be imagined. Indeed, from
wherever you see it, the towers, pinnacles, and large
spire over the centre give it an air too grand to be
described by pen. The whole is of freestone. 'Twas
built by Sir William Cecil in the time of Elizabeth.
He was afterwards by her created Baron Burleigh.
There are many good pictures, but then not hung up
as intended to be. Having spent some time in seeing
Burleigh Hall, we proceeded on to Stamford, a town
in Northamptonshire, about a mile distant. We went
thro' part of Rutlandshire. That afternoon drank tea
at Colesworth,[3] and got to Grantham, in Lincolnshire,
that night. The next day, being Sunday, we propos'd staying at the above place till Monday morn.
The church[4] at Grantham (at which we were twice on
Sunday), is a Gothic structure deserving observation,
and would have made a very fine appearance, had they

[1] Brownlow, ninth Earl of Exeter.
[2] Antonio Verrio, celebrated painter, time of Charles II.
[3] Colsterworth ; Sir Isaac Newton born there.
[4] Dedicated to St. Wulfram; a church here before the Conquest.

1757 not concealed it from view by other buildings till one is within a few steps of the grand entrance. This for the honour of the town is rather unfortunate, as 'tis eclipsing its only beauty. In the evening we went to Belton House, the seat of Lady Cust. 'Tis nothing more than a good family house. Two things relative to it we were desired to remember, viz., that the original of sash windows was at the erecting of this edifice in Charles I.'s time; the second, that from a temple in the garden called Belle Mount you may see seven counties at once, a thing from one spot thought very remarkable. Having stayed pretty late at Belton, we only got back just at supper-time, and early next day quitted Grantham, breakfasted at Newark, Nottinghamshire, an ancient and neat town situated on the Trent; formerly, though now ruinous, there was a castle there, built by Alexander, Bishop of Lincoln.[1] We dined at Carlton, drank tea at Tadcaster.[2] From this place we had nine miles only to go before we reached a city so famous that our expectations had form'd an idea of a place that would almost equal the grand Metropolis; but, York, I must depreciate you so far as to give it as my opinion that by many degrees you merit not the title of the least resemblance. We entered its gates about seven in the evening, not an hour so late (at this season) as to give the city the dull aspect it then seem'd to wear; but we had a reason assigned to us for this, that I believe might be a just one, viz., that in summer all the principal inhabitants retire into the country. However to us it appeared a most indifferent town. 'Tis situated on the confluence of the Ouse and Foss rivers,

[1] Time of King Stephen.
[2] Ancient market-town in West Riding.

and reckon'd a wholsom and clear air. The streets (hardly deserving such an appellation), are extremely narrow, the houses seemingly very indifferent, and indeed the whole city, three things excepted (viz. the Cathedral, Castle, and Assembly Room), a perfect contrast to what we thought it had been. The Minster is indeed a building curiously magnificent. I think it surpasses, at least on the outside, Westminster Abbey. 'Twas rebuilt in the reign of Stephen, having been burnt down with the whole city before the Conquest. The carving in stone is excessively fine, and what with the solemnity of the structure, joined to that of the organ, which at our entrance was playing, I think I never experienced a more pleasing awful satisfaction than at the first view of this noble Cathedral. From hence we went to the Castle. 'Tis now a prison, and may be styl'd a grand one, the felons having a large place by day allotted for them in the open air, a liberty at other places they have not room to allow these wretches. We saw above forty then there. The sight of so many unhappy objects greatly depress'd us, tho', strange as it appeared, but one, of so great a number had a countenance even seemingly dejected, nor look'd as if they felt for themselves, what even our pity for their supposed distress made us experience. Having staid at the Castle a very short time, we went next to the Assembly Room, the third and last place worthy our notice. 'Tis in form an Egyptian Hall; its dimensions 112 feet by 40, and 30 in height; the seats crimson damask, and all the furniture quite in taste, and 'tis called the completest ball-room in England. By Wednesday noon we had gone over the renown'd city. It was, it seems, before

B

1757 it was burnt down almost four times as large as at
present. We quitted it about six on Wednesday
evening, proposing in our way to Malton that night
to see the seat of Lord Carlisle. Castle Howard[1] is
fifteen miles distant from York; the situation pleasing.
The house is of vast extent (340 feet), and makes a
fine appearance at the distance, but I think the rooms
in general too small, though in the wing now building there seems by the plan some fine apartments to
be intended. The whole is of stone, the furniture
is magnificent, and there are many curiosities that
my Lord[2] brought over with him fifteen years since
from Italy and other countries, such as pictures, busts,
figures of oriental alabaster, and above thirty different sorts of Egyptian marbles, with other things too
numerous to mention, as valuable as ornamental,
having a fine effect as one passes through the several
apartments. The house stands in a wood; the park
is a very fine one; in that is a grand mausoleum, but
it was unfortunately too late for our walking to it,
as the evening drew on before we had hardly seen the
house. We lay at Malton, five miles from thence, breakfasted next at Yettingham, and so on to Scarborough.
'Tis impossible to conceive a sweeter prospect than
one has of this town when at about half a mile distant. The ruins of a fine old castle on a prodigious
eminence forms a most pleasing point of view, the
town seemingly scatter'd on the brow of the same
hill to complete its beauty, and the sea at a small
distance terminates the whole. We got there about
two; after adapting our dress to that of a public place,

---

[1] Castle Howard, built about 1702 by Sir John Vanbrugh for Charles,
third Earl of Carlisle.

[2] Henry, fourth Earl of Carlisle.

call'd on some friends then there, who shew'd us the 1757
rooms, inform'd us of the customs of the place, and
made the short time we stay'd pass most agreeably.
In the evening we walked up to the Castle, but the
fogg was so great from the sea as totally to hinder
the extensive view they assured us the immense
height afforded. About a mile from the town is their
famous medicinal springs,[1] said to partake of the
different qualities of vitriol, alum, iron, nitre, and salt.
The company meet here before breakfast to drink the
waters. The next morning we were of the group in
this agreeable walk on the sands, though fatiguing
to invalids, as from the town one descends above a
hundred steps. At the Spaw is two rooms, one call'd
the gentleman's, the other the ladies', and a terrass
commanding a most delightful prospect. At our
return to our lodgings we found Mr. and Mrs.
Handley, but had their company only for that
evening, tho' some hopes of again meeting in Yorkshire. As we left Scarborough the following day,
lay at Whittwell, the morning after breakfasted at
York, dined at Ferry Bridge, where Mr. Pem. Milnes
and Miss Slater met us to conduct us to the house of
the former at Wakefield, the end of our intended tour
for the present, as we were there to meet our friend
Mrs. Hooper, and had promised to spend a month
with her in visiting her nieces, the two Mrs. Milnes.
She was got there a day or two before us, and we
arrived just as the family were sitting down to supper.
We had great pleasure in the meeting after a very
long absence, and spent our time most agreeably
during our stay, tho' we could have wished not quite

[1] There are two springs. They consist of carbonate and sulphates of
lime and magnesia, not *vitriol*.

1757 so much visiting as we were obliged to give way to.
A few days after we came, my father went with the
gentlemen to Lord Rockingham's, and returned vastly
pleased with his visit, which was two days, and with
Wentworth House. Another day they took him to
dine at Sir Roland Whin's. We went one day to
Westerton, Mr. Birt's, a gentleman of large fortune,
who has since bought and rebuilt in a superb manner
Wenvo Castle, in Glamorganshire—I hear a most
delightful spot. I cannot say as much for Westerton,
or village, surrounded by coal-yards ; but as sinking
these pits raised Wenvo Castle, neither Mr. Birt or
his family, I dare say, think them odious. We had
the curiosity to walk and take a near outside view of
one seventy yards deep. The manner they work
them is strange, and not a little dangerous, as they
are obliged to have candles, and sometimes with a
roof so low that the men dig on their knees. This
in a place where there is nothing but coal makes it
surprising there is not frequent accidents. They have
two boxes which are alternately pulled up and down
by pullies worked by a horse, which goes round and
round in a sort of a well. In short, the whole process is
curiously frightful, and yet Mr. Birt told us many ladies
even venture down the pits to see the entire manner
of it. This I think one should rather be excused.

At our return home that evening we were talking of the Moravians and the oddness of their worship, and Mr. Milnes, who most obligingly wished
us to see everything worth observation, told us
he really thought we should be entertained. To
see anything of their manner one must be there
on a Sunday, and the morrow being so, we agreed
for once, as we none of us usually travell'd on

Sunday, to make it a day of amusement—a thing 1757
always to be avoided, in my opinion, by people of
a station in life to make any day their own, and
I ever am surprised 'tis not thought rather vulgar
than fashionable by the great to make that day a
day of travelling, as it always is done, when 'tis the
only one the lowest traders can spare to take their
pleasure in.   Early the next morning we set out and
got to Pudsey [1] about ten.   The situation is charming.
On a pleasing eminence commanding the most delightful prospect they have erected three houses.
The centre one is their chapel and house of their
clergyman, in which he only and all their children
constantly reside.   The house on the one side is all
for unmarried men, that on the other for the single
Sisters, as 'tis call'd.   Those bound by the matri-
monial shackles reside in or near the village of
Pudsey, but send all their children to the centre
mansion to be properly educated in their religion.
What that is, I never heard determinéd; some people
imagine it borders on the Roman Catholic.   As we
ascended the hill their band of music struck up, and
in my life I think I never was so charmed.   It consists of organ, French horns, clarinets, and flutes,
hautboys, and every kind of instrument, joyn'd by
the most harmonious voices one ever heard.   The
congregation were just enter'd the chapel as we did,
their men ranging themselves on forms at one side,
the women on the other.   They were extremely civil

---

[1] The Moravian settlement here was founded in 1748. The Bohemian
or Moravian Brethren date back to the tenth century, but were not
established in England till the middle of the eighteenth century.   Their
belief is very like the Church of England. They have an episcopate,
and claim to be an original Church, uncontaminated with Roman
doctrine.

1757 to us as strangers, seating us according to the above
method. The clergyman at first got into the pulpit
and read some sentences from a book which the
people made responses to, and often sang in chorus,
accompanied by the full band of music, which had an
effect most amazingly fine indeed. After, the same man
preach'd a sermon replete with incoherent nonsense,
all extemporary; the text was "My Lord, and my
God." After the sermon the children are admitted,
and not till then; they walk in two and two, and the
clergyman being come down from the pulpit, they
are placed before him on forms. They first sang
very prettily; he afterwards talked to them near a
quarter of an hour, but on subjects far above the
comprehension of their tender years. After this they
sang again, and then retired in the order they came,
looking most beautifully, being most sweet children,
and the dress of the female infants adding to their
beauty. The men and boys have nothing unusual
in their dress, but that of the women has something
in it extremely odd yet pretty, plain to a degree yet
pleasing, because accompanied by the utmost neatness, an ornament ever adorning to the meanest habit;
their gowns white linen, close to the shape, their
cap comes over the face like our largest French
nightcaps, rounding over the cheek and coming
down in a peak over the forehead, and sets close
to the face, no hair being seen. To distinguish the
ladies, all married Sisters tie the cap under the chin
with a large bunch of blue ribbons, the widows white,
and the single Sisters with pink, but the knots round
the caps of all is muslin, broad-hemmed. We were
now told the service of the morning was over. We
wanted to see the sleeping-room of the women, but

were told it could not be seen till after dinner, and 1757
we had much too far to go home for us to stay longer.
We had been told it was well worth seeing.   The odd
description we had of it is as follows :—Eighty beds,
each just large enough for one person, all of white
dimity, and a most perfect neatness all throughout
the apartment.   Every night one woman walks up
and down this gallery with a lighted taper in her
hand till daybreak, and this ceremony they perform
by turn.   We spent an hour in walking round and
making all inquiries about this odd sect of people, and
came away charmed with the situation and music,
if but little edified with their religion.   So far indeed
we agreed that the Moravians and monks, bore a
resemblance to each other, as both chose the finest
spots for their monastic residences, that the most
pleasing objects without, might compensate for the
gloomy ones within.   We dined at Leeds on our way.
     The next morning my father left us, being obliged
to return to London, but he went round by Mr.
Slater's in Derbyshire for a few days.   That day we
dined at a family's near Leeds, a town very popular,
and carrying on a vast trade in the woollen manufactures, but nothing extraordinary in its appearance.
Having spent a fortnight now at Mr. Pem. Milnes,
Mrs. Hooper, Mr. and Mrs. Handley (who were
guests come from Scarborough), Mr. and Miss Slater,
my mother and myself, adjourn'd, according to promise, to the other Mr. Milnes, where we spent a second
most pleasing fourteen days, the two families being
always together in a continual state of visiting ; but
the destin'd time of our party leaving Yorks for
Derbyshire being arrived, we set off to see other
obliging friends, tho' not without concern at quitting

1757 these who had so hospitably entertain'd us. We got
to Mr. Slater's the day following. We found Derbyshire not indeed so extensive a county, but as more
romantic it's more pleasing than Yorkshire, and though
at the same time remarkable for producing many
commodities in great plenty. The finest lead in
England, iron, &c., 'tis full of quarries of free stone,
greatstone, brimstone, black and grey marble, crystal,
alabaster, and sometimes there is found antimony.
The vales produce great quantities of corn, and the
mountainous parts coal-pits; but what adds beauty to
this county is the parks and forests, and inequality of
hills and dales that so diversify the landscape. About
a week after our large party arrived at Mr. Slater's
there came two other ladies and four gentlemen to the
races, which were to begin on the next day. One of the
later was Mr. Pem. Milnes, whose pleasure at seeing
his only child, a sweet girl of three years old, gave us
all the highest satisfaction. She had been here ten
months with her grandmama, on account of the small-
pox being at Wakefield. On the Wednesday, having
dined early, we set off in different carriages, and seven
gentlemen on horseback for the course, about three,
came back to tea about eight. Sir Harry Hemloak,
his two sisters, and more company returned with us,
and about ten we went to the Assembly Room, where
the Duke of Devonshire[1] always presided as master
of the ceremonies, and after the ball gave an elegant
cold supper, where, by his known politeness and affability, it would be unnecessary for me to say how
amiable he made himself to the company. We got
home about five. The next evening were at the
concert, as the same company usually met at that on

[1] William, fourth Duke of Devonshire.

the second night, and on the third day again went to 1757
the course.   There came back with us to tea the
Duke of Devonshire, Mr and Miss Simpson,[1] and two
Miss Bourns, the first young lady a most beautiful
girl indeed.   That evening's ball was equally brilliant
as the first night, and both gave us as strangers a
high idea of these annual assemblies at Chesterfield,
which town in itself has but a poor appearance.   I
must not forget to mention, what indeed I had before
read of, the oddity of the spire of the church there,
which, indeed, 'tis hardly possible not to observe, as
from whatever side of the town you view it, it always
appears leaning towards you, and *very crooked.*
Whether at first purposely contrived so as to raise
wonder at the builder, or, as it is lead, whether the
sun may not have warp't it, seems uncertain, as the
country people differ greatly in their sentiments on
the subject.   One afternoon we were most agreeably
entertained at Mrs. Bourn's, where we went to tea.
Their gardens are charming, and as we drank tea in
one of the buildings, the family being very musical
and charming voices, the young ladies sang, while the
gentlemen accompanied on their German flutes.   This
little concert took up the heat of the day, after which
we walk'd over the grounds.   When in a little temple,
on entering we laughed exceedingly at the rural
politeness of our beaux ; but as gentlemen of the
army are always gallant, we were the less surprised at
our elegant collation of fruit, cakes, cream, placed in
the most neat and rustic manner imaginable.   This
made us rather late home ; but we had passed the
afternoon and evening too agreeably to repine at that.
      Some of our race party had now left us, among

      [1] Afterwards Lady Bridgman.

1757 them a most agreeable young lady, Miss Gisbourne. I remember that day the neighbourhood were a little alarmed at hearing above a hundred and fifty men, with oaken clubs, had entered Chesterfield, and were making a vast riot. The gentlemen were assembled on a turnpike meeting, and these fellows were certain it was about the Militia Act[1] which it seems they had a most unconquerable aversion to, and were determin'd to oppose. It was some hours before they would hear at all; but when convinced they had been misinformed, retired very peaceably. Poor Mrs. Slater was soon after the races taken very ill, and confined to her bed and room some days. We feared, as no doubt it was, her over-attention to her friends, having the house so very full of company; but we had soon the pleasure to see her perfectly recovered, when she was, as she was ever, attentive to our entertainment. She took us to see a house of the Duke of Devonshire's, called Hardwick, nine miles from Chesterfield. The situation is fine. It was built in 1578 by Elizabeth, Countess of Shrewsbury. Of course it is antique, and render'd extremely curious to the present age, as all the furniture is coeval with the edifice. Our ancestors' taste for substantialness in every piece makes *us* now smile; they too would, could they see our delicateness in the same articles, smile at us, and I'm certain, if any one was to compare three or four hundred years hence a chair from the drawing-room of Queen Elizabeth's days and of the light French ones of George II., it would never be possible to suppose them to belong to the same race of people, as the one is altogether gigantic, and the

[1] This Act, passed by the Commons, was eventually thrown out by the Lords.

other quite liliputian. This house was rendered famous, 1757
too, as Mary, Queen of Scots, was most of the seventeen years she was a prisoner to the Earl of Shrewsbury confin'd here; her rooms of state and chamber
are shewn, her bed only remov'd, as that was seized
for plunder in the Civil Wars. Everything else
remains as it then was, and the apartment hung with
the unfortunate Queen's work, representing in symbolical figures and allusive mottoes all virtues; but after
all far more celebrated for beauty than goodness; but
how much so ever her conduct deserves censure, she
certainly deserved not the fate she met from the hand
she received it, which greatly sullies the memory of the
otherwise ever to be admired Elizabeth, who one hardly
can think had a right to deprive her so long of liberty,
much more of life. But not to revive a subject which
so long has lain dormant, I'll bid adieu to that and a
place which afforded us vast pleasure from the unusual
antiquity of the whole, and from being kept so exceedingly neat as it was throughout. . . .

The next day we went to visit a family at
Walton Hall,[1] another sweet situation, and a few
mornings after went to see Mr. Rhodes of Barleborough Hall. The approach to the latter is as fine
an avenue of ancient elms as I ever saw, from the
bottom of which the old mansion is very striking,
it being built by Judge Rhodes in the reign of
Elizabeth; there is a church here, a curiosity from
its being so diminutive; 'tis hardly possible to conceive its smallness. Mr. Rhodes, by fitting it up
with mahogany pulpit, his own seat, &c., has made
it so elegantly neat, that 'tis as well worth seeing
as a magnificent cathedral!

[1] Since the seat of Charles Waterton, the naturalist.

1757   After having spent our time most agreeably with our Derbyshire, as we had before done with our Yorkshire friends, our London party set out on our return to the Metropolis, but in our way back was to stay a few days at Matlock and see Chatsworth; the latter we did the morning we left Mr. Slater's, it being about ten miles distant. This celebrated seat in the Peak of Derbyshire of his Grace of Devonshire I must own does not quite answer what report had taught me to expect, tho' undoubtedly striking; but I was told it would appear less so to us than to strangers in general by the Slaters having a key to go through his Grace's grounds, a better and much shorter road than the public one, but that did not give one near so picturesque a view of Chatsworth's situation as if we had gone down to it all at once from the barren moors. The house is of stone, and the architecture thought very fine, twenty-two rooms on a floor; the windows of the principal storey, seventeen feet in height, are all looking-glass, of panes two feet wide, the frames double gilt; the door, and window-frames, and staircases of marble; ceilings and some apartments painted by Verrio and other celebrated artists; there is some fine tapestry, and in one chamber a most elegant bed, and furniture of fine old print set upon Nankeen, which has a very pretty effect, as the colour of the ground sets off the work. There are many fine pictures; one range of rooms they still style Mary, Queen of Scots, as she was some time here, as well as at his Grace's other seat of Hardwick; there is a very elegant chapel, the altar and font fine marble, seats and gallery cedar, the walls and ceiling painted. The front towards the garden is esteemed a most

regular piece of architecture. The frieze under the 1757
cornice has the family motto upon it, in gilt letters
so large as to take up the whole length, tho' only
two words, "Cavendo Tutos," which are as appli-
cable to the situation of the house as the name of
the family.   The waterworks, which are reckoned
the finest in England, were all played off, may be
said to be more grand than pleasing, as there is a
formality in them, particularly the grand cascade,
which takes off every idea of the rural scene they
are supposed to afford one, and a kind of triflingness
(if I may make a word), in the copper[1] willow-tree,
and other contrivances beneath the dignity of the
place. The gardens are fine. The very disadvan-
tages of the situation contriving to their beauty.
On the east side, not far distant, rises a prodigious
mountain, so thick planted with beautiful trees that
you only see a wood gradually ascending, as if the
trees crowded one above the other to admire the
stately pile before them. 'Tis said that Marshal Tallard
when he returned to his own country, when he
reckoned up the days of his captivity, said he should
always leave out those he spent at Chatsworth ; and
I must own this magnificent (tho' at the same time
gloomy), place may justly be stiled one of the wonders of the Peake. . . . In speaking of the waterworks,
I forgot to mention the length of the great cascade,
220 yards long with twenty-three falls. In prose-
cuting our journey of about eleven miles, 'tis hardly
possible to describe the variety of beauties ; sometimes we were like Don Quixote, almost imagining
ourselves enchanted, at another terrified by the huge

[1] On pulling a string this sham tree deluges the stranger with a
shower-bath.

1757 rocks, which by their stupendous height seemed to
threaten every minute to crush us by their fall. In
the greatest of our terrors (when in a very narrow
road, the above-mention'd rocks on one side, and
an immense precipice down to the river on the
other), we could not help laughing at the calm
answer of one of the postillions, who by often
going, I suppose, had not an idea of the danger
we apprehended, for only calling out to beg he'd
let us walk, and saying, "Where, friend, are you
going?" "Only to Matlock Baths, ladies." So indeed
we knew, but at that moment doubted the wisdom
of our driver, who, however conveyed us very safe
to the destined spot. Ceremony seems banished from
this agreeable place, as on entering the long room
strangers as well as acquaintances most politely made
inquiries about the terrors of the way, &c., which
themselves had before experienced. The very early
hour of rising at Matlock, gave us the next morning a
still finer idea of the uncommon beauties of the place,
as a most glorious day gave it additional lustre. The
time of bathing is between six and seven, the water
warm, and the pleasantest to drink that can be ; at
eight the company meet in the long room to breakfast
in parties. This room and baths were built in 1734 by
Stephen Egglinton. 'Tis a very good one, fifty feet
long, windows all the way on each side, commanded
the most romantic views, one way a fine terrace,
beyond that a lawn extended to the river Derwent,
which latter is a continual pleasing murmur by the
current forcing itself over large pieces of rock ; over
this rises a most picturesque and natural shrubbery,
to an immense and perpendicular height on the crag
of rocks. On the left is seen Matlock High Torr, a

rocky mountain which, from the surface of the water 1757
to the top, is 445 feet.   As there is always a cool spot
among the woods, walking seems the particular amusement of the place.   At two the bell rings for dinner,
and, as before said, ease without unnecessary ceremony reigns here.   Every one sits down without any
form, those who come first by the rule taking the
uppermost seats at the long table.   There is a gallery
for a band of music, who play the whole time of meals,
The fatigue of dress, too, is at this public place quite
avoided, as hats are general, as the company walk
again till evening, when there is a ball in the long
room till supper, and sometimes after.   Every one
retires very early, as few card-tables are seen, gaming
not having yet reached this rural spot.   The Boat-
house, as 'tis call'd, we went one afternoon to drink
tea at, where we bought curiosities of spars, &c., of
the miners, men employed to the number of above ten
thousand about Matlock only.   We went, too, one
morning to see them melt lead at a village near, call'd
Cumford, but the heat was so intense we did not stay
long among them ; and the poor souls told us was
often very prejudicial to them.   That evening we
went in a barge on the river, but it being not navigable, 'tis but in few places the stones and craginess
of the rocks will allow of boats.   Every evening
almost we found new company on our return to
supper.   Tho' the numbers perhaps were lessn'd, as
most likely as many were gone off the same morning,
about a hundred generally assembled at dinner.   I
heard Miss Slater, who sometimes makes a stay there,
say that two or three days has made a total change
of inhabitants.   We tried one evening to ascend the
prodigious rock I before spoke of, call'd Matlock

1757 High Torr. Many do, it seems, perform it, but I own
I was frighted before I had got a quarter of the way up,
and each object below began to appear so diminutive
that I, even with some others, consented to be ridi-
culed for my fears, and with vast joy got down again
as soon as possible, and even thought I felt giddy for
hours after, and thought myself most happy when I got
into the grove, one of the sweetest walks in Matlock.

And now I think 'tis time for me to quit this
sweet place, on which fame indeed has always been
so lavish of encomiums that one almost fears com-
mending what one must injure by one's praise. We
spent five most agreeable days there. Mr. Slater
and his sister, accompanied us as far as Derby,
where we lay that night; a town of great antiquity, very large, neat, and populous, and now of
great note from its silk-mills, which are indeed most
exceedingly curious, but it seems they don't let
strangers view them with great attention, nor show
the whole works, as the first person that set up these
mills at Derby, they say, brought the whole from
Italy by memory, having got a sight of these three
times, once in the habit of a gentleman, the second
in that of a Jesuit, and the third as a common soldier.
Supposing this true, he must have been a man of
most extraordinary genius, the machine consisting of
99,947 wheels, and all these turned by one.

The next morning our London party left Mr. and
Miss Slater to return home, desiring our joint thanks
to all the branches of the family for all the civilities we
had received among them, in both the agreeable visits
we had paid in Yorks and Derbyshire. We slept at
Loughborough, and lay at Leicester, a very ancient-
looking town indeed, so much so 'tis said by some to

have been a city. The next day we breakfasted at 1757
Market Harborough and dined at Northampton, one
of the prettiest towns I ever saw. It happen'd to
be the race-time, and a vast concourse of company
might add to the liveliness of the place. The next
place of note was Newport Pagnel, the most noted
place, it seems, in this kingdom for making lace.
Next came to Woburn, then Dunstable, the place
Rapin mentions, where the sentence of divorce was
pass'd against Queen Catherine, wife of Henry VIII.,
by Archbishop Cranmer. We that night (the last of
our tour), lay at St. Albans. The next day we breakfasted at Barnet, and got to London about two,
where, being once more arrived, I've brought to a
conclusion my too tedious narrative of our ten weeks'
excursion. An able pen would have given a more
pleasing description of the many fine places we were
at, but as 'tis the sentiments of an admired author,
" That 'tis false modesty to make apologies for doing
indifferently, that, in which one is not supposed to
excel," I shall only add, that innumerable civilities,
delightful countries, weather the most pleasing, all
combin'd to render our journey agreeable.

N.B.—We set out on the 8th July and return'd
the 9th September. Travel'd 665 miles.

The next event Miss Girle chronicles in her diary 1758
is in 1758. "Great rejoicings and illuminations on
the taking of Louisbourg, and the 16th of September
everybody went to see the Cherbourg cannon carried
thro' the city of London."

She also chronicles the admiration of the public 1759
for Roubiliac's two monuments in Westminster Abbey
to General Hargraves and Sir Peter Warren. She

1759 visits in 1759, from her relation Mr. Mount's place
at Epsom, Lord Baltimore's seat, a Mr. Belchier's
also, which she describes as very curious.

"Literally contained within the circumference of
a chalk-pit. Its owner had a very fine seat called
Durdens, in Surrey, burnt to the ground, but, instead
of rebuilding that, has collected not only the neces-
saries, but even the luxuries of life into the above
small compass, a good house, one room 30 feet by
20, and 15 feet high. In his gardens (all within the
pit), is hothouse, greenhouse, orangery, vineyard,
pinery, a grove, terrace, fish-ponds, fountain, with
rock-work and the largest gold and silver fish I ever
saw, a hot and cold bath, a pretty shrubbery; in short,
one cannot name anything that is not in this wonderful chalk-pit." This same year, 1759, Miss Girle, on
the 13th of August, set out with her family, "a lady
of our intimate acquaintance," and a cousin, on a fresh
tour to Oxford, &c.

After setting out early from London, they stayed
some three hours at Salt Hill, then proceeded to
Reading, reaching the town about six o'clock. She
says : This town, in my opinion, may be styl'd a
pretty town, but residing three years near may perhaps
have made me partial. 'Tis finely situated on the
rivers Thames and Kennet. There are several good
streets, and the market-place is neat and spacious.
They have three extremely good churches. The
adjoining Fourbourg,[1] which commands one of the
most delightful views I ever saw, contains the venerable ruins of an ancient abbey, found'd by Henry I.,
who was there buried, but his bones (as Rapin says),
were thrown out to make a stable, and the monastery

---

[1] Now called the Forbury.

is now a dwelling-house. We staid at Reading all 1759
Tuesday, having the pleasure of seeing there many
of our friends. We quit'd it early on Wednesday,
travelling that morn thro' part of Oxfordshire. Our
road for some hours was chiefly through the most
pleasing woods. For beautiful variety, a place called
Berring's Hill[1] exceeded all we that day saw. After
having breakfast'd and spent some time at a town
named Benson,[2] we went on to Oxford, that University so famous thro'out the world. We enter'd it
not till near the approach of evening, but found its
appearance striking and noble to the stranger's eye.
On account of its grand and numerous buildings, the
High Street, which for length and breadth, it seems, is
hardly to be parallel'd, is render'd particularly magnificent by the fronts of four colleges and the churches
of St. Mary, and All Saints. The city itself is of great
antiquity, it having been consecrated to the Sciences
by the ancient Britons ; and tho' it has suffer'd cala-
mities, 'tis now arriv'd at a very high state of grandeur,
adorn'd with twenty colleges, five halls, fourteen parish
churches. Coming into it pretty late, as I before
observ'd, we had time that night only to see one of
its colleges, and having fixed on that of Christchurch,
proceeded to the view, on which Dr. Hunt (Professor
there of Arabic), was so obliging to attend us. This
fine Gothic structure extends 382 feet. Originally
'twas founded by Cardinal Wolsey, but on his disgrace
Henry VIII. seiz'd on the foundation, and that he
might not be thought to derive his fame from others,
called it Christchurch. Over the entrance is a very

---

[1] Berin's Hill, supposed to be derived from Berinus, first Bishop of
Dorchester, Oxon, hard by.
[2] Bensington, pronounced Benson, site of an ancient British city.

1759 beautiful tower, and in it hangs the great bell called "Tom." On the sound of its hundred and one strokes (the number of students in this College) at nine every night, all the gates are to be shut, and every gentleman in the University must repair to their respective societies. The bell[1] is 5 feet 9 inches high and 7 feet in diameter. The great quadrangle has a handsome terrace round it, and in its centre is a fountain with a statue of Mercury,[2] and in arches over three of the entrances are those of Queen Anne, Archbishop Fell, and Cardinal Wolsey. Under the latter we enter the stately stone staircase,[3] whose beautiful roof, tho' very extensive, is supported by only one curious pillar. On our entering the hall, the Doctor told us it was reckon'd one of the largest in the kingdom, tho' its dimensions are no more than 120 feet by 40 feet, and in height 80. The ceiling is a grand frame of timberwork finely carv'd, and adorn'd with arms properly blazon'd. The Gothic fretwork roof of a large window at the upper end of the room demands particular observation from its elegant lightness. The hall on each side is decorated with the portraits of bishops and others educated at Christchurch; but what, in my opinion, greatly enhances the beauties of this ancient hall is, that at this day 'tis just the same (except the forty-five pictures above mention'd) as in the time of its founder, the Cardinal, in 1525, without the least addition of more modern ornaments, except such as cleanliness ever demands. The chapel of this College is the cathedral of the Bishop of Oxford, remarkable for some remains of painted glass of a most brilliant

---

[1] "Great Tom" weighs 17,000 lbs., the clapper, 342. It came from the Abbey of Oseney.

[2] The statue now removed.

[3] Built in 1640.

colour, and the fine stone roof of its choir. Having 1759
seen thus far and the evening advancing, we return'd
for the night to our lodgings; but Thursday's morn
had not many hours been visible before our sex's
characteristic, as 'tis call'd, *curiosity*, made us, I must
own, rather impatient to be traversing over the
charming buildings of this fine city; and our breakfast repast was no sooner over than we got into our
vehicle, which for hours incessantly whirl'd us o'er
the rattling pavement, stopping tho' at the most
remarkable edifices for us to view the grandeur of
in, as well as outside.   The first College we were set
down at was that of Trinity, which we went to see
on account of the peculiar elegance of its chapel,
which was built A.D. 1693.[1]   The screen, rails, and
altar-piece is cedar inlaid (the fine scent of which on
entering is very agreeable), besides other embellish-
ments.   There are many festoons of carving so finely
executed that 'tis unnecessary to inform any that has
seen his performances that they were done by *Grindeline* Gibbons.[2]   The chapel is pav'd with marble,
and under an alcove near the altar is an elegant
Gothic tomb, with the effigies of Sir Thomas Pope[3]
(the founder), and his lady in alabaster.   The roof
is enrich'd with painting and fretwork.   From the
chapel we went into the gardens, which are prettily
laid out, and remarkable for the fine yew wall that
surrounds them.   From Trinity College we went to
the Museum, a building sixty feet in length, with a
grand portico of the Corinthian order.   At entering
this apartment, a smile, I fancy, takes place on the
features of the most grave philosopher from the odd

[1] Rebuilt.   [2] Grinling Gibbons.
[3] The College was founded by Sir Thomas Pope in 1554.

1759 contrasted view that lies before them. There may,
and no doubt there are, many curiosities in this collection ; but I must own some I should have thought
too minute to be preserved by gentlemen of such a
University ; but ignorance ought always to be silent,
and therefore I'll criticise no more! A present of
Lady Pembroke's deserves mentioning, which is a
magnet, the finest now in England, attracting a
200 lb. weight. Then there is an ivory carved ball,
enclosing three of the same sort, one within the other,
all cut out of one piece, which I think is extremely
curious, as is a band of paper prick'd by a young lady
in imitation of lace ; and many other things which
would give entertainment could one be certain they
really were what they now have, I fancy, only the
name of ; as, for instance, we were present'd with a
view of the skull of Oliver Cromwell, when at the
same time history informs us his body was never
found ; but his head indeed, for all I can tell, may have
travelled to Oxford solo, and there lies among other
curiosities, as the shield of Achilles, &c., &c.

From the Museum we next visit'd the Bodleian
Library (which is over the divinity school, where Miss
Blandy [1] was tried), this library consisting of three
lofty rooms, dispos'd in the form of the Roman H ;
on all sides are the books arrang'd, each volume being
chain'd to the cases. In the picture gallery con-
tiguous to it are many valuable portraits. Two I
must mention, that of Dr. Walls, by Sir Godfrey
Kneller, which is reckon'd the masterpiece of that
fine lymner, and one of Johannes Duns Scotus, who

[1] Miss Blandy, a native of Henley-on-Thames, was tried at Oxford
in 1752 for poisoning her father by administering powders given to her
by her lover. She protested her innocence, but was hanged at Oxford
the same year.

made a resolution to fast till he had finish'd a book 1759
he was translating, and died writing the last page, is
a figure most striking. In this gallery, on a pedestal
of black marble, stands the brass effigy of the Earl
of Pembroke in complete armour, who was chancellor
of the University in the reign of James I. 'Twas
design'd by Peter Paul Rubens, and supposed to be
the finest statue in England.

We next went to New College, found'd by
William of Wickham.[1] The first court is 168 feet
long ; in the centre is the statue of Minerva. At
the north-west corner we enter'd a chapel, which
by far (as we were told), exceeds all in Oxford, and
'tis indeed a fabric most magnificent. The ante-
chapel is supported by four pillars of fine proportion, and thro' a curious Gothic screen you come
into a choir grandly striking, render'd more so by the
noble flight of marble steps, and their iron rail-work
surrounding the altar, the ornaments, paintings, and
crimson velvet embroider'd communion cloth all adding lustre to each other. The organ is fine, erect'd
by the famous Dolham, and the stalls esteemed the
finest Gothic finishing for its lightness anywhere to
be met with. The gardens of the College are large,
and from a very high mount the Gothic spires, &c.,
of the building has a fine effect, and the area before
this eminence is reckon'd a curious specimen of the
old parterre taste ; 'tis divided in quarters. In one
(cut out in box), are the arms of England, garter,
and motto ; in another, those of the founder, with
this, " ' Manners make the man,' says William of
Wickham 1379 "—and things after the same manner
in the two others. There is a fine bowling-green,

[1] In 1380.

1759 shady'd on one side by tall sycamores, whose branches
are so enwoven from end to end as render them
justly admired as a natural curiosity. From New
College we went to the Clarendon Printing House, a
magnificent structure with a Doric portico. This
edifice was erected A.D. 1711 [1] by the profit arising
from the sale of Lord Clarendon's History, as the
copy had been present'd by his son to the University.
The letters are all solid metal, and the manner of
placing, sorting, and taking the impression all gives
entertainment, making one at the same time thank-
fully happy that an art so charming has a being in
our country ; for what pleasure so delightful as that
of reading ? We next went to the Theatre, erect'd
at the expense of Archbishop Sheldon,[2] cost £15,000 ;
the front is adorn'd by Corinthian pillars, with the
statue of him and the Duke of Ormond. On entering,
the mind is struck with an idea of grandeur. The
roof is flat, and not being support'd by columns or
arch-work, rests on the side walls, which are seventy
and eighty feet distant ; this roof is covered with
allegorical painting. The room is, besides, furnish'd
with full-length portraits ; 'tis in form a Roman D,
and contains 3000 people. From the Theatre we
went to the Schools to take a survey of the statues,
Lady Pomfret's present to the University, and which
are styled an inestimable collection.[3] I've no doubt
by connoisseurs in ancient antiquities they may be
thought so—their number is 135—but I must own to
have a taste so refin'd as to have no pleasure in the
sight of so many dirty, frightful, maimed figures,
some having unfortunately lost heads, others legs,

[1] By Sir John Vanbrugh.   [2] In 1669.
[3] This is an amusing account of the Arundel marbles !

arms, hands, or eyes. Being at a little distance 1759
from a Grecian Venus, the beauty of her face greatly
struck me, but how was I forc'd to call my own
judgment in question when on a nearer view I found
it a new head, stuck by a late statuary on the dirty
shoulders of a lady who seem'd to have no other
merit but her having been form'd so many years ago.
Strange repositories these, and the only places, I fancy,
where beautiful features are pass'd by unregard'd, and
the men stand in admiration at the majestic air of
ladies far past their grand climactericks.

From the schools we went to the Radcliffian
Library, which is a circular building situated in a square.
It stands on arcades in which lay several pieces of the
ruins brought from Palmyra. Ascending a flight of
spiral steps, you come into the library itself, which is
said to be a pattern of elegance ; it rises into a capa-
cious dome ornament'd with compartments of stucco.
The pavement is of a two-coloured stone brought
from Germany. The room is enclos'd by a circular series of arches, beautified with festoons and
pilasters, behind these, in two galleries above and
below, are the books in elegant cases, facing each
other ; over the door a statue of Dr. Radcliffe by
Rysbrack, and indeed the whole room is finished in
so high a taste as exceeds description. After seeing
it we went to the College of All Souls, and saw first
the chapel, which we could not help thinking in-
significant after that of New College or Trinity, tho'
at any other city but that of Oxford might be styl'd
grand. We then went to their library, a room that
from its ornaments and size must be call'd a fine
one ; 'tis 200 feet in length and 40 in height. About
the middle of the north side is a recess equal to the

1759 breadth of the room, in this is the statue of Colonel
Codrington.[1]   There are two arrangements of books,
the upper one being in a superb gallery, over which
is a series of bronzes consisting of vases and busts
interchangeably disposed.   The ceiling and other spaces
are adorn'd with the richest of stucco.   The lock and
key to this apartment, tho' seemingly too minute an
object, deserves mentioning, it having cost sixteen
guineas, and really may be styl'd a curiosity.   Their
hall at this College is an elegant modern room.   The
next place our vehicle set us down at was the Physick
Garden,[2] which is five acres, surround'd by a wall
with rustic portals at proper distances; on each side
the grand entrance is a greenhouse, besides there's
a fine hothouse, containing and raising for the garden
many thousand plants for the improvement of bota-
nical studies and vegetable philosophy.   There are
many very curious ones, the sight of which gave me
a very high entertainment, as particularly the coffee
shrub, the caper tree, the plantain, cotton, cinnamon,
creeping cerus, with many others too numerous to
mention.   We saw the trunk of an aloe that blew
there some years ago.   From this garden we went
to Magdalene Walks, as the gardens of that college
are called, indeed they are charmingly pretty, having
a lawn, grove, and paddock stock'd with forty head
of deer, besides a most agreeable walk shaded by
lofty trees, and its banks wash'ed by the river Cher-
well.   At the hall of this College we saw the gentlemen at dinner, which was the last sight I think that
we travers'd after in this city of curiosities, and having
seen, tho' not all, yet those buildings that were deem'd

[1] The library was built with money left by him for that purpose.
[2] Established in 1622.   An earlier one founded by Linacre.

most deserving observation, we quitted a place which 1759
I think every native of England once in their lives at
least ought to visit.

We lay at Woodstock the evening we left
Oxford, and the next morning went to the Palace
(or Castle), of Blenheim, the seat of his Grace the
Duke of Marlborough, the royal gift of Queen
Anne, who built and gave it to the family in commemoration of the battle of Blenheim in France.   It
cost near £300,000.   On entering the park thro' a
portal of Corinthian order, the magnificent pile strikes
the eye, and gives one the idea of grandeur from a
view so superb.   Then the Rialto bridge, the lake,
its valley, and other beautiful scenes are not less
delightful.   Here you are about half a mile distant
from the house, and have only an oblique prospect of it,
but on a nearer approach you find the front a semi-
circle, its centre a portico elevated on massy columns ;
over the door is the figure of Pallas.   This entrance
admits you to a hall which is fifteen feet in height,
supported by Corinthian pillars, on the recesses of
which are casts from antique statues ; over them paintings.   The ceiling represents the Duke crown'd by
Victory.   In the arcades on the right and left is a fine
arrangement of marble termini.   The hangings of
the first apartment are the achievements of Alexander.
In this room are two crayon pieces finely executed
by Lady Bolingbroke (sister of the present Duke [1]) ;
in the third apartment is that charming picture of
Rubens' family by himself; here, too, is that principal
one of Vandyke's, Lord Stafford dictating to his secretary ; in the fourth apartment the hangings conclude
Alexander's battles ; the fifth is a cabinet of pictures by

[1] George, third Duke.

1759 the most eminent masters ; the tapestry of the sixth,
seventh, ninth, and tenth are the battles of the great
Duke of Marlborough, and nothing can be a more striking ornament to the rooms they adorn than these fine
hangings ; the eighth apartment is grac'd by the most
pleasing specimens of Rubens' luxuriant pencil, and
the eleventh by other masters. The saloon is answerable in magnificence to the rest ; its dado is lin'd with
marble, the doorcase is the same (and so are all in
the other rooms, each a different sort) ; the walls are
adorn'd with paintings by La Guerre ; 'tis in compartments, each of which contains people of a different nation in their proper habits, as the English,
French, Italian, Spaniards, Turks, Chinese, Dutch,
and Moors ; they are finely executed and have a
charming effect, each portrait seeming in admiration
of the noble room. From a series of smaller tho' magnificent apartments one is suddenly struck at entering
the library, which is indeed superb ; its dimensions
add greatly to its grandeur, it being 180 feet long
and proportionately broad and lofty ; the Doric pilasters of marble, the complete columns of the same,
supporting the rich entablature, the window frames,
and surrounding basement of black marble, and the
stucco'd compartments of the vaulted ceiling are all
in the highest taste.   This room contains the best
private collection of books, as we were inform'd,
in England, amounting to 24,000 volumes, which
cost £30,000; they are under gilt-wire lattices ;
on the top of the cases is a series of bronzes,
and over them paintings from Italy, Germany
and Flanders, with the cartoons copied by Le
Blaud from those of Hampton Court ; the furniture of the library is answerable to itself, part of

which is a very fine orrery and planetarium, two 1759 curious tables of agate inlaid, on each a pair of urns of oriental alabaster ; at the upper end of the room is a statue, very highly finish'd, by Rysbrack of Queen Anne. Leaving the library, we had then gone thro' the body of the house, which consists of fifteen principal rooms. One of the state bed-chambers is point furniture on a buff-coloured holland, the hangings, bed, window curtains, and chairs all the same, and nothing can be more neatly elegant than this apartment. In one of the wings is the chapel, where there is a grand monument to the old Duke and Duchess by Rysbrack, and their two sons, who died young ; underneath, basso-relievo, is the taking of Marshal Tallard. The park and gardens are extremely fine, the former near eleven miles circumference, containing innumerable scenes of rural variety. This park has been many years famous, it being that where Henry II. erected the house and labyrinth for his mistress,[1] the romantic retreat that was styl'd Fair Rosamond's Bower. 'Twas situated in the sweet valley I mention'd at our entering the park. The celebrated poet Chaucer[2] was born and liv'd in a house very near the Corinthian portal, the ruinous remains of which are still visible. The gardens of Blenheim are laid out with taste, embellish'd by natural beauties. The south front of the palace is towards them ; on the pediment in its centre is a bust of Louis XIV. larger than life, taken from the citadel of Tournay. About two miles before we got to Mortenhenmarsh (the place where we that

[1] In vain did Vanbrugh plead with Sarah, Duchess of Marlborough, to retain this. She pulled it down in 1709, leaving only an old wall.

[2] Chaucer lived at Woodstock, and much of the scenery of "The Dream" is taken from there.

1759 day din'd) is a pillar erect'd, call'd the four Shire
Stone, as there the counties of Worcester, Gloucester,
Warwick, and Oxford meet, a circumstance not a
little extraordinary, that at the same time one may
be in all four! In the evening we went down Broadway Hill, the summit of which commands a prospect
terribly delightful by reason of the surrounding vales.

We lay that night at Broadway, and the following
morning went thro' the Vale of Evesham, a place
I've often heard prais'd for beauty, and which indeed
is extremely pleasant.   By dinner-time we got to
Worcester, a city of great note, built by the Romans ;
it contains twelve churches and a cathedral, has a
very grand Town-Hall, and is really a neat place.
The next morning papa and myself went in a chaise
to Lulsley,[1] a situation I think so sweetly romantic ;
none I ever saw except Matlock in the Peak of
Derbyshire exceeds it.   From thence we had a fine
view of Malvern Hills, which are rather mountains,
they rising one above the other for seven miles.   We
return'd to Worcester to dine, and about two hours
after set out to Tewkesbury, the neatest and best
pav'd town we had yet been at.   About a quarter of
a mile from this place was fought the famous battle
between the Houses of York and Lancaster, on the
4th of May 1470, to this day styl'd the Bloody
Meadow.   Edward IV. totally overthrew Henry VI.
of the latter House, taking him and his son prisoners,
the latter of whom was murder'd by order of the
Duke of Gloucester.   The great old abbey at Tewkesbury may be call'd one of the largest churches in
England that is not cathedral, it having two spacious

[1] Miss Girle inherited a portion of this estate of Lulsley from her
mother's family.

aisles, a stately tower and large chancel; the com- 1759
munion table is one entire piece of marble fourteen
feet long, its cloth a present from the Dowager Lady
Coventry, her own work. This church was first built
in the year 711,[1] but William the Conqueror added
to it greatly; it contains many curious monuments
of antiquity, some few of which I shall mention.
An abbot lies here in a stone coffin, which about
fifty years since was opened by some persons (as
was thought, only for his crozier and ring). The body
was there entire, and the diaper he was wrapt in
perfectly fresh, an incident that seems surprising.
George, Duke of Clarence, who was order'd by his
brother Richard to be smother'd in a butt of
Malmsley, is buried in this abbey, and the great
Earl of Warwick in Edward IV.'s time, who was
styl'd the king-making Earl. The tomb of a Lord
O'Brien deserves attention for the curious Gothic
workmanship wherewith 'tis adorn'd, as does still
more the magnificent little chapel dedicat'd to Mary
Magdalene, where private mass used to be said.
Two other monuments I remember is Edward (son
of Henry VI.), who I before mention'd was murder'd
at the battle of Tewkesbury, the other was that of
a monk,[2] who in time of rebellion had run into a
hollow tree, and endeavouring after the battle was
over to get out, found it impossible to extricate himself, and was starv'd to death; but why so very a
coward should have been honour'd by a fine monument seems extraordinary, as every one must think
a mind so selfishly mean almost deserv'd the punish-

[1] A.D. 715, founded by Odo and Dodo, Dukes of Mercia.

[2] This must have been a verger's fiction at that period; the monument is to Abbot Wakeman, erected for himself as a memento mori,
when Abbot; he was afterwards Bishop of Gloucester.

1759 ment it met with.   It took up some time to view
the old abbey with the attention it deserv'd, but the
agreeable survey over, we got into the coach and
proceed'd to Cheltenham.   This place has been for
many years frequented on account of its Spaw waters ;
there was then the season, but little company.   We
breakfasted with some friends who were there, after
which, having seen the place and everything deserving
notice, we set out for Gloucester, got there by dinner-
time.   Gloucester is the capital city of the county,
and lays stretch'd, as it were, along the river Severn.
There is nothing except the Cathedral[1] I think worth
seeing ; that on the outside is a fine Gothic structure,
with a tower remarkably light and pretty ; the inside
of the church most excessively heavy, being support'd by plain pillars of a size most enormous.   The
most particular monuments are these : Robert, Duke
of Normandy, eldest son of William the Conqueror ;
Edward II. ; then there's a tomb of one Parker, who
was the last Abbot and first Bishop, and another of
a man and his wife with their nine sons and seven
daughters.   I must not forget to mention the clois-
ters of this cathedral, which are reckon'd remarkably
beautiful.

We left Gloucester about four, and being pretty
late in the evening, we could proceed no farther
than a place call'd "Cambridge Inn," where indeed
necessity oblig'd us to put up with lodgings sufficiently
inconvenient ; but as it was for a few hours only, we
made ourselves as easy as 'twas possible in a situation
disastrous enough, rejoicing only at the approach of
the next morn, which no sooner arriv'd than we
quitted with pleasure "Cambridge Inn."

[1] Founded in A.D. 679 by Wolfhere, first Christian king of Mercia.

We breakfasted at Amesbury Hill, where is one of 1759
the sweetest prospects imagination can conceive, commanding an extensive view quite to the Severn Sea,
which adds no little beauty to the whole.   After staying some hours at this charming spot, we went on to
Bristol, reaching that place about six in the evening.
This city is seat'd between the rivers Avon and
Frome, contains nineteen churches and a cathedral.
The streets are but narrow.   The new Exchange is a
handsome building, and the quay for its length, and the
crane, is not, we were inform'd, anywhere in Europe
to be equall'd.   Queen Square, and College Green, are
the two prettiest places in Bristol.   In the former is a
statue to William III. by Rysbrack, and in the latter
a curious cross, suppos'd the most ancient and well-
preserv'd now in England.   The Cathedral is not
very extraordinary, and upon the whole, the city
itself, I fancy, would not be greatly injured by having
the same character ; not that 'tis near so bad a place
as report has taught me to expect.   They there draw
all their goods on sledges, which they say is a great
inconvenience, tho' I thought it seem'd much less so
than the way they convey them from place to place
in the Metropolis.   The next morning we went to the
Hot Well on St. Vincent's Rock, which indeed is a
sweet romantic place.   This was the fullest season
has been known for years.   The company meet here
.to drink the waters at eight and twelve, then walk in
the rooms, which is a little way distant from the well.
After dinner meet there for the evening, and on
Tuesdays and Fridays there are balls.   This is a
short description of the employment of the Bristol
season, which was then at its height, and a prodigious
deal of company there then indeed seem'd assembl'd.

1759 Mr. Ford's family were so obliging to give us their
company to dinner, and in the evening we once more
prosecut'd our tour, and got to Bath that night.
This is a place of great antiquity, lying in a valley,
surrounded with amphitheatrical views of hills, from
which hills spring the water so fam'd, and which are
of such advantage to this city—a city, in my opinion,
more worth seeing than any I was ever at, the great
Metropolis excepted. Twice I have been there before,
but 'tis infinitely improv'd by the building the circus,
and the whole street by which 'tis approach'd from the
square. They seem to fear the former's ever being
finished, its progress is so extremely slow; nine houses
only are yet erect'd. There is intended to be three
times that number, and the openings between give a
fine view of the country. Those that are complet'd
give one an idea of the elegance of the whole, they
being in a magnificent taste in the Doric, Ionic, and
Corinthian orders. . . .

   We employ'd our morning as is usual at Bath in
going to the Pump, the Abbey Church, and the rooms,
tho' each were but little frequented, there being but
two or three families besides that of the Duchess of
Marlborough. The heat of the waters is very extraordinary, and people attribute it to different causes,
but most to its passing thro' certain sulphurous veins
of the earth. In taste 'tis not so agreeable as those
at Bristol. Thursday afternoon we went to Mr.
Busby's at Walcot; we had paid in the morning a
visit to Mr. and Mrs. Pierce, and early on Friday we
quitted this agreeable place, and lay that night at
Devizes. At this town then were quarter'd our
Berkshire Militia, which, to the honour of their officers
and county, we really thought came much nearer to a

resemblance to the regulars than any we had yet seen. 1759
After having breakfasted on Saturday, we quitted this
town, and in a few hours had the pleasure of seeing
that famous monument of antiquity on Salisbury Plain,
call'd Stonehenge. But as I should be able of myself
to give but a very incoherent account of this noble
work, eminent from the remotest ages, I shall here
insert a very short abstract indeed, as I took it down
in reading Dr. Stukeley's book concerning it. His
words are as follows :—" 'Tis more than probable that
it was a temple of the British Druids, and the chief
cathedral (as it may be call'd), of all their temples in
this island. 'Tis thought to be of an extraordinary
antiquity, perhaps three thousand years old, executed
not long after Cambyses' invasion of Egypt. When
the Saxons and Danes came over, they wonder'd at
Stonehenge then, and were at as great a loss about
the founders and intent as we are now. Camden saw,
with excellent judgment, 'twas neither Norman nor
English. Inigo Jones endeavour'd to prove it the
former ; but whoever is acquaint'd with Roman architecture must be of a different opinion. After passing
a circular ditch by which 'tis enclos'd, about 30 yards
distant is the work itself, being 108 feet in diameter.
On entering and casting your eyes around the yawning
ruins, you are struck with an ecstatic reverie. The
temple was compos'd of two circles and two ovals,
the whole number of stones 140 ; the great oval
consisting of 10 uprights, the inner, with the altar, of
20 ; the great circle of 30 ; the inner of 40, and 5
imposts of the great oval ; 30 of the great circle ; 2
stones standing on the bank of the area, 2 others
lying down, and one there seems to have been by the
barrow nearest this place. The largest stones beyond

1759 controversy were brought from those called grey-
wethers[1] on Marlborough Downs, and a piece brought
to the Royal Society, and examined with a microscope, 'tis found to be a composition of crystals, red,
green, and white.   The extravagant grandeur of the
work has attracted the admiration of all ages.   Indeed
a serious view of it puts the mind into a kind of ecstasy
at the struggle between art and nature, and 'tis truly
entertaining to consider the judicious carelessness
therein ; for notwithstanding the monstrous size (the
stones of the adytum being 30 feet high), 'tis far
from appearing heavy, and no one ever thought it
too great or too little, too high or too low.   The
trilithon at the upper end was an extraordinary beauty,
but the noble impost is dislodg'd from its airy seat and
fallen on the altar.   The two uprights that supported it
are above 30 feet long ; one is entire, but leans upon
one of the stones of the inward oval, the other is
broken in half lying on the altar."

Such is the account Dr. Stukeley gives us of
Stonehenge.   The original indeed is a folio volume ;
mine only a few lines taken from different parts of
his, to serve as a help to memory should time
obliterate the idea of these very striking ruins from
my mind.   Having spent some time in viewing this
magnificent wonder, and endeavouring with some
tools our servants had, to carry some pieces of it with
us, which with great difficulty we at last accomplished,
and have since had them polished ; but in reading the
above, altho' we were rather mortified, as 'tis his
sentiments that 'tis an absurd curiosity for people to
wish the remains of this temple further ruinated, but,

---

[1] The stones of Stonehenge are sarsen (or grey-wether), syenite, and
diastyte.

[28] Martha Ray was r
Fielding and commi
found guilty and ser
the British Evening
Sandwich: *General*
publication costing
1779; *Gazetteer an*
Morning Post and L
[29]Cradock, pp. 117-
[http://oxforddnb.cc
been serious about
one ending a letter '
Augustus to Lord S
Sandwich: First Lo
execution at Tyburr
Hackman had been
Gentleman Compos

[30]Montagu, pp. i-xl.
voyage, in fact, he c
J.M. Rigg, 'Cooke,
accessed 6 Dec 201

A. Clark, Pompeo Batoni a complete catalogue of his works with an introduction text

ND 623 . B2 C4A

Oxford, Phaidon, 1985

however, we have the comfort to think the very small 1759
bits we took could not greatly endanger the work, and
that, tho' our party were chiefly female, we had not
more curiosity than the learn'd gentlemen of the
Royal Society, who, it seems, with Dr. Stukeley, had
some brought for their inspection thro' a microscope.
. . . We once more enter'd the attending vehicle,
highly entertain'd by the sight of what in the same
moment gave one sensations pleasingly awful.   By
the number of barrows on Salisbury Plain people
(says Dr. Stukeley), injudiciously conclude there have
been great battles fought there, and the slain buried
in them, but they are really no other than family
burying-places.

From Stonehenge we went to Wilton House.
This seat of the Pembroke family has been theirs
two hundred years, but originally a monastery.   Part
of it was rebuilt in the reign of Henry VIII. and part
in that of Elizabeth.   This charming tho' ancient
mansion is situated in a garden of sixty acres, which
a river runs thro' ; a delightful lawn lays before the
house, which has the view of the canal ; a grand
arcade at the upper end, where the fall of water is
very fine.   On the contrary, when you are at this
building, the eye has still greater beauties to admire,
as the magnificent old structure, a Palladian bridge,
Gothic seats, temple, and numberless pieces of the
watery element, which ever is one of the most pleasing
objects in a fine prospect.   The late Lord Pembroke
had thought, it seems, of erecting in his gardens a
Stonehenge in miniature, as 'twas suppos'd to have
been in its first glory. . . . The late Earl was—so
I'm told—a man of great genius and a master of
antiquity, by which he was enabl'd to collect such

1759 valuable pieces of painting and sculpture as made a
perfect museum. The busts, statues, and relievos,
in all 335, are deem'd very fine. There are ten state
apartments, the chimney-pieces of which were carved
in Italy ; the decorations of the wainscot are gilt, the
stuccoed ceilings are answerable to the splendour of
the rest. 'Twas at this seat Sir Philip Sidney wrote
his " Arcadia." In the bottom panels of one of the
rooms are several incidents of that romance in miniature, but very ill painted. The bed-hangings of one
of the state rooms is bugles, which by candlelight
must look, as we imagin'd, extremely pretty. 'Twas
worked by some ladies of the family. But what most
deserves a particular observation is the celebrated
picture of the Pembroke family by Vandyke. This
very large piece is at the upper end of the great room.
It consists of ten whole lengths, besides two sons and
a daughter, represented in the clouds, who died young.
'Tis so fine a performance as I imagine it has few
equals, and at 60 feet distance (the length of the
room), one almost sees each portrait animated into
that life the limner has so well endeavour'd to express.

.   .   .   .

We quitted Wilton just time enough to reach
Salisbury before the close of day, so had not the
opportunity that evening of seeing a place every one
talk'd of for its peculiar neatness. The next morning we went to the Cathedral, a fine fabrick, the spire-
steeple very beautiful. This building, founded A.D.
1220, is thought remarkable for having as many gates
as months in the year, windows as days, and marble
pillars as hours—a circumstance for which the architect is justly found fault with if in his plan so whimsical a thought had preference to others much more

material in a design so great. After the Cathedral 1759
service we return'd to the inn, and, dinner over,
quitted this celebrated town. . . . We lay that night
at Andover, the next at Hertford Bridge, and early
on Tuesday got to Mr. Baker's at Mattingley, which
family obligingly insisted on our staying with them
till the next morn. . . . Wednesday morn only too
soon began its dawn, almost with which we quitted
their friendly mansion and set out for Lincoln's Inn
Fields, which place, after having dined at Staines, we
reach'd in the evening of the 29th August, which day
was the concluding one of an excursion as agreeable
as everything seemingly contributing to our pleasure
could render so delightful a tour.

The number of miles we travell'd :—

From London to Reading.	39
Reading to Benson	15
Benson to Oxford	12
Oxford to Woodstock	8
Woodstock to Moreton-hen-Marsh	20
Moreton-hen-Marsh to Broadway	8
Broadway to Worcester	21
Worcester to Lulsley and back	16
Tewkesbury to Cheltenham	10
Gloucester to Cambridge Inn	12
Cambridge Inn to Amesbury	46
Bristol to Bath.	17
Bath to Devizes	19
Devizes to Wilton	25
Wilton to Salisbury	3
Salisbury to Andover	17
Andover to Basingstoke	18
Basingstoke to Hertford Bridge.	10
Hertford Bridge to Mattingley	3
Mattingley to Staines	23
Staines to London	17

359

1759   Miss Girle paid a visit to the Tower in December
1759, breakfasting with the Governor.   Her description has nothing remarkable in it, with the exception of seeing the wild beasts then kept there.   The
next extract of interest is on May 6, 1760 :—" Earl
Ferrers was carried from the Tower to Tyburn,
escorted by a party of Horse and Foot Guards ; a
clergyman, and two sheriffs were in the coach with
him.   The poor unhappy man was drest in his
wedding suit, dating, as he himself said, his whole
unhappy conduct from a forced marriage.[1]   He
observ'd that the apparatus, and being made a
spectacle of to so vast a multitude was greatly worse
than death itself; the procession was two hours and
three-quarters from setting out, the landau and six
in which he was, the sheriffs each in their chariots,
one mourning coach, and a herse attended and
return'd thro' Lincolns Inn Fields about one.   I
think I never shall forget a procession so moving ;
to know a man an hour before in perfect health, then
a lifeless corpse,[2] yet a just victim to his country, for
the abuse of that power his rank in life had given
him a title to—his rank, indeed, caused his punishment, as the good old King in answer to the
numerous petitions of his greatly to be pitied family
made this memorable speech, ' That for the last years
of his life he had been beyond his most sanguine
hopes successful, for which he should ever return
thanks to God, and on his part he had and always
would endeavour to administer justice as he ought,
as events had shown by the punishment of his most
exalted subjects.' "

[1] He had murdered his steward in a peculiarly brutal manner, for
refusing to falsify some statements as to the Earl's financial position.

[2] For his rank's sake he was hung by a *silken* rope.

Miss Girle concludes with thinking the unhappy 1759
Lord's intellect was more at fault than his heart, in
the murder for which he suffered. Her account of
the British [1] Museum, just opened, 1759, and its
contents are amusing.

"Montagu House [2] as a noble one is of itself
worth seeing. The apartments are all fitted up
with bookcases, and cabinets for Sir Hans Sloane's
curiosities, purchas'd by the public for £10,000;
there are 30,000 volumes of manuscripts. Six rooms
are Sir Hans' collection of books, many valuable ones
no doubt—four is here shown as greatly so: 1. "In
thy own old age," one of the first books printed; 2.
Queen Mary's Mass-book, finely painted; 3. The
first Bible ever printed in English, a present to
Henry VIII. on his permitting it to be in that
language; 4. A manuscript Bible, wrote by a lady
named Theclea, very valuable for its antiquity. In
one room, with many other drawings, were two
volumes of insects, by Mariana,[3] in their several
states, with the plants they feed on, cost Sir Hans
£500. In other apartments are rang'd Egyptian
figures, found with mummies, &c., &c. . . . One
room of curious things in *spirits* (but disagreeable).
Indeed Sir Hans seems justly to have gain'd the
title of a real virtuoso in the above collection.

October 25, 1760, His Majesty George II. died 1760
at Kensington, in the 77th year of his age, and 34th
of his reign, taken from a people by whom he was

---

[1] 1753 was the year Parliament purchased Sir Hans Sloane's Museum,
which with the Harleian Library, formed the nucleus of the present
British Museum. The Museum was opened 1759.

[2] Had been the residence of the Dukes of Montagu; built 1677.

[3] Maria Sibilla Merian, one of the earliest delineators of insect life;
she was born 1647, died 1717.

1760 sincerely loved, fortunately for himself, at the most shining period of his life. 'Twas astonishing to see the amazing consternation, bustle, and confusion an event like this, quite unexpected, made in a metropolis such as London. I happened to be out that morn before it was known : it was published about twelve, when instantly the streets were in a buzz, the black cloth carrying about, and in half an hour every shop was hung with the appendages of mourning, which was not put on till the Sunday se'nnight following. The bowels were brought privately from Kensington, and buried in Henry VII.'s Chapel, and the night after, the body was brought and deposited in state for interment ; on the next day, Tuesday, November 10th, the great bell of St. Paul's, and every other church in London, toll'd from 6 to 11, and minute-guns fired ; all which form'd the most melancholy sounds 'tis possible to imagine.

December 9, 1760.—The scene of joy as usual soon succeeded, and every one went to see their new young monarch go in state to the House of Peers, really a pretty sight, by the multitude of coaches and concourse of populace that attended. The acclamations of joy and approbation were excessive, tho' I imagine not more than every sovereign receives on the like occasion. Novelty was, and ever will be pleasing to people of all ranks in life, as well as the mere vulgar. The procession was as follows :—

12 Grenadiers.
A coach, six bay horses, decorated.
A coach, dun horses.
12 Grenadiers.
14 Yeomen of the Guard.
10 Footmen.
4 other men.

The King in the state coach, drawn by 8 cream-coloured horses,
long tails, and manes ornamented with blue ribbons.
A Company of Horse Guards.
In the return, all the Members of both Houses
of Parliament in their coaches.

In 1760 occurs the fourth journal of travel by Miss
Girle, entitled—

"PLYMOUTH JOURNAL"

1760

If the rusticity of a dull pen, like a piece of rough
marble, may be polish'd by exercise, then (as I've
scribbled o'er much paper), may I in time, perhaps,
have the honorary title of an expert journalist. Here
am I now commencing my fourth essay on our
summer's rambles. . . . Our party assembled and
our morning fine, we once more bid adieu to the
Metropolis. Our first day's place of breakfasting was
the Orkney Arms, Maidenhead Bridge. All within a
few miles of this place the road, I think, is disagreeably unpleasant, the grounds surrounding it wearing
that dreary flat aspect which, in my opinion, generally
denotes those bordering on the great city ; but when
once Windsor Castle is in view, then the whole country
is fine, and is so quite on to Newbury. The prospect
in particular is very delightful from the hill just after
you leave Maidenhead, commanding Clifden, Lord
Inchiquin's, and the houses of several other gentlemen. We that evening reach'd Reading, the county
town of Berks. 'Tis large, well built, and during the
Civil War in England was strongly fortified. The
remains of the bastions, &c., are still seen ; formerly was
noted for a famous abbey in the adjoining Fourbourg

1760 (erected, as 'tis said, by a Saxon lady).   Here the
Parliament of England has been sometimes held.   Its
venerable ruins even now strike the beholder with an
awful pleasure.   'Tis most charmingly situated ; but
that, indeed, is no wonder, for who ever heard or read
of a society of religieux in former days whose thoughts
were so entirely fix'd on the other world, as to make
them neglect erecting their earthly residence on the
most delightful spot.   Indeed, this Fourbourg must
have been ever beautiful, and since the above mention'd time render'd more so by having in view the
seat of Lord Cadogan,[1] Captain Forrest's, &c.   The
abbey was built of flints, the remaining walls eight
feet thick, tho' the stones that fac'd them are gone,
but 'tis amazing to see how hard 'tis cemented.
Reading has three handsome churches built in the
quincunx fashion ;[2] and within a furlong of the town,
to the south-west, within a hundred yards of the
Kennet, on a rise call'd Cat's Grove Hill, is a stratum
of oysters,[3] five or six inches thro' the hill, many large
and entire, others mould'ring and decay'd, suppos'd to
have been there buried at the Deluge.

On Tuesday we set out early for our farm at
Beenham,[4] papa being obliged to go there on business
with his tenants, and we, not a little fond of the place,
chose to accompany him in the excursion.   It was a
very agreeable one.   Beenham lays about a mile out
of the great road to Bath, on a pretty steep ascent, and
near nine from Reading, which nine miles is allow'd
to be as fine a ride with regard to the prospects on

[1] Caversham Park.
[2] Probably she means one at each corner of the town.
[3] Fossil bed of oysters.
[4] Underwood Farm.

each side as almost anywhere met with.   As thro' my   1760
journal I intend to mention every seat we pass nigh
to, I must not omit that fine old mansion call'd Ingle-
field House,[1] now Mrs. Brathawit's, and a little farther,
on the same hand, is Mrs. Zinzan's, a very delightful
situation.   We there call'd, and had the pleasure of
finding them all well.   After a short visit we proceed'd
to the farm, which is only three-quarters of a mile
distance from their house. . . . In the evening we
return'd again to Reading, which we left on Wednesday by six, and in our way, to Basingstoke went to
see Mr. Baker's new purchas'd estate in Hampshire.
'Tis prettily situated on Heckfield Heath (near Mr.
George Pitt's).   The family, as we knew, were gone
into Norfolk, so that we went on to breakfast at
Basingstoke, which in itself, and surrounding country,
I think very indifferent; from thence thro' a road
equally unpleasant, we went to Andover, there lay.
This place, on the borders of Salisbury Plain, is a
great thoroughfare on the direct western road, is
tolerably built, tolerably neat, and intolerably paved ;
but the art of sticking the streets with the points of
stones upwards greatly flourishes in every town almost—you perceive they're proficients in this trade,
but what end (except 'tis a 'shoemaker's plot), it can
answer, 'tis difficult to imagine.   On Thursday we
went on to Salisbury, a city in Wiltshire, laying at
the confluence of the two rivers Avon and Willy.
When at this place the last summer, I own I thought
it not in beauty what report had taught me to expect ;
but now, by not having my expectation rais'd, which
ever diminishes the lustre of new objects, it really
wore an aspect much more striking ; it was indeed the

[1] Englefield House.

1760 race-time, which gave it an air of unusual gaiety. . . .
The streets are all at right angles, according, as 'tis
said, to the model of old Babylon, the market-place
spacious ; but as to their canals, as they style them, I
must say that in my opinion they deserve not so fine
a title.   The cathedral, begun by Bishop Poore, is in
figure a cross ; above the roof, which is 116 feet high,
rises the tower and spire, the highest and grandest in
England, being from the ground 410 feet, yet the wall
at top less than five inches diameter; its ornaments
are rich.   The tower has sixteen lights, four of a side.
The inside of the church cannot, I think, be admir'd ;
the outside is simplicity with elegance, tho' some think
this cathedral light and slender to a fault, for the
building be strong, yet, having not the appearance of
strength is as great a defect in beauty as being over-
clumsy.   This fabrick is remarkable for having an
equal number of gates as months in the year, windows
as days, and marble pillars as hours, a circumstance
for which the architect is greatly found fault with, his
plan so whimsical. . . . We went on to Woodyeates
Inn, where we stay'd that night ; 'tis a single house, a
few miles after entering Dorsetshire, with a country
round it very disagreeable.   The next morning from
this place we went to see' the seat of the Right Hon.
George Doddington.   The house, gardens, and park
called Eastbury are eight miles in circumference.
When we got to the park, choosing to walk, we
quitted the vehicle.   The building, as you see thro' a
fine lawn, may be styl'd an elegant fabrick ; 'tis of
stone, extending in length 570 feet, of which the main
body of the house takes up only 144 ; the rest is
arcades and offices.   Having ascended a grand flight
of steps, you come under a Doric portico, whose pedi-

ment extends 62 feet, with pillars 46 feet high ; from 1760
thence you enter a noble hall, adorn'd by statues and
busts, the saloon painted olive, the ornaments, as the
cornice, &c., rich gilt ; the sofas in this apartment are
very fine tapestry, On one side the saloon is the
common dining and drawing room, on the other the
best drawing-room, hung with and furnished with cut
velvet ; the state bed-chamber, hung with crimson
velvet furniture ; the same, the bed with gold, and
lin'd with a painted India satin ; the dressing-room
hung with green satin. The marble tables in all the
principal rooms are fine, purchas'd, the housekeeper
inform'd us, out of one of the Italian palaces. I was
much surprised to see in a house like this so few
pictures, only one—which was Lord Stafford dictating
to his secretary—worth remarking, a thing surprising
at a time when it seems to be the peculiar taste of the
gentlemen of this age to make collections, whether
judges of paintings or ambitious to be thought so.
The *Managareth*, or Chinese bedroom and dressing-
room in the attic storey, is excessively droll and pretty,
furnish'd exactly as in China, the bed of an uncommon
size, seven feet wide by six long. In the common
breakfast-room, fixed over the chimney is a clock
which I think may be called curious, the dial white-
flowered glass, the hand of the same material but of
colours various, altogether forming a pretty ornament.
The gardens are laid out as well as is possible without
a view of water. . . . From Eastbury we went on to
Blandford, a town about four miles distant ; 'tis well
built and populous, more so indeed at that time, as
it was their fair and visitation time. . . . Blandford
is seated on the river Stour. I've heard that formerly 'twas the greatest manufactury in England of

1760 bone lace, but what is remarkable is that the poorer sort of its present inhabitants told us they never knew that it ever was so.

As we prosecuted our tour, about a mile from this town, we saw the seat of Mr. Portman Seymour,[1] and so on after two of Mr. Pledwell's,[2] the one a new handsome house, the other the ancient family seat—a fine old mansion; and as they are only three miles apart, I think the gentleman must have some difficulty (his father being lately dead), to determine at which to reside. We pass'd to a house of Mr. William Pitt's near Dorchester, which place we reached in the evening. This town has a neat appearance; I believe, tho', only from being built entirely of stone, for the houses in general, except one or two in the High Street, are mean: 'tis, I think, a place of the least bustle I was ever in; it seems serenity itself; no one appear'd agitated by hurry or confusion. Quite round the town is a very pleasant walk of sycamores, which must be very agreeable to the inhabitants. Mr. Hawkins, a gentleman of the place, gave us the favour of his company for the evening, and early the next morning we again set out. Near Dorchester[3] are the remains of a Roman amphitheatre,[4] and one[5] of their encampments able to contain about 30,000 soldiers. The country here begins to wear a fine aspect, and every mile brings additions to its beauty; our road from this morn was nothing but ascents or descents, no level, all a range of hills, no sooner at the foot of

---

[1] Bryanston Park.

[2] Mr. Pleydell's, Whatcombe House.

[3] Dorchester, the British Dwrinwyr, afterwards Roman Durnovaria. These walks were made by the Romans.

[4] Amphitheatre called Maunbury, reckoned to hold 12,960 spectators.

[5] Poundbury, or Maiden Castle, both near Dorchester.

one, but a still higher offer'd for us to mount. Our 1760
prospects must, of course, be charming, the sea adding
to its grandeur. We breakfasted at Bridport.[1] 'Tis
large, on the seashore, stone built, chiefly cottages, but
they are neat, and therefore the town cannot be styl'd a
bad one. Once this was the only place for twisting ropes
for the Royal Navy. They still carry on the trade, and
'tis charming to see how industrious their poor are—
every child of five years being able to earn threepence
or a groat a day. At this town we breakfasted ; and
not far from it is a hill call'd after it by the name of
Bridport. This hill it was that gave us sensations too
difficult to describe, and impossible to say whether
pleasure or terror was the predominant passion of our
bewilder'd senses. We got out of the coach, trusting
more to our own steadiness than to our seemingly compos'd animals, and had then in view a prospect, if I may
use the expression, terribly pleasing. . . . The scene
continued for a mile and a half. Its length made us
grow courageous, and we left it more in admiration
than in fear, reaching that night Axminster. We
found ourselves in a town of a very poor appearance,
nothing in it worth a stranger's notice, except the
carpet manufactory to see ; that is indeed well worth
while ; the weaving of it is extremely curious, and gave
us ladies the more pleasure, I believe, as our sex are
here admitted to be artists—an uncommon privilege[2]
at this time of day, when the men seem to engross
every possible branch of business to themselves.
Axminster is on the great Western road, and the first

[1] A seaport and municipal borough. Pop. in 1896, 7000.
[2] The carpet-weaving is now removed from Axminster to Wilton.
Miss Girle would have been satisfied with the present progress in
occupation for women, and, for 137 years ago, seems to have been before
her age in thought.

1760 town in the county of Devon. We were led by
Camden, and curiosity to take an inside view of the
church, he having told us of the monuments of two
Danish princes slain at the battle of Bruneburg in
this neighbourhood,[1] fought by King Athelstane, with
seven princes, over whom he obtained victory; but
really the sight of their highnesses afforded us great
entertainment, nor should I have had the least notion by
their present clumsy appearance such uncouth lumps
of stone were once design'd to represent royalty. We
left Axminster next day. Near it is a seat of Mr.
Tucker's,[2] so sweetly situat'd that none can, I fancy,
exceed it. Indeed the country here is most amazing
fine, and the Vale of Honiton, a few miles farther, so
far exceeds any idea one can form of a landscape, that
'tis in vain to endeavour at the description. The
inhabitants of Dorsetshire, they say, pique themselves
on what Charles II. said of their county, which was,
"that in or out of England he never saw its equal;"
but sure he had then, I should imagine, never been in
Devonshire; the former is very charming, but still in
my opinion exceeded by the latter. At Hainton we
made a stay of some hours. 'Tis really a very pretty
town. Five miles from it is a seat of Sir William
Young's, which we pass'd that day in our way to
Exeter. And now I must give some account of this
the capital of Devon. It stands on the east of the
river Exe, which washes its walls, on a hill of a gentle
rise, encompass'd with a ditch and strong wall a mile
and half in circumference. I must own myself greatly

---

[1] Battle of Brunedune in 937, fought against Anlaf the Dane. In
this were slain five kings, seven princes, a Bishop of Sherborne, and
5000 of the enemy. (Vide *Saxon Chronicle*.)
[2] Coryton House.

disappointed in this city, styl'd the " London of the 1760
West." That title, I suppose, it derives from its
trade, for its inhabitants appear very industrious, and
'tis infinitely to their credit to say that business seems
their chief employment; but 'tis the place I imagin'd
so much superior to what it is.   It principally consists
of one very long street, tolerably broad, but not very
straight, the houses every one of which are shops of
a most ancient model; indeed we saw not any that
can be call'd good in this grand city, consisting of
fifteen parish churches (besides a cathedral), several
of which in the Civil Wars, they told us, were ex-
posed to sale by the common cryer.   The Romans
are supposed to have been here,[1] among other probable proofs, from many of their coins dug up there.
Their Cathedral is in general, I believe, thought
a good one.   It exceeds, in my opinion, either Worcester, Bristol, Gloucester, Winchester, or Salisbury in
the inside; but none I've ever seen equals that of
York.   This at Exeter was thirty years building;
the choir, by Bishop Wharleward,[2] in the year 1150;
the body, by Quivel, in 1280.   Grandison consecrated
the two last arches at the west end in 1327, and
covered the whole roof; and Courtenay completed
the north tower in 1485; and 'tis very remarkable to
observe the uniformity of the whole, for no one can
discover the least incongruity in the several parts, so
much does it appear the work of the same architect.
I must not omit to mention as a curious piece of
antiquity the Bishop's throne[3] of Gothic woodwork
carving.   Indeed it may justly be admir'd, the canopy

---

[1] Its Roman name was Isca Damnoniorum ; British, Caer Isc.
[2] Bishop Warelwast.
[3] Made in 1470 under Bishop Stapleton.

1760 being carried up in a light taste for above sixty feet.
'Tis thought to be coeval with the See, and at the
demolition of Episcopacy in the time of Charles I.
was remov'd, but 'tis suppos'd privately order'd to be
carefully preserv'd, as since it has been replac'd without having receiv'd the least damage.   I think they
don't at this Cathedral perform the choir service at all
well.   There are many ancient monuments ; some of
those shown to us as most deserving notice I must here
mention.   The first discoverer of Newfoundland he's
here, Captain Gilbert ; Bishop Stapleton,[1] who founded
and laid the first stone of Exeter College, Oxon ;
Bishop Bidgood, who originally was only a Blue-coat
boy of this city ; Bishop Oldham's effigy, with his
hands nail'd together ; he was excommunicated for not
turning Catholic, but died before the time design'd for
his execution ; Lady Barret, in a little chapel, now
called by her name, because she there lay in state ; a
skeleton effigy of Bishop Lacy, who in endeavouring
to imitate our Savour in fasting forty days, on the
thirty-ninth fell a martyr, I think one may say, to his
presumption ; and in the library belonging to the
Cathedral is Judge Doddridge and his lady, who was
maid of honour to Queen Elizabeth.   In the body of
the church is a clock very remarkable for its antiquity
and workmanship.   'Twas made some hundred years
since,[2] has three dials; as for the hour, minute hand,
and moon's age, 'tis really curious.   The organ[3] is
esteem'd a fine one.   The choir has two sets of
hangings, tapestry and velvet, and gilt plate for the

[1] Murdered in a mob at Cheapside for espousing the cause of Edward
II.

[2] Made time of Edward III., minute dial added in 1760, same year as
this Journal.

[3] Built by Loosemore, 1665.

communion service. The altar-piece, representing the 1760
inside of the church, is reckon'd a fine painting well
preserved, except some little injury it received by
three or four bullets fired at it in the great Rebellion
in Oliver Cromwell's time. The painted glass, the
figures of the patriarchs, kings, &c., were greatly
damaged by the Reformers' zeal. Here, I think, finishes
my account of the Cathedral.

In the north angle of the city, on the highest
ground, stand the ruins of a castle called Rougemont,[1]
formerly the residence of the West Saxon kings, afterwards the Earls of Cornwall. It was surrounded by
a high wall and deep ditch ; had a rampart of earth
parallel to the top of the wall overlooking the city and
county. The inhabitants have for some years been
filling up the ditch and on it planting trees, which on
one side of a fine terrace form a grove, and the
other being what one may style a natural hanging
shrubbery, beyond which the rising country forms a
charming prospect, which together makes the walk
(called Northern Hay), very delightful. . . . On the
Monday morning we left Exeter, and breakfasted at
the town of Chidley,[2] of which, as nothing can be said
in its praise, I'll make no further mention.

We were surpris'd in our travels thro' Devonshire to see their cottages of an appearance really
meaner than in any county is usual ; and indeed, as
by fatal experience, they have found residences terribly
unsafe ; for on July 2nd, at Offington, near Exeter,
more than twenty were demolished ; the poor people
were in their beds, and one old woman in hers

---

[1] Built by William the Conqueror on an older site, given by him to
Baldwin de Brionne, husband of William's niece, Albreda.
[2] Chudleigh, now celebrated for its caves, with prehistoric bones, &c.

1760 drowned by the rain being prodigious heavy; it came pouring in such torrents from the hills behind, and hurl'd down so great a quantity of stones of such amazing size, that soon broke down walls built only of a composition of clay and straw, call'd cob. The houses were instantly overflow'd and tumbling to pieces ; all were in the utmost consternation, as one may easily imagine, from the ruinous state their habitations are still in.   But to quit a subject so dismal.

We that night lay at Ashburton,[1] a tolerable market-town on the great road ; the next morning we breakfast'd at a pretty rural place call'd Ivy Bridge,[2] and in the evening reach'd Plymouth.   As we were strangers at the place, and rather fatigued that day with travelling, we choose to limit our curiosity by deferring our rambles till next day, papa that night only sending to a gentleman of his acquaintance (there quarter'd), desiring the favour of his company at breakfast. He came early next day, and it being propos'd to spend great part of it at Lord Edgecumbe's,[3] he was so obliging as to procure us a safe and large boat for our little voyage ; but first, breakfast being over, we went to view part of the town.

Plymouth (as must be generally known), is a place of great consideration and note, situated between two large outlets of the sea, in the bottom of a very large Sound, which on every side is encompass'd with hills, the shore steep, and in the entrance into the bay has a most dangerous rock, which, being cover'd at high water, many ships have there been lost when they thought themselves perfectly safe ; but, as I

---

[1] One of the old Stannary towns of Devon, on the edge of Dartmoor.
[2] A romantic spot on the river Erme.
[3] Mount Edgecumbe.

learn'd at Plymouth, on the above-mentioned rock, 1760 call'd the Eddystone, was erected two years ago a new lighthouse,[1] so contriv'd as it can't take fire, which misfortune happen'd to the last there built, which was burnt down. Having walk'd about some time, seen the Victualling Office (in which the bisket bakehouse performers gave us great entertainment), with the parade, quays, markets, &c., except the garrison, which we left for the evening, and now went to our boat, which lay ready for us. 'Tis by water to my Lord's not quite a league, yet by land, tho' in Devonshire, more than fifty miles, being obliged to go so far round and thro' part of Cornwall.

We had not been ten minutes on the watery element when Mount Edgecumbe present'd a view which none could exceed. It lies on the opposite shore from Plymouth, on the other side of Hamoaze. In less than half-an-hour we quitted the boat, and, entering the park, were then at the seat indeed justly stil'd one of the grandest spots in our charming isle. The gardens, which we first went over, seem in the taste every one could wish. In the orangery are some of the largest fruit I have ever seen. In the Maze, twenty-five orange-trees brought from the Straits, that for height, tho' lopp'd, are really curiosities. In one part of the gardens next the sea my Lord[2] has erected a small battery, where, on any particular occasion of rejoicing, they can fire twenty-one pieces of cannon, call'd a royal salute. Here is a pavilion, from which is a very fine view.

---

[1] The third. The first was washed away; second burnt in 1755; Smeaton's, finished in 1759, now removed to the Hoe; fourth opened 1882.

[2] Richard, second Baron Edgecumbe.

1760   Having walk'd over the gardens, we ascended a fine
lawn, at the top of which stands the ancient mansion
(a stone building), and both within and without bearing testimony of the antiquity it boasts.[1] Leaving the
house, we mounted a steep ascent, and for about a
mile and a half went on in a walk, where on one side
we had a rising, the other a hanging wood, thro' the
latter a very delightful prospect, and the whole being
park, and the number of deer, no small addition to a
scene so pleasing. The extent of our rambles that
way was to a rustic arch of stone erected at the top
of the hill, from which the view of the sea is indeed
noble, and from this point we see the Eddystone.
Farther beyond the arch is a zig-zag walk, which goes
quite down again to the shore; but we now pursu'd
our way back thro' the park, and reach'd very soon a
little temple which afforded us a repast very agreeably. This spot, commanding a sweet view of the
winding harbour underneath, and being in the midst
of a wood guarded from sun-influence, was fixed on
by a large party of gentlemen and ladies, who came
that day on a scheme of pleasure to Mount Edgecumbe, as a place to enjoy in the most rural manner
the cold collation they brought there. Captain Marriott was to have been with them, but at our arrival
insisted on accompanying us to my Lord's : there we
met his friends, who, with the greatest civility, desir'd
us to refresh ourselves. With thanks we accepted the
obliging offer, and the day being extremely hot, we
received from it a new recruit of alacrity to pursue our
rambles, and took leave of the company, sorry not to
have it in our power, but in words, to return the
receiv'd obligation.

[1] Original portion built in 1550.

In our way back thro' the grounds we saw many 1760
fine prospects, too great a number to give description. From one place the views have a very pretty
effect from seven vistas that surround you; at the end
of each is a different object; from one the town of
Plymouth, with its churches and spires; another, the
Isle of St. Nicholas, on which is a castle commanding
the entrance into Hamoaze and Cutwater; from the
third you see Mount Batten; the fourth, Plymouth
dock; fifth, the county of Cornwall; and at the end
of the two others, rising at the end over the top of
trees, are a round and square tower at a great distance.
More than five hours, I think, we spent at my Lord's,
admiring its several beauties. We at last reach'd the
shore, and, entering into the boat, soon were wafted
to the dock, the place we were next to see. The dock
is two miles from Plymouth, and is, as I was inform'd,
as compleat an arsenal as any the Government are
masters of. Here ships are built or brought to be
repair'd, and there are all sorts of warehouses for
naval stores for those ships appointed to lay there,
besides military stores and handsome houses for the
officers. They are now building a new dry dock (a fit
size for the " Royal George," [1] our largest man-of-war),
which 'tis suppos'd to excel any of the kind, it being
hewn out of a solid rock of marble, and lined with
Portland stone. We once more took boat, and went
round several men-of-war; saw the " Formidable," a
fine ship of ninety guns, taken by Sir Edward Hawke.
After viewing the shipping, we were all landed at the
hospital, which is recently erected, consisting of six
separate buildings of stone, makes a fine appearance,

[1] This vessel sank in Portsmouth Harbour, with over eight hundred
souls on board, in 1782.

1760 and, what is more to the founder's honour, will afford
a most happy relief to the sailors and soldiery. Near
here is the place where part of the French prisoners
are kept, of which there are at Plymouth between four
and five thousand. We saw them at some distance,
amusing themselves in a field adjoining their prison.
From the hospital we walk'd to our inn, not having
any curiosity to see the inside; but the gentlemen
walk'd over it, and afterwards overtook us at our
entering the town. 'Twas then five o'clock, and having
been out from before ten, and, I suppose, walk'd more
than nine miles, we found ourselves ready for dinner,
which waited only our appearance. We that day had
procur'd for us those celebrated fish John Dorees, and
red mullet. As I'm not in the least fond of fish, I
can't be a judge of its excellence; but really the latter,
which, on account of the trail, is styl'd the " Sea
Woodcock," is beautiful to the eye and has a flavour
most remarkably fine. The former is a creature of
an aspect rather horrible ; nor does the goodness, in
my opinion, at all compensate for its figure, tho'
Quin [1] (who now lives at Bath), often, it seems, comes
from thence to Plymouth to eat them in perfection ;
therefore I suppose them deem'd curious, as he is said
to deserve in some degree that unmanly title of an
epicure. Provisions here, except fish, by the continual resort of company, are dearer than one should
imagine. Quin, I suppose, thought so, by the following droll essay of his wit, which Captain Marriott was
giving us an account of. The last time of his being
there, after a fortnight's stay at his inn, and being
kept in his usual magnificent table, on viewing his

[1] James Quin, celebrated actor and gourmand, born 1693, died 1766 ;
spent his last eighteen years retired at Bath.

bill, thought it, I fancy, a little extravagant, for, after 1760
discharging it, on going away, in an arch tone, " Herbert," says he, " give me the watchword." " Sir,"
replied the landlord, " I don't understand you." " No,"
said Quin ; "and hain't you robb'd me, and is it not
customary for highwaymen to give the watchword ? "
The joke caused a smile, which I suppose made its
author go off in good-humour, tho' eas'd of his money.

After we had din'd, it then being the cool of the
evening, we went to take a view of the citadel or
garrison, a small but regular fortification over against
the Isle of St. Nicholas. In my description of this
place I fear (from not having a knowledge of that
science), making a mistake ; but that reason, I hope,
will plead my excuse ; but the terms of fortification
are quite out of female knowledge ; and what with
many other things the men would perhaps say, we
should not endeavour to understand ; yet I must own
'tis my opinion that women might be made acquainted
with various subjects they are now ignorant of, more
for want of instruction than capacity, and what at first
may appear intricate, after a quarter of an hour's
converse might give entertainment. But is it anything surprising the sex should amuse themselves
with trifles [1] when these lords of creation will not give
themselves the trouble (in my conscience, I believe
for fear of being outshone), to enlarge our minds by
making them capable to retain those of more import-
ance ? But to digress no further, but proceed with my
account of the citadel. From what I learn'd, by over-
hearing the gentlemen discourse in their view of the
works (being as unobserv'd as our grandmother Eve

---

[1] Pity our heroine could not have had a peep at women's progress at
the end of the nineteenth century.

1760 listening to the angel's tale to Adam, to whom she afterwards told her hearing the story—

> " As in a shady nook she stood behind,
> Just then return'd, at shut of evening flowers."
>
> —*Milton.*

'Tis, as I said before, a regular fortification, inaccessible by sea, not exceedingly strong by land, only, by being of a stone hard as marble, they say it would not soon yield to the batteries of an enemy. 'Tis surrounded by a deep trench three-quarters of a mile in circumference, out of which was dug the stone the whole was built with. It has three hundred great guns on the walls, which stand thickest towards the sea. Several are planted lying almost level with the water, which gives the greatest security to ships in harbour.

From the town, which lies sloping on the same rock towards the east of the sea, call'd Catswater, we ascended the glacis, pass'd the trench by the drawbridge, and thro' the bastions, and came into a sort of field, where are the barracks for the soldiers, which really may be styl'd huts, just to shelter them from the inclemency of the weather. Here, too, are the guard-room and casements, as I think they are called, buildings of such prodigious strength as to be perfectly safe from the reach of bombs, and here, in case of a siege, the soldiers off guard retire.

Having now seen all here mention'd, we last went to walk on the ramparts, where the prospects of the sea, the shipping, the lower battery, &c., was so delightful, that it detain'd us till night had near drawn her sable mantle o'er the whole. 'Twas near ten when we return'd to supper, and the remainder of our evening was spent in conversing of the day's diversion, and of

how much more pleasure we had receiv'd than even 1760
we expected from the town of Plymouth and the places
that surround it.

The next morning, soon aften ten, we set out
again for Ashburton, after returning thanks to Captain
Marriott for the civilities we receiv'd the preceding
day. Accompanying us to the end of Plymouth, he
took his leave, and we went on to Ivy Bridge, and in
the evening reach'd Ashburton ; reach'd Exeter early
on Friday, stay'd there the whole day, and got the
next morn by twelve to Honiton. When we before
were at this town, knowing we were to return thro' it,
we defer'd till then seeing the making of bone lace ;
so now, as soon as we had breakfasted, went to view
this their chief manufacture, which really gave us
great pleasure, and much more to see 'twas our own
country-women that could arrive at such perfection
in this work, as I hope will prevent our ladies from
forming the least wish to have the right Flanders ; for
really, on comparing two pieces, ours had the first
preference ; and if so, how very cruel not to encourage
the industrious poor of our native land. After seeing
the lace-making we went to the broad-cloth weaving,
which, tho' in a different way, is still curious ; and
from thence, it being market-day, we stroll'd round
inquiring the price of several commodities, and, ignorant Londoners as we were, quite astonish'd to hear
we might have a couple of fine chickens for sixpence,[1]
a pound of veal for three-halfpence, and other provisions in proportion cheap. What a surprising difference from the Metropolis ! From the market we went
back to our inn, and there, for the remainder of our

---

[1] This account shows how railways have almost equalised the price
of provisions, &c., throughout the country.

1760 stay, amus'd ourselves with the transcription on the wainscot, which, at such places, I think every idler seems to subscribe their unit for the entertainment of the next idle gazer.   I found the following four lines, which perhaps by many have been found too true in their pursuit of grandeur :—

> " How wretched is our fate,
> What hazards do we run ;
> We are wicked to be great,
> And great to be undone."

After a stay of nearly five hours at Honiton, we pursued our journey ; and having mounted one of those hills which surround this pretty town, we had again in view the fine vale I've mention'd before, than which I think no prospect of the mind can surpass in beauty.   We that night lay at Axminster, and from thence, to have the pleasure of variety, the next morn we took the other road to Salisbury from that we came.   Soon after we got out of Axminster we came into Somersetshire.   A mile from Chard, and not far from Crookhorn,[1] where we breakfasted, lies the seat of Earl Powlet,[2] on the brow of the Serene Hill.   The house appears good tho' ancient, the grounds of vast extent, commanding fine prospects.   We got that night to Yeovil,[3] a really pretty town, and the country round it very delightful.   We pass'd a seat of Mr. Fane's,[4] near this place.   At our arrival we failed not going to Mr. Forbes's, an inn[5] so very famous for a most extraordinary kitchen, that we were told it was worth going miles to see it ; and indeed it answer'd

---

[1] Crewkerne.
[2] Hinton St. George.
[3] Celebrated for its glove manufactories.
[4] Brimpton Hall.
[5] " The Angel."

description, and may be call'd a general repository for 1760
curiosities of every sort its owner can collect—as china,
pictures, shells, antiques, &c., all rang'd in order.
There is two dishes of Roman earth, very handsome,
and of great value, having been in this town three
hundred years; and in another corner lay a lamp,
which Mr. Forbes said was really dug out of the ruins
of Herculaneum, and therefore esteems it highly. But
'tis not only the kitchen at this inn deserves notice;
the whole house for neatness is a curiosity.

'Twas rather late next day when we left Yeovil;
two miles from the town we ascended a long steep eminence called Babylon Hill; the origin of its title none
could inform us of, but papa imagin'd it was from the
resemblance it bears to the Hanging Gardens of that
place. At the top the view is very pleasing. As we
pass'd Sherborne we saw the ancient seat of the Digby
family,[1] seeming a vast pile of building. Just before
we got to Shaftesbury we had a prodigious hill to go
up, so steep the horses could hardly gain the top.
There stands the town,[2] the only one I ever saw on
so high a situation, as generally for the convenience
of water they lay low. The prospects surrounding it
are indeed charming, more so, I suppose, from the
novelty of the place. They have two sweet walks,
one call'd Park Hill, and Castle Hill; from the former
is a zig-zag way down the hill, which is a common
footpath to the inhabitants, tho' to us it appear'd
perpendicular, and even frightful to see them un-
concernedly descend. The day following we went
for many miles over the plains, to which we arriv'd
by a terrible hill, five miles off Shaftesbury, called the

[1] Sherborne Castle.
[2] Of great antiquity. The British Caer Palladwr.

1760 White Sheet.   We breakfasted at Salisbury, and that
night lay at Stockbridge, getting to Winchester early
the next day.   No place this summer is more gay
than this, prodigious deal of company resorting to the
camp, his Highness the Duke of York[1] was there
then, and excessively admir'd for his civilities to all
ranks.   The first night of his arrival, so wonderful a
mortal is a prince, the streets were throng'd to see
him, upon which he threw open the window and with
universal applause was gazed at.   Winchester is a
mile and a half within its walls, has at some distance
a venerable appearance, but in itself nothing remarkable ; here is no manufacture, no nagivation, and of
course no trade, but what is naturally transacted by
its inhabitants and the neighbouring villages.   The
Cathedral on the outside is extremely plain ; on
the in, 'tis esteem'd fine ; the oddity of the tower
greatly strikes the eye ; they say indeed 'twas never
finish'd and 'tis suppos'd to have been intended to
support a spire, as it has strength for one higher than
that at Salisbury.   On the south side of the west gate
of the city was formerly a castle, and in the place
where that stood Charles II. began a noble design
for a royal palace[2] in 1683 ; a large cupola was intended 30 feet above the roof for a view of the sea ;
the shell is said to have cost £25,000.   I think there
are 27 windows in front, and the apartments on the
principal floor 20 feet high.   His late Majesty George
I. gave to the Duke of Bolton the pillars, of Italian
marble, which were to have supported the staircase,
said to be a present from the great Duke of Tuscany.

[1] Edward, Duke of York, third son of George II.
[2] Architect, Sir Christopher Wren.   The portion completed made
into barracks in 1810.

The centre of the palace being exactly in a line 1760
with the centre of the west end of the Cathedral,
there a street 200 feet broad was to have been built,
houses for the nobility ; the parks were to have been
ten miles round. Winchester, if this grand work had
been compleated, would indeed have been a city of
magnificence. They have now eight regiments en-
camped there, seven militia, one of regulars. We saw
the Berkshire exercise, who really perform'd well ;
the view of a camp and their martial music is very
pleasing. I was in Colonel Vansittart's [1] tent, furnish'd in the taste adapted to the place ; those for
the soldiery are of a much smaller size, and besides
them are a great number of sutler's tents, or rather
hovels. From Winchester we had propos'd ourselves
great pleasure by going from thence to Gosport, to
pay a visit to a Berkshire family residing there during
the war, with whom we had been extremely intimate.
We that night lay at Wickham,[2] one of the most
rural pretty towns I ever saw. The next day, as we
drew nigh to Gosport, our fear of not seeing Mr.
Percy's family increas'd, as they might possibly be
gone on some travelling excursion, but on our arrival
we found them at home, and the additional pleasure
of finding Mrs. Durell and Mrs. Percy's sister, from
their house from Southampton, to which place we
once intended to go on purpose to see them. The
reception we met with from these our agreeable
friends show'd the sincerity of the many wishes
they've express'd that we would, while they continued
there, make Gosport be listed among our other tours.

[1] Of Shottesbrook, Berks.
[2] Birthplace of the celebrated William of Wykeham, Bishop of Winchester.

F

1760 . . . Mrs. Durel, Miss Brown, Mr. Percy, papa,
and myself, accepted an invitation from Mr. Jones,
(agent of the Hospital) (we three were the only
ladies); the invitation was to see the Royal Hospital
at Haslar. The building is grand, taking up within
its walls 32 acres. It commands a fine prospect of
the sea, Spithead, Southsea Castle, and other points
of view. After an agreeable day, in the evening we
returned in a six-oar'd boat to Gosport. Friday morn
we went to Stokes Bay to see them take shrimps and
other fish; here is a fine dry heath commanding the
sea and the Isle of Wight. We had in a former
journey been on that very charming island, so were
now satisfied with the pleasing view of it from this
place. Here, having spent two hours, we return'd to
the town, and in walking round employ'd another.

Gosport, like most seaports, is a place of very indifferent appearance, and where we should not choose
to reside, except it were at Coal Harbour, which,
laying by the waterside, is pleasant. After having
dined, our large party, in a man-of-war's boat, were
wafted over to Portsmouth. The crossing is short
but agreeable, by the having several remarkable
points of view, as Block House Fort and Point, the
round tower opposite, the Royal Hospital at Haslar,
the two neighbouring towns, Spithead, &c. Having
landed at Sallee Port, we walked over the town, which
I think can hardly boast of a superior elegance to
Gosport, and having gone thro' the ordnance or gun
wharf, been round the ramparts, and taken a view of
the inside of the church, we next went to the dock,
where we had been invited to tea at Mr. Moriarty's
there, by his lady and himself. We were treated
with great politeness, and after a visit that appear'd

too short because so agreeable, we again sallied out 1760
to satisfy our curiosity, a passion very prevalent in most
minds, tho' by the men deem'd the characteristic of
the female one *only*, but to which of right belonging
I'll leave to abler pens and pursue my tale.

In the yards, the dock, and storehouses of Portsmouth the furniture they say is laid up in the most exact
order, so that the workmen may find anything they
want even in the dark.   The remains of the dreadful
fire, July 2nd, was then smoking, and terrible is it to
behold anywhere the ravages of this merciless enemy.
'Tis computed that the loss here was not less than
£90,000, and storehouses, a rope-walk that was a
room 170 feet long partly demolish'd, a 1000 tun
of hemp, with other magazines.   Most people really
think this destruction was caus'd by lightning [1] and
some affirm they saw a ball of fire fall on one of the
storehouses, while others imagine it was a premedi-
tated design to destroy the whole yard. . . . We
next went on board a man-of-war ; 'twas the " Tartar,"
that has done so great execution when commanded
by the brave Lockhart.   From this ship we went into
the hull of the " Britannia," now building ; it is 170
feet long on the inside by 50, and is to carry 100
guns.   The bulk of these prodigious bodies seems to
the eye amazing.   We next went to view the three
ships of Thuroe's [2] squadron, laying then at Portsmouth, and after that proceeded to the Academy to
see the model of a 100-gunship call'd the " Victory,"
which was cast away in the year '46.   This model
cost more than 100 guineas. . . . 'Twas pretty late

---

[1] It is now asserted to have been lightning.
[2] Thurot, the Captain of the French squadron ; these three ships
were taken by Capt. John Elliot off the Isle of Man.

1760 before we got home to Mr. Percy's, but the remainder
of the evening we spent very happily with our obliging
friends; but the next morn arriv'd, and on that we
were to quit their hospitable mansion.   The 12th hour
of that day was a witness to our parting, and we then
quitted Gosport and set out for the Metropolis.

About five miles after leaving Gosport we found
ourselves on those delightful eminences call'd Portsdown Hills.   They extend into Sussex; the soil is
chalk, and the face of the country greatly to be
admir'd.   The ports, creeks, bays, ocean, ships, Isle
of Wight, Porchester Castle, towns of Gosport, Portsmouth, Southampton, Chichester, and in short under
one view all the coast from Portland Isle to Sussex,
gentlemen's seats scatter'd here and there to make the
prospect still more beautiful.   We that night lay at
Liphook, and the next morn came down Hind Hill,
an old romantic spot, to which is given the nickname
of the Devil's Punch Bowl, and indeed one seems
to travel round a basin of amazing size, which road
appears from the inside of a vehicle rather frightful
than pleasing.   We went thro' the neat town of God-
alming, and pass'd a seat of Lady Oglethorp's.   We
breakfasted at Guildford, which is well built.   We then
went to see some painted glass,[1] which is esteem'd
curious.   'Tis in the chapel of the Hospital, founded by
Bishop Abbot, 1619, for twelve old men and eight
women, who were all to be above sixty years of age.
The road to Leatherhead is, by most people, thought
to be more than agreeable; 'tis, indeed, thro' a series
of cornfields, and in the miles one passes at least ten
seats, tho' to my eye, who in the course of three

[1] Supposed to be of Flemish origin, and more ancient than the
Hospital's foundation.

weeks had seen so many places where Nature shone 1760
with such superior lustre, poor Surrey to me seem'd
dull, flat, and totally void of the all-enlivening faculty
of pleasing. . . . The owners of the ten mansions
above mentioned, the first from Guildford, was the
Lord Onslow's,[1] the second, Admiral Boscawen's,
third, fourth, and fifth, Lord Pennant's, Lacy's, and
General Howard's, and the rest were Lady Mary
Tryon's, Lord Effingham's, Mr. Warren's, and two
more, about the owners of which I was not so fortunate to gain intelligence. . . . We that night reach'd
Leatherhead, pay'd our compliments to Mr. Dowsett's
family there.   The next morning having breakfasted
and spent some hours, we set out for my Uncle
Mount's at Clapham, and after a short visit to them,
we proceed'd to London, reaching our Lincoln's Inn
Fields early enough in a very delightful evening,
almost to regret our arrival at the Metropolis at a
season when the country was in the height of beauty,
and the great city dull, dusty, and abandon'd.

		Miles we Travell'd from London.
July 7.	Monday, Breakfasted[2] at Maidenhead at "Orkney Arms"	25
	Lay at Reading, "Black Bear" . . .	14
,, 8.	Tuesday, went to Beenham. and return'd to Reading	18
,, 9.	Wednesday, Br. at Basingstoke, "The Crown"	17
	Lay at Andover, "The White Hart" . .	18
,, 10.	Thursday, Br. at Salisbury, "The King's Arms"	18
	Lay at Woodgates Inn	11

[1] Fell Hill.
[2] The reader must remember breakfast here stands in place of
modern luncheon, tho' earlier—virtually *déjeûner à la fourchette*.

Miles we Travell'd
from London.

July 11. Friday, Br. at Blandford, "The Greyhound"	12	
Lay at Dorchester, "The Antelope" .	.	16
„ 12. Saturday, Br. at Bridport, "The Bull"	.	16
Lay at Axminster, "The Green Dragon"	.	12
„ 13. Sunday, Br. at Honiton, "The Dolphin"	.	10
Lay at Exeter, "The New Inn" . .	.	16
„ 14. Monday, Br. at Chudleigh, "The King's		
Arms"	.	11
Lay at Ashburton, "The New Inn" .	.	11
„ 15. Br. at Ivy Bridge, "The Prince George"	.	13
Lay at Plymouth, "The Prince George"	.	11
„ 17. Lay at Ashburton, "The New Inn" .	.	24
„ 18. Lay at Exeter	.	22
„ 19. Br. at Honiton	.	16
Lay at Axminster	.	10
„ 20. Sunday, Br. at Crewkerne, "The George"	.	15
Lay at Yeovil, "The Angel" . .	.	9
„ 21. Monday, lay at Shaftesbury, "The George"	22	
„ 22. Br. at Salisbury, "The King's Arms" .	.	20
„ 23. Br. at Winchester, "The Chequer"	.	10
Lay at Wickham, "The King's Head"	.	14
„ 24. Thursday, lay at Gosport . . .	.	9
„ 26. Br. Saturday, din'd at Petersfield, "White		
Hart"	.	23
Lay at Liphook, "The Anchor" .	.	8
„ 27. Sunday, Br. at Guildford, "The White Hart"	16	
Lay at Leatherhead, "The Swan"	.	12
„ 28. Monday, got to London . . .	.	20
We travell'd in all . . .	514	

The next year, 1761, our heroine was destined to
lose her beloved father. In her diary she says :—

"*July 5th.*—This year I had the inexpressible loss
of one of the best of fathers. Having been ill long, and
London not agreeing with his constitution, he had
just purchas'd a house in the Circus, Bath, and our
goods were packing to remove there, but on his death
my mother and I, preferring the country, took a house

of Lady Buck's at Caversham, in Oxfordshire, having 1761
formerly lived in that neighbourhood."[1]

On September the 8th Miss Girle notes :—

" Her Royal Highness Princess Charlotte of Mecklenburg came to London. The marriage was perform'd the same evening." This was the marriage
of George III.; and on the 22nd of September Miss
Girle writes the following interesting account of the
coronation, entitled—

THE JOURNAL OF A DAY

Tuesday, Sep^{ber.} 25th, 1761.

The journal of a day, or short abstract of more
than twenty hours pass'd by one of the innumerable
parties assembled at their Majesties' coronation. In
a letter to a friend in the country.

Safe, perfectly safe from the dreaded coronation
is your Caroline ; but take the promis'd journal as it
follows. On Monday last I set out from my Uncle's
in Kent, very early in the morn, and thro' as much
rain as I believe ever fell in one day, arriv'd at the
Metropolis by the hour of dinner ; a gloomy prospect
the badness of the weather, as I then thought of the
morrow. On entering Mr. M——'s, was surpris'd to
see the whole company in all the elegance of dress,
but soon was inform'd that we were to go that evening
to our seats—this at Mr —— request, a poor timorous
mortal, not unlike another gentleman of my acquaintance in Hants county ; for as we were to have a file
of musketeers for our guard, the danger of going in

---

[1] One of Miss Girle's homes was at Beenham, only about nine
miles off.

1761 the morning could not have been great. However
'twas settl'd, and about five parts of our company left
us. When they were gone and I was drest (in *my*
coronation robes), we drank tea, and others of our
party coming to sup at Mr. M——'s, we left not this
house till near eleven, at which time three more coaches
set out, and without difficulty join'd the rest long before
twelve. Our room in the Broad Sanctuary (for which
was given 120 guineas), was commodious, our party,
consisting of twenty-four, quite agreeable, and our view
of the procession (in our own opinion, which you'll own .
a very material point), the very best of any of the surrounding multitude ; for we were just at an angle of
the platform fronting the band of music, and the Con-
duit, which ran with wine for the day. Thus situat'd
and all assembl'd, not having couches sufficient for the
repose of all (tho' there were in an adjoining apartment
two beds for the most delicate of our ladies), conse-
quently the most of us were to sit up, and of course
cards (the usual triflers of the time of idle people), were
propos'd, and the remaining dark hours employ'd at
commerce and lottery. The morning's dawn, however, was most impatiently expected, and tho' curiosity
is only stil'd a characteristic of the female mind, I
think the gentlemen were equally with the ladies desirous of its approach. At last it came, and sufficiently
were we then diverted by various artificers finishing
the platform for the expected ceremony. At five, an
early hour, we breakfasted ; that of six brought the
Guards, the foot rang'd on each side the platform, the
Life and Grenadier Horse in a double row under our
windows, making a most fine appearance, join'd to a
view of the scaffoldings ; they were form'd over each
other as the side-boxes at the theatre, lined as these

with red or green cloth, and the company of the 1st,
2nd, and 3rd rows were extremely brilliant, the day,
a most glorious one, adding to their splendour. From
this time we waited, but not with impatience, till twelve,
for there was a diversity of objects to satisfy the most
unbounded curiosity, nor could anything be conducted,
as far as was within our sight, in better order ; even the
very mob (tho' such amazing multitudes), seem'd that
day to have forgot their native rusticity, and seem'd
willing to be rul'd and kept in exact order. 'Twas in
this interval of time I exercis'd my pencil and took
the sketch you my friend and Mr. B. requested. . . .

I now come to the procession itself. You know,
my dear, how highly were my expectations rais'd, and
that in imagination I'd form'd a sight most magnificent.
To give you now my opinion of it, I need only say
that the reality was even more superb than the idea.
The coronation robes are a dress extremely becoming
to the ladies. I wish I could pay the same compliment
to their noble partners in the splendid group, but truth
will not allow my silence on the occasion, knowing
they made a far less illustrious appearance, tho' likewise deck'd in all their pageant grandeur ; but each
female shone indeed, in jewels, gold, silver, past description fine; and the sun, by casting his all-piercing
influence on these their dazzling ornaments, gave all
a double lustre in each beholder's eye; their head-
dress was genteely fancied, their diamonds and
coronets, with the hair in falling ringlets, so elegantly
dispos'd, that most look'd pleasing, but there were
eight or ten who must attract more notice from their
native figure than it was in the power of all their
glittering gewgaws to bestow. Pembroke [1] I thought

---

[1] Elizabeth, daughter of the second Duke of Marlborough.

1761 first in this list of lovely ones. Richmond,[1] Rockingham, Marchmont, and Harrington deserv'd not to be
the last. But now, my friend, what am I to say of our
new Queen? You desir'd me to be particular, but shall
we, who have yet only seen her in her coronation
procession, pretend at the description of her person?
Justice permits it not, as she then, by all accounts,
appear'd to a disadvantage, and was hid (being not
very majestic), by the number of her attendants; in
fine, the King's Charlotte is a woman by all accounts
that will ever rank among the good, not the handsome,
and with this her George, being the sensible man he
is, must be more happy than if a beauteous idiot like
a Coventry[2] was the partner of his crown. That she
has no title to praises due to a fine form or face, every
one agrees, but that she has every requisite to adorn
an amiable mind is as generally allow'd; and does she
not then deserve to be Queen of England? As to our
King, he look'd as a monarch ought, with dignity and
sweetness almost peculiar to himself. 'Tis said that
Quin[3] (who you know taught him to play), never acted
Majesty better than he performed the reality. At first
coming on the platform, as if astonish'd at sight of such
amazing multitudes, he clasp'd his hands, and lifting up
his eyes to heaven, stood for some moments in a profound silence, and I dare say (for great is his humility),
he never had a meaner opinion of himself than at that
instant, to think that all this bustle was for one poor
mortal, an earthly king. When he proceed'd, 'twas
with a slow and exact pace, thro' increasing acclama-

---

[1] Mary, daughter of the third Earl of Aylesbury.
[2] Lady Coventry was one of the beautiful Miss Gunnings.
[3] Quin, on being asked if he had taught the King to act, replied, "Yes,
I taught the boy."

tions, after stopping as if to give his subjects the pleasure of gazing on their monarch. One should hardly
imagine, my dear, this a sight to excite tears even in
the midst of royal pomp, splendour, and magnificence,
but it did mine; 'twas moving to see the excessive
joy of the surrounding throng, when one knew the
good young King deserv'd their every acclamation,
not from being born to the crown he was going to
receive, but by his own intrinsic merit.

The Knights of the Bath made a sumptuous
appearance; their plumes, as they went, each carried
in his hand, as did the peers and peeresses their
coronets.

The Herb maids I must not forget to mention;
they were first in the procession, viz., six very fine
girls (they said young ladies of distinction, each giving
twenty guineas for her place). Their dress was neatly
elegant, white calico gowns and coats, blue and white
stomachers, sleeve knots, lappets, no hoops, white
shoes, white mittens turned with blue, and earrings
and necklace of the last colour. A little basket on
their left arm, and with their other hand they strewed
the platform with flowers. When the procession had
entered the Abbey, a great deal of the company left
their seats in the scaffolding and met on the platform;
and I believe walked there for two or three hours,
so that we there had the opportunity of seeing numbers
of persons of distinction who were at the coronation.

'Twas about this time we ourselves dined; the
gentlemen had before provided an elegant cold collation, with burgundy, champagne, claret, and other
wines; and because they were perfectly polite throughout that day, we were obliged to sit down first, while
they waited behind our chairs (as Uncle Selby would

1761 have had Grandison on his wedding-day) ; indeed, I
believe our beaux were the most polite of the day, for
I've since heard of parties where gentlemen, as well
as ladies, drew lots for seats, and if the front ones fell
to the men, down sat they, *sans cérémonie*, and left
the ladies to see as well as they could over their
unmannerly powder-puffed pates, while our heroes
thought themselves happy (at least had the complai-
sance to tell us so), with a third row.   I fortunately,
as one of the youngest, and (I suppose), one of the
shortest (the only time I ever remember the diminu-
tiveness of your Caroline stand her in any stead), had
two undisputed titles, (tho' I claim'd them not), and
was placed in the front seats.   About six we were
once more inform'd by the shouting populace of the
approach of the procession at the return from the
Abbey.   Their Majesties had on their crowns, the
nobility and knights their coronets and plumes, so
that if the sun had shone out as when they went, the
ceremony would now have been still more magnificent.
We saw it pretty well, but those who were not in the
Broad Sanctuary must have been greatly disappointed
they were so late.   The crew of the "Charlotte" yacht
were determin'd to be conspicuous at this return, for
with their colours flying, and notic'd by the pink
cockades, they in an instant made a lane thro' the
multitude, and with loud huzzas attended their Queen's
canopy from the door of the Abbey to that of the Hall.
The procession once more over, our whole party with
great ease got to our attending vehicles, and without
any difficulty, except the exercise of our patience,
reach'd home.   Sometimes, indeed, we went not ten
steps in half an hour's time, yet the way seem'd not
tedious, for the streets were so illuminated.   The

Guards, who were all over the town, and the throng of 1761
carriages were so amazing, as to keep up our attention.
We however reach'd Mr. ——'s about ten. (I wrote
to mama the instant of my safe arrival there, as I
knew her so kindly apprehensive of any accident
happening.) After my letter finish'd, to supper.
Retired about one to our several apartments, and not
much before that hour met at breakfast the next
morn. I stay'd that day and the next at Mr. ——'s,
and yesterday came down here. And now, my dear,
my journal ends. You desir'd a very particular account
of the day's entertainment. If I've been tedious, I
hope you'll pardon me ; for tho' a dull journalist, you
are sensible I must ever be your sincere and oblig'd
friend,   CAROLINE GIRLE.

In the spring of 1762, Miss Girle in her diary 1762
mentions a visit to see the seat of Mr. George Pitt,[1]
afterwards Lord Rivers, and called Strathfieldsaye,[2]
saying, "'Tis an ancient white house, habitably good,
the park, shrubbery, and grounds laid out prettily, and
a menagery[3] exceedingly so, one of the first that was
made in England, shows the pheasants, &c., to great
advantage, being of a circular form with pens all round
it. Colonel Pitt's[4] (his brother), house and park almost join the above, both within a quarter of a mile of
Mr. Baker's, which makes Heckfield a most delightful
situation."
The next entry is August 5th, 1762. "I was

[1] First Baron Rivers.
[2] Purchased by the nation in 1815, and presented to the Duke of
Wellington, held by the tenure of yearly a tricoloured flag presented on
June 18th at Windsor.
[3] Old-fashioned name for aviary.
[4] Sir William Augustus Pitt, K.B., of late seat of Lord Eversley.

1762 married to Philip Lybbe Powys of Hardwick Hall, Oxfordshire."

Before giving extracts from a letter of Mrs. Lybbe Powys describing her husband, &c., mention must be made of the family he belonged to. The Powys family derives its lineage through the Barons of Main-yn-Meifol of Powysland from Iorwerth Goch, Lord of Mochnant in Powysland, younger son of Meredith, Prince of Powys, third son of Rhodri Mawr, King of Wales. Meredith Ap Bleddyn, Prince of Powys, bore arms thus : Shield argent, on which a lion rampant sable, armed and langued gules (called the Black Lion of Powys); these arms have been altered in Baron Lilford, now head of the family, to : Or, a lion's gamb erased, in bend dexter, between two cross crosslets fitchee, in bend sinister gules. Circ. 1250, William Powys was born, from him in direct descent, for which I must beg the reader to refer to the Powys pedigree, was Thomas Powys of Snitton, County Salop, born in 1558; he married Elizabeth, daughter of Richard Smyth of Credenhall, Hereford, by whom he had nine children, and was succeeded on his death in 1639 by Thomas, his eldest son, who was Serjeant-at-Law and a Bencher of Lincoln's Inn. This Thomas of Henley Hall, near Ludlow, married Anne, daughter of Sir Adam Littleton of Stoke Milbourne, Chief-Justice of Wales, a descendant of the celebrated author of the " Treatise on Tenure." By this lady he had six children, four sons and two daughters. His first wife died, he re-married Mary Cotes of Woodcote, Salop, by whom he had five sons and one daughter. By his first marriage the eldest son, Littleton, born 1647, a Bencher of Lincoln's Inn, received knighthood

from William III., on being made Chief-Justice of 1762
North Wales in 1692. In 1695 he became a Baron
of the Exchequer, and in 1702 a Judge of the King's
Bench, which he resigned in 1726. He married Anne
Carter of London, by whom he had no issue; she
died November 28, 1720. Sir Littleton, died March
13, 1731, aged eighty-one, and was buried at Bitterley, Salop; having outlived his brothers and eldest
nephew, he left his estate to his great-nephew Thomas
Powys. Sir Littleton's next brother, Thomas, was also
bred to the bar, was Solicitor-General in 1686, when
he was knighted, the next year Attorney-General
—was at the trial of the seven Bishops, at which
his impartiality was greatly admired; constituted one
of the Judges of Queen's Bench in 1713, removed
from this in 1714. Sir Thomas purchased the manor
of Lilford in Northamptonshire in 1711; it had long
been held by the family of Elmes, also resident at
Bolney Court, Oxon; the last survivor, William Elmes,
sold it to a Mr. Adams, a money-scrivener, whose
estates being afterwards in Chancery for his debts,
Sir Thomas Powys purchased it. Sir Thomas married
twice, first to Sarah, daughter of Ambrose Holbech,
Esq. of Mollington, Warwickshire, and by her had
three sons and three daughters. Secondly, to Elizabeth, daughter of Sir Philip Meadows of Bentley,
Suffolk, by whom he had one surviving son, Philip.
This Philip married Isabella Lybbe, sole child and
heiress of Richard Lybbe, Esq. of Hardwick Hall,
Oxon. The issue of this marriage was three sons,
Philip Lybbe, born October 26, 1734, married to
our heroine in 1762; Thomas, born 1736, in holy
orders; and Richard John, born 1741, a captain in
the Guards. (*Vide* Lybbe Pedigree, and narrative of

1762 family in account of Hardwick House.) I will now copy a letter of the bride to a Derbyshire friend describing her husband.

HARDWICK HOUSE,
October 24th, 1762.

If my dear Bessy has still the friendship for her Caroline I used to flatter myself she had, the known superscription of this letter will, I'm certain, give her pleasure. To make excuses when silence has been so long is impossible, therefore I shall only say the change of scene I've undergone since last I corresponded with my friend has engrossed my every thought. The newspapers, I imagine (tho' I have not), may have inform'd you that I've dropped my former name for that of Powys, but I'll give you a short history of myself for some months. Months past, in November, my poor mother's health wanting country air and exercise after the death and fatigue she experienc'd during the long illness of my dearest father, we took a house at Caversham, one mile from Reading and five from here, round which place you know formerly we had an agreeable set of acquaintances, which after some time we were happy to renew, and at an assembly (for assemblies, you know, are often productive of matrimony), Mr. Powys and I met, and soon after agreed—he to love, I to love and obey for life ; indeed, we had often heard of each other, and years ago the families were intimate, but the children of each then too young to think of those weighty matters. However, my mother approving in every point, for tho' of age, I think one is never at liberty to make those unhappy who gave us being, so the deed was done the 5th of last August! My mother admires her son ; his father, the best of men, doats on her daughter. As to my Philip, as all new-married ladies say, he is in every respect the man I wished, and I do really think I shall tell you the same seven years since. As many say who have known him from his infancy, he was never guilty of any vice, and hardly of any fault. A rare husband, you'll say, my Bessie; but we will allow for the partiality of the character given by friends; but his father has often told me his two eldest boys never gave him one moment's uneasiness by their conduct; so you find I've two brothers, two both younger than Mr. Powys—the eldest a clergyman (then twenty-six years old), who is in every respect what a clergyman and a gentleman ought to be, and has just been given a living by Mr. Freeman, of Fawley Court (Bucks), on a sweet spot thirteen miles from us,[1] and two from his patrons. The different pursuits may serve to characterise the minds of each, as our young officer is what I fear too generally young men in the army are, gay, thoughtless, and very handsome; but what boy of fourteen having a commission in the Guards can be otherwise? and one rather pities than blames this inconsiderateness, and as he has good sense and good temper, we hope he will soon be all we wish. My being first introduced to him was rather unpleasant, as he was but just came from abroad, and got to Hardwick by breakfast the morning after we were married; but we soon became acquainted, and not to like him is quite impossible. We live at Hardwick (our father[2] with us), in a large old house, about twelve rooms on a floor, with four staircases, the situation delightful, on

[1] Sambrook Freeman presented Fawley, Bucks, to T. Powys, October 30, 1762.
[2] Mr. Philip Powys, ætat 62, had lost his wife May 1761.

G

1762 the declivity of a hill, the most beautiful woods behind,
and fine views of the Thames and rich meadows in
front. Hardwick Woods you may perhaps have heard
of, as parties come so frequently to walk in them, and
request to drink tea in a cottage [1] erected for that purpose in a delightful spot commanding a noble view of
the Thames. My mother has taken a house in Reading, which adds to my happiness her being so near,
and for which I am much obliged to her, as she has a
house in London,[2] and loves the Metropolis so much
better than her daughter, whose utmost ambition, you
may remember, was to marry a gentleman who always
resided in the *country ;* but this I dare say is generally
the case where girls have not been debarr'd in early
life from seeing in moderation all the diversions of
that gay world. You'll want, I dare say, some description of the person of my dear Phil. He's tall
and thin. Tall men, one generally sees, marry little
women ; as to myself, the compliments I am paid
here by my poor neighbours is, ' that I am a very *little*
madam, indeed !' But to proceed. My father and all
the tenants tell me there never was so beautiful a
boy as the young Squire ; but I think (fortunately),
the small-pox has given him now a good, rough, manly
face. His age, twenty-eight, tolerably adapted to mine
of twenty-four ; but I had rather he should have been
past thirty. Our tempers—you are acquainted with
mine—I flatter myself, will agree ; but I hardly ever
saw one so excellent as his appears to be. And
now, my dear, I think it is time to conclude this
long epistle ; but mind you give me joy soon, and
remember me to all Derbyshire and Yorkshire

---

[1] Called "Straw Hall."
[2] In Lincoln's Inn Fields.

acquaintances, and believe me, tho' a bad correspon- 1762
dent, not a dilatory, but most sincere friend,

CAROLINE POWYS.

A minature existing in the family of "my Phil"
represents him as a fine man, with good features, a
high forehead, an aquiline nose, bright blue eyes ; but
the complexion (a rosy one), shows signs of the rough-
ness produced by the ravages of small-pox. Young
ladies of the end of the nineteenth century are advised
to read, and take to heart this letter, so descriptive
of an honest, suitable, and loving courtship, so different from the inculcations of Society novels of the
fin de siècle.

Besides an excellent husband, our Caroline had
become the mistress of one of the most beautiful
estates on the banks of the Thames. Hardwick
House, near Whitchurch, Oxon, was, and is, of unique
interest, equally to lovers of history as to admirers of
scenery. Situated on a grassy slope leading down to
the river, commanding fine views of the same, and
yet elevated sufficiently to avoid the river fogs, backed
by a steep hill, richly clad with exquisite hanging
woods, which protect the house from the north and
east winds, it possesses an unrivalled aspect, whilst
its exterior presents a crowd of picturesque gables,
surmounted by the quaint clock-tower, rising from
mellowed red walls, adorned with stone mullioned
windows—a most pleasing style of architecture. In-
ternally its interesting and comfortable apartments
combine to form a *tout ensemble* hard to beat.

As to its ancient history, the Manor of Hardwick
was amongst the list of twenty-eight lordships given
by William the Conqueror to his favourite, Robert

1762 D'Oyley, on his marriage with Aldith, the daughter of
Wigod, Thane of Wallingford (the faithful friend and
cupbearer to the Conqueror).[1]   Maud, the daughter of
Robert D'Oyley and Aldith, carried the manor in
marriage to Miles or Milo Crispin.   Canon Slatter,
in his "History of Whitchurch," says Hardwick seems
to have been a separate manor to Whitchurch, and
states that Milo Crispin gave its tithes to the Abbey
of Bec, in Normandy.   He dying, his widow re-
married Brien Fitzcount.   She was supreme lady of
the honour of Wallingford, in which Hardwick was
included.   Brien Fitzcount was an ardent supporter
of the claims of the Empress Matilda to the English
crown.   By his wife, Maud, he had two sons, but
they were both unhappily lepers.   After the accession
of Stephen, and the Treaty of Wallingford, signed in
1153, Brien Fitzcount took the Cross and went to the
Holy Land.   His wife, Maud, had already, circ. 1149,
embraced a religious life in the Abbey of Bec, the
poor leper sons being immured in the Priory of Ber-
gavenny, provision being made to the monks for their
maintenance.   Robert D'Oyley the second, nephew
of the original Robert, now held the honour of Wallingford.   It is stated in a paper of Bransby Powys,
grandson of our heroine, and who may be deemed
the archæologist of the family, that the family of De
Herdewyke held Hardwick soon after the Norman
Conquest.   Canon Slatter derives the name Hardwick
as Hard Spring, *wick* or *wyke*, used for *wich* an'd
wych, being Celtic for a spring.   This spring is named
in the old Saxon boundaries of Whitchurch.   As
proper names were frequently derived from the place
persons lived in, doubtless the De Herdewycks adopted

[1] *Vide* "The House of D'Oyley," &c.

theirs from their abode. They would hold the estate 1762
from the Lord in capite (or supreme lord), under
feudal tenure. In the Rotuli Hundredorum, com.
Oxon, in Langtre, temp. Edward I., under the head of
Whitchurch, we find Ralph de Anvers held two parts
of a fee therein in capite, and that William de Herdewycke held of him one virgate of land given in frank-
marriage, and that Walter de Herdewycke held of
him a half virgate of William de Herdewycke by the
annual rent of 21s. Ralph de Anvers is mentioned
in a Fine Roll of 13 Henry III., memb. 4, of the
men of the honour of Wallingford, begging to be
excused from going to war. "Who made a fine of
100s. for the same to have his scutage of two knights'
fees, &c., of the same honour." In an inquisition
taken at the death of John de Herdewycke, in the
18 Richard II., it states Hardwick was held "with
demesne lands of the crown of the manor of Whitchurch, in honour of Wallingford, for 11s. per annum
and suit of court for all services." At the death of
Richard de Herdewycke in the reign of Henry VIII.,
Hardwick passed by the female line to the family of
Crochefelde, and tenure was reaffirmed by inquisition
of 12 Henry VIII. (1521), on the death of William
Crochefelde, therein styled "cousin and heir to Richard
de Hardewycke." In 1526 Hardwick was sold by
"William Davy and Allys, his wife (late wife of
William de Crochefelde), and Allys Preston" (cousin
and heir of the said William Crochefelde), to Rich-
ard Lybbe, originally of a Devonshire family from
Tavistock, but then seated at Shinfield, in Berk-
shire (*vide* Lybbe Pedigree). Richard Lybbe married
Bridget, daughter of William Justice, of Reading.
He died in 1527, and was buried at his other property

1762 at Shinfield. He was succeeded by his son, another Richard Lybbe, who married Joanna, daughter of John Carter, of Checkendon, Oxon. This Richard was sewer to Queen Mary, and a stirrup of a curious shape, and large enough to hold two feet, said to be hers, is still possessed by the Lybbe Powys. It must have been during this Richard Lybbe's life that Queen Elizabeth paid a visit to Hardwick.

A fine coloured and gilt monument exists in Whitchurch Church to Richard Lybbe and his wife. He is represented, clad in armour, kneeling at a prie-dieu; his wife opposite, in a ruff and quaint head-dress. A fine coat-of-arms and crest surmount the monument, the date of which is 1599. A tablet to their son, another Richard Lybbe,[1] and his wife, Ann Blagrave, daughter of Anthony Blagrave, of Bulmarsh, Berks, has this quaint inscription :—" To Richard Lybbe, of Hardwick, Esqre. and Anne Blagrave, united in sacred wedlock 50 years, are here againe made one by death. She yielded to the change Jan. 14. 1654, which he embracied July 14. 1658."

Epitaph.

" He, whose Renowne, for that completeth Man,
Speaks louder, better things than Marble can;
She, whose Religious Deeds makes Hardwick's Fame
Breathe as the Balme of Lybbe's Immortall Name,
Are once more Joyned within this Peacefull Bed,
Where Honour (not Arabian Gummes) is spred.
Then grudge not Friends who next succeed 'em must,
Y' are Happy, that shall mingle with such Dust."

During this Mr. Lybbe's life occurred the dreadful period of the Civil Wars. In 1642, at its commencement, loans were levied by King Charles I. on his

[1] This Richard Lybbe was High-Sheriff of Oxon in 1640.

faithful subjects.   The following is a copy of the loan 1762
levied on Richard Lybbe :—

"1642. Declaration to raise £100,000 from subjects
in loans.   £40 demanded from Mr. Lybbe on plate.
Toucht plate at 5s., untoucht plate at 4s. 4d. per
ounce.   Seven days given to find and give to the
High Sheriff (then Sir Thomas Chamberlayne), who
is to pay back at Corpus Christi, Oxford."

The King's signature is at the top of this paper, the
rest in print, containing the signatures of the Earl of
Bath, Lord Seymour, John Ashburnham, John Fetti-
place.   It was addressed "To our trusty and well-
beloved Richard Lybbe."   The King acknowledged
the receipt of the loan, and Mr. Lybbe eventually
endorsed the paper at the back, "Was never paid back,
nor expected it, but the document would have a *value
of its own.*"   But this was only the commencement of
levies of money for the Royal cause ; besides the levies
soon enforced by Parliament added to the latter a real
case of plundering.

In 1643 the Parliamentary troops from Reading
sacked the house at Hardwick, "taking awaie," as Mr.
Lybbe piteously describes it, plate to the value of near
£200 (a list of which will be found at the end of this
work), and other goods, including a fine bed with
velvet hangings, to a total of £800.   Mr. Lybbe
meanwhile being obliged to conceal himself for fear
of being taken prisoner.   He, however, managed to
save his best horses, and sent three for the King's
service to Captain Tom Davis, who was in a troop
under the Marquis of Hertford.   Mr. Lybbe's son,
Anthony, who had married in 1637 Mary, daughter
and heiress of Leonard Keate, of Checkendon, Oxon,
was in arms attending the King.   Mr. Richard Lybbe

1762 pleaded after this for remission of further loans to the King, stating, first, that he had been High Sheriff for Oxon in 1640, by serving which office he had incurred debts to the amount of £300, which prevents his furnishing the King with more money; secondly, he had already voluntarily paid £40; thirdly, driven from home by fear of rebels, who plundered him of £800 in money and plate; fourthly, his revenue of £600, £200 of which was settled in marriage on his son Anthony, and with what he had settled on other children, only £200 per annum left for himself. Parliament enforced their payment, as in December 1644 there is a receipt given him for £6, 10s. and six bushels of wheat for Hardwick, and £11, 18s. for Whitchurch property. Twice he has to pay this year, twice in 1645, and twice in 1646. No wonder, in a paper dated 8th March 1646, he says: "Since which time, by this unnatural war, my house and study being plundered by soldyers, and among my many and great losses I lost my accounts, and many writings of great concernment."

There is a tradition in the family that at the commencement of the war a large sum of money was buried for security, and every subsequent generation of descendant children have dug for the same, but without success! Richard's son, Anthony, was attached by Parliament for his support of the King and his estate sequestrated, but in a paper dated 14th April 1646 is discharged from sequestration. This was signed at Reading Abbey by Francis Pile, Tanfold Vachell (of Coley, Berks), Daniel and John Blagrave. The two latter, being his near relatives on his mother's side, were doubtless of great use in rebutting the charge; but even as late as 1649 he is again reported,

but through Mr. Blagrave's influence got off. This 1762
was the year of the execution of the unfortunate King.
In one of the memorandum books of the Lybbes is
this entry: "King Charles the First was prisoner at
Causham Lodge,[1] and bowled in Collin's End Green,
19th July 1648, attended by a troop of horse of
Colonel Rossiter's." Collin's End[2] is on the top of
the hill at the back of Hardwick, and belonged to the
Lybbe estate. There was a bowling-green attached
to an inn there, afterwards called the " King's Head."
The original house is now Holly Copse, but there is
an inn near bearing the same sign.

Charles I. was at Caversham,[3] from July 3rd to the
22nd in 1647. Mr. Jesse, in his " History of the
Stewarts," says : " He (the King), frequently went to
the bowling-green at Collin's End, Mr. Lybbe Powys'
possession. There was a small building for shelter
and refreshment near. Mr. Powys has a picture at
Hardwick of the old lady who lived in the house near,
who used to wait on the King when he visited the
green." This picture is now at Holly Copse, near
Collin's End, belonging to Mr. Lybbe Powys, as well
as Queen Mary's stirrup.[4] The bowling-green is now
an orchard. Lord Augustus FitzClarence, Rector of
Maple-Durham, gave to this inn, years after, a portrait-
sign of the King, copied from a Vandyck, under which
the following lines by Mr. Jesse were inscribed :—

> " Stop, traveller, stop ; in yonder peaceful glade
>   His favourite game the royal martyr played ;

[1] Caversham Park, was then called " Lodge."
[2] It belongs still to the Lybbe Powys, being made into a shooting-box.
[3] Then Lord Craven's property.
[4] The stirrup is of iron heavily gilt, and would hold four ladies' feet ;
eight holes at the bottom to let rain out.

Here, stripped of honours, children, freedom, rank,
Drank from the bowl, and bowled for what he drank ;
Sought in a cheerful glass his cares to drown,
And changed his guinea ere he lost his crown."

But to return to Anthony Lybbe. On the Restoration he borrowed, in 1672, £500 in order to restore Hardwick, which had been lamentably injured during the war. In a paper of Bransby Powys he states of the house : " Some portions are evidently of a very early period, and were probably existing in the time of Richard II., but the south front or river front was built by Anthony Lybbe after the restoration of Charles II., when the house appears to have required great repairs, in consequence of the dilapidations occasioned during the Civil War, the known loyalty of its owner having subjected it more than once to the pillage of the Parliamentary forces." For the more minute details of these and subsequent repairs, the reader must turn to a note at the end of this book. The debt on the house was discharged March 24, 1676, two years after Anthony's death, by his son, another Richard Lybbe. This Richard married first Sophia, daughter of Sir Thomas Tipping ;[1] she died in 1682, and he re-married Mary, daughter of Sir William Hill, who died the year after. Mr. Lybbe founded, in 1714, the almshouses for old men at Goring, Oxon, where he had property. He died the year after, and was succeeded by his son, another Richard, who in 1712 was High Sheriff for Oxon, and the same year married Isabella, daughter of Sir William Twysden of Roydon Hall, Kent. From this union was born Isabella, sole

[1] Made baronet by William III. Lady Tipping was sister of and co-heiress with Dame Alice Lisle of Moyles Court, Hants, who was condemned to be beheaded by the infamous Judge Jeffreys for sheltering two fugitives from Sedgemoor. See note at end of book.

child and heiress, who on December 19, 1730, married 1762 Philip Powys, only surviving son of Sir Thomas Powis of Lilford, by his second marriage with Elizabeth, daughter of Sir Philip Meadows[1] of Bentley Hall, Suffolk, thus bringing to her husband Hardwick. From this union were born three sons, Philip Lybbe, born October 26, 1734, the husband of our heroine; Thomas, born September 26, 1736, afterwards Dean of Canterbury; and Richard John, born August 1741, subsequently captain in the Guards; and one daughter, Elizabeth, who died in infancy.

To return to a description of Hardwick House. The general architecture is Tudor, though, as mentioned before, a portion is far older, supposed to be of Richard II.'s reign. Time has mellowed the bricks it is built of into a colour that fascinates the artist's eye; the windows picked out with stone, a few modernised, but the majority retaining their original shape. The south front of the house has been extended considerably by the present lessee, Mr. C. Day Rose, but very judiciously; he has also built new stables, a covered tennis-court, cottages, &c., but the modern portion of the house I do not purpose to describe. At the end of this book will be found a note (No. 2) of all the dates known of alterations; but as these details are less interesting to the general reader than the family, I do not insert them here. On the south side of the house runs a broad terrace, beneath this a flower-garden on a gradual slope to the river Thames, with fine trees scattered around—notably a fine cedar on the east side, and opposite Queen Elizabeth's bed-chamber a large mass of clipped yew, through which

---

[1] Some Peerages spell it " Medows," but in Sir Thomas Powys' epitaph it is Meadowes. See note at end of book.

1762 an arch is cut, forming a quaint object. The entrance
is on the north side of the house, under the clock-
tower, but another door has been made close by. On
this side the ground rises in a steep grassy slope for a
great height ; on either side this vista hang the most
exquisite woods, forming a complete shelter from the
north and east. On the top of the slope is a fine
natural terrace, from which is a superb view. Here
stands a cottage called " Straw Hall," once a favourite
resort of picnic parties, but since game has become
more strictly preserved is closed to the public. Written
over "Straw Hall," in 1756, is a verse by Thomas
Powys, brother of Philip, and afterwards Dean of
Canterbury, who had a great turn for rhyming :—

> " Within this cot no polished marble shines,
>   Nor the rich product of Arabian mines ;
>   The glare of splendour and the toys of state,
>   Resigned, unenvied, to the proud and great ;
>   Whilst here reclined, those nobler scenes you view
>   Which Nature's bold, unguided pencil drew."

" Straw Hall " has always been a favourite resort of
the family, and innumerable are the mentions of teas
held there in Mrs. Powys' journals. Near the other
end of the terrace in a grotto lies buried " Muff," long
the beloved dog of the Dean's, who erected this epitaph on a stone :—

> " From insults rude thy poor remains to save,
>   Thus faithful Muff thy master makes thy grave."

At the west end of the terrace is a cottage disguised by a church-like gable called " The Baulk."

Returned to the house, the spectator enters from
the porch a square panelled hall, hung with many
family portraits and furnished with old oak ; to the

left of this is a drawing-room.   A very fine room used 1762
as a dining-room is beyond the Queen Elizabeth's
staircase.   The wainscoting of the walls, most elegant in design, a very handsome plaster ceiling, and
in the mantelpiece is a stucco head, said to be a likeness of King Alfred.

One of the principal staircases, which is shut off
from the hall, is extremely handsome, the balustrades
all oak richly carved, the plaster ceiling most exquisitely modelled.   This staircase leads to Queen
Elizabeth's bed-chamber, now used as a drawing-room,
and both staircase and room were decorated for the
visit paid by the Queen to Mr. Lybbe.   Queen Elizabeth's room looks east, is very large, with a splendid
oriel window at east end.   The whole of it is panelled
with most richly carved oak, the details of which
would take too much room to describe.   The door
and its case are remarkably ornate.   Over the fire-
place, which has a carved back and contains very
ancient dog-irons, is a most curious over-mantel, which
represents Abraham offering Isaac as a sacrifice.   An
angel is seizing his arm to prevent this.   In niches
at the side are large figures of Faith, Hope, Justice,
and Charity.   Above these are the Lybbe arms.   But
what makes this very noteworthy is that the whole is
carved in chalk, which retains its original sharpness
of outline in a remarkable manner, and is, I believe,
in these days a lost art.

The plaster ceiling is elaborately modelled, and
in the centre, at intervals, are three portrait medallion
heads of Queen Elizabeth.   Four other heads in
medallions are placed at the corners, of the following
incongruous personages, viz., Joshua (dux), Jeroboam,
Fama, and Julius Cæsar, all fully inscribed, so that no

1762 doubt may exist as to their personalities, though why they are selected, with the exception of Fama, is a mystery. Some years ago, unfortunately, the bedstead was disposed of, but a pencil-drawing of it exists in one of Bransby Powys' big family scrap-books, and represents a huge handsome carved four-poster, in which we can imagine the Virgin Queen reposing under her own medallion portraits.

The bedrooms are numerous and comfortable, retaining old-fashioned names, such as the "blue room," "mahogany room," &c., &c., the "powder room," a very essential apartment when people loaded their head or wigs with powder. This is now made into a dressing-room. There are several staircases, many sitting-rooms, and long corridors filled with pictures, the principal of which are Sir W. and Lady Twysden, by Sir Peter Lely, A.D. 1693. He is represented in armour. Their daughter married Richard Lybbe (*vide* Pedigree). Sir Littleton Powys, in a black cap, red furred gown, and white upper cloak ; also his brother Sir Thomas, by Sir Godfrey Kneller ; Sir Philip Meadows, father of the second Lady T. Powys, 1717, by Dahl ; three-quarter length portraits of Philip Powys and his wife Isabella, by Davenport, and many others, amongst them Mr. and Mrs. Girle, by Vanderbanck, Caroline Powys' parents. Mrs. Girle has a sweet round rosy face, with an abundance of soft brown hair, of small stature, according to her picture. The only picture of our heroine is a miniature painted by Spornberg at Bath in 1807, when she was sixty-nine. In this a curious sort of turban-cap conceals all her head, with the exception of a fringe of hair on the forehead. She has pleasant eyes, a well-shaped nose, and a rather

prominent chin, denoting firmness of character. We 1762
know from her own showing, our Caroline was dubbed
"a very little Madam," and in later life, from her
diary, that she was rather embonpoint.

One curious discovery in her time must be noticed.
In a recess in the corridor leading to the breakfast-
room was found a bronze jug, inscribed "Edward,
Rex Anglia." It is 7½ inches high, 5¾ at base, with a
straight handle of 4 inches. It holds exactly a gallon
of wine. This was considered by General Conway
and Lord Frederick Campbell, connoisseurs in antiquities, to be a standard measure of the reign of one
of the Edwards.

To return to Caroline Powys' diary. September 7, 1762, is the next entry of a first visit to a
place and people destined henceforth to be intimate
friends.

"We went to see Park Place,[1] the seat of General
Conway, and one of the most capital situations in
England. The house stands agreeably, but is too
indifferent for the surrounding grounds. They have
a pretty cottage near the river, which the General
took the idea of from 'Straw Hall,' in Hardwick
Woods." A note added in later years: "*N.B.*—
In July 1793 Gen'l Conway alter'd the house, and
whiten'd it, and 'tis now an exceeding good one."

As we shall come to frequent mention of General
Conway, a short sketch must be here given of him.
Henry Seymour Conway, the second son of the first
Lord Conway, was born in 1720. Educated at Eton,
he entered the army; was aide-de-camp to the Duke
of Cumberland at the battle of Dettingen; present
at those of Laffeld and Fontenoy; at the latter was

[1] Park Place, Henley-on-Thames, now the seat of Mrs. Noble.

1762 taken prisoner. About 1747 he married Caroline, daughter of John Campbell, fourth Duke of Argyll, and widow of Charles Bruce, Earl of Aylesbury. By her first husband Lady Aylesbury (who retained her first married name after marrying General Conway), had one daughter, married to the Duke of Richmond;[1] by her second marriage she had another daughter, Anne,[2] born in 1745, married to the Honourable John Damer. General Conway bought Park Place after the death of Frederick, Prince of Wales, in 1752, who had been its previous owner. The General commanded the British forces in Germany in 1761. In 1765 he was dismissed for persistent resistance of war and rejection of corruption. He opposed vigorously in Parliament (which he now entered), the taxation of America, &c. ; became Secretary of State ; in 1768 returned to his military profession ; in 1782 became Field - Marshal, and in 1785 Governor of Jersey. General Conway and his wife were devoted to Park Place, and from the commencement of their ownership endeavoured in every way to improve and adorn a spot so romantically beautiful. The General was first cousin on the maternal side to Horace Walpole, who was also his dearest friend. Walpole took deep interest in all the improvements at Park Place, and eventually made his young cousin, Anne Damer, his heiress. Lady Aylesbury was remarkable for her beauty, as well as her daughter, the Duchess of Richmond. Horace Walpole mentions the exquisite picture she and this daughter made, sitting in a seat shaped like a shell at Strawberry Hill, and fondly termed the Campbells "huckaback beauties," a homely

[1] Charles, third Duke of Richmond.
[2] See note at end of book.

term, but meaning that they were beautiful always, 1762
and for daily use, owing nothing to fictitious charms.

Mrs. Powys' first child, Caroline, was born June 1763
14, 1763. On the 14th July the same year, " My
brother (-in-law), Captain Richard John Powys, married
to the daughter of General Bedford ; they met at
Bristol, both so ill of consumption that 'twas thought
neither could recover, but in a few weeks they went
off to Scotland."
A Gretna Green match !

In March 1764, Mrs. Powys lost her little Caro- 1764
line, and in April she, her husband, and father-in-law
went to Bath for a little tour to recover her spirits.[1]
" *September 6th*, 1764.—Died in childbed, and likewise the infant, my sister, Richard Powys, just sixteen
years of age, a most amiable young creature in mind
and person, the latter particularly elegantly pretty.
The General and Mrs. Bedford had been reconcil'd
from almost the first, and lived with them at the time
of her death."
" *April 27th*.—Our boy Philip Lybbe born ! "   1765
" *August 16th*, 1766.—We all set out on an ex- 1766
cursion for a day or two, and went first to Hedsor,
Lord Boston's, near Clifden ; but I think a still finer
situation, a very indifferent very old house,[2] but stands
on such an eminence as commands a beautiful view
of the Thames and fine country round that spot. We
din'd at March's, and in the evening went by water
to drink tea at Monkey Island, belonging to the Duke

---

[1] She never forgot her first child, but as each year came round noted
its birth and death in her diary.
[2] New house built in 1778.

H

1766 of Marlborough.[1] On this little island are two buildings, richly decorated on the inside. We went back
to Maidenhead Bridge, and next morning went to
Windsor. First we went to the Duke's Lodge[2] in
Windsor Great Park (which is twenty miles round);
the avenue leading to the lodge is three miles and a
half long, a perfectly straight line; when at the upper
end, the castle at the other makes a noble point of
view. The late Duke, son of George II., built to it
a number of new rooms, and began a pretty chapel.
. . . The late owner (the Duke of Cumberland), seem'd
regretted as his merit deserv'd; for, tho' a year after
his death, every domestic he was mentioned by paid
the grateful tribute of tears to his beloved memory.
Having seen the house, we went to the Tower, call'd
Shrubs Hill. The plantations the Duke made here on
a soil so barren appear wonderful; but firs will grow
almost anywhere. The building is pretty, commanding a most extensive prospect. In the principal room
is a chandelier of Chelsea china, the first of that
manufacture, and cost £500. From hence we went
to the Chinese Island, on which is a small house quite
in the taste of that nation, the outside of which is
white tiles set in red lead, decorated with bells and
Chinese ornaments. You approach the building by a
Chinese bridge, and in a very hot day, as that was,
the whole look'd cool and pleasing. The inside consists of two state rooms, a drawing-room, and bed-
chamber, in miniature each, but corresponds with the
outside appearance; the chamber hung with painted
satin, the couch-bed in the recess the same; in the
drawing-room was a sort of Dresden tea-china, most

[1] Built by third Duke of Marlborough.
[2] Duke of Cumberland.

curious indeed, every piece a different landscape, 1766
painted inimitably; in short, the whole of the little
spot is well worth seeing.   We dined at Windsor,
and then went to the Castle, where, I think, there is
but little worthy one's observation; the furniture is
old and dirty, most of the best pictures removed
to the Queen's palace,[1] and the whole kept so very
un-neat that it hurts one to see almost the only place
in England worthy to be styled our King's Palace
so totally neglected.[2]   The fine carving of Grindeline
Gibbons in St. George's Chapel is still left there.
The view from the terrace, I know, is generally admir'd, but tho' I may show my want of taste, I must
own it never strikes me with the idea of beautiful.
Shenstone has a pretty idea of distinguishing between
landscape and prospect, but says mere *extent*, is
what the vulgar admire.

"We lay again at Maidenhead Bridge, and the
next morn went to see Lady Orkney's at Taplow,[3]
where is a terrace more, I fancy, adapted to the
word landscape, as that of Windsor is to prospect;
'tis two miles and a half in length, a hanging wood
below you; all the way the Thames runs along the
bottom; the country all round highly picturesque;
a Gothic root-house which hangs pendant over the
river is exceedingly pretty; the building is like
'Straw Hall' in our woods, only the inside is
Gothic paper resembling stucco; the upper part of
the windows being painted glass gives a pleasing
gloom."

"*October* 1766.—Went to dine at Sir John Cope's,

[1] Buckingham House, bought by George III. in 1761, and given to
the Queen.
[2] Very different in 1899.
[3] Taplow Court, now H. Grenfell's, Esq.

1766 Bramshill, in Hampshire, a most immense pile of building now, tho' I think he told us hardly the half of what was erected first by the Lord de la Zouch in the reign of Elizabeth.[1] The range of apartments are so vastly spacious that one generally sees Sir John toward the winter put on his hat to
1767 go from one room to another."

"*March 23rd*, 1767.—Went to see what is rather a difficulty to see at all, the Queen's Palace.[2] The hall and staircase are particularly pleasing ; the whole of the ground-floor is for the King, whose apartments are fitted up rather neatly elegant than profusely ornamental. The library consists of three rooms, two oblong and an octagon. The books are said to be the best collection anywhere to be met with. The Queen's apartments are ornamented, as one expects a Queen's should be, with curiosities from every nation that can deserve her notice. The most capital pictures, the finest Dresden and other china, cabinets of more minute curiosities. Among the pictures let me note the famed cartoons from Hampton Court, and a number of small and beautiful pictures ; one room panell'd with the finest Japan. The floors are all inlaid in a most expensive manner, and tho' but in March, every room was full of roses, carnations, hyacinths, &c., dispersed in the prettiest manner imaginable in jars and different flower-pots on stands. On her toilet, besides the gilt plate, innumerable knick-knacks. Round the dressing-room, let into the crimson damask hangings in a manner uncommonly elegant, are frames of fine impressions, miniatures, &c., &c. It being at that time the coldest weather possible, we were amazed to find so large a house

[1] James the First.   [2] Buckingham Palace.

so warm, but fires, it seems, are kept the whole day,   1767
even in the closets, and to prevent accidents to furniture so costly from the neglect of the attendance,
there is in every chimney a lacquered wire fireboard,
the cleverest contrivance that can be imagin'd, as
even the smallest spark cannot fly through them,
while you have the heat, and they are really ornamental.   By the Queen's bed was an elegant case
with twenty-five watches, all highly adorn'd with
jewels.

"*May* 12*th*, 1767.—Went to see the so-much-
talk'd-of church built by Lord Le Despencer,[1] near
his own seat at West Wycombe, Bucks; but as Mr.
Young in his six weeks' tour has so well described
this place, I shall set it down in his words as follows :
'On the summit of a hill which overlooks the whole
country, his Lordship has erected a church, and adjoining to it a mausoleum, the latter a six-angled
open wall of flints, with stone ornaments and row
of Tuscan pillars ; on the inside runs a quarter stone
around it, two of the six divisions are occupied with
dedications to the late Earl of Westmoreland and
Lord Melcomb.   There is not much to recommend
in the taste of this building ; it is either unfinish'd,
or the idea very incomplete, and situation such as
to appear from many points of view to be one building with the church, which has a bad effect ; and
had even St. Paul been to preach here, he must
have furnish'd the neighbours with more than mortal
legs to have become his auditors, for it was with

---

[1] Sir Francis Dashwood, afterwards Lord Le Despencer, founder
of the mock Monks of St. Francis at Medmenham Abbey.   Their
proceedings are chronicled in *Chrysal, or The Adventures of a Guinea.*
For real characters in this book *vide* note.

1767 the utmost difficulty I could gain the top. I consider
this church, therefore, much in the same style as
Beatrice did Don Pedro for a husband, "fit only for
festivals, with another for common use, too elevated,
for every day."[1]   I agree with Mr. Young that the
difficulty of this ascent must be dreadful on the
ancient and decrepid parishioners.   The inside of the
church is striking as a fine *concert* or *ball* room, 'tis
indeed an Egyptian hall, and certainly gives one
not the least idea of a place sacred to religious
worship, having no pews or pulpit, but two sort of
ornamented writing - desks for the clergyman and
clerk, and the font is shown as an elegant toy ; the
congregation sits each side on rows of forms, as at
an assembly.   The house and grounds of this nobleman are, I think, indifferent."

This extraordinary church was built by Lord Le
Despencer in 1763, just after the break up of the
sham Franciscan Brotherhood at Medmenham, of
whose doings the least said the better.   A . full description of this church, too long to insert here, will
be found in Chambers' "Book of Days."   See note
at end of this book.

"*July* 28*th*, 1767.—Went to breakfast with Mr.
Clayton at Harleyford,[1] near Marlow, in Buckinghamshire, to see his place, justly esteem'd one of the
prettiest of that neighbourhood.   He has lately built
an elegant brick house, less, but after the model of
Lord Harcourt's ; his library one of the most pleasing rooms I was ever in, the eating-room good, but
I think the entrance, drawing-room, and apartments
above stairs on too contracted a plan.   The situation
is beautiful (except one meadow before the eating-

[1] Built in 1715 by the first Baronet, Sir William Clayton.

room, from which I should imagine the rushes might 1767
easily be remov'd), the approach to the house uncommonly pleasing, and the whole of the offices so
contriv'd in a pit, as to be perfectly invisible—a great
addition that to the look of any place, and certainly
adds infinitely to the neatness so conspicuous round
Harleyford."

"*September* 16th, 1767.—We went to meet many
families at a turtle-feast at Colonel Vansittart's at
Shottesbrook,[1] Berks, a good old house, a most notable collection of pictures, but the place and country
round it exceedingly dreary. Mr. Vansittart is reckon'd
to have the best fruit and kitchen garden, better
arrang'd than most others."

January 1768, Captain Richard Powys, whose 1768
Gretna Green marriage has been before noted, tho'
in very precarious health, re-married a Miss Gibson,
grand-daughter to the Bishop of London. He did
not long survive his second marriage, dying on February the 7th. Mrs. Powys says: "There could not
be a young man of a more amiable, sweeter dispo-
sition, tho' in the very early part of life had been gay
and extravagant to a degree; but how readily was
that to be pardoned in a youth exceedingly handsome,
in the Guards at fourteen years of age, keeping company with persons of the highest rank." He was
only twenty-six when he died. Bransby Powys says
in one of his journals of his uncle Richard: "A large
bundle of papers bearing the unvarnished title ' Dick's
Debts' exists at Hardwick, forming perhaps the most
complete catalogue of the expenses of a dandy of the
court of George II., consisting chiefly of swords,

---

[1] A most ancient manor, held by Alward the goldsmith, temp. William
Rufus. Church dates from 1337.

1768 buckles, lace, Valenciennes and point d'Espagne, gold
and amber-headed canes, tavern bills, and chair hire!"
The chairs would be Sedan chairs.

On Michaelmas Day 1768, Mrs. Powys' second
son, Thomas, was born. In the same year occurs :
"Master Pratt, only son of the Lord Chancellor,
came to my brother Powys at Fawley." This boy
was John Jeffreys, afterwards second Earl, and first
Marquis Camden. Born in 1759, he was conse-
quently nine years old when he became pupil of the
Rev. Thomas Powys, Rector of Fawley, and the
next year the Lord Chancellor Camden[1] made Mr.
Powys a Prebendary of Hereford and Bristol, whilst
the King presented him to the living of Silchester,
Hants.

1769   On July 13, 1769, Mrs. Powys says : "We went
with a large party to see Bulstrode, the seat of the
Duchess-Dowager of Portland, in Buckinghamshire.
This lady was daughter of Harley,[2] Lord Oxford,
mention'd in the late publish'd letter of Swift. This
place is well worth seeing, a most capital collection[3]
of pictures, numberless other curiosities, and works
of taste in which the Duchess has displayed her well-
known ingenuity. Among the pictures most famed
are a Holy Family as large as life, by Raphael ;
'The Building of Antwerp,' by four eminent hands,
from Sir Luke Shaub's collection. The hall is surround'd by very large pieces of every kind of beast,
by Snyders. The menagerie, I had heard, was the
finest in England, but in that I was disappointed, as

---

[1] Charles Pratt, an eminent lawyer, born 1713.
[2] Margaret Cavendish Harley, only child of Edward, second Earl of
Oxford ; Prior's "My noble, lovely, little Peggy."
[3] When sold in 1786, the collection took thirty-seven days to sell.

the spot is by no means calculated to show off the 1769
many beautiful birds it contains, of which there was
great variety, as a curassoa, goon, crown-bird, stork,
black and red game, bustards, red-legg'd partridges,
silver, gold, pied pheasants, one, what is reckon'd exceedingly curious, the peacock-pheasant. The aviary,
too, is a most beautiful collection of smaller birds—
tumblers, waxbills, yellow and bloom paraquets, Java
sparrows, Loretta blue birds, Virginia nightingales,
and two widow-birds, or, as Edward calls them, 'red-
breasted long-twit'd finches.' Besides all above mention'd, her Grace is exceedingly fond of garden-
ing, is a very learned botanist, and has every English
plant in a separate garden by themselves. Upon
the whole, I never was more entertain'd than at Bulstrode.

"On our return we went to see Mr. Waller's[1] at
Beaconsfield. Fine gloomy garden quite in the old
style, but I never saw anywhere so well-grown a
collection of firs and every sort of evergreens as at
this seat of our famed poet, Waller.

"This summer we spent a week at Shotover, in
Oxon, the seat of Mr. Schutz, whose father, Baron
Schutz, came over into England with George II. It
is within four miles of Oxford, a magnificent place,
an elegant stone house, which stands in the centre
of very fine gardens, something in the style of Mr.
Waller's ; straight avenues terminated by obelisks,
temples, porticoes, &c. ; it has an air of grandeur.
Mr. Schutz is now every year making openings to
an extensive country before altogether excluded.
While at Shotover we visited at Lord Harcourt's.[2]
An exceedingly fine situation, and reckon'd a good

[1] Hall Barn.   [2] Nuneham Park.

1769 house; but though lately built, and of stone, coming from Shotover made it, I imagine, not to appear so good a one as 'tis generally esteem'd. Lord Harcourt had just finish'd a pretty church,[1] which he rebuilt near his own house."

Mrs. Girle this year presented her daughter with a new coach, made by Poole of Longacre.

1770 January 1770, Lord Camden resigned the seals. This year Mrs. Powys visits her aunt Mrs. Mount at Clapham, and with her, visits Hampton Court Palace, which she pronounces neater kept than Windsor Castle, a better collection of pictures, but considers the situation dull; but she is enraptured with a visit to Richmond Hill.

She mentions in May being at the Exhibitions of pictures in London. "The Royal Academy is always stil'd the only one worth seeing, at least 'tis unfashionable to say you had been to any other; but while Elmer excels so in dead game, still life, and droll portraits, and Stubbs in animals and trees, I must own I've pleasure in seeing their performance, tho' not exhibited at the Royal Academy."

She also visits the model of the city of Paris, "a most ingenious piece of workmanship. We were taken to see the wedding-chair of Lady Craven,[2] then exhibited as curious, the first of the kind, being of red morocco leather, richly ornamented with silver, lined with white satin, fringed and tassel'd; it cost £250. Seems too superb to meet the inclemency of the weather, but 'twas only meant as a Court chair, and tho' exceeding elegant, I question if, when occu-

[1] All Saints, built 1764.
[2] Elizabeth, daughter of the fourth Earl of Berkeley, wife of the sixth Baron Craven; married subsequently the Margrave of Anspach.

pied by its still more elegant mistress, it takes the 1770
eye for more than an instant from her beautiful form.

"Took some friends to see Sir Harry Englefield's [1]
and Mr. Birt's, two places in Berks stil'd pretty; the
former I think little deserving the epitaph, the latter a
good house and grounds."

"*July* 13, 1771. — Being at my brother Powys' 1771
at Fawley, one I suppose of the most elegant par-
sonages in England, commanding from a very good
house [2] a prospect uncommonly noble, he took us
to Mr. Michell's new house, [3] which makes so pretty
an object from his own place. The house was not
finish'd, stands in a paddock, rises from the river on
a fine knoll commanding a view which must charm
every eye. The hall, and below-stairs, if we could
then judge, seem too minute, the plan of the bed-
chambers exceedingly convenient and pleasing, kitchen offices are all very clever. About a mile from
the house, through a sweet wood, you mount a vast
eminence which brings you to an exact Chinese house
call'd Rose Hill, [4] from being built in the centre of a
shrubbery of roses, honeysuckles, &c. The situation
of this commands what some call a finer prospect than
the other house, but the variety of each is pleasing.
A poor woman lives here, and 'tis a sweet summer
tea-drinking place inside and out, in the true Chinese
taste."

1 Englefield House, a most ancient manor.
2 Built by Rev. John Stevens, circ. 1740 ; two vicars before Mr.
Powys. Old vicarage made into stables. Mr. Powys was presented
in 1762.
3 Culham Court, Berks.
4 Rose Hill, built for General Hart in Chinese style.

SHROPSHIRE JOURNAL

1771

Taken from three letters to Mrs. Wheatley, cousin to Mrs. Powys.

COURT OF HILL, WORCESTERSHIRE,
Aug. 28th, 1771.

Your kind partiality to your friend when last at
Hardwick, my dear Margaretta, in professing yourself
entertain'd by journals of my former excursions, makes
me suppose, vainly imagine, I may give you pleasure
by a concise account of our present journey into
Shropshire. Mr. Powys, myself, and our eldest boy[1]
set out on Monday the 26th, went in our carriage
to Benson,[2] from thence in post-chaises as more
expeditious than coach or phaeton, as we purpos'd
laying at Worcester the first night, tho' eighty miles
from Hardwick. From Benson we went to Oxford.
As to this city, so strikingly noble, I shall say nothing,
as I know you have seen it. Blenheim, too, we now
pass'd, both of us having often seen that heavy pile
of Vanbrugh's, tho' we talk of reviewing it on our
return, to see the fam'd Brown's so-much-talk'd-of
improvements in the gardens. Near Euston, on the
right, you see a seat of Lord Shrewsbury's.[3] Seems
not remarkable, except for an avenue of clumps, the
first trees so planted in England. The roads here
are turnpike, but not good, the country unpleasing,
stone wall hedges, and the heaps of same materials
lie so scattered about for mending as gives a most
litter'd appearance ; but from Chapel House[4] to Broad-

---

[1] Then six years old.   ·
[2] Bensington, Oxon.
[3] Heythrop Park, now Albert Brassey's, Esq.
[4] A celebrated coaching inn.

way all is still worse. I never saw a country wear 1771
a more melancholy aspect, and yet were we highly
entertain'd by a "Turkish Spy." Don't you recollect charging me to read it soon. I took the first
moment to comply with your request. 'Tis amazing
clever. The'going down Broadway Hill is still formidable, but I remember it horrid. They have just laid
out £200 on it, and by dragging we got safe to the
bottom. At Broadway[2] dined. Our next stage to
Pershore, through the Vale of Evesham, so famed of
old for fine grain of all kinds. Our last stage that
night was by moonlight. Got to Worcester about
nine, ourselves nor little companion in the least
fatigued, tho' a long journey for a boy of six years old,
but novelties took up his attention, and the day pass'd
agreeably even without sleep.

Worcester city in some parts well built, fine
assembly-room, excellent town-hall, Cathedral indifferent, and a large infirmary now building. As to
its china manufacture, 'tis more worth seeing than
anything I hardly ever did see. They employ 160
persons, a vast number of them very little boys.
There are eleven different rooms, in which the employment is as follows : First room, a mill for
grinding the composition to make the clay ; second,
the flat cakes of clay drying in ovens ; third, the
cakes work'd up like a paste, and form'd by *the
eye only* into cups, mugs, basons, tea-pots, their
ingenuity and quickness at this appears like magic ;
fourth, making the things exactly by moulds all
to one size, but they are seldom different, so nice
is their eye in forming ; fifth, paring and chipping
coffee-cups and saucers in moulds, a boy turning the

---

[1] 1086 feet high.   [2] Worcestershire.

1771 wheel for each workman; sixth, making the little
roses, handles, twists, and flowers one sees on the
china fruit-baskets, all these stuck on with a kind of
paste; seventh, scalloping saucers, &c., with a pen-
knife while the composition is pliable, and in this room
they make the china ornamental figures; these are done
in moulds, separate moulds for the limbs, and stuck
on as above; eighth, the heat of this eighth room was
hardly bearable, filled with immense ovens for baking
the china, which is put in a sort of high sieves about six
feet long; ninth, glazing the china, by dipping it into
large tubs of liquor, and shaking it as dry as they can;
tenth, some sorting the china for painting, others
smoothing the bottom by grinding; eleventh, painting
the china in the different patterns.   I rather wonder'd
they did not in one room exhibit their most beautiful
china finished; they did, it seems, till finding people
remain'd in it too long, and so took up too much of
the men's time, so now they send it to the shops in
Worcester for sale.   You pay for seeing the manufacture by putting what you please in a box at the
gate.

   We left Worcester about one the morning after we
got there, and instantaneously entered a fine country.
Their race-ground is a mighty pretty meadow, of
an oblong shape, but thought dangerous, as the horses
going round it on one side are absolutely close to
the river Severn.   Glasshampton,[1] a house of Mrs.
Winford's I've heard her speak of, lies below on the
right, Lord Foley's[2] on the left.   Within a few miles
of Worcester we dined at what they call the "Hundred

   [1] Old family seat of the Winfords; afterwards burnt down by a
careless drunken workman.
   [2] Whitley, now Earl of Dudley's.

House," a most lonely but sweetly romantic situation,
accommodation dreadful ; but the pleasures of travelling in my opinion ever compensate for inconveniences
on the road, and ladies too delicate should remain at
their own seats ; but the inns on the Bath road really
make one think others so bad, that people used to
those, may the more easily be pardon'd.   Sir Edward
Winnington has a sweet place call'd Stanford Court
near the "Hundred House," which we passed in our
way to Court-of-Hill, which we reached about seven
o'clock, and were received by that family with that
cheerful ease characteristic of real friendship.   I don't
think we merited such a reception, as 'tis now nine
summers we have intended to return the visit politely
made me by these relations[1] of Mr. Powys, the following one to that in which we were married ; but I
don't know how it is, but one is apt to think a journey
of a hundred miles so vast an undertaking, when in
fact when once set out 'tis trifling.

Court-of-Hill is an ancient building, spacious, not
uncomfortably so, situation particularly fine, the house
stands on a steep knoll which is laid into paddock,
from three sides of which 'tis impossible to conceive
a prospect more beautiful, except for the want of water.
You look from a vast eminence down on valleys so
sweetly diversified, then the country rising mountain
above mountain, almost reaching the clouds ; Malvern's
famed hills just in front, and as you look round
part of eight counties are at once in view—Worcestershire, Gloucestershire, Herefordshire, beyond these
the Welsh ones of Brecknock, Randor, Monmouth,

[1] Andrew Hill, of Court-of-Hill, married Anne Powys in 1679,
daughter of Thomas Powys of Snitton and Henley Hall, Salop. The
Mr. Hill here mentioned was their grandson.

1771 and Montgomery.   Behind the house is a fine grove,
bounded by a vast mountain called Clee Hill,[1] which
produces stone, lime, and coal in great abundance.
This rock or hill is dreadfully steep to *ascend*, but
dismally so to *descend*, tho' they make nothing of it in
their coach or on horseback.   At the top indeed one
is rewarded for all frights and trouble in the view
around you ; but don't imagine that, noble as this place
is, I give up the sweet softness and natural simplicity of
our Hardwick. . . .   And then our Thames may be set
against their wooded mountains ; but how many truly
beautiful situations are there in England, and why not
give each its due praise without depreciating the rest ?
Sir Charles Grandison, you know, had the art of com-
plimenting twenty women in the same company on
their peculiar accomplishments, and yet left them *all
satisfied!* a much more difficult task than mine.   As
to our relations here, I need say no more than to say
they bear a most astonishing resemblance to our relations in Kent, and express a real friendship for us,
and prove the reality by conspicuously treating us
without form or ceremony.   Their manner of living,
as I've before heard, is always in the superb style
of ancient hospitality, only their winters are spent in
London.   You see generosity blended with every elegance of fashionable taste ; but they have a vast
fortune, and only two children, both girls, one ten,
the other five.   Their house, Mrs. Hill[2] says, is ever
full of company, as at present   Our present party, sixteen in all, relations ; but they have nine good spare
chambers.   Among the number is our elegant cousin
Conyngham, who, I believe, you have heard me men-

---

[1] Titterstone, the highest of the Clee Hills, is 1780 feet.
[2] Was Lucy, daughter of Francis Rock, Esq.

tion as so very pretty. Nay, General Conway, and 1771
Mr. Freeman, say the handsomest woman they ever
saw in France or England. What makes her still more
lovely is, she has not a grain of affectation, tho' only
eighteen. He is an agreeable little man, heir to about
£5000 a year. I could not help liking him, he is so
very like in manner, tho' not near so handsome, as
my brother, Captain Powys,[1] whose sweetness of dis-
position must ever make one regard his memory.
Our little Phil, for person and ease, is next in admiration ; indeed, behaves cleverly, and is no trouble,
which is lucky, as we have only our man-servant (Mr.
Powys, you know, loves not travelling with female
attendants). Indeed, Phil might be spared a nurse
or two. The Miss Hills have each a servant. I've
already seen eight maids ; how many more there be I
know not. The roads about here are wonderful to
strangers. Where they are *mending*, as they *call it*,
you travel over a bed of loose stones, none of less size
than an octavo volume ; and where not mended, 'tis
like a staircase. There are turnpikes—some of the
roads not better than where we have none, but some
are good, and Mr. Hill and other gentlemen are so
laudably anxious for the improvement of them that
I imagine in a few years there will be none bad ; for,
by all accounts, the worst of the present is fine to
what were formerly. They appear unfit for ladies
travelling, but they mind them not ; and I thought
if the delicate Mrs. Conyngham had no fears, such
a one as your Caroline ought not. So I mounted
"Grey," Mr. Powys' great horse—luckily a native of
Shropshire—and up I went the tremendous hill before
mentioned. The fashion here is to ride double. How

[1] Captain Richard Powys, died 1768.

I

1771 terribly vulgar I've thought this; but what will not
fashion render genteel. 'Tis here thought perfectly
so.   As to carriages, they make nothing of going a
dozen miles to dinner, tho' own to being bruised
to death, and quite *deshabbiller'd* by jolts they must
receive.   Here I shall conclude my first epistle.

FROM LETTER 2ND.

COURT-OF-HILL,
September 8, 1771.

. . . Wednesday, the day after we came, and
Thursday, company to dinner.   Friday morn a large
riding cavalcade set forth to see Henley, a seat of
their uncle's, Sir Littleton Powys,[1] two miles from
Ludlow.   You've heard us mention, I believe, Mr.
Powys[2] of Lilford, in Northampton; he has just sold
it, rather to the concern of the family, particularly
the Hills, who were most of them brought up there.
They indeed could have no prospect of its coming
to them, being even after us in the entail; but they
think it a pity to go out of the name that has been
in possession such a number of years.   'Tis really a
fine old place, badly situated, but I find 'tis far from
every part of Shropshire that resembles Court-of-
Hill.   What a monopoly of beauty else would be that
county!   The house and furniture of Henley are quite
antique, but one receives pleasure in these reviews
of former times.   In a gallery are the portraits of

---

[1] Sir Littleton Powys, Baron of Exchequer in 1695; Chief-Justice of
Wales, 1697; Judge of Common Pleas, 1700; Judge of Queen's Bench;
died at Henley Hall, Salop, 1731.

[2] Thomas Powys, great-nephew of Sir Littleton, and his heir, father
of first Baron Lilford.

our family (not yet removed), for some generations, 1771 down to the present possessor of Lilford,[1] among them that of the famous Lord Keeper Littleton.[2] On our return we rode through a fine park belonging to Witton Court,[3] one of the two finely situated seats Sir Francis Charlton has near Ludlow. Saturday we dined at Bitterley, at Mr. Rocke's. Met with no accident but breaking a splinter bar. Mighty fortunate, too, I thought, considering the roads. There seems such confusion with the intermarriages of our cousins, that I give over recollecting who they were, and rest satisfied with who they are. Mr. Hill married a Miss Rock, and Mr. Rock a Miss Hill, &c., &c., just at the same period ; so that, as a smart gentleman said on paying the wedding visits, " Really, the Rocks having turn'd into *Hills*, and the Hills into *Rocks*, it was utterly impossible to distinguish them so as to pay each his proper compliments on the occasion."

Sunday at church ; but their own clergyman being on a tour of pleasure, we had one too thoroughly versed in the Welsh language for us to understand the least of what, poor man, he no doubt thought English !

Monday, you perhaps, who have not a shooting husband, may forget was the first day of September, but Mrs. Conyngham and I lost ours by six that morn ; they were out with their guns, and being both excellent shots, were useful in Mrs. Hill's

---

[1] Lilford, Northamptonshire, had been bought from the Elmes family, who had possessed the property from Henry VII.'s time, by Sir Thomas Powys, in 1711, grandfather of Mr. T. Powys, who sold Henley Hall, and brother of Sir Littleton Powys.

[2] Sir Edward Littleton, born 1589, made Lord Keeper 1641, died 1645.

[3] Whitton Park ; the other place was Ludford House, at Ludlow.

1771 numerous family ; others of the gentlemen rode with the ladies.

Tuesday, Sir Walter and Lady Blount to dinner ; she was a daughter of Lord Ashton's—very agreeable people. I was bid to take notice of a present his cousin the Duchess of Norfolk made him at their wedding, viz., an exceedingly fine pair of diamond buckles, very handsome indeed they are. They are Catholics. They obligingly insisted on our dining there next week ('tis a mighty fine place, it seems), if we would not spend some days there ; but our party being so large, we would all have excus'd ourselves if possible even from a dining visit.

Wednesday morning, I mounted double, but found it utterly impossible, as I thought, to keep on, so had again recourse to my tall horse and side-saddle, provok'd beyond measure to follow Mrs. Hill, who sat knotting on her pillion with such unconcern, while we were going up and down such places as I imagin'd our necks in danger each step. That evening we walk'd up the Clee Hill to see the whole process of making lime at Mr. Hill's kilns.[1] To see the quarries of solid rock is rather tremendous, not made less so by seeing the men standing on its sharp points. They make a small hole with a chisel, in which they place gunpowder, light it, and retire to a safe distance ; you instantly hear the report of its blowing up that stone, or rather it only cracks, and then the labour is immense before the stone is thrown down ; when it does fall, they have to break it in pieces very small, and for doing this use hammers 30 lbs. weight. Only think of labouring with tools so ponderous, and these poor fellows work for about a

[1] These kilns are still in work.

shilling a day. Next a deep round hole is dug, in 1771
which is regularly laid bit by bit the pieces of stone
till raised above the ground five or six feet; underneath is an oven easily set fire to. As these kilns are
on the slope of the knoll, they burn four or five days
and nights, and there being several at a time, have a
pretty effect from the house in a dark evening.

Thursday being the first day of Ludlow races, we
were all to set out for that place. The Pardoes,[1]
at whose house some of us were to be, went the
evening before to prepare for our reception, and to
take lodgings for those their house could not hold.
Ludlow is ten miles from Court-of-Hill. We did
not set out earlier on the Thursday morn than to
reach Ludlow just as dinner was ready; that over,
we re-enter'd our carriages and proceeded to the
course,[2] that is most exceeding pretty, so calculated
for a race. 'Tis a circular spot one mile round, and a
perfect flat, so that the horses are in your view the
whole time, and the field itself is so beautifully surrounded by such fine wooded hills that you seem
in an amphitheatre, surrounded by a country most
delightfully cultivated. On one side of the course is
a large mount cut into the turf seats, and one fine
tree on the top; this being cover'd by the multitude
had the drollest effect, and put me so much in mind
of an ordinary painting I've often seen in cottages of
a genealogical tree of poor Charles I. The race over,
we flew back to dress. Here I was better off than
the rest of the ladies, except Mrs. Conyngham; her's
and my man are clever in the hair-dressing way, so
that we were ready long before those who waited for

---

[1] They were cousins of the Hills, an old Shropshire family.
[2] Bromfield racecourse, near Ludlow.

1771 the hair-dresser. We got to the ball about nine, a
very agreeable one, tho' 'twas said not near so brilliant
as formerly. This, indeed, I can easily conceive by
our race-assembly at Reading, which used to be
thought the next to York ; but the fashionable resort
to water-drinking places every summer takes from
each county those young people who otherwise would
be ambitious of shining at these annual balls. However, Ludlow's assembly, with two lords and six
baronets' families, might be stil'd tolerable, tho' it
seem'd a mortifying thing that Lord Clive's[1] family
were at Spaw, and Lady Powis[2] ill in London. Mr.
Conyngham and Greenly, as stewards, were of course
masters of the ceremony, assisted by their ladies.
Mrs. Conyngham must be ever most elegant, but
such a figure ornamented by dress and jewels must
be still more conspicuous. There were many pretty
women—Miss Pardoe greatly admired ; indeed these
two cousins, Harriot and Lucy, put me not a little in
mind of Richardson's " Harriot Byron, and Lucy
Selby ; " Lucy Pardoe, like the latter, a very fine girl,
all pleasing vivacity ; Harriot Conyngham, sweetly
delicate in manners, with every advantage of person,
and, if any advantage to us females, I might say
learn'd, as her father instructed her in the Greek and
Latin from her earliest years. But to return to and
then adjourn from the assembly to Mr. Pardoe's,
where our whole company came to supper, not a-bed
as you may suppose till near five.

The following morn 'tis the custom of the place
for all the company to meet at the theatre, which is a

---

[1] Of Oakley Park, Salop.
[2] Wife of first Earl of Powis, of Walcot, Salop, and Powis Castle,
Montgomeryshire.

very pretty one, and always a good set of actors;
the play always bespoke by the stewards' ladies.
It was now "The Author and the Citizen," indeed
perform'd exceedingly well.   This was not over till
dinner-time.   All the gentlemen in town dine at the
ordinary, and every lady of any consideration is invited to a Mr. Davis's, a gentleman of large fortune
in Ludlow, and having been formerly an eminent
attorney, of course acquainted with the surrounding
families.   She is a very clever, agreeable woman, and
we had everything in the highest elegance, but it
look'd so odd sitting down three- or four-and-twenty
ladies, and not one man (but my very little one, Phil).
We had not time to sit long at the dessert, tho' consisting of every kind of fruit, ice, pines, and fine wines,
as the race-time again drew near, to which we got
just as the horses started.   When over, we return'd to
dress, and then to the assembly, and about four in the
morn a very large party indeed (being double our
usual one), met at Mr. Hill's lodgings, where he had
order'd a supper for a very numerous company.   We
here staid some hours talking over, as usual, the incidents of the day, and were most exceedingly gay;
for I don't agree with Miss Paget (in the novel of
"The Card"), that a ball when over, "is a horrid
thing."   I rather think a most diverting one, in recollecting the droll figures that generally contribute to
make the group,   I can't say it was early that we
met next day, and I had then to walk about what is
esteem'd the prettiest town in England.   It stands on
an eminence, or rather brow of a hill, which renders
every street as remarkable for neatness as they are
for the goodness of their houses.   It was formerly a
principality of Wales, and their prince resided in the

1771 now ruinated castle standing at one end of the town. From the castle terrace, under which runs the river Teme, you look down on it from a vast height, while the fine nodding ruin hangs over you on the other side, making a landscape the most picturesque. As to your little Phil, I believe he was almost in every house in Ludlow, as Mrs. Hill stil'd him one of the race-week sights.   Three or four times a day he acted Prince Henry to audiences of twenty or thirty people with vast *éclat.*   Luckily he don't mind strangers, indeed it has been my endeavour he should not, for I think shy children of his age are dreadful.   One day at the course Lord Bateman came up to the coach, and says to Mrs. Hill, "What is the name of that beautiful boy?"   He gave her no time to answer, but says "My name is Philip Lybbe Powys, of Oxford-shire."   "Why then, Philip," replied his Lordship, "you are the very finest fellow I ever saw in my life."   Poor man! he is, it seems, remarkably fond of children, and wrongly miserable that he has none.   Indeed, one finds them most agreeable *douceurs* when with one. But now, for instance, my little Tom, at the distance he is now from me, makes me feel for him each moment lest he should not be well as I left him. . . . I find it impossible to finish my journal while here, as we go so soon, but you shall, if you desire it, have the conclusion in a third letter as soon as I get home.

LETTER 3RD.

HARDWICK,
September 22nd, 1771.

Here we are, my dear Margaretta, once more return'd to our beloved Hardwick, happy that, not-

withstanding the noble prospects we have seen, this 1771
still appears more beautiful than ever, and doubly
happy were we to find those well we have been so
long absent from. . . . We quitted the very pretty
town of Ludlow with our large party on the Saturday
evening, all of whom had promis'd to return to Court-of-
Hill for the time we were to stay there.   Indeed, the
set was a most agreeable one, never less than sixteen
or eighteen of ourselves, and most days additional
company. . . . Sunday pass'd, as usual, with people
cheerfully thanking for the enjoyments of life.   We
now heard an excellent preacher in Mr. Bowles.

Monday, the morning as usual divided into parties
of riding, walking, shooting, reading, working, drawing.
Never met at dinner till after four (this, too, you
know, is the usual Hardwick hour), tho', indeed, in
the shooting season seldom before five.   A walk in
general after tea, and in the evening a large pope
table,[1] another quadrille, and many lookers-on besides ;
never supp'd till near eleven, or a-bed till near two.   So
as I generally had letters to write at night, and Phil's
rising to shoot with Conyngham by seven, I don't
really think I could say I had a night's rest while
there.

Tuesday, the family of Bowles to dinner.   This
name you know, as the father,[2] who lives near
London, is, I think, tenant of Mr. Wheatley's, his
eldest son not married.   This is the second, and a
clergyman,[3] married a Miss Hale, a Herefordshire
beauty of very large fortune.   He has, indeed, a good
income, £12,000, as one of the younger children, and

[1] Game of Pope Joan.
[2] Humphrey Bowles of Wanstead, Essex.
[3] Rev. George Bowles, ancestor of Baron Northwick.

1771 the two livings here in their own gift. I never saw anything so handsome, too much so for a man, I think. It seems he is the image of his sister, who married Sir John Rushout's son when Becky Bowles, I've ever heard talk'd of as a perfect beauty. These Bowles live at Burford, a fine house badly situated.

Wednesday, a Miss Strahen came for one night on her way to Shrewsbury races. This daughter of Sir Patrick Strahen's I've long known by name, being almost a proverb for plainness. Two gentlemen once laid a wager that each could name the ugliest woman in London, the company were to judge, and poor Miss Strahen was mention'd by both! She came the moment before dinner, and Mrs. Conyngham happening to sit next her, and I opposite to both, it was hardly possible to suppose those two of the same species; but would you imagine with such a countenance she had a hand and arm the most beautiful, nay, she is so agreeable, so exceedingly clever, so everything but handsome, that before she left Court-of-Hill next day, I had lost the idea of her bad person. She must have been sensible in her youth her chance for society was the cultivation of her mind; in that she succeeded; no one's company is more sought. You can't imagine a person of rank she is not intimate with. They told me that in person she was really every year more agreeable, and I fancy if Miss Strahen would take a more matronly title, as her person is genteel, she'd soon pass for a good comely woman, an excellent exchange for that of an ugly Miss, in my opinion.

Thursday we were to dine at Sir Walter Blount's. We had all been invited, but it being utterly impossible for all to go, Mrs. Hill left eleven, besides

children at home, and attended three of us ladies in
the coach, Mr. Hill, Mr. Conyingham, and Mr. Powys
on horseback. Mawley, the seat of Sir Walter, is
ten miles from Court-of-Hill ; the road over the Clee
Hill more horrid than any I had yet seen, literally
mended with the iron-stone. We were, however
shook mighty merry, and only forced to get out once.
Had the sweetest views. In about two hours and
three-quarters we got there. Mawley is indeed a
very fine place. They begged us to be early, to go
over the house before dinner. The floors are most
of them inlaid like those of the Queen's palace, as
is the grand staircase ; that and the hall being exceedingly pleasant. Every room is carved in the
most expensive taste. In what is call'd the little
drawing-room, the wainscot, floor, and furniture are
inlaid with festoons of flowers in the most curious
manner with woods of different colours. In this room
is a cabinet of ivory and ebony, a present to the late
Sir Edward from China. It would take hours to
examine it. Out of this is the state bed-chamber, bed
and furniture crimson velvet and gold lace. The
library, eating-room, and large drawing-room all good.
Lady Blount's dressing-room you may imagine elegant ; fine India paper on pea-green, put up by
Spinage, with equal taste as Mrs. Freeman's (at
Fawley Court, Bucks), by Bromwich. The chambers
all good, spacious, and well-furnish'd. I think Lady
Blount has more chintz counterpanes than in one
house I ever saw ; not one bed without very fine
ones. But she seems to have everything very clever,
and a thousand nick-nacks from abroad, as one generally sees in these Catholic families. The elegance of
their table you may suppose not inferior to that of

1771 their house; genteelest service of plate, and everything that was in season. The gentlemen at dinner,
speaking of the present dearness of provision and rise
of meat, Sir Walter said they indeed were exempt
from the imposition of a butcher, as they kill'd all
their own, and did not go to market for one thing.
This must be exceedingly comfortable to a man of
large family and large fortune, both of which he is
possessed of. I believe I told you she was a daughter of Lord Aston, and co-heiress of £200,000. Sir
Walter and Lady Blount are both about thirty, both
rather handsome—would be more so if both were not
too inclined to grow fat; are most agreeable and
easy in their manners, and have three charming boys,
the eldest not three years old, and a fourth coming.
Never did three little creatures look so pretty; the
two youngest in fine sprigg'd muslin [1] jams, the eldest
in a vest and tunic of tambour (Lady Blount's own
work), large sprigs of gold on a thin muslin lin'd
with pink. I much wanted to see their chapel, as I
imagine it must be superb. There were many pictures about, and one small room with many fine religious subjects.

We were talking of the amazing wit of Pope, who
was often at Mawley, tho' much oftener at our neighbours the Blounts of Maple-Durham, where there is
such fine portraits of himself and Patty Blount. One
day Sir Walter's father was in his company and
talking of punning. Pope said that was a species of
wit so triflingly easy that he would answer to make
one on any proposed subject offhand, when a lady in
the company said, "Well, then, Mr. Pope, make one
on keelhauling." He instantly replied, "That, madam,

---

[1] Jamdari, a figured Indian muslin.

is indeed putting a man under a *hard ship!*" Keel- 1771
hauling is drawing a man under a ship. What a
ready invention must the man have had! One could
hardly have found a more crabbed word to exercise
the punster's faculty.

They would fain have persuaded us to come
there for some days, obligingly saying it was far
the nearest road in our way home, but we had
already exceeded our intended stay from Hardwick.
The next day we had an invitation to Croft Castle,[1]
Mr. John's, and for the day after to Burford,[2] Mr.
Bowles', but as we had fixed the next Monday for
our departure, we got Mrs. Hill to make our proper
compliments for not waiting on these families. We
all had a very high entertainment for some days
in finding Mr. and Mrs. Evans at Court-of-Hill the
evening we came from Mawley. Mr. Evans is, or
rather was, a poor Welsh clergyman, having £18
only a year, till Mr. Hill gave him a small living
which made his income to about £80, making him
and his wife the most happy as well as most grateful
couple in all Wales. They are always desired to pay
an annual visit to their benefactor, and not knowing
the house was full of company, or having sense enough
to make inquiry, they came, and at first, I verily
believe, were near frightened to death; but as all
insisted on their stay, and took the utmost pains to
encourage them, they soon seem'd, at least the wife,
charm'd to a degree. Indeed ours was the most
difficult task, for while she was a novelty, it was

---

[1] The Crofts had been seated here from Edward the Confessor till
the reign of George III., when Sir H. Croft sold it to Mr. Johns.

[2] Burford House, once the Mortimers', then Barons of Cornwall, sold
to William Bowles, M.P., ancestor of Lord Northwick, the present owner.

1771 hardly possible to keep one's countenance—a very large, far from ugly woman, continually inquiring about fashions, and not willing to be out of it. Having, I imagine, heard ladies wore curls, she had literally an amazing frizzed black wig; her clothes were good and in great variety, but you may guess how made and how put on. With all this finery she keeps no maid, nor he a man. At sitting down to supper, she takes out a flaming coloured linen handkerchief, and pinn'd it by way of bib on each shoulder. Mrs. Hill, being aware that this usual ceremony must have nearly killed the most of the company with laughing, had whisper'd it about before we left the drawing-room, and we were all weak enough to imagine politeness would come, if not by instinct, yet by example. But we were miserably mistaken, for this badge of meal-time was daily three times display'd; so you may judge of what with her figure and determination to taste of every "nice thing," as she term'd them at table, if it were hardly possible to keep our countenances free from a smile. As to venison, she did not seem tired either with the sight or taste, as we most of us were, as Mrs. Hill once was obliged to give us a haunch for five days running, they had such quantities sent them; but in Shropshire they have not yet come into the saving method of disparking, as about us, where venison now is absolutely a rarity. I've had but two haunches at Hardwick this summer, not even our annual buck from Blenheim. The *poor* Duke[1] of Marlborough is forc'd some years to send his excuses, tho' from the old Duchess my father had an unlimited warrant for both bucks and does, as many as he chose to send

[1] The second Duke.

for.[1] Mr. Evans, poor man, tho' equally illiterate, 1771
had not the drollness of his wife, and rather chose
breakfasting on cold pasty with "the gentleman,"
as he styl'd Mr. Hill's servant out of livery, than
with our gentlemen. But she was really diverting,
laugh'd so hearty, and seem'd so happy, particularly
when Conyngham talk'd Welsh to her.

One evening at tea Mrs. Pardoe, who is exceedingly droll and clever, whispers Mrs. Evans that
now she had been so long with all the ladies, she
wanted to know how she lik'd them. "Oh, to be
sure, 'tis a fine sight to see so many, and so well
dress'd too." "But give me your opinion of them.
My niece Conyngham, is she not exceedingly handsome?" "Why, ah! mighty well, to be sure."
"Mighty well. Why, she is reckon'd quite a beauty."
"Yes, yes, I've heard—I have heard so. To be sure
she is very well, for all that she is so spare." "My
sister Hill, then, she is fatter. What is your opinion
of her?" "Oh, Madam Hill is mighty well look'd."
"And Mrs. Powys?" "Mrs. Powys is a mighty
clever lady. Has a good eye." (I told Mrs. Pardoe
I suppose they only saw my profile, or else both eyes
might have come in for a compliment.) Miss Galaher
comely, Miss Pardoe very smartish, and so she
went on. Then, turning to Mrs. Pardoe, "But,
indeed, indeed, you yourself are far the handsomest." Once, indeed, Mrs. Pardoe was pretty to
a degree, but we begg'd her now not to be vain on

---

[1] There is a warrant from the great Duke of Marlborough to Mr.
Powys extant. "May 1, 1739.—To the keepers in Woodstock Park,
Stone, Ashworth, and Wyatt. This is to order you to send to Mr. Powys
whenever he pleases to command them, every season, without any
new directions from me, one brace of bucks and another of does.—
J. MARLBOROUGH."

1771 the given preference, as it was size only that made her obtain it!

On Monday we quitted this every-way agreeable Court-of-Hill. I cannot say we set out so early as we ought, as they all insisted on seeing us at breakfast, which afterwards we ladies at least repented, as most of us rose from the table in tears at the breaking of a circle in which for three weeks we had with so little ceremony and sincere friendship experienced the real enjoyment of a large society. The day, unfortunately, was the only bad one we had had, and that of course seem'd to participate in one's gloomy ideas; but by the time we reached the Hundred House the day and ourselves brightened up; for you know Phil and your Caroline cannot be long unhappy when not separated, and we had an agreeable journey to Worcester, there dined, and walk'd about a good deal, taking the boy to the Cathedral. On our way to Broadway, where we lay, we were surprised at the amazing numbers of Quakers we met, but afterwards heard they were going to Evesham. Once in seven years 'tis their rule to meet at four different places to settle their accounts. The next morn we walk'd up Broadway Hill, from the top of which is seen Ragley (Lord Hertford's), Overbury (Mr. Martin's), and many others. We pass'd that morn the four-shire stone,[1] at which point Worcester^{re}, Gloucester^{re}, Oxfordshire, and Warwick^{re} meet. Near Woodstock you see at one view Blenheim, Lord Lichfield's, and Sir James Dashwood's. The first, as I told you, we intended to spend some time at. The inside of the

---

[1] A stone pillar, which also stands on the site of a battle between the Saxons and Danes, in which Canute was defeated by Edmund Ironsides.

house I've given a description of in a former journal. 1771
The new piece of water is a grand design of Brown's,
tho' I think one too plainly sees that 'tis only a *piece*
of water, which I should have thought might have
been conceal'd by a genius so great as Mr. Brown's
in design. We dined and stay'd a vast while in
Oxford ; indeed it is a place so entertaining one can
hardly ever quit it, and our little fellow-traveller was
so diverted with the grandeur of it, that we did not
reach Hardwick till between nine and ten, when, as
I before, I believe, told you, we had the inexpressible
satisfaction of finding all that we could wish. . . .

From Hardwick to Benson	10 miles.
Benson to Oxford	12 ,,
Oxford to Woodstock	9 ,,
Woodstock to Chapel House . .	10 ,,
Chapel House to Broadway . . .	17 ,,
Broadway to Pershore	12 ,,
Pershore to Worcester	10 ,,
Worcester to Hundred House . .	11 ,,
Hundred House to Court-of-Hill . .	15 ,,
	106 ,,

October 1771.—Mrs. Freeman's,[1] Fawley Court,
Bucks, I've deferred mentioning, tho' so frequently
there, till it was more finish'd. 'Tis in Buckinghamshire, built by this gentleman's father,[2] but, though
always an excellent house, had no ornaments till now,
when Mr. Freeman has laid out £8000, I believe, in
inside decorations, besides having the celebrated Mr.
Brown[3] to plan the grounds. We spent a week there

---

[1] Once the seat of Sir Bulstrode Whitelock. Sold to the Freemans
after the Restoration.

[2] Wrong ; his great-uncle, William Freeman, in 1684.

[3] Lancelot Brown, nicknamed "Capability" Brown, eminent landscape gardener.

K

1771 this year in the shooting season, and tho' one had
seen it so frequently while the improvements were
going on, one could hardly have imagin'd either house
or its environs could have been so embellish'd by the
artist's hand. Every room is of a good house size,
being fitted in an elegant, and each in a different
style. The hall is a very noble one ; round it statues
on pedestals, some fine ones large as life. It's stucco'd
of a French grey. The saloon answerable to the hall,
with light blue and gold cord. In this room are many
fine pictures, a magnificent organ at the lower end,
inlaid with many curious woods ; a fine chimney-
piece, two very beautiful marble tables, on each an
elegant candlebranch of ormolu ; the paper cost fifty
guineas ! The ceiling of this room is very fine old
stucco, which Mr. Freeman thought too good to be
destroy'd. On the right hand is the drawing-room,
fitted up with every possible elegance of the present
taste, hung with crimson strip'd damask, on which are
to be pictures ; a most beautiful ceiling painted by
Wyatt ; the doors curiously inlaid, the window-shut-
ters painted in festoons, a sweet chimney-piece, a
grate of Tutenar's, cost 100 guineas ; two exceedingly large pier glasses, the chairs and confidant sofa
in the French taste. This room leads to the eating-
room, in which the colour of the stucco painted of a
Quaker brown. The ceiling and ornaments round
the panels all display such an elegant simplicity of
neatness that I almost prefer this to any room at
Fawley Court. On the left hand of the saloon is a
large billiard-room hung with the most beautiful pink
India paper, adorn'd with very good prints, the
borders cut out and the ornaments put on with
great taste by Broomwich, and the pink colour, be-

sides being uncommon, has a fine effect under prints. 1771
From this room you enter the breakfast-parlour, a
sweet apartment, peagreen stucco, gold border, elegant
chimney-piece, green marble with gilt ornaments ; the
sofa and chairs, Mrs. Freeman's work, a French pattern, pink, green, and grey ; curtains, peagreen lute-
string.   In recesses on each side the chimney are two
elegant cases of English woods inlaid, glazed so as to
show all the curiosities they contain of fossils, shells,
ores, &c., &c., in which Mr. Freeman [1] is curious, and
has a fine collection.   On one side of the room is a
large bookcase of the above woods, and at the
bottom of the room is a table in which the maker
has amazingly display'd his genius in disposing the
different colours.   Near this is a small library.   The
staircase, now separated from the hall, is a superb
one, and the apartments above nobly spacious as the
rooms below.   The best room is furnish'd with bed,
&c., of the late Mrs. Freeman's work.   One is seldom
partial, I think, to ladies' work of this kind, as it
generally carries the date of the age it was perform'd
in, but this is peculiarly fine, differs from any one ever
saw, and certainly does her honour.   Her own picture
is properly placed over the chimney of this room.
The dressing-room to this is prettier than 'tis possible
to imagine, the most curious India paper as birds,
flowers, &c., put up as different pictures in frames of
the same, with festoons, India baskets, figures, &c.,
on a peagreen paper, Mr. Broomwich having again
display'd his taste as in the billiard-room below, and
both have an effect wonderfully pleasing.   The next
bedchamber is furnish'd with one of the finest red-

[1] This was Sambrook Freeman, great-nephew of the first Freeman
owner.

1771 grounded chintz I ever saw, the panels of the room painted, in each a different Chinese figure larger than life. In the dressing-room to this, an exceedingly pretty tent of Darius bed. The third capital apartment is furnished with bed, counterpane, &c., of yellow damask, the room hung with India paper, buff ground. Over the chimney in this dressing-room a droll picture of a Chinese pauper.

There are numberless other more common rooms, but Mrs. Freeman's own dressing-room must be mention'd as most elegant. The room is a dove-color'd stucco, ornamented with pictures and a thousand other curiosities, as one might expect to see in the particular apartment of the mistress of Fawley Court.

The grounds laid out by Mr. Brown with his usual taste. Though Mr. Freeman's own house unfortunately cannot boast a situation so uncommonly eligible as his parsonage, yet tho' at the bottom of the hill, it stands on a fine knoll, commands a beautiful view of the Thames and surrounding hills, cover'd with the finest beech woods. Mrs. Freeman has a pretty menagerie and most elegant dairy in the garden, ornamented with a profusion of fine old china.

N.B.—Since the above, Mr. Freeman has erected an elegant building in his island,[1] planned and executed by Wyatt,[2] and the room is ornamented in a very expensive manner.

In December 1771, being at my cousin Wheatley's in Kent to spend Xmas with a very large party, they were so obliging as to take us to see many places, the weather being remarkably fine. We set out first for Knole, that fine old seat of the Dukes of Dorset . . .

---

[1] This is now the so-called "Regatta Island."
[2] James Wyatt, eminent architect, born 1743 ; died 1813.

It stands in a park of eight miles circumference, and 1771
not a little resembles the old stone Colleges of Oxford.
Part of it was built four hundred years since, and part
in the reign of Queen Elizabeth. 'Tis a double quadrangle, spacious to a degree that's hardly credible,
having, as the groom of the chambers inform'd us,
five hundred rooms, tho' he own'd he never had patience
to count them, tho' he often had the thirty-five staircases. In the old Duke's [1] time, he said, the company
us'd to be as innumerable as the apartments, and made
us laugh by an instance of this, having desir'd the
housekeeper to count the sheets she gave out, having
delivered fourscore pairs, she said, she would count no
longer! One is almost sorry the present owner has it
not in his power to keep up this ancient hospitality,
but everything possible was left from the title—a great
pity with such a seat as Knole. One goes through
the apartments with concern that this young Duke
cannot refit the furniture of each. One longs to repair
every old chair, table, bed, or cabinet, exactly in its
former taste, particularly in the room call'd the king's
bedchamber, the furniture of which was a present from
the royal family, and certainly had been equal to the
rank of the donor and splendid to a degree. The
bed and chairs cost £8000,[2] the outside cloth of gold,
the inside that of silver, the beakers, jars, &c., on the
cabinets of most curious filigree, the frames of all the
glasses, sconces, tables, and chairs, of solid emboss'd
silver. In that, and many other rooms likewise, old
cabinets very fine with silver emboss'd frames. The
pictures I should imagine to be the finest, and no
doubt the largest collection in England. The portraits

[1] Charles Sackville, second Duke. His nephew succeeded him.
[2] The bed alone cost £3000. The whole fittings of room, £20,000.

1771 of the family for many generations. One parlour is hung round with all the English poets only. 'Tis amazing and impossible to enumerate the many fine pieces in each room, and the present Duke has just brought many, being just return'd from abroad, particularly a Lucretia, by Titian, from Rome. The chapel here is pretty and adorn'd with some fine painted glass.

The Powys also visited Sir Gregory Page's, Blackheath; Sir George Young's at Foots Cray Place; and Sir Sampson Gideon's villa called Belvidere, lately Lord Baltimore's. Of this it is stated :—

"Commanding a noble view of the river Thames for above twenty miles. Thirty or forty sail constantly passing and repassing before you. The house is very small, except two rooms built by Mr. Gideon, Sir Sampson's father, for his pictures, which, tho' numerous are exceeding pleasing. In the eating-room, two paintings by Teniers over the door you enter. Van Tromp over the other, Rembrandt by himself, two fine heads; the creatures entering the Ark, by Rubens; two insides of churches, very fine. The Genealogy of our Saviour by Albert Durer, capital tho' not pleasing; two views of Venice by Canaletti; two small landscapes with horses, beautiful, by Wouvermans; two landscapes by Poussins; a fine piece of dead game with a dog barking at it; Boors at cards, and other Dutch pictures of Teniers. In the drawing-room on one side of the chimney, the Duchess of Buckingham and three children large as life, and one of Rubens' children with them, all by Rubens; on the other side Mars and Venus, the latter face the most pleasingly beautiful I ever saw; opposite, at the bottom of the room, the Assumption

of the Virgin Mary, the Flight into Egypt, both 1771
large as life, by Merelli;[1] over the door, Snyders,
his wife and child, by Rubens; Our Saviour in the
Temple amid the Doctors; on the other, Venus and
Cupid, an allegorical piece; the rest of the house
very small—two small parlours, in one, panels painted
of monkeys, another *Scaramouches*, which the old
Lord Baltimore used to call the Monkey and Scara-
mouch parlours. (*N.B.*—Since I was at Belvidere,
I hear Sir Sampson has rebuilt the house in a most
magnificent taste, and immensely large)."

1772.—On January 2nd Mr. Wheatley took us 1772
to see Mereworth, built by Lord Westmoreland in
1715, and left at his death to Lord Despencer, the
present owner.   The plan is in the Italian taste,
for coolness as we were informed; but, in a country
so different as ours from Italy, 'tis a plan, I think,
unnecessary to adopt, as it seems to make one's
residence uncheerful.   As you enter from a vast flight
of steps, a large hall of an octagonal figure, lighted
only from a dome on the top, so entirely excluding
the sun; opposite the great doors the saloon or
picture gallery—many capital ones.   The staircases
are made in the corners of the octagon hall—of
course, winding, narrow, and steep.   At the top is
a gallery round, and looking down on the hall;
round this are the chambers, more spacious and convenient than one would imagine, but on the whole
'tis not a pleasing house.

January 18*th*, 1772.—At court on the Queen's
birth-night, her Majesty dressed in buff satin, trimmed
with the sable just made her a present of by the
Empress of Russia.[2]   The Princess of Brunswick[3] was

[1] Murillo.   [2] Catherine II.   [3] Augusta, sister of George III.

1772 there, coming on a visit to her mother, then ill. We used to think her, though not handsome, a good figure, but she is now grown so fat and plain, that, tho' cover'd with jewels, I never saw a woman that look'd more unfashionable.

January 28th, 1772.—This week the town was in a vast bustle at the opening of the Pantheon, and Mr. Cadogan was so obliging to send me his tickets for the first night. As a fine room I think it grand beyond conception, yet I'm not certain Ranelagh struck me not equally on the first sight, and as a diversion 'tis a place I think infinitely inferior, as there being so many rooms, no communication with the galleries, the staircase inconvenient, all rather contribute to lose the company than show them to advantage.

February 8th, 1772, died the Princess Dowager of Wales, mother to the present King George III., was buried the 15th, and Sunday the 16th began the public mourning, twelve weeks in crape and bombazine, broad hemm'd linen, a fortnight black silk, fringed linen, drest and undrest greys, or black and white, and another fortnight colour'd ribbons, white and silver, &c. ; went quite out the 10th May.

1773   *January 6th*, 1773.—Mr. Powys, myself, and our eldest boy went to Bath for five weeks for Mr. Powys' health, and the waters were of infinite service to him. While there we saw King's Weston, a fine place of Mr. Lenthall's ; breakfasted at the Hot Wells, Bristol, which I always think a most melancholy place out of the season ; saw the Bristol glass-houses, which are really curious. The celebrated Miss Linley (afterwards Mrs. Sheridan), was now a capital singer at Bath. We heard her in "Acis and Galatea," and

nothing but the elegance of her figure can equal her 1773
voice.

November.—Being then in London, went to see
Mrs. Wright's waxworks, which, tho' exceedingly well
executed, yet being as large as life, if of one's particular
friends, 'tis rather a likeness strikingly unpleasing.

February 5th, 1775.—Caroline Isabella born at a 1775
quarter after two in the afternoon.

On July 5th went to Stowe.[1] Sir Charles,[2] Lady
and Miss Price, Mr. Powys and myself, set out in
our two phaetons.   On our way to Abingdon, we
stopped to see Mr. Phillips,[3] the builder's house, Culham
House. From there to Abingdon, dined there, and
got to Oxford early in the evening. It happen'd, as
we before knew, to be the time of Commemoration,
but we none of us chose taking different dresses for
that occasion, as we had been at that and the oratorios
the year before, when at Mr. Schutz's of Shotover.
The performers were the same as Miss Davis, and
Linley, Gerdini, Ficher, &c. But tho' we did not go
to the music, we did to Merton Gardens after the
assembly was over, and it being a beautiful evening,
it was really a most pleasing sight to observe the
variety of dress. Those from the theatre full drest,

[1] The seat of the Duke of Buckingham and Chandos.

[2] Sir Charles Price of Blount's Court, Oxon. His second wife, Mary
Brigham, of Cane End, Oxon.

[3] Mr. Phillips was a remarkable person, and undertook the public
works and buildings, now occupying a whole department, for the sum of
£53,384 per annum. He built Battersea and Culham Bridges over the
Thames. Was a great collector of pictures and china. He lies buried
in Hagbourne churchyard with this epitaph, "Here lyeth the body of
Thomas Phillips, son of Matthew Phillips of this parish, whose known
skill, and diligence in his profession, joined with great probity in his
dealings, gained him that reputation in business which recommended him
to be carpenter to their majesties King George I. and King George II.
He died the 14 August 1736, aged 47 years."

1775 accidental travellers in riding dresses, the Oxonians in
their gowns and caps. It had almost the appearance
of a masquerade. Thursday, we went to Bicester,
a most dismal and unsafe road as I ever travell'd in
my life. Soon after we pass'd Sir James Dashwood's
at Cadlington,[1] which seems a melancholy situation.
I rather fancy we lost our way, as the roads were so
bad. I often thought the phaetons could not stand
the ruts, and to complete our miseries it was impossible
for Macbeth's Witches to have been in a worse storm
of thunder, lightning, and rain, after a most unpleasing
morning. We got to Bicester in a torrent of water.
The people at the inn seeing us in phaetons thought
only of beds for us, but we ourselves most luckily were
the least wet. I can't say the same for our servants,
all four nearly drowned, but by taking great care of
them none were luckily ill, and in the evening we got
to Buckingham ; but hearing there was an inn
quite at the park gate at Stowe, we chose to lay
there to take the first fine weather for seeing the
place. This we afterwards almost repented, as never
were accommodations so wretched. The next morning, very fortunately, was exactly such a one as we
wished it to be. The garden being a five-mile walk,
which we accomplish'd with great ease, as you go
over the house when just half round the grounds.
These more than answer'd my expectation, as I had
always heard it represented as a perfect flat, which
it by no means is, as you ascend the whole two-
miles avenue from Buckingham. The buildings used,
I know, to be thought too numerous, but in such an
extent I do not think even that, and the fine plantations now grown up to obscure them properly, must

[1] Kirtlington Park.

add infinitely to many picturesque views of porticos,
temples, &c., which when originally were expos'd
at once, with perhaps three or four more seen from
the same point, must have had a very different and
crowded effect. The house, which will be one of
the most noble in the kingdom, we then saw to
infinite disadvantage, as entirely altering, a fine new
saloon not even cover'd in, scaffolding around the
whole building, every room unfurnish'd, all the fine
pictures taken down. There is some of the fam'd
Gobelin tapestry at Stowe, which (I own I may
be partial to English manufacture), is not in my
opinion anything equal to Saunders, at Lord Cadogan's, Caversham Lodge.

We lay that night at Aylesbury, pass'd Lady
Tent's, Sir William Stanhope's, and Sir William
Lees,[1] both near that town. The next morning by
Wendover is Mr. King Dashwood's,[2] a brother of
Lord Le Despencer's; two miles from thence is
Hampden[3] Lord Trevor's, and at Missenden[4] is the
fine old abbey of that name sweetly situated. At
High Wycombe Lord Shelbourne has an odd pretty
place just at the end of the town. We went on to
dine at West Wycombe, as the Prices had never seen
the so-much-fam'd church of Lord Le Despencer's.
The house,[5] which we first saw, is nothing remarkable,
tho' very habitably good; you enter it sideways thro'
a portico—odd and uncommonly pleasing, some good
pictures, the gardens and park pretty, those and the
house much improved since we were there before.

---

[1] Hartwell House.
[2] Wycombe Park.
[3] Belongs to the Earl of Buckinghamshire.
[4] Formerly Abbey of Austin Canons, founded circ. 1133.
[5] West Wycombe House.

1775 The new church and mausoleum, on an immense eminence, dreadful for the old people at least to ascend; the former gives one not the least idea of a place sacred to religious worship. 'Tis a very superb Egyptian Hall, no pews, pulpit, or desk, except two ornamental seats which answer the two latter purposes. The font is shown as an elegant toy; in fine, it has only the appearance of a neat ballroom with rows of forms on each side. The mausoleum is a six-angled open wall of flints, stone ornaments, and rows of Tuscan pillars, two of the six divisions are occupied with dedications to Lord Melcomb and Westmoreland, and in the centre of the mausoleum is a monument for Lady Despencer, lately dead. On the whole this extraordinary building is well worth the observation of strangers. We that night went to my brother at Fawley,[1] parting near there with the Prices, who, as ourselves, seem'd greatly pleas'd with our little tour.

1776   1776. — The most severe frost in my memory began January 7th and lasted till February 2nd. It began to snow about two in the morning as we were returning from a ball at Southcote, and kept snowing for twelve days, tho' none fell in quantities after the first three days, but the inconvenience from that on the ground was soon very great, as strong north-east winds blew it up in many places twelve to thirteen feet deep, so that numbers of our cottagers on the common were oblig'd to dig their way out, and then hedges, gates, and stiles being invisible, and all hollow ways levell'd, it was with vast difficulty the poor men could get to the village to buy bread; water they had none, but melted snow for a long

[1] Fawley Rectory.

while, and wood could not be found—a more parti- 1776
cular distress in Oxfordshire, as our poor have always
plenty of firing for little trouble.   As to our own
family, we were fifteen days without the butcher from
Reading being able to get to us, and then he came
on foot, but luckily we had sheep, hogs, and poultry ;
our farmyard looked like a picture I've seen of all
animals collected to enter the ark, as all our sheep,
cows, horses, &c., were oblig'd to be fodder'd there.
We could have no news or letters from Henley or
Reading for ten days, but then we began to be so
impatient we got a man to venture on foot ; no horse
passed for a month, or cart for two.   On the fifteenth
day the butcher sent over two men with a little beef
and veal, which then began to be scarce even there ;
not one team at Reading market the Saturday after
it began — a thing never known.   The two London waggons came in with sixteen and fourteen
horses ; but one horseman that day thro' the turnpike ; all stages and machines stopped for ten or
twelve days on the very best roads.   It kept on
freezing intensely after it had done snowing, the river
being froze over from Whitchurch to Maple-Durham.
Some of our people were silly enough to walk over
it.   Two hundred and seventeen men were employ'd
on the Oxford turnpike between Nettlebed and Benson to cut a road for carriages, but then a chaise
could not go with a pair of horses, and very dangerous, like driving on glass.   A waggon loaded with
a family's goods from London was overturn'd, a deal
of damage done in china, &c., but 'tis astonishing
any one would venture to send any goods in such
a time, or venture themselves.   We wish'd much to
have had some company in the house, but we were

1776 even so unfortunate, as not to have Mr. Pratt, my
brother, and our boy Phil, as they were all at my
Lord Camden's for the Christmas. Our gamekeeper
measured a piece of ice from a pond on the 29th;
it was nine inches and a half thick. The beer and
ale froze as they drew it, and the cream was forced to
be put in the oven to thaw before they could churn
it for butter, all my tender greenhouse plants died,
did not save one geranium, the oranges and myrtles
not hurt, or any shrubs or flower-roots out of doors,
the snow no doubt preserved them. Every one
dreaded the so-much-wish'd-for thaw; we by the
river expected a deluge, but, thank God! never could
such severe weather end more moderately. On the
2nd February began a most gentle thaw, and the
immense quantities of snow melted away by gentle
degrees to every one's astonishment. The road to
Reading continued impassable till the 15th, after
that the way was shovell'd, but when I went long
after, it was in many parts a lane of snow above the
coach windows. There was a deal of snow on the
20th March! I fancy the weather of 1776 was very
like what Sir William Temple in his works mentions
of 1678 in Charles II. time: "I was going," says
Sir William, "from the Hague to Niemegen, the
inclemency of the season such as was never known
in any man's memory, the snow in many places nearly
ten feet deep, and ways for my coach to be digg'd
through in many places; several postboys died upon
the road. I pass'd both Rhine and Weal with
both coaches and waggons upon the ice, and never
suffered so much from weather in my life as in
this journey, in spite of all I could do to provide
against it, yet was it perfectly ridiculous to see

people walking about with long icicles from their 1776 noses."

Before resuming Mrs. Powys' experiences, it must be acknowledged, from notes of her various occupations, and collections of objects of varied interest still owned by her family, that few people could be more fitted to amuse and employ herself usefully when confined to the house.   She was a skilled needlewoman ; [1] later on we shall find Queen Charlotte taking interest in her work, and asking if she was working anything new.   She embroidered, worked in cloth, straw plaited, feather worked, made pillow lace, paper mosaic work, &c., dried flowers and ferns, painted on paper and silk, collected shells, fossils, coins, and was a connoisseur in china, &c. ; besides this, she was an excellent housekeeper, and as a specimen of the patience exercised in the careful preparation of household drugs in those days, I give the following receipe as made by her :—

"LAVENDER DROPS.

" Six handfuls of lavender flowers stript from stalks, put them in a wide-mouth glass, and pour on them four quarts of the best spirit of wine, stop the glass very close with a double bladder tied fast down that nothing may breathe out, let it stand in a warm place six weeks, keep it circulating about, then distil it in a limbeck.   When all is run off, put to this water sage flowers, rosemary flowers, bugloss flowers, betony flowers, burrage flowers, lily of the valley

---

[1] Her mother, Mrs. Girle, excelled in needlework, and in 1753 finished a bedquilt for her daughter, which had taken several years to work.   It had her coat of arms in the centre, and crest (a wheat sheaf), in each corner.

1776 flowers, cowslip flowers, each a handful gathered in
their seasons in dry weather ; let this stand six weeks,
then put to it balm, motherwort, spike flowers ; cut some
small bay leaves, orange leaves, and the flowers of each
an ounce ; distil all these together again, then put in
citron peel, lemon peel, dried single piony seed, and
cinnamon, of each six drams, nutmeg, mace, candimums,
cubels, yellow saunders, of each half an ounce, lignum
aloes, one dram ; make these into a fine powder and
put them into glass, then take juinbes,[1] new and good,
a pound stoned, and cut small, stop all quite close for
six weeks more, shaking it often every day, then run
it thro' a cotton bag, then put in prepar'd pearl two
drams, ambergrease ditto, of saffron and saunders and
yellow saunders each an ounce, put these in a bag and
hang them in the water, and close up the glass well ;
at three weeks' end it will be fit to use.

"*N.B.*—When you find any indisposition, or fear
of any fit, take a small spoonful with a lump of sugar ;
it helps all palsies of what kind to cure."

She also adds that in 1782 she had still some drops
made years before by her father-in-law, Mr. Powys,
made by this receipt, and notes, " They are far superior
to any one buys ; " so they ought to be, for they contained thirty-two ingredients, and took twenty-one
weeks to make !

1776.—Mr. Pratt[2] left my brother this March,
having been with him seven years and some months ;
he soon after went to Cambridge. The parting was a
most melancholy one on both sides, as I believe never

---

[1] A fruit with a stone.
[2] Only son of Lord Camden, the Lord Chancellor, pupil to Rev.
Thomas Powys at Fawley Rectory, Bucks.

was there a tutor and pupil who had a more sincere 1776 affection for each other.

On the Queen's birthday Mr. Hanger,[1] brother to Lord Coleraine, was drest in a sky-blue Paduasoie, the seams work'd with gold, gold cuffs and waistcoat, a velvet muff trimmed with cheneal blonde, and long streamers of the same, a large white feather in his hat ; and the next summer another standard for dress, Mr. Bamfield[2] (now Sir Charles), at Exeter Races, had a blue trimm'd with Devonshire point, and olives of fine pearl ; the coat cost £800.

When in London this spring (1776) we had the very high entertainment, at a private concert, of hearing the celebrated Mrs. Sheridan sing many songs, accompanied by Giardini on the violin. I had never had that pleasure since she was Miss Linley ; was then charmed, but more so now. I think indeed her voice, person, and manner are more than one generally sees combined, and then her being so totally unaffected, render each ten times as pleasing as otherwise they would be.

June 1776.—Tho' we never have any friends at Hardwick that we don't take them to see Caversham Lodge,[3] yet I've not here mentioned it, as I knew it was to undergo many alterations ; those are nearly finished, and from always being a pleasing, 'tis now a very fine place, the situation beautiful, and these grounds laying out were the first performance of the since so celebrated Brown, who made a just tho' droll observation on the vast number of trees of an amazing

[1] George Hanger, last Lord Coleraine, an early boon companion of the Prince Regent, nicknamed "The Hanger On."

[2] Sir Charles Bamfylde, ancestor of Baron Poltimore.

[3] Then the seat of second Lord Cadogan, now of W. H. Crawshay, Esq.

1776 growth all through the whole spot, "that it was impossible to see *the trees* for wood." Indeed they stood so thick that this was literally true, they hiding each other. But by taking some down and leaving conspicuous the most noble, he has made it one of the finest parks imaginable, and at the time of the white-thorns being in blow, which at Caversham are by far the oldest and most beautiful I ever saw, 'tis hardly possible to describe the scene it offers. The terrace at Caversham (next to Lord Lincoln's), I've heard is the finest in England. On this stands the house, now white, formerly of brick and infinitely larger than at present; you enter a charming hall (lately new), the old hall now a very elegant library, which you go through to a breakfast-room adjoining the saloon, in both of which are many good pictures, but the drawing-room beyond the saloon is one of the most pleasing apartments I ever saw, being fitted up with the English tapestry, which in most people's judgment exceeds the Gobelin. This history is a pilgrimage to Mecca, the camels, horses, dogs, amazingly well executed, the attitudes of the people fine, the colours of the finest tints, and all the figures of a pleasing size. Over the chimney-piece is a piece of the same, which represents a Sultan going into the private apartments of his women, his handkerchief in his hand to cast at the favour'd one, an attendant behind, and a most beautiful girl holding up a festoon curtain through which he is to enter. This piece is reckon'd inimitable; in short, the whole does great credit to Saunders. There is a little fire-screen of it, groups of flowers which show the different kinds of tapestry. From this room you go through a pretty lobby into the eating-room, a very good one. Among the pictures is a remarkable one

which belonged to General Husk, who made a present 1776
of it to the family, as 'tis taken from a circumstance in
the Duke of Marlborough's wars in which General
Cadogan[1] was present. The Duke, General, &c., are
on horseback in conference with the French General,
and the Duke has dropp'd his glove which his aide-de-
camp is dismounting to pick up, and mark privately
the spot, as they had before agree'd that just where
that fell he would have the battle. . . .

JOURNAL OF A FIVE DAYS' TOUR, IN A LETTER TO A FRIEND

1776

We have some years wish'd to see Stourhead, so
at last suddenly fix'd on the 5th of August, the fourteenth anniversary of our wedding-day ; our party
small, Mr. Annesley, my brother,[2] Mr. Powys, and
myself in two phaetons. We call'd at our friends the
Rushs of Heckfield; their place a very pretty situation,
close to two pleasing parks, Lord Rivers', and his
brother's, General Pitt. Basingstoke is only ten miles
from thence. We got too early there to remain the
night, and as we found afterwards, too late to reach
Overton, eight miles farther. Fortunately the road was
good and safe, as we were literally benighted travellers
in an unknown country ; many times I could not see
any horses to the phaeton. We sent one of the servants on for a light, and so by the light of a lanthorn
we were ushered into the town at near eleven. The

---

[1] William Cadogan, first Earl, succeeded the Duke of Marlborough
as Field-Marshal.

[2] Rev. T. Powys, her brother-in-law, always styled "brother."

1776 next morning we pass'd the house of Capt. Jennings
at Laverstock, near that a house and mills of a Mr.
Portal, at which is made the Bank paper.[1] Near the
town of Whitchurch, in Hampshire, is the seat of
Lord Portsmouth, call'd Hurstbourne, a large and very
ancient pile, standing in a park eight miles in circumference, but at present not one modern improvement
about its environs; we then pass'd a hunting-seat of
Mr. Delmé's named Redrive; and seven miles from
Salisbury, the spot where Lord Holland's house was
burnt down the year before. We had breakfast at
Andover, and got to the above-mention'd city (Salisbury), by three. Tho' we had all been there often,
'twas agreed to spend that evening in a review of it.
We of course laid out money in the famous steel-work
of this place, and paid as much again for it as in
London, at which place they have told us they could
not even make a pair of scissors. On Wednesday
morning we went three miles on the other side of
Salisbury to see Longford Castle, the seat of the Earl
of Radnor, situated in a pleasing valley, the river
Avon running thro' the garden. The house, built in
the reign of James I.,[2] is in a triangular form, round
towers at each angle, which are the eating - room,
library, and chapel, these rooms are octagon in the
inside; there is a fine gallery; the fitting up and
pictures of that only, is said to have cost £10,000; at
each end are the two celebrated pictures of Claude
Lorraine, of the rising and setting sun, amazing fine
landscapes indeed, and which we went on purpose to
see; but there are many of the most capital masters

[1] Still made there.
[2] Long before this, in 1591, by Sir T. Gorges, but enlarged by late
Lord Radnor.

dispers'd all over the house, some inimitably fine ; a 1776
boy, whole length, by Rubens, in the breakfast-room,
is almost life itself ; but I cannot enumerate half, for
tho' there is a catalogue to every room, we could not
allow ourselves time to see them with just attention,
not having imagin'd this house near so much worth
seeing as it really is, and from its triangular form 'tis
so singular[1] (there being but one more in England, built
by the same person, six miles distant), that it has an
agreeable effect ; it neither looks modern or ancient
but between both ; stands in the middle of the garden,
only one step from the ground, so that you may instantly be out of doors.   The park is fine, the environs
in taste, the furniture elegant, the pictures a most
noble collection, so that we were quite pleased that
Claude Lorraine had tempted us these three miles
out of our first propos'd excursion.   We return'd back
thro' Salisbury, and so to the inn at Wilton,[2] where
we breakfasted, as we could not resist seeing Lord
Pembroke's, tho' we all had often been there before ;
indeed I fancy few people pass by, as at the porter's
lodge, where he desired us to set down our names and
the number of our company, we saw by the book there
had been to see it the last year 2324 persons.   Merely
to *see*, 'tis certainly one of the finest sights in England ;
but to reside at, 'tis too grand, too gloomy, and what
I style *most magnificently uncomfortable*, the situation
bad, the rooms, except one, too small, and I want
three or four more considerable ones.   Were I Lord
Pembroke,[3] I'd have two superb galleries, one for

[1] It was built after the model of the Castle of Uraniberg, designed by
Tycho Brahe.
[2] Seat of Earl Pembroke.
[3] Wilton has been much altered since this account was written, at the
beginning of the nineteenth century by Wyatt, and since.

1776 pictures, the other for statues, busts, &c., of which
many here it seems are nowhere else in the world
to be met with; they would then appear with advantage, whereas now the whole house gives one an idea
of a statuary's shop. 'Tis universally allowed that
the one grand apartment[1] I before mention'd is the
noblest can be seen—60 feet by 30 and 30 feet high.
The celebrated family picture by Vandyke every one
has heard of if not seen—20 feet long, 12 feet high—
contains thirteen figures large as life, and at the farther
end of the room one could imagine them animated.
'Tis well known that of late years the most capital
pictures of the best masters have been brought into
England; many indeed were taken away in Charles
I.'s time, but now there's hardly a gentleman's seat
without a good collection. At Wilton they are fine
indeed, tho' I think a good deal hurt by being too
highly varnish'd in a late cleaning. The building was
begun in the reign of Henry VIII., the great quadrangle finish'd in that of Edward VI., and the porch
design'd by Hans Holbein; the hall-side being burnt
down, was again finished by Inigo Jones, 1640.

From Lord Pembroke's we went to Fonthill, the
seat of Mr. Beckford, now a minor. The old house
was burnt down about twenty years ago,[2] and this
just finish'd as this young gentleman's father (the
great Beckford, as he is usually styled), died. 'Tis
a large stone house, eight rooms on the principal
floor, but, as a contrast to Lord Radnor's, which we
had that morning admir'd for being so near the
garden, the ground apartments at Fonthill[3] by a most

---

[1] Called the Double Cube.   [2] June 1755.
[3] Cost Alderman Beckford £240,000. His son sold it and built the
still more magnificent Abbey, commenced in 1796.

tremendous flight of steps are, I believe, more distant 1776
from the terrace on which the house stands than the
attic storey of Longford Castle; and the housekeeper
seems to show it to a disadvantage, I think, taking
us under these steps through a dark and gloomy
hall, from which she mounted us to the second storey
of bed-chambers first. The state bed and furniture
crimson velvet, gold frames to the chairs, tables,
and cornice to the bed. Mrs. Beckford's dressing-
room has in it numbers of superb and elegant nick-
nacks. From thence we descend'd to the principal
floor, where is display'd the utmost profusion of magnificence, with the appearance of immense riches,
almost too tawdrily exhibited. There are many good
pictures and many very indifferent. Cassaulis I never
admire; the best at Fonthill are of the small kind,
fit only for lady's cabinets; of these there are many
capital ones. The chimney-pieces all over the house
are elegant to a degree; even those in the attics must
have cost an immense sum, all of statuary or Sienna
marble; but what hurts the eyes most exceedingly is
that every hearth, even the best apartments, are common black and white, which seems such a saving of
expense in the very article where profusion has been
so lavish'd that 'tis perfectly amazing. A fine grove
of oaks, with clumps of evergreens on the left of the
house, is very picturesque, and there is a fine piece
of water, otherwise the situation is disagreeable.[1]

From hence we went to dine at Hendon, the
borough which was then so talk'd of on General Smith's
account, then in the King's Bench for bribery there.
'Tis a horrid, poor, thatch'd, dirty-looking village, not
a tolerable house in the place; we could hardly pro-

[1] William Beckford shifted the site to build his splendid Abbey.

1776 cure a dinner. We intended laying at the inn at
Stourton, built by Mr. Hoare for the company that
comes to see his place, but to our great mortification,
when we got there at near ten o'clock, it was full,
and we oblig'd to go on to Meer, a shocking little
town three miles off. There too the best inn was filled.
The other, or rather ale-house, was bad indeed, but
the landlord so anxious to accommodate us with beef
steaks or anything of that kind for supper, that,
as we could not do better, we laugh'd ourselves into
good-humour, tho' his only parlour, the man said, was
taken by two gentlemen from the other inn, belated
too, and whom he begged we would join, he was sure
they would be willing; but as we imagin'd the gentlemen, like ourselves, liked their own company, and might
not be of the landlord's sentiments, we stuff'd ourselves
into the bar-room till bed, when the above heroes were
so kind as to resign the best bed, as the maid styled it to
me, and getting two more in the village, we did tolerably, and in the morn return'd to Stourhead, which
answered every difficulty we had met with the preceding evening, as both house and grounds are so
vastly well worth seeing. The inn I mention'd is
just at the entrance of the garden. We there left
our horses and carriages, and walk'd for about two
miles; the pleasure-ground in all is seven; Alfred's
Tower, at the extent one way, which is seen for miles
round Stourhead. The first building after the gardener's cottage is the Bristol Cross,[1] a present from that
city to Mr. Hoare, a very light Gothic structure, but
its kings and queens in the niches round it would,

---

[1] Erected in that city in 1373 in gratitude for grants made to the city
by Edward III. Contains eight statues, four last added in 1633. Removed
in 1733, and sold to Mr. Henry Hoare.

in my opinion, have look'd better of the original stone 1776
colour than so ornamented with red, blue, and gilt
clothing; but still 'tis pretty through this profusion
of finery, and I believe it may in some measure be
more strikingly gaudy from its nearness to one; could
it be plac'd on an eminence at a little distance, it
surely would have a more pleasing effect. Fifty
men are constantly employ'd in keeping the pleasure-
grounds, rides, &c., in order, in all about 1000 acres.
It was a park when Mr. Hoare purchas'd it of Lord
Stourton, but all the buildings and plantations are the
present owner's own doing,[1] without any assistance
but common workmen to plan or lay out the whole
seven miles' extent, nor could Brown have executed
it with more taste and elegance. Nature indeed had
been profuse in giving a spot the most beautifully
irregular, without which no grounds can be laid out
pleasing to the eye. These were nothing more than
naked hills and dreary valleys, which now are so
beautifully adorn'd by art, assisting Nature with trees,
her greatest ornament, where hills and water only were
before. This indeed might be discovered by the
disagreeableness of the country the instant you are
out of Mr. Hoare's domains. The next building after
the Cross is a greenhouse, prettily adorn'd outside
by stone or burnt cinders from the glass-houses at
Bristol, the inside black gravel stones mixed in the
mortar; it looks like pounded flints and has a pretty
effect. We then pass'd over what the gardener
called a Palladian bridge, but he certainly mistook,
as I think Palladio's bridges were cover'd over.
This is open top and sides, pretty at a distance;
when near, the idea of going over a kind of ladder

[1] Mr. Richard Hoare, afterwards made a Baronet in 1786.

1776 only is frightful. Another party of company could not bring themselves to venture, but 'tis not so bad after you have brought yourself to venture a few of its steps, tho' its perpendicular appearance and seeing the water through at first looks formidable. We saw many pretty seats at the stems of trees of stones piled like rock-work on each other. The next building is the Pantheon,[1] in which are seven niches with statues large as life, over them seven alto-relievos. From the Pantheon colonnade you have a fine view of a constant cascade which is very beautiful; from this we went to the Temple of Apollo.[2] On the outside niches with statues, on the inside a gilded sun with a skylight to illuminate it. From thence we cross'd another bridge leading to a stone alcove, then to the Temple of Flora. In general these edifices are so alike at all gardens, and the seats and buildings here put one greatly in mind of Stowe, if it were not for the much more beautiful spots each is here erected on, to what that flat situation can boast. The Turkish tent at Mr. Hoare's is very pretty; 'tis of painted canvas, so remains up the whole year; the inside painted blue and white in mosaic. We thought it best for our horses to take them at this time to Alfred's Tower, three miles off, that they might again rest while we walk'd the remainder of the tour. They sent a guide with us over the top of the hill, which commands so many fine views of this now cultivated spot. One of them looks down an immense valley, where is the head of the river Stour. It rises in six different springs at a piece of rock-work where the figure of Neptune is striking, and the river gushing

[1] A copy of the famous Roman temple.
[2] Temple of the Sun, designed after that at Baalbec.

out.   The tower[1] is lately finish'd, cost above £4000, 1776
yet we thought it the least worth seeing of any one
building at Stourhead.   It being brick in a country
of stone is rather wonderful.   The form triangular,
150 feet 10 inches high, one of the angles round a
stone pillar is a spiral staircase of 225 stone steps
before one gains the top, and then there being no seat
or enclos'd room, only an iron at such a distance that
people may just pass in walking round, and those who
can, may look down the tower from top to bottom on
the inside.   It does take in an immense tract of
prospect, and our guide inform'd us of twenty different
things he saw and meant us to see.   The tower was
erected in honour of Alfred the Great, as an inscription over the entrance mentions that on this summit
his standard[2] was erected against the Danes.

After seeing the tower we descended the hill, and
by the banks of the river came to the Convent, an
elegant building, painted glass in the upper part of the
windows in miniature.   Nuns in their different habits
in panels round the room, very pretty Gothic elbow-
chairs painted in mosaic brown and white.   Two very
ancient pictures found in the ruins of Glastonbury
Abbey—the Wise Men's Offerings—well painted.
From this place we came back to the house, again
put up the horses while we saw indoors, which in
itself answers the situation, and contains a thousand
curiosities of furniture, pictures, &c.   You enter a
noble hall, round this in panels are whole-length portraits, very capital ones, one in particular by Carlo
Maratti.   He is drawing the portrait of a young nobleman standing by him, other figures behind as large as

---

[1] Built by Henry Hoare, Esq.   The hill is 800 feet above the sea.
[2] In A.D. 879.

1776 life. Opposite the chimney, Mr. Hoare, when a youth,
on horseback.   There are ten rooms on the principal
floor, the saloon finely proportioned, 50 by 30, and 30
high.   The paintings here large and fine, some his-
torical.   In the third room shown is the so-much-
talked-of cabinet [1] that once belong'd to Pope Sixtus,
which Mr. Hoare purchased at an immense sum, so
great that he says he never will declare the sum.   It
is, indeed, most beautifully ornamented, as well as
valuable, for on the outside are many fine gems.   A
border goes round the frame four feet from the ground,
here set in frames.   Pope Sixtus's picture, and those
of his family, drawn, you may be sure, after he was
raised from his original obscurity.   Some time after
the purchase was made, in some inner private drawers
were found seventy-two other miniatures, some in the
old English dress, others of Spain and Italy.   The date
on this curious antique cabinet is 1677.   In a closet out
of this room is a most inimitable portrait of Titian by
himself, at ninety-two years old.   Round this are hung
the seventy-two miniatures above mention'd.   There
are a number of fine paintings, and they are hung in a
most clever manner, the frames having hinges fasten'd
to the walls on one side as a door is, and may be
pulled forwards as the light is required.   The best
picture at Stourhead is, I think, over the chimney in
the picture gallery, a Rembrandt—Elijah restoring the
widow's son to life, Elijah as large as life, and a most
striking figure.   There are many of Rembrandt,
Canaletti, Claude Lorraine.   There are two from the

---

[1] This cabinet was left by a nun, the last of Pope Sixtus' family, to a
convent at Rome, where it was purchased by Mr. Hoare.   It is made of
ebony, agate, and lapis-lazuli, fronted by pillars of precious stones, and
inlaid with gold.

last master by Wotton, well executed ; one fine land- 1776
scape by Gainsborough, of Bath, some cattle of
Cuyp's.   The state bed and furniture are of India
painted taffeta.   In the eating-room is a most curious
emboss'd piece of plate,[1] a present from the City of
London to Sir Richard Hoare when Mayor, intended
for the sideboard, but 'tis now in a frame over a table,
on which stands three fine pieces of the Sevres manufactory, reckon'd superior to Dresden ; 'tis immensely
dear.   I forgot to mention a sweet picture of Angelica
Kauffman's, a lady in a white and gold Turkish habit,
working at a tambour.   But for all my encomiums
about this charming place, I cannot think it equal to a
situation in our own neighbourhood.   I mean Park
Place,[2] General Conway's, which has more of the soft
and beautiful, with the addition of a fine country every
way round, while the charms of Stourhead are literally
confin'd within itself.   We dined that day at Dedford
Marsh, and from thence to Amesbury, so dreary a
road as quite from Mr. Hoare's I never went over ;
dismal downs, not a cottage or tree to enliven the
scene.   Here and there a melancholy looking shepherd,
attending, as they told us, flocks, sometimes of three
to five thousand ; some farms having two or three such
flocks.

When we got to Stonehenge, we drove up and got
out of the carriages to see "this stupendous piece of
antiquity," as Dr. Stukeley stiles it ; the number of
stones, he says, are 140.   Our coachman informed us it
was impossible to tell them, and no one ever did, as
they would actually die if they attempted it.   Our
sagacious servant told us "the Devil brought them

[1] Represents the story of Cyrus and Queen Ismaris.
[2] Park Place, near Henley-on-Thames, Berks.

1776 there from Ireland, tied up in a withe, which breaking,
is the reason they are so scatter'd, and one fell just at
the river at Amesbury." He told us this with the
gravest countenance, and seem'd angry at our laughing.
We had only one mile to Amesbury from Stonehenge.
We were this night too unfortunate, for being late, the
inn was full, and as we were settling with the landlady
to get us beds at private lodgings, our servants came
and whisper'd us that the two gentlemen from the inn
at Meare were now in that front room. We then
look'd in, and so they were. Sitting with candles, we
saw our former night's facetious landlord's "two agreeable gentlemen," were Mr. Walpole[1] and Mr. Adams,
who we were exceedingly well acquainted with. You
may be sure we now made ourselves known, and
passed a very pleasant evening with them, laughing
exceedingly that none of us chose the evening before
to join company. The Duke of Queensberry's seat
borders on this town; seems a most dismal, dreary
situation.

We left Amesbury next day, came most shocking
roads thro' a new turnpike to Kingsclare. On the top
of Kingsclare Hill we saw the clouds pass below in
the valley with great velocity; rather shocking, but
that hill is a vast height, looks very romantic with the
big town just under it. We see this hill, you know,
from Straw Hall, in Hardwick Woods. We din'd
at the town, and reach'd home that evening, perfectly
pleased with our excursion, and perfectly happy to
return here. As you know, tho' we have great pleasure
in seeing fine places, we are so vain as to think few
surpass our own, I mean in natural beauties. Hardwick's merits is all its own, never has been indebted

[1] Horace Walpole and Adams, the architect.

to modern improvements, and in this age may, for 1776
that reason, be thought more uncommon, as the rage
for laying out grounds makes every nobleman and
gentleman a copier of their neighbour, till every fine
place throughout England is comparatively, at least,
alike! Miles travelled, 174.

October 11*th*, 1776.—From my brother's at Fawley
we went to see Hurley Priory,[1] Berks, an immense old
white house near Marlow. Formerly it belong'd, with
a vast tract of land, to Lord Lovelace, but now is in
possession of a Mr. Wilcox, who purchas'd it, with
little of the ground remaining except the gardens.
This gentleman is a nephew[2] of Bishop Wilcox (Rochester), is a man curious in antiquity, and seems
deserving of so fine an old mansion by the care he
seems to take of it. I own I never was better pleas'd
with any house I ever saw. You enter from the
garden one of the most pleasing halls you can imagine,
vastly large, amazingly light, in which is a fine staircase, with a gallery looking down into the hall; the
rooms all large, windows immensely so, all glazed with
a multiplicity of little panes, but no casements, so that
'tis the most cheerful house possible. In a large drawing-room upstairs is the fine paintings of Salvator
Rosa,[3] every panel a distinct landscape, shades of

[1] A Benedictine foundation, on the remains of which Sir Richard
Lovelace built or added to largely. He accompanied Sir Francis Drake,
and was fortunate, capturing a galleon containing much Spanish gold.
His son, in 1626, was created Baron Lovelace.

[2] Mrs. Powys is wrong. He was son of the Bishop, and inherited it
in 1791 from his aunt, Mrs. Williams, who, winning two prizes in a
lottery, one of £500 and one of £20,000, was enabled to buy it. Her
daughter, Mrs. Lewin, dying, the place went to the nephew.

[3] These panels, 32 inches long, 14 broad, green, grey, and brown,
lights in silver lacquer. In modern times these pictures have been attri-
buted wrongly to Pietro Tempesta. Mr. Lane, of Badgemore, bought
some; Mr. Budd, of Newbury, thirty panels; also Mr. F. Maitland
some.—Vide *Gentleman's Magazine*, 1731 to 1868.

1776 greens and browns, the large trees inimitable. Salvator lived in Charles II.'s time. He never was in England; but this work of his was sent over in separate panels. In one of the windows in this room are 365 panes of glass. The cellars of this house have long been famous for their goodness, tho' they are uncommonly so, but because in them was plann'd the Revolution. The servant inform'd us two kings had dined there. They might indeed, as they are light, answerable to the rest of the house;[1] but we could see no reason for such an entertainment. The following inscription is plac'd against a wall :—

"The Priory of St. Mary's, Hurley, founded in the reign of William the Conqueror, by Geoffrey and Lecelina Mandeville, A.D. 1086."

Mrs. Powys' account of this most interesting place, about which a volume could be written, ends here. An inscription in these vaults existed till 1831, now removed, to this effect :—

" *Mortality and Vicissitude to all.*

" Be it remembered that the Monastery of Lady Place, of which this place is the burial cavern, was founded at the time of the great Norman Revolution, by which Revolution the whole state of England was changed.

" Be it remembered that in this place, 600 years after, the Revolution of 1688 was begun. This house was then in the possession of Lord Lovelace, by whom private meetings of the nobility were assembled in this vault, and it is said that several consultations for calling in the Prince of Orange were held in this recess, on which account this vault was visited by that powerful Prince after he had ascended the throne."

---

[1] They were visited by William III. after his accession, and George III. and his Queen in 1785.

When William the Third arrived in England, Lord 1776 Lovelace, with seventy followers and gentry and others, rode to welcome the King, but were stopped at Cirencester, where Lovelace was taken prisoner, and young Bulstrode Whitelock, grandson of Sir Bulstrode Whitelock, of Fawley Court, Bucks, and son of Mr. William Whitelock, of Phyllis Court, Oxon, was shot, and died November 14, 1688. On Lord Lovelace's liberation from prison, he was made captain of the band of gentlemen pensioners to William III. He lived in such a costly state that he involved himself in debt, and Lady Place was sold in two portions under a decree in Chancery. The direct title was extinct in 1736, but the present Earl of Lovelace, by his first marriage with Ada Byron, daughter of the poet, she being nearest heir to the Lovelace's line, assumed the title.

In 1838 three bodies of monks, clad in their Benedictine habit, were found in the vaults, and reinterred in the churchyard. The fittings of the house were sold in December 1837. Mr. Budd bought staircase, columns, hall fireplaces. The house was pulled down, and materials sold by public auction. There is a picture of the house in "Illustrated Thames," by G. Leyland, published in 1897 by G. Newnes. The vaults of the priory, refectory (now a stable), some out-buildings, ponds, and walls, are the sole representatives of the once magnificent mansion. The tithe-barn and ancient pigeon-cot of the monks exist as well, whilst the Church of Saint Mary,[1] built in 1086, is deeply interesting. To return to Mrs. Powys.

[1] Mentioned as a church in Domesday Book, probably then rebuilt and freshly endowed by Geoffrey de Mandeville.

1776 ACCOUNT OF A GALA WEEK IN THE NEIGHBOUR-
HOOD OF HENLEY-UPON-THAMES, OXFORDSHIRE,
JANUARY 1777 (which I wrote of in two letters
to Mrs. ——).

December 1776.—But I must take up no more
time, my dear, on other subjects, as we have one in
this county at present will furnish out a letter of
length sufficient to *tire you*. 'Tis of a play to be perform'd by Lord Villiers [1] and some company at their
house about ten days hence. You know Lady Grandison, [2] his mother, who married Sir Charles Montagu,
took Phyllis Court (Oxon) of Mr. Freeman [3] some
time since. The Villiers live with them, and their
house is generally full, and to make it gayer than
usual this Christmas, they talk'd of performing "The
Provoked Husband," at first, I imagine, intending the
audience to be merely their own family; but such
interest has been making among people of fashion
for admittance, that at present 'tis the sole object of
the neighbourhood for miles round. We thought
ourselves not the least likely to be of the fortunate
number invited, for, as in their case, there must be
limitations, they properly give none but to those they
visit (and you may remember when first Lady Grandison came we never went, as we imagined a family so
deeply engaged in the fashionable game of loo, could
never wish an intimacy with one who never play'd at
all); but my brother [4] at Fawley is very intimate
there, who as a clergyman may, you know, easily keep

[1] Afterwards Earl Grandison.
[2] Elizabeth, Countess of Grandison in her own right.
[3] Sambrook Freeman, of Fawley Court, Bucks.
[4] Rev. Thomas Powys, rector of Fawley, Bucks.

clear of gaming, even with the approbation of the 1776
most polite. When Lord Villiers sent him his ticket,
there were some for us, but as my father chose not to
be in the scene of gaiety, the tickets were returned,
but Lord Villiers desir'd the Camden family to be
invited, for whom he'd send more.

The plan of the week is as follows : Three
nights the play is to be perform'd. The first only
as rehearsal, on Saturday the 4th, it being young
Mr. Hodges' birthday, and the day of Mr. Hodges'
tenants' feast, to whom 'tis supposed 'twill be a high
entertainment, and perfect the performers for the
grand exhibitions of the Monday and Friday following, when there are to be balls, and supper given by
Lord Villiers at the "Bell,"[1] at Henley, after the
plays, and a grand ball at Freeman's on the Wednesday after the plays. The famous Monsieur Tessier
is to perform Pygmalion ; if you inquire what theatre,
I must inform you a very neat one, fitted up by Lord
Villiers at Bowney [2] (Mr. Hodges')—a barn and coach-
house laid together, hung with green baize, the seats
the same, scenes from the Brighthelmstone Company,
and the whole to be lighted with wax. It holds 300,
so that number of tickets is given for each night.
My brother has much to do in it, as they begg'd him
to write two prologues, one for the play and another
for Pygmalion, besides to assist Mrs. Howe (sister to
Lord Howe), in prompting them. Hedley's, the inn
where the balls are to be, is already so fully engaged,
that he has bespoke forty private beds in the town ;

[1] The "Bell" Inn is now the Royal Grammar School, an interesting
building, with a curious secret chamber on the roof. It was a great
coaching inn, once had stables for a hundred horses. Prince Rupert
during the Civil War had a spy hung on the tree still opposite it.

[2] Bolney Court, Oxon.

1776 the other great inn,[1] too, entirely bespoke, and every
lodging in Henley ; fourteen and sixteen guineas given
for the three nights.   A band of ten musicians have
been down at Sir Charles Montagu's these ten days,
the best hands from Italy.

Lady Grandison was telling my brother yesterday
they had about thirty set down to dinner every day
in the parlour.   "And yet, Mr. Powys, you shall
judge if my larder will not hold out.   I've three does,
a warrant gone for a fourth, three brace of pheasants,
eight hares, six brace whistling plovers, twelve couple
woodcocks, ten brace partridges, a peafowl, two guinea-
fowls, snipes and larks without number, and most of
'these sent for the occasion, as I suppose, without
names!"   This is all I can send you word about it
at present ; only that poor Sir Charles Montagu and
Garrick (who was to have been there), are both ill
with the gout ; but as I'm certain female curiosity will
wish for the conclusion, I'll write again when I return
to Hardwick, till when I am at *this* and *every* season,
most affectionately your   CAROLINE POWYS.

HARDWICK,
January 13th, 1777.

1777   And now, my dear, for my promise, which I fear'd
with all our airy schemes of pleasure would have been
buried in a deep snow, for just at this time last year
how many weeks were we kept prisoners, and now we
live in continual apprehensions as it fell daily, and
the very night before we were to set out, so much as
to fill up the track of our usual way to Fawley, how-

[1] The "Red Lion." At this other historic inn Shenstone wrote his
celebrated lines "On an Inn," on a pane of glass. The great Duke of
Marlborough had a room there, fitted for himself in his journeys to and
from Blenheim.

ever, by going some miles round we got into the 1777
Henley turnpike, and at last, to our great joy, safe to
my brother's,[1] where we heard of every house in the
neighbourhood being full of company, even Freeman's[2]
were obliged to put up five new additional beds; yet
we afterwards heard of many tickets returned on
account of the weather, which was indeed bad to a
degree. The Saturday, as I said before, was only a
rehearsal before Mr. Hodges' tenants, and as they
found it was wish'd, many of the town people of
Henley, from which it was about three miles; however, the house was filled even that night. On Monday, the 5th, we got there in time, you may be certain.
The two first rows were left, by desire of those who
were first there, for the Grandison family, and tho'
Lord Villiers' servants said he had express orders
none should be kept, however, common politeness was
sure to counterbalance such a command. The house
was very soon filled, and you'd hardly imagine such
an audience in the country. As the company was
nearly the same both nights, I'll set down those I
knew to be there on either, tho' there were numbers
of fine men behind, whose faces I was not acquainted
with. The Duke of Argyle,[3] Lord Frederick Cavendish,[4] Count Brule, the Lords Tyrconnel, Beauchamp,[5]
Harrowby,[6] Sefton, Rivers,[7] Camden,[8] Macclesfield,[9]
Barrymore,[10] Parker,[11] General Conway,[12] Sir George

[1] Fawley Rectory.   [2] Fawley Court.
[3] John, fifth Duke of Argyll.
[4] Field-Marshal, son of third Duke of Devonshire.
[5] Third Earl Beauchamp.
[6] First Earl Harrowby, then renting Shiplake Court from Henry
Constantine Jennings.   [7] First Earl.
[8] Lord High Chancellor.   [9] Thomas, third Earl.
[10] Richard, the celebrated Earl of Barrymore.
[11] George, Viscount Parker.   [12] Of Park Place.

1777 Warren, Sir Thomas Stapleton,[1] Sir Michael Fleming, Sir Harry Englefield,[2] Sir George Beaumont;[3] the Ladies Grandison, Aylesbury,[4] Egremont, Hertford, Macclesfield, Villiers, Dowager, Tyrconnel, Sefton, Powis, Harrowby, Lady Almeria Carpenter, Lady Louisa Clayton,[5] Lady Caroline Herbert, Lady Harriot Herbert (daughters of Lady Powis), Lady Cecil Price, Lady M. Churchill, Lady Elizabeth Conway, Lady M. Parker, Lady Isabella Conway, Lady Warren, Lady Englefield, Lady Cornwall; Sir Thos. Clarges, and the families of Onslow, Churchill, Conways, Rivers; John Pitts and General Pitts, Howes, Pratts, Claytons, Freemans, Prices,[6] Tufnels, Vanderstegens,[7] Jennings,[8] Eliots, Rices, Mortons, Stonors',[9] Tilsons, Englefields, Norths, Monsons, Winfords,[10] Herberts, &c., &c. The curtain drew up about half after six o'clock, when Lord Villiers did great justice to my brother's prologue, which was much applauded. The play really amazingly well done throughout. "Sir Francis Wronghead" inimitably; "Manley," as well as it could be possibly; "Lord and Lady Townly" both shone. Miss Hodges, who is a most beautiful girl, had every advantage of dress, a pink satin suit of clothes, elegantly trimmed with gauze and flowers, all Lady Villiers' diamonds, valued at £12,000; four large

[1] Of Grey's Court, Oxon.
[2] Of Englefield House, Berks.
[3] Seventh Baronet.
[4] Wife of General Conway.
[5] Wife of Sir William Clayton of Harleyford, Bucks, sister of George, Earl of Pomfret.
[6] Sir Charles Price of Blounts Court, Oxon.
[7] Of Canons End, Oxon.
[8] Shiplake Court and Shiplake House, Oxon.
[9] Mr. Thomas Stonor of Stonor, Bucks.
[10] Of Thames Bank, Marlow.

bows making a complete stomacher, two of the same
as sleeve knots, a superb necklace and earrings, her
head almost cover'd, and a girdle of jewels, the ends
hanging down a quarter of a yard ; besides these a
complete bouquet, so that her angelic form was as
fine as it was *beautiful.* " Lady Grace "[1] (a sweet
girl), acted her part so well that I daresay she is the
character in real life ; and I could not help supposing
" Manley " *really* as much the *lover* as he appear'd to
be, especially as they had been in the same house for
so many weeks.

After the play, as I before inform'd you, was perform'd, a piece, taken from Ovid's *Pygmalion,* wrote
in French by the famed Rousseau,[2] and Tessier spent
some weeks with him, perfectly to comprehend the
author, as he declar'd he wrote it to express by action
every passion to the eye. We had first my brother's
second prologue, spoke by Lord Malden,[3] and the
audience a second time gave a great share of applause
to both the *speaker* and *writer.* When the curtain
draws up, Tessier (the Prince), is leaning on a table
in the most melancholy mood, dress'd in a most superb
habit. At the further end of the stage was a canopy
and curtain of gold and silver gauze (which cost £10),
behind which, on a rise of four steps was conceal'd his
beautiful statue. He was, I suppose, twenty minutes
in all the attitudes of tragic woe, deliberating whether
he should withdraw the veil, so fearing the sight of
this too lovely object. His powers are certainly astonishing ; 'tis said no one equals him. Some *partial
English* flatter themselves *their Garrick* might come
up to him. I own myself of that number ; but then

---

[1] Miss Clark.   [2] Jean Jacques Rousseau.
[3] George, afterwards fifth Earl of Essex.

1777 as not a perfect mistress of the French, I fear one's
opinion would go for nothing, tho' he speaks so just
and distinct, I understood by far the greater part of
the *whole*. At last he ventures most gently to draw
aside and fasten back the curtain, discovering a figure
which seem'd to captivate the audience almost as much
as it did the inamorated Pygmalion. Indeed she was
the sweetest statue imaginable ; clothed in a white lute-
string close-bodi'd, flowing train, her hair in ringlets
down to her waist, just tied behind, a white fillet
across her head, a long veil of white gauze button'd
on the shoulder and one side. Her first appearance
was in the finest attitude, leaning on a pedestal, one
hand hanging over it, holding in both a wreath of
flowers. Standing first in this posture almost an hour,
not her eyes (as far as one could perceive) *mov'd*. It
was quite astonishing to her audience ; such claps you
never heard, as between the woe and raptures of *her*
now almost distracted lover. He once tried to proceed
with his work, but throws away his implements as if
fearful they must injure a frame so *delicate*. At last,
by his prayer to Venus, she becomes animated, turns
her head, moves a hand, and at last, with vast seeming
apprehension, *descends* the steps. Her attitude so
pleasing, his admiration 'tis not possible to express on
paper. She speaks, he kneels down, grasps her hand,
and while both seem under the most *indescribable*
surprise, the curtain drops. It was really the finest
scene imaginable, and you see avoided every indelicacy.
Most of the company had privately express'd their
apprehensions of, from the well-known story in Ovid,
for the sake of our sweet actress, who was so much
admir'd, that I found most were of my sentiments of
its not being the thing for a girl of fashion to appear

in an affair of this very public nature.   After the play 1777
we returned to Fawley, as my brother excus'd us to
Lord Villiers for the ball *that* night, as I had then no
young people.   I also rather fear'd not being able to
go thro' *all* the diversions of the week, and it was
then twelve o'clock.   The rest of the company (invited
by his Lordship), went to the ball and supper at Hedley's, the inn at Henley.[1]

The next morning we expected Lord Camden,
Mr. Pratt, and two of the young ladies, but unfortunately poor Miss Jenny had too bad a cold to
venture, so my Lord stay'd till Thursday, in hopes
she would then be better.   Lady Camden, too, was
not well enough to come down, the weather being
terribly cold.

On the Wednesday, Mr. and Miss Pratt, my
brother, and ourselves got to Freemans' a little after
eight.   So great a crowd, or so fine a house[2] to dispose them in, you don't often see in the country.   I
need not mention the company, as it was nearly the
same as that of Monday night, as they sent cards
to all the people of fashion who were at the play.
Their usual eating-room not being large enough, the
supper was in the hall, so that we did not come in
thro' that, but a window was taken out of the library,
and a temporary flight of steps made into that, from
which we passed into the green breakfast-room (that
night the tea-room), thro' the pink paper billiard-
room, along the saloon, into the red damask drawing-
room.   Though none set down, this room was soon
so crowded as to make us return to the saloon.   This
likewise very soon fill'd, and as the tea was carrying
round, one heard from every one, "Fine assembly,"

[1] The "Bell."   [2] Fawley Court, Bucks.

1777 "Magnificent house," "Sure we are in London."
They danc'd in the saloon. No minuets that night;
would have been difficult without a master of the
ceremonies among so many people of rank. Two
card-rooms, the drawing-room and eating-room. The
latter looked so elegant lighted up; two tables at loo,
one quinze, one vingt-une, many whist. At one of
the former large sums pass'd and repass'd. I saw
one (nameless here), lady of quality borrow ten pieces
of Tessier within half-an-hour after she set down to
vingt-une, and a countess at loo who ow'd to every
soul round the table before half the night was over.
They wanted Powys and I to play at "low loo," as
they term'd it, but we rather chose to keep our features less agitated than those we saw around us, for
I always observe even those who have it to lose have
no less a tinge of the rouge in their countenances
when fortune does not smile. Oh! what a disfigur-
ing thing is gaming, particularly to the ladies. The
orgeat, lemonade, capillaire, and red and white negus,
with cakes, were carried round the whole evening.
At half an hour after twelve the supper was announced, and the hall doors thrown open, on entering
which nothing could be more striking, as you know
'tis so fine a one, and was then illuminated by three
hundred colour'd lamps round the six doors, over
the chimney, and over the statue at the other end.
The tables were a long one down the room, terminated by a crescent at each end, and a crescent table
against the two doors in the middle; the windows
were sideboards. The tables had a most pleasing
effect, ornamented with everything in the confec-
tionary way, and festoons and wreaths of artificial
flowers prettily disposed; all fruits of the season, as

grapes, pines, &c. ; fine wines (Freeman is always 1777
famous for) ; everything conducted with great ease—
no bustle. Their servants are particularly clever on
these occasions, indeed are annually used to it, and
none of those of the company admitted, which generally creates confusion. Ninety-two sat down to
supper. Everybody seem'd surpris'd at entering the
hall. The house had before been amazingly admir'd,
but now there was one general exclamation of wonder.
This, you may be certain, pleas'd the owners, particularly as many of the nobility there now never saw
it before. The once so beautiful Lady Almeria, I
think, is vastly altered. She and Lady Harriot Herbert had the new trimmings, very like bell-ropes with
their tassels, and seemingly very inconvenient in
dancing. .Lady Villiers had a very pretty ornament
on, which was the girdle "Lady Townly" wore,
fasten'd round the robing of her gown, and hung
down as a tippet. After supper they return'd to
dancing, chiefly then cotillons, till near six.

On the Thursday, we were hardly up and breakfasted at the genteel hour of three, when Lord Camden
and his other daughter came from London, the latter
with such a cough, that I was in a continual fright
about her going ; but the disappointment of Freeman's
ball had been so great, Lady Camden ventur'd to let
her try for the last night, but she was really the next
day infinitely mended.

The Friday morn Henley town was just like any
public place, such different sets of company walking
about it. Never before was it so gay, or so much
money spent there ; provisions rose each day immo-
derately. The gentlemen walk'd down. (We were
engaged in hair-dressing, of which fraternity five from

1777 London were at Lady Grandison's, three at Freeman's,
and others in the town no doubt).   In Henley our
party meeting that of Lord Villiers, my brother told
his Lordship he had sent to Lord Camden at his
desire, who was happy in the thoughts of seeing their
performance of that evening.   My Lord Villiers said :
—"Since they had been flatter'd in having some little
merit in the theatrical way, 'twas impossible but they
must wish to have such an orator as Lord Camden
approve if just, or blame with his unerring judgment
if otherwise."   My Lord, pleas'd with the compliment,
return'd one as flattering.   The graces (as Chesterfield
says), are never wanting to persons of true politeness.
We dined early, and got to the theatre in time.   Most
of the same people of fashion as the first night, and
the sweet little Lord Barrymore being very near us.
From being so very young,[1] my boy could not conceive
to be of any consequence, and made all round us laugh
by telling Lady Villiers he was much too small to be
a Lord !   Phil luckily is a great favourite with her
Ladyship, otherwise he would have seen no more than
you did, sitting just behind her head, whose feathers
were full three quarters of a yard high.   All the
Conways, too, are so immensely tall ; one of the boys
of an amazing height is to be a clergyman,[2] and my
brother telling him he must have all the sounding
boards raised wherever he preached, it put Lord
Camden in mind of a *bon mot* of Princess Amelia's,
who asked a remarkably tall young man what he was
intended for ; he told her Highness, "the Church."

---

[1] He was born in 1769, hence only eight years old then.   Phil Powys
was fourteen.

[2] Edward Conway, one of seven sons of Earl Hertford, and nephew
of General Conway of Park Place.

"Oh, sir," replied the Princess, "you must mistake ;
it's certainly for the steeple!" The performers again
surprised the audience. It was indeed vastly well
acted. Lord Villiers had a different and still finer
dress, buttons and buckles quite in ton, viz., large to
an excess, all the very fine men wear two watches—
Lord Villiers, Lord Malden, and Tessier had. The
play over, we wondered not to hear the coaches call'd
up, but were soon inform'd there was to be a dance.
This, as there seem'd no performers, we all wonder'd
at, but the curtain drawing up, three characters only
appear'd. Those, tho' disguised, we soon found were
Tessier, Churchill, and Englefield. The first an excellent figure as an old woman playing on the violin,
the second, a girl with a brandy bottle, looking rather
delicate, as Churchill is a pretty young man exceedingly fair, she and her *pero* danc'd the *fricassée*, a most
robust performance, an excellent burlesque on fine
stage dances. Tessier who is a fine hand on the
violin, play'd to them, and afterwards came forward,
and in broken English said he knew not our language
well enough to sing in that, but would with our leave
give us a little French song made by himself since
dinner, which he did in a most droll manner, sings
well, and the thought was clever, the whole turning in
compliment on the Grandison family and their neighbourhood, showing so splendid an audience as that he
address'd. Everybody was much pleas'd, particularly
as none but the three concerned knew of it till the
instant. All over, the performers joined the company,
and compliments you may be sure were liberally
bestow'd ; those of the morning between the Lords
Villiers and Camden renewed and added to. The
family insisted that none that night be excus'd from

1777 ball or supper; we wanted to send Phil home (not because he has not yet learned as you may suppose of Gallini), but as too young; but Lord Camden would have him at the whole, and introducing him to Lady Grandison she obligingly said she would not only now but always look on him as her particular guest. When the company was all got to the inn, tea was brought round the ball-room, a most comfortable thing after the play, tho' then twelve o'clock or later. The conversation was for some time on a subject you'd hardly imagine—robbery. Post-chaises had been stopped from Hodges to Henley about three miles; but tho' the nights were dark we had flambeaux. Miss Pratt and I thought ourselves amazingly lucky. We were in their coach, ours next, and the chaise behind that, robb'd. It would have been silly to have lost one's diamonds so totally unexpected ; and diamonds it seems they came after, more in number than mine indeed. It seems it was well known Mr. Hodges would not let Lady Villiers' jewels be kept at Bowney,[1] so that each night her woman was sent in a hired chaise to bring them home, and we found only hired chaises had been stopped. On the alarm, Lord Villiers sent a guard of six arm'd men for the Duenna, and so to the great joy of the company we soon heard of her being arrived in safety. After this there were two dances before supper; that ready, the family desired the company to go down just as nearest the door, without ceremony, and fill the rooms below, in all which were tables ready, as they came to them, so that there was not the least confusion. The suppers were very elegant, provision of every kind, wine, fruits, &c., &c., as at Freeman's. No servants but those of the

[1] Old spelling for Bolney Court, Oxon.

Grandisons and Villiers; indeed they have such 1777
numbers no others could be wanted. Everything was
sent from their house, and their own three cooks to
dress it. Soups and game as usual hot, the rest cold.
We hear cost Lord Villiers £1000. The dancing,
with cotillons, we heard continu'd till near six. We
took our leave rather sooner, as Lord Camden was
oblig'd to be in town that day to dinner, so that
returning to Fawley, we took not quite three hours'
sleep before we sat down to breakfast; that over, my
Lord and family set off for London, and us for Hardwick, and thus ended this agreeable week. . . .—I am
your sincere friend and affec.,   CAROLINE POWYS.

HARDWICK,
January 14, 1777.

DRAMATIS PERSONÆ.

In Play of " The Provoked Husband," acted at Bolney Court, Oxon.

Manley	Mr. MILLS.
Count Bosset	Lord MALDEN.
Sir Francis Wronghead .	Mr. FURZE.
Squire Richard . .	{ Mr. ONSLOW, second son { of Lord Onslow.
Poundage	Mr. CHURCHILL.
Lord Townly . . .	Lord VILLIERS.
Lady Grace	Miss CLARK.
Lady Wronghead . .	Miss HERVEY.
Miss Jenny	Miss HOPKINS.
Myrtiller	Miss P. HOPKINS.
Mrs. Motherly . .	Mrs. JOHNSON.
Trusty	Miss NEWEL.
Lady Townly . . .	Miss HODGES.

PYGMALION.

Pygmalion	Monsieur TESSIER.
Statue	Miss HODGES.

Prologue by the Rev. T. POWYS, *spoken by* Lord VILLIERS.

Most raw recruits in times of peace appear
To brave all dangers, and to mock at fear,
But, when called forth to tread the embattled plain,
They fairly wish themselves at home again,
Whilst hardy veterans long inured to arms,
Hear unappalled the battle's loud alarms.
Thus *we, unpractis'd* in the stage's arts,
Have fearless oft *rehears'd* our various parts,
Talk'd wondrous big of our theatric feats,
And dared the censure of the vacant seats.
And now alas ! the case is altered quite
When such an audience opens in our sight ;
Garrick himself in such a situation
(Tho' sure to please), might feel some palpitation.
Our anxious breasts no such presumption cheers,
Light are our hopes, but weighty are our fears.
We then ('tis too late to quit the field),
Must to your judgment at discretion yield.
Oh ! then be merciful ; the fault's not ours,
If, with a wish to please, we want the powers.

The following prologue was alter'd by Mr. Powys
as it was first wrote by Mr. Coleman, to be spoke by
" Lady Wronghead." The lines mark'd with commas
were in the original :—

Spoken by Mr. MILLS *in the character of* " MANLEY."

I fear the ladies think my last night's dealing,
Betray'd a heart quite destitute of feeling :
Who to my married friends such lessons gave,
As made each husband think his wife a slave.
So doctor like, I've took an early round,
And just stept in to tell you what I found.
My Lady Townly's quite to health restor'd :
And cousin Wronghead's *pulse* is vastly lower'd.
The first whose bosom grateful friendship warm'd,
Thus spoke the dictates of a heart reform'd,
" Sick of my follies, faithful to my vows ;
" I'm now remarried to my former spouse.

"Ladies *there are* at this might feel remorse,   1777
"And find perhaps more charms in a divorce.
"I've trod the giddy round, and don't deplore
"That the gay *dream* of dissipation's o'er.
But Lady Wronghead still *bewailed* her fate,
And sigh'd for splendour, equipage, and state.
Farewell, dear scenes! she cried, was ever wife
Born with a genius for the gayest life,
"Like me untimely blasted in her bloom,
"Like me condemned to such a dismal doom.
"No money when I just know how to waste it,
"No London when I just began to taste it.
"Farewell the high-crown'd head, the *cushioned tête*,
"Which takes the cushion from its prop'rer seat.
"'*Seven the main*,' that sound must now expire,
"Lost at hot cockles round a Christmas fire.
"Farewell, dear scenes, where late such joys I knew;
"Dress, cards, and dice, I bid you all adieu.
"These joys thus banish'd I shall taste no more,
"For Lady Wronghead's occupation's o'er.
"How shall I drag out life, and how, alas!
"Shall tedious country winter evenings pass?
"Dear ma'am, I said, your groundless fears dismiss,
I have a thought—a new one—it is *this*.
Shall we come down and try to act a play?
A play? and what d'ye think the wits will say?
Unheard with keenest satire they'll decry it.
Turn all to *farce*, and swear 'tis vain to try it.
Avaunt such wits, who with ill-judging spleen,
Shall rudely strive to blast the well-meant scene.
Far happier he his faults like us he stops,
And *checks* his follies when the curtain drops,
No more in vice or error to engage,
And play the fool at large on *life's great stage*.

Prologue by Mr. T. POWYS *before* MONSIEUR TESSIER'S *performance of* ROUSSEAU'S *French piece of* PYGMALION.

Spoken by LORD MALDEN.

As some there are who may not know the story,
Which the French poet means to lay before ye,

1777

I'll tell you in plain English what he says.
A young unmarried prince in former days,
Long rail'd at wedlock, and could never find
In all the *sex*, a woman to his mind.
Some were too *short*, and others were too *tall*,
Too *fat*, too *thin*, there was some fault in *all*.
Tir'd with the fruitless search, at length he cried,
Art shall supply what Nature hath *denied ;*
I'll make a *faultless maid :* so said so done ;
Just to his taste he made a maid of *stone*.
Th' enraptur'd artist, as her charms he view'd,
Stood, by the magic of his art subdued.
But still she was a piece of mere still life,
And something more he wanted in a wife.
A wife, he thought, some little warmth should share
Are there none here *whose wives have some to spare*
He kissed her oft, but ah ! how cold the kiss?
Especially in such a night as *this*.[1]
Vain was his art, for, do whate'er he could,
There was no comfort without flesh or blood.
To Venus he address'd his fervent prayer,
That she would animate the obdurate fair ;
For Venus *can*, whene'er she will, impart
A yielding softness to the hardest heart.
His prayer was heard, she *gently* turn'd her head,
And o'er her limbs the glow of life was spread.
Convinced at last, he feels her pulse beat high,
And wanton seem'd to roll her am'rous eye.
Loos'd was her tongue ! she was *indeed* a wife,
And he no *more complain'd* she wanted *life !*

1778
May 1778.—We went when with Miss Ewer at Clapham to see Panes Hill,[2] late Mrs. Hamilton's. The grounds are seven miles round, which we went in little chaises. . . . The finest as well as the most strikingly beautiful grotto, all made of Derbyshire spar.

August 12*th.*—We went to pay a visit to Mrs. Annesley, Bletchingdon House, Oxon. In this part

[1] January 6–10th, *snow* then on the ground.
[2] Grounds made by Hon. Charles Hamilton.

of our county [1] there are more fine houses near each 1778
other than in any, I believe, in England. We were
reckoning nineteen within a morning's airing worth
seeing. I must say something of that we were at,
as Mr. Brown [2] would style it, " A place of vast
capabilities," stands high, the ground lays well, and
the views round it far preferable to most in that
county. Mrs. Annesley's is large, tho' only seven
windows in front, the present approach thro' a fine
stone gateway with iron rails, you ascend a large
flight of steps into a large hall, opposite you a second
flight carries you into a second or larger hall, in which
fronts you by far the noblest staircase I ever saw.
'Tis of *Manchineale* wood, and after going up about
twenty steps it turns to the right and left, making a
gallery at the top which looks down into the hall,
this gallery leads to all the chambers. On the ground
floor are four parlours, library, and state bedroom ;
many rooms were fitted by the Lord Anglesey who
built it, but which Mr. Annesley was going to finish,
but his sudden death prevented, and as his lady
justly observes, it would be absurd in her to lay out
money there, as her eldest son will have so immense
a fortune, it would only be injuring her younger
children, and she is too good a mother to do that ;
indeed, hers and their happiness seem'd centr'd in
each other. I think I never felt more for any one
than I did for her at hearing an account of his death
(tho' now years since), from a lady who is there every
year, and was at the time. I own I am always foolish

---

[1] Bletchingdon was held for King Charles I. by C. C. Windebank,
who, however, surrendered it hastily to Cromwell, for which he was shot,
April 3, 1644.

[2] "Capability" Brown, the great landscape gardener.

with regard to dreams, and now from these worthy good people, whose veracity I cannot doubt, I fear I shall in future be still more superstitious.

Mr. and Mrs. Annesley were a most happy couple, had known each other from childhood, had been married, I suppose, about ten years, had two sons and two daughters. She waked herself and him one night with crying so violently in her sleep that he was quite alarm'd. He insisted on knowing what dream she had had; she only said she had dreamt he was not well, but it was, that he fell down in a fit. He laughed at her as she lay crying for an hour or two, and going to sleep again, she again dreamt the same. 'Tis impossible, the lady says, to tell her anxiety the whole next day, he laughing it off, and at dinner he said, "Well, my dear, I'm not sick yet, I think, for I never was so hungry in my life;" she answered, "Indeed I am very foolish, but I shall be better in a day or two." That night pass'd over, but, poor man, next day at tea-time he was nowhere to be found; when she heard this, she flew about like a wild creature into every room. Going into their bed-chamber and not seeing him, she was running out of it when the youngest child says, "Mamma, perhaps papa is in the closet," and throwing open the door, there he lay dead; she immediately fainted, and what she must that instant have felt is hardly to be imagined. She has never been in that room or the library since, and if anybody mentions dreams, only says, "Pray don't talk on that subject." We spent a most agreeable week there, there being a good deal of company, fourteen of us in the parlour, but tho' our party was large, it did not hinder our seeing places every day we were there, and the first place,

as the nearest, we went to was Blenheim. . . . The 1778
environs of Blenheim have been amazingly improved
by Brown since I was last there, many rooms furnish'd
and gilt, and as there are many fine pictures, must
be always worth seeing.   A fine ride round the park
of five miles which we went, and afterwards three
round the shubbery.   The Duke, Duchess, and many
of their children, with other company, were driving
about in one of those clever Dutch vehicles call'd,
I think, a *Waske*, a long open carriage holding fifteen
or sixteen persons.   As forms are placed in rows so
near the ground to step out, it must be very heavy,
but that, as it was drawn by six horses, was no inconvenience, and 'tis quite a summer machine [1] without any
covering at the top.

The next morning we went to Middleton Park,
Lord Jersey's.   As Lady Jersey was Miss Twysden,
daughter of the Bishop of Raphoe, so nearly related
to my father,[2] we had a curiosity to see the place,
tho' the family were abroad, and tho' on a small
plan, I hardly ever saw so clever one for its size, as
every room is good, tho' only four in the whole.
You enter a hall, the staircase behind; on one side
an eating-room 36 by 22, on the other side a drawing-room the same dimensions, with a most excellent
library out of the first, behind the hall, 70 feet long.
In this room, besides a good collection of books,
there is every other kind of amusement, as billiard
and other tables, and a few good pictures.   As her
Ladyship is, according to the present taste, a botanist,

---

[1] The parent, apparently, of the modern char-à-banc !

[2] The father-in-law, Mr. Powys (whom she always calls father).   His
wife's mother was a daughter of Sir William Twysden, hence Lady Jersey
was her cousin.

1778 she has a pretty flower-garden going out of the library; upstairs is an elegant small dressing-room, the window down to the ground, and, what has a pretty effect, the shutters are looking-glass which reflect the prospect very pleasingly. The beautiful Duchess of Devonshire and many of the principal nobility are hung round the room in miniature pictures, and some very good etchings by the present Lord Harcourt.

The next day we were to pay a visit to Sir James Dashwood's, Kirklington Park, two miles from Bletchingdon; 'tis not finished yet; when complete will be a most noble one. In the drawing-room are some good pictures, among them those of their daughters. I always thought Lady Galloway[1] the most pleasing, but in these portraits the Duchess[2] is by far the handsomest. As to Sir James, we could not help saying at our return, that he was at sixty-three, one of the finest men we ever saw. Lady Dashwood's chinaroom, the most elegant I ever saw. 'Tis under the flight of stairs going into the garden; it's ornamented with the finest pieces of the oldest china, and the recesses and shelves painted pea-green and white, the edges being green in a mosaic pattern. Her Ladyship said she must try my judgment in china, as she ever did all the visitors of that closet, as there was one piece there so much superior to the others. I thought myself fortunate that a prodigious fine old Japan dish almost at once struck my eye. The next morning we set out very early, in a very large party of several carriages to see both Ditchley and Heythrop. The first, the seat of the late Lord Lichfield, a large

---

[1] Wife of the eighth Earl of Galloway.
[2] Elizabeth, wife of eighth Duke of Manchester.

house,[1] fourteen rooms on a floor, and not one good
one. A bed-chamber with hangings, bed, and furniture of crimson and yellow velvet is shown as a great
curiosity, but I think ugly. The pattern is all pagoda.
It was a present of Admiral Lee, my Lord's brother,
who had it taken out of the loom in China, and the
loom broke that no one else might have the same.
The drawing-room chairs are Gobelin tapestry, each
one of Æsop's Fables, and an exceeding fine carpet,
the work of Lady Lichfield.[2] The bed-chambers are
very good, and on that floor an excellent library. We
there saw a fine book of plants painted exceeding
well, which Lord Bute got for Lord Lichfield, and I
must mention a leather chair in this room, which from
its construction seems the greatest treasure to a gouty
or sick person, as if their hands are at liberty they
move themselves most easily to any part of a room.
It has four wheels, two within the four I believe.
The housekeeper could not tell where bought, but cost
seven guineas.

From Ditchley is not more than an hour's drive
to Heythrop,[3] Lord Shrewsbury's, a place well worth
seeing indeed, tho' the country is bad. You enter a
hall which appears infinitely larger by three arches
fronting you. The middle one only is an arch, the
other two are windows of plate-glass which reflect
the grand avenue of clumps (the first of the kind in
England), by which you approach the house.[4] The
deception is strikingly pretty. There has within these
few years two rooms here been fitted up at vast

[1] Now Viscount Dillon's, a descendant.
[2] She brought Ditchley to her husband, being a Lee, a descendant of
Sir Henry Lee, mentioned in "Woodstock."
[3] Now seat of Albert Brassey, Esq.
[4] Burnt down in 1831 whilst occupied by the Duke of Beaufort.

1778 expense, one of them the most noble library, eighty-three feet long, twenty feet high, the colour green, very fine stucco ornaments by the famous Roberts, of Oxford. There are nine venetian windows, two fine statuary marble chimney-pieces. In the arches over the doorway are fables of Æsop's, finely executed in stucco, with wreaths of vine leaves, the ground round them Artois colour—the sofas, chairs, and curtains fine chintz, a present of the late Lord Clive, a bed and furniture of the same above stairs. The other room is the drawing-room, which Sir James Dashwood informed us Lady Shrewsbury had often told him the furnishing of that only cost £6000 — the two sofas ninety guineas each, each chair thirty. They are of tent stitch-work at Paris, the carved frames made there and gilt in England. The grate, polished steel, cost £95 ; the statuary marble chimney-piece, £1500. This room is 47 feet by 25, and 20 high. Its hung with Brussels tapestry, representing the four quarters of the world. Four fine drawings in chiaro-obscura over each door are most striking, done by Garrety, Antwerp.

One morning while at Bletchingdon we went to see a fine steel manufacture at Woodstock, made some purchases, but 'tis all amazing dear. Saw some scissors at fifteen guineas a pair, very curious no doubt, but not answerable to the price ; sword-hilts and stars for the nobility are beautiful—the latter not dear, about twenty guineas each, but scissors at fifteen guineas are extravagant to a degree, as the steel, they told me, is equally good at 2s. 6d., the *open work* above adding to the price.

1779   On Monday, the 15th March 1779, my brother (-in-law), Powys was appointed a Prebend of Bristol

by the Lord Chancellor Thurlow, by recommendation
of my Lord Camden.

On September 14th, 1779, we had the great loss
of a friend, as well as parent, in my Father Powys,
who died about six in the morning. 'Tis a most self-
pleasing reflection, as a daughter-in-law, to know that
in the seventeen years we lived together we never
had the shadow of a dispute, and his own sons have
now the inexpressible consolation of considering they
ever made it the study of their lives to make him happy.
Indeed he was so good a man that no one could be more
deserving of the happiness he seemed always to have
enjoy'd in a life rather uncommonly fortunate, as he
lived to seventy-five years of age without knowing
what illness was till that which carried him off, for
by *great* temperance, and *great* exercise, he was certain of a *great* share of health, and for fifty years
he had liv'd with different branches of his family of
all ages, from one year old to fourscore, and never
known to quarrel with any.

Caroline Isabella[1] inoculated October 13th, 1779.

In April 1780 we went to Bath for Mr. Powys'
health.   He soon received benefit from the waters,
and having numbers of our old acquaintances there,
we passed six most agreeable weeks.   We went from
there one day to Corsham,[2] Mr. Methuen's, to see
one of the finest collections of pictures now in England—indeed they surpass expectation.   In two rooms
the value of those only are £30,000, consisting of
only sixty-eight pieces.   'Tis an old house, and badly
situated.   Among the above-mention'd fine pictures it
hurts me to mention two portraits of children in the
hall by our so famed Sir Joshua Reynolds, whose

---

[1] Mrs. Powys' daughter.   [2] Ten miles from Bath.

1780 portraits when first done seem so inimitable, and in the course of a very few years are absolutely without the least colouring left. Sure if he would be shown some of these gone pieces, he would, for his own fame's sake, try to obviate this horrid appearance of his works.[1]

We spent one agreeable day at the hot well,[2] Bristol; dined there, walk'd up those fine rocks, and staying to see the tide come in, had the most beautiful view of that sweet place; crossed over the river to see a place just taken by Mr. Hussey, who married a daughter of Lord Walpole's—a sweet situation. The dismal brown pump-room (at the hot wells), always strikes one with horror. I'm certain its being so dull a one, must strike the miserable concourse of invalids always assembled in it with a melancholy not to be erased.

In July this year, being at Mrs. Winford's, near Marlow,[3] we went to pay a visit at Lord Boston's.[4] I've before mention'd the situation of this charming place, and gave it far the preference to its neighbouring one, Clifden. I must now say how complete the whole is now made by his present Lordship's having built a new house, which tho' not to be styled large or magnificent, is altogether the most elegant one I've seen for a vast while. The drawing-room a white flock paper; the chairs and curtains lute-string, white ground, a faint stripe, and fringed. My lady's dressing-room octagon, the corners fitted up with the cleverest wardrobes in inlaid woods; their own bed the

---

[1] This is written twelve years before Sir Joshua's death, which was in 1792.

[2] Clifton hot well.

[3] Thames Bank.

[4] Hedsor. This house built, 1778, by first Lord Boston.

Dutch cord white dimity, Devonshire brown fringe, 1780
curtains and chairs the same; all over the house a
thousand elegant neatnesses and contrivances.

The next day we went to see the Queen's bed,
lately put up at Windsor, a most curious piece of
work indeed.   Miss Hudson (who teaches the new
patchwork at Bath), was one of the workers, and she
was regretting, as every one might, that poor Mrs.
Wright died just before it was finish'd.   The colours,
designs, and work are all beautiful.   It was fourteen
years about working, but I should fear would not last
many years without fading exceedingly.   The Castle
is now kept much neater than when I was there last;
the pictures have been all clean'd, many more brought
there, some new furniture, and indeed the whole noble
place looks much more like the residence of royalty
than it did some years ago.

In September we were at Mr. Mount's,[1] in Berkshire, Wasing Place, a most elegant new house, built
of the white brick—fine pictures, and the fittings-up
in the modern taste—a contrast to the fine seat of
Mr. Chute's,[2] about twelve miles from them, in Hampshire, a place we had long wish'd to see, as we were
acquainted with the family, though at too great a
distance to visit from Hardwick.   We were happy
to accept their obliging invitation to dine there with
our friends at Wasing.   The Vine is indeed a noble
old house; the number of rooms immense; two long
galleries, one full of whole-length portraits; the other
they make a greenhouse of in winter, and they say

[1] Mrs. Powys' uncle by marriage with her aunt, Miss Elizabeth
Girle.
[2] The Vine, long the residence of the Sandys family, bought by
Chaloner Chute in the Commonwealth.   He was then Speaker of the
House of Commons.

1780 has a most pleasing effect to walk thro' the oranges, myrtles, &c., ranged on each side.   The room we dined in, of a vast length, is painted dark blue, small old panels, in each of which is a gold star, the cornice gilt.   It has not a bad appearance in a house of that antiquity; but what is most curious at the Vine is a chapel [1] in which are three large windows of the finest painted glass.   'Tis exquisitely beautiful; we might have spent hours in viewing the different histories of the several compartments, and there is likewise a fine ancient pavement [2] well worth observing, and good carving.   Mr. Chute [3] is now erecting a most superb monument [4] of statuary marble in an inner chapel to the memory of Chaloner Chute.   It's finely executed, indeed; has already cost him £1000, tho' not near finished.   He has got from abroad a screen, I believe 'tis called, or folding doors of most curious open carved work, which is to part the outward and inner chapels.   At the Vine are numberless curiosities, among which a service of finest delf, much more valuable than any china, each plate a different view of Venice.   In the gallery library are many portfolios of the finest prints, and in a closet below, out of the suit of rooms, is a most elegant cabinet, very valuable.

[1] Built by first Lord Sandys, who brought the glass from Boulogne after the siege, temp. Henry VIII.

[2] Also from Boulogne.

[3] John Chute, the friend of Horace Walpole.

[4] Sculptured by Banks, after a portrait by Vandyck in the house.

JOURNAL OF A SECOND NORFOLK TOUR

1781

WE set out to Mr. Slaney's,[1] in Norfolk, Mr. Powys 1781
and Phil in the whisky. My mother, Caroline, myself,
and Triphosa[2] in the coach. Lay that night at March's,
Salt Hill; breakfasted the next morning at Turnham
Green, and got to Mr. Creuzé's,[3] Leytonstone, to
dinner by four, where we had promised to pay a visit
on our way. The next morning they were so obliging
as to take us to see Wanstead House,[4] the seat of the
Earl of Tylney, reckon'd one of the finest houses in
the kingdom. There are nineteen rooms on the principal floor, and most furnish'd and fitted up in the
ancient taste, with Brussels tapestry, in Flanders and
cut velvet, the sofas reaching the whole side of the
rooms. The hall very magnificent, 50 feet high, the
ceiling painted by Kent, whose portrait is over the
chimney. The rooms seem all small, at least comparatively so. In the first into which we were shown is
a good picture of Titian, a Holy Family, and six
whole-lengths of the Tylneys, by Sir Godfrey Kneller.
The ball-room 75 feet long by 30, olive and gold
wainscot; two compartments of Brussels tapestry, one
the battle of Telemachus, the other his shipwreck in
Calypso's Island. To look through the suite of apart-

[1] Mrs. Powys' cousin on maternal side.
[2] The maid.
[3] Francis Creuzé, Esq., a cousin of Mr. Slaney's and Mrs. Powys's, a
banker in Lefevre & Co.
[4] Built for first Earl of Tylney in 1715; pulled down in 1822. The
Earl of Mornington, who married the heiress of Tylneys, spent all her fine
fortune of £80,000 a year. The sale of the contents of Wanstead lasted
thirty-two days, conducted by the celebrated George Robins.

1781 ments has a fine effect, 360 feet, the length of the house.

We return'd to Mr. Creuzé's to dinner. The next day Mr. and Miss Ewer came to Leyton, and on the Friday morn we left it. My mother staid there till our return from Norfolk. We breakfasted at Brentwood.[1] Near that town was Warley Camp,[2] but at this time camps had been so numerous, and the rage for seeing them had been so great, that we did not think it worth while to go out of our way for a view of it. We dined at the " Black Boy," Chelmsford, and meant to lay at Kelverden. Got there about nine, and found the two inns quite full. When proceeding six miles farther to Stanway, every soul in the village were in their beds ; nor could all our vociferation awake them, which, after some time endeavouring in vain, we were oblig'd, with tired horses and fatigued very much ourselves, to go on to Colchester, in as dark a night as any in July ; but the road was fortunately good. Just at eleven we got to the " King's Head " Inn, and there rested ourselves and animals till ten the next morning. Colchester is an exceeding pretty town, full of good houses. We stopped to take a second breakfast on the road on Saturday, and got to Ipswich about seven in the evening, where we stayed most of the next day at the " White Horse,"[3] the most nasty, noisy inn I think I was ever at in my life. But indeed the town itself is dreadful—narrow streets, poor-looking old houses, and altogether a most melancholy place. We went to a good church, and

[1] On highway to Chelmsford. Forty coaches a day traversed it then.
[2] This camp, on the site of an ancient one, was re-established during the French Revolution.
[3] Immortalised by Dickens in " Pickwick."

tolerable preacher ; but we were not the least concern'd 1781
to leave Ipswich, which we did in the evening, and
went to Sewell Inn, within twenty miles of Norwich,
which inn seemed a perfect palace after our miseries of
the preceding evening.

Monday we breakfasted at Long Stratton's, and
got to Mr. Slaney's, Norwich, soon after three.   His
house is a very good one ; stands on the Tomblands,
so call'd, as imagin'd, by its having formerly been a
burial-place ; but this is mere conjecture.

Tuesday, Mr. Slaney took us to see the usual sights,
as the City Hall, a fine building, formerly a church.[1]
The light Gothic pillars are beautiful.   There are full-
length pictures of all their mayors in their robes round
the hall.   In the evening went to see a garden of Mr.
Ives' in a village call'd Bishopthorp, near Norwich,
from which there is a fine view of the country and the
navigable river that comes up to the city.   This gentleman has lately built a new house here.   The garden
was a marl pit.   We took a further drive to a place
called the " Grove " ; the prospect from it is pleasing.

Wednesday we went up the Castle Hill.   The
castle is now the county gaol, the finest that can be ;
commands a noble prospect of the city and country
round, with the thirty-six churches, and elegant light
spire of the cathedral.   We then went to see the new
hospital, where the poor patients are kept in so perfect, neat, and comfortable a manner ; 'tis hardly con-
ceivable.   We then paid a visit to Mr. and Mrs.
Chambers, who have just built a new house.   In the
evenings walk'd to the tea-gardens, a Vauxhall in
miniature.

[1] St. Andrew's Hall, nave of the Black Friars' Church, given at Dissolution to the city.

1781   Friday, we went to see the cathedral, a very fine
Gothic building.   The Dean's lady, Mrs. Lloyd (who
was Miss Grey, the celebrated worker in worsted), has
just put up a fine east window of stain'd glass, about
thirty portraits of the Apostles, &c., full-length; a
window underneath of the Ascension.   That evening
we drove out some miles to an old Roman encamp-
ment.[1]

Saturday, we went about ten miles from Norwich
to a place called Hoveden Hall, the seat of Mr.
Ofrier, a relation of Mr. Powys.   We had the mortification to find they had gone to Tunbridge.

Sunday, after church, Mrs. Green, the clergyman's
lady, took us to the Deanery to see Mrs. Lloyd's
work, which is indeed quite amazing,   A whole-
length of a hermit with a folio prayer-book open, is
beyond description, though some think an old gardener at his stall, with a young girl, is superior to
that.

Monday morn we receiv'd and paid visits.   About
one the Sheriff, Mr. Doughty, came into the city in
great state.   That office is here attended with great
expense, at least £300, whereas with us in Oxfordshire I have heard my father Powys say it cost him
between one and two.   After his fatigue of conducting
in the Judges was over, we met him at his lodgings
and drank tea with him and his lady, who was Miss
Powys of Northamptonshire.[2]   She desired I'd go
with her to the Assize ball the next day, but I had
been asked by Mr. Slaney to go with Lady Astley,[3]
Mrs. Ives, Mrs. Bacon, and Mr. Jerningham,[4] &c., &c.,

[1] Caister St. Edmund.
[2] Anne Powys, sister of the first Lord Lilford.
[3] Wife of Sir Edward Astley, of Melton Constable.
[4] Of Costessey Hall, Norfolk.

so was obliged to decline the obliging offer. Tuesday 1781
the procession of the Judges, Mayor, Corporation,
Sheriff, and neighbouring gentlemen made a capital
cavalcade as they came over Tombland by Mr.
Slaney's window. In the evening our very large
party met at the ball, a very numerous assembly, and
numbers of the ladies profuse in jewellery, particularly
the Ladies Buckingham[1] and Astley. The High
Sheriff's lady always stands the top couple, the second
was Miss Bacon and our son Philip. We got home
about two, after being highly entertained.

The next morning we went to see Yarmouth, but
I must not forget a church we pass'd on our way. At
the top of the tower you may, as you go by, perceive
a tomb, the anecdote of which is, "that two maiden
ladies always had declar'd that, as they never had
lain by man on earth, they never would after death,"
so were really enclos'd on the top of the aforesaid
tower. We got to Yarmouth about four. 'Tis a very
pleasing town, and numbers of good houses, and their
quay reckon'd the prettiest in England—a mile long,
very broad, and numbers of handsome houses. The
view from the sea from thence very fine, from the
numbers of ships always laying in the road. They
are now raising new fortifications in the vicinity of
Yarmouth, as they daily expect to be surpris'd by the
Dutch. The loss by the Dutch war[2] to this town was
really terrible, as malt and herring houses that did let
for £70 a year now let for less than £30.

We went to see the use of the drying-houses for
herrings, which is really curious. They are sheds

---

[1] Wife of first Marquis of Buckingham.
[2] The Dutch war in 1660, also in 1778, when Admiral Parker re-
pulsed the Dutch, but with heavy loss.

1781 round a little court.   Under the sheds the herrings
are laid three deep.   The shed holds three lasts.   A
last is 10,000, and a vessel generally brings about
eight lasts.   When they have hung out of doors two
days they are wash'd in tubs of brine, then brought
to an inner house to the gang of women—twelve is
a gang—who spit them on sticks, which sticks hang
from the ceiling to the floor, on cross-band beams
from the top, about 40 or 50 feet high, then fires are
made under them by sticks of 4 feet long, the size
according to Act of Parliament, and when dry'd put
into barrels.

We walked and rode upon the sands, from which
is a most picturesque view; no shells, but pretty
pebbles, many white cornelians, and quantity of pretty
sea - weeds.   The jetties or wooden platforms are
thrown out into the sea.   The most droll thing in
Yarmouth are their little carts, alias hackney-coaches,
in which everybody goes about, as their rows,[1] or
what in London we should call alleys, are too narrow
for any other carriages to pass, as the broadest are
only 4 feet 8½ inches, some only 3, or 3 feet 2 or 3
inches.   The riding in these Yarmouth carts is truly
comic, and their uncommon jolting hardly to be borne,
and those not used to driving them would immediately
overturn them, as the wheels are underneath and no
farther out than their shafts, the whole lower than
our garden-whisky—in short, just upon the ground.
There is one fine church[2] and chapel, the former built
about eight hundred years, with a spire so dreadfully

[1] One hundred and fifty-six of these rows still exist in the old part of
the town. These carts date from Henry VII.'s reign.

[2] Dedicated to Saint Nicholas, the patron saint of sailors; second
largest parish church in England.   First built circ. 1091 by Herbert de
Losinga, Bishop of Norwich.

crooked it hurts the eye of every beholder, and verses 1781
are written to ridicule that and the Yarmouth females—

> "The Yarmouth girls are one and all
> Straight as their steeple, tho' not quite so tall."

It was reported the whole day we were there that
the Dutch were to land and burn the town that night.
I cannot say we were greatly alarm'd, though certainly the Ministry, by the preparations they are
making there of three batteries, the gates and walls
repairing, do expect them, and the Dutch knowing
the coast so well, 'tis, they say, very easy. In the
evening we went to the camp at Hopton Warren,
about four miles from Yarmouth, on a hill commanding a most noble view of the sea, and a very dry,
healthy situation. Lowestoffe, a town near where the
camp is now, is the most eastern point of the kingdom. The Duke of Manchester is there, and Colonel
Bullock commands the Essex, and Major Tinon
commands the camp. We dined at Blowfield, and
return'd to Mr. Slaney's in the evening.

Saturday we din'd at Mr. Ives', a party of seventeen—a most superb dinner, eighteen dishes the first
course, including the two soups. In the evening we
all went to the play ; a very pretty theatre. Sunday
went to church at St. Andrew's. The altar-piece, full-
length portraits of Moses and Aaron, reckon'd a very
capital one.

Monday morning we left Mr. Slaney's with great
regret. He was so obliging as to go with us some
part of our journey. We breakfasted at Blickling,[1]
the village where Lord Buckingham's house is—a fine

---

[1] Was begun building in James I., completed 1628; now the Marquis
of Lothian's.

1781 old seat and noble park, and a very fine piece of water. They told us Anne Boleyn was born here. We dined at " The Feathers " at Holt, and lay at Walsingham, and the next morning went to see that fine old ruin call'd Our Lady of Walsingham,[1] supposed to be the finest in England. They are in the gardens of a Mr. Warren.[2] It even now (with every disadvantage of an owner who has no pleasure in being possess'd of such a great curiosity), gives one the highest gratification ; but if the garden was laid out with the best modern taste, this noble arch would stand clear of all the rubbish with which it is surrounded. I there saw a most beautiful tree call'd the trumpet-ash. Mr. Slaney was so good as to procure me a fine young one, which I planted at Hardwick in remembrance of him and Walsingham Abbey.

From thence we proceeded to Holkham, now the seat of Mr. Coke. When I was in Norfolk some years ago, it was Lord Leicester's, then not near finish'd. I shall say nothing of this place, as in a journal in 1756, in a letter to my father, I've given a description of it.

At Houghton we proposed again seeing Lord Orford's, a seat once so famed for the most capital collection of pictures in England, lately purchased by the Empress of Russia.[3] We had most fortunately seen them in the year 1756, and I then took a written catalogue of them all from one Lord Orford had given Mr. Jackson. 'Tis really melancholy to see the hangings disrob'd of those beautiful ornaments, and only

---

[1] From the famous image of the Virgin once here. An Augustinian Priory founded early in the twelfth century.

[2] Now in the Lee Warner family.

[3] Sold by George, third Earl of Orford, for £40,500 to Catherine II., to the annoyance of his uncle, Horace Walpole.

one picture now there, a portrait of the Empress 1781
herself, which she made my Lord a present of; but
though 'tis said to be a striking likeness, and well
painted, it rather gives one pain to see the person
who must deprive every one who now visits Houghton of the entertainment given to them by these
pictures, and their going out of the kingdom makes
it still worse. The house is good, but situation unpleasing, as most are, I think, in the county of
Norfolk. We din'd and lay at Swaffham. The
next day we call'd at Mr. Chute's, who has a house[1]
in this country, but they were then at "The Vine,"
in Hampshire, generally residing half the year at that
fine ancient seat. I had forgotten to mention that
near Yarmouth is the famous ruin of Sir John Old-
castle's tower. It was said in Shakespeare's time
that the character of Falstaff was drawn by him from
that gentleman.

At Swaffham, to our infinite regret, we parted with
our amiable friend and relation, Mr. Slaney, after
spending three weeks with him in the most agreeable manner possible. We breakfasted at Brand, in
Suffolk. All about that place is, I think, one of the
most horrid countries I ever beheld, and near here
is the new purchase of our Oxfordshire neighbour,
Lord Cadogan,[2] call'd Sandy Downham;[3] indeed,
nothing but sand is visible—no tree, or hardly a
bush. The road styled Brand Sands, for about
thirteen miles, deep sand over the horses' hoofs, but
they are endeavouring to mend it by mixing it with

---

[1] South Pickenham Hall.
[2] Charles Sloane, third Lord Cadogan, had just sold Caversham Park
to Colonel Marsack.
[3] Santon Downham.

1781 chalk. But for his Lordship to sell so beautiful a spot as Caversham Park to purchase the above dreary wild spot is certainly beyond one's ideas.

1782 In the middle of September 1782, my mother (Mrs. Girle), made us all happy by coming to reside at Hardwick. She had long talked of leaving Reading and taking a house at Bath; but we could not reconcile ourselves to her being at so great a distance, so in the end fixed on a scheme agreeable to us all, of living with her at Bath in the winter if she would consent to be at Hardwick the other part of the year.

1783 We went to Bath the first week in February for three months, my mother taking a house in Russel Street.

Our eldest son, Philip,[1] was at Lochée's Academy this year for six months. General Conway gave him a commission in the army, cornet of 50th Foot.

1784 Went to Bath February 6th for three months with my mother; had a house in Gay Street.

The Ewers came to us at Hardwick. Our youngest son, Thomas, was in July this year chosen Fellow of St. John's College, Oxford, tho' only fifteen years old.

This summer (1784), we came to reside with my brother[2] at Fawley, August the 10th, as we found Hardwick too large for only Mr. Powys, myself, and Caroline, after being used to so large a family, for my mother finding she did not like Bath so well as she imagined she would, intended to take a house near London. Our two sons too, being out in life, and my brother Powys, after educating them with

---

[1] Philip was then eighteen.
[2] Her brother-in-law, Rev. Thomas Powys, Rector of Fawley, Bucks.

the most parental tenderness, was left too by himself, 1784
as Mr. Pratt, Robertson, Watson, and Annesley[1] had
all left him some years.   It was not without the utmost
regret I left Hardwick.   Even tho' we proposed to
let[2] it but for a few years, one must be partial to a
spot so beautiful, where one had lived in the utmost
felicity for two-and-twenty years ; but as the situation
of Fawley is likewise delightful, and the house, tho'
small, compact and elegant, it had ever been a
favourite place with us all, and of course we removed
with less regret as it in many respects was certainly
much more eligible.

However suitable for size and economy, we can
imagine Fawley Rectory seeming like a doll's house
to Mrs. Powys after her splendid mansion at Hardwick.   The situation of Fawley Rectory is certainly
very fine.   Perched on a ridge of the Chilterns, it
commands to this day most extensive views, Windsor
Castle being included in the panorama.   Great numbers of trees had been cut down throughout the
country before and during the Civil War.   Many points
of view which Mrs. Powys could then see are hidden
now by the vast growth and plantations of modern
years.   The approach to Fawley Rectory from the
Marlow high-road is a gradual ascent of about two
miles, through the typical beech-woods so familiar to
all dwellers near the Chilterns.   These woods, exquisite as they are in spring and summer, are dreary
enough in the winter, and the extremely steep ascent
is inconvenient, particularly in frosty weather.

The Rev. Thomas Powys had been presented to

[1] Pupils of Rev. T. Powys.
[2] Hardwick was soon let to Mr. Gardiner.

1784 the living of Fawley in October 1762 by Mr. Sambrook Freeman, of Fawley Court, Bucks. There existed a well at Fawley Rectory of the immense depth of 369 feet. In 1765 Mr. Powys planted a number of firs, shrubs, &c., given to him by Lord Cadogan from Caversham Park, which place he soon afterwards sold to Major Marsack. Mr. Powys built a root-house or summer-house the same year. Henceforth we must consider our Mr. and Mrs. Powys as residing at the Rectory.

This autumn they all spent a week at Bletchingdon Park (Mr. Annesley's). His mother, mentioned before in these pages, had died the previous year at Bath (1783). The eldest Miss Annesley married the same year Mr. Charles Warde, and early in 1785 Mr. Annesley [1] was married to Miss Catherine Hardy, daughter of Admiral Sir Charles Hardy. To return to the diary.

1785   "*February 1st*, 1785.—Our eldest son, Philip Lybbe, was appointed sub-brigadier and cornet in the 2nd troop of Horse Guards."

In October 1785 Mrs. Powys gives the following amusing account in a letter to a friend, describing a visit of George III. and the royal family to Mrs. Freeman, widow of Sambrook Freeman, of Fawley Court, Bucks, who was residing then at Henley Park, having given up Fawley Court in 1782 to Mr. Strickland Freeman, nephew of her late husband, and constituted his heir in default of issue.

[1] Father of first Viscount Valentia.

Well, my dear, as I've given you so long a detail
of our concerns, I think I ought to endeavour to
entertain, as you say I always do, by my anecdotes of
this social neighbourhood, but I must then go back
from December to October last. Perhaps you may
have seen in the newspapers that our Fawley environs
was then honour'd by the royal visitors. The servants
at Fawley Court heard of them about two miles off;
of course thought they were coming there, as they
often did in his uncle's[1] time, but to the no small disappointment of the nephew, as well as the domestics,
they pass'd by, and went up to the Dowager Mrs.
Freeman's at Henley Park, not so noble a house, but
all elegance, and one of the most beautiful situations
imaginable. She most unluckily had been some time
confined to her house with a violent cold; and the
butler came running up to her dressing-room, saying,
"The King and Queen, M'am." "Don't alarm me,
William" (you know her delicate manner); "they are
not coming here, but to Fawley Court, no doubt."
However, another footman followed immediately, saying the carriages were just driving up, and he had got
a good fire in the drawing-room. She had only time
to say, "A smart breakfast, William," and to throw on
a huge cloak, and was down just as the King, Queen,
two Princesses, Lady Louisa Clayton, and two gentlemen entered. They stayed two hours and a half,
talked incessantly, seemed vastly pleased, and knew
every family and their concerns in this neighbourhood,
Mrs. Freeman said, better than she did herself! The

[1] Sambrook Freeman.

1785 worst of these great visitors are that no servants must appear, and you are obliged to wait on them yourself; this, ill as she then felt, was very fatiguing; besides, not knowing the art, one must do it awkwardly. Mrs. Freeman, after standing up in the corner to make the tea in the same spot, she handed a dish to her Majesty, and was carrying one to the Princess Royal, who laughingly said, "I believe you forgot the King." Mrs. Freeman, in some agitation, was ready to laugh too, as she says she had at the moment completely forgotten that kings were to be served before ladies; but immediately rectified her mistake, and it was received in perfect good-humour; but what next vexed her sadly was that she had no opportunity of giving the least refreshment to Lady Louisa, and the two gentlemen, who stood behind all the time, and were out so early in the morning, and to be at home so late, but she knew in the same room with their Majesties it was not to be attempted; therefore if you know of it, another breakfast is prepared in another room in case opportunity offers to let their attendants partake of it. But the King seeing Mrs. Freeman was really ill, would not let her stir, and a servant she could not call in. That such distressing etiquette must be kept up is rather uncomfortable. After breakfast the King said they must see the house. "Certainly," Mrs. Freeman said, and was going to the door to attend them, but he kept her back, and shut her in, saying, "You shall not go out with such a cold; we will go by ourselves." And so they did wherever they chose, as no servant was to attend. The ladies, you know, are great workers, and admired some beautiful chairs Mrs. Freeman is now working. The Queen, too, I'll assure you, asked what work her neighbour, Mrs. Powys,

was about, as she knew she was very ingenious by 1785
some painting she had seen some years ago of hers.
This, I am sure, was a great compliment to me, as I
should have thought her Majesty must have forgotten
my gown, which I painted on white satin, which a
lady begged me to let the Queen see. Just before
Mrs. F.'s company departed, Lady Louisa had just
time to whisper her that she was quite unhappy not
to let her know of their coming, but they never tell,
and love to take people by surprise. They had sent a
note to her the night before to desire her company at
nine the next morning to go driving, never mentioning
where they were going. Certainly a visit to Mrs.
Freeman's cottage, as she calls it, at Henley Park,
tho' all elegance, was a great honour, and at the same
time a mark of their Majesties good-natured attention, as they had so often visited her in her former
splendour at Fawley Court. Well, my dear, here
ends the royal visit ; but I've not got done with the
bustle of that morn, tho', I think luckily, I've got
a frank, or my letter would come to a sum from its
length. Our family was put in the idea of royal visitors, not ourselves, for we were all rode or walked
out different ways. It happened to be market-day
at Henley, so, of course, all the country some miles
round heard of the great event, and our servants were
not a little surprised to see two teams come galloping
uphill, not the usual stile of waggons, travelling at a
great rate. The carters stopped at our gate, saying,
"We cannot stay, as the King and Queen are just behind." Our housekeeper was in such a fuss. "Oh dear,
oh dear! what must I do now the family are from
home?" But no time had they for consultation, as
immediately a coach and six drove up the avenue, but

1785 was soon found to be only Earl Macclesfield[1] coming to pay us a morning visit, and returning thro' Fawley village, passed for King and Queen, and their daughter, Lady Mary,[2] for the Princess Royal. When I went to Shirburn Castle I made them all laugh heartily at this account. Mrs. Freeman returned, or as it is termed, went to thank their Majesties for their visit, the next court-day. Mrs. Freeman thought it would be a sad worry to her, as she had not been to court since Mr. Freeman's death, and was fearful no suit she had would do; but luckily on her going to the mantua-maker's she found no alterations in the fashions for court dress for years, whereas common ones change every month. Flounces and trimmings, tho' quite out elsewhere, trebled ruffled cuffs and long dangling ruffles as formerly.

The following extract from a letter of Mrs. Powys will show the old-fashioned *Sangrado* form of doctoring.

"*December* 30, 1785. — We have now confined ourselves fifteen weeks with our dear son Philip, nor paid one visit but of a morning. You have not heard of his unfortunate journey here, as his tedious illness was owing to that. I've often told you what a good young man he is, and that he always chooses to be with us in the country except the four days at a time when he is upon guard. On the 15th September we had a letter to say he would come down the next day, as he believed something had flown in his eye as he was walking in the Park, and it gave him great uneasiness. He had shown it to the surgeon of his regiment, who said he would bleed him in the morn,

[1] George, 4th Earl.   [2] Afterwards married the Earl of Haddington.

gave him a cooling mixture, and desired him to go 1785
into the country; not on horseback, but in a chaise,
keeping his eye from the air, and it would soon be
well. All this was done; but it being a very dark,
rainy evening, that, tho' the postboy and himself knew
the road perfectly through our wood, they lost it, and
found themselves in a horse-way of Mr. Freeman's, near
the root-house, where they knew there were many pits.
Phil got out; they put the horses behind, and with
much difficulty dragg'd the chaise down again into the
coach-road; but he had not gone above ten minutes
when he was overturn'd over a stump. The chaise,
glasses, &c., were now broke. They did not attempt
to raise it, but each took a horse, and at last reach'd
home, and found they had been about an hour and a
half in the wood, when twenty minutes is the usual
time! Poor Phil went immediately to bed, being
greatly fatigued, and the pain in his eye vastly increased, as he had lost his bandage, and his arm, too,
had bled again; in short, he was a most miserable
object, and gave us all infinite anxiety, and for many
days the inflammation increased. He was in too much
pain to return to London, but fortunately a Mr. Davenport, an eminent surgeon, has bought an estate near
Marlow, and retired from town, and he was so kind as
to come immediately, and has order'd our surgeon
here how to proceed, and is so good as to come
to him every two or three days. He now mends
amazingly, as all the faculty tell us. Time and warm
weather only can make a perfect cure; but as for many
weeks we were apprehensive for the sight, we are
most thankful. . . . It is hardly possible to imagine
with what fortitude he bears the sufferings he has gone
through, though he has not since the *accident tasted a*

1785 *bit of meat or drunk a drop of wine, had a perpetual blister ever since, and blooded every three or four days for many weeks.* His health is certainly better than even I knew it, most probably from the *discipline,* some of which might be necessary for a young man in full health with a good appetite, and who never minds over-heating himself in shooting, cricket, &c."

Truly, Mr. Powys' enduring this treatment was a *survival of the fittest!*

On December 31, Mr. Pratt, only son of Lord Camden, was married to Miss Molesworth by Mr. Powys. This is the account :—

1786 "*January* 13*th,* 1786.—A great wedding is over, in which my brother Powys did his clerical part in marrying his pupil, Mr. Pratt, to a most beautiful young lady, Miss Molesworth, niece to Lady Lucan, and a fortune of nearly £40,000. Their income will be increased, as Pratt's is now large, and will be so increased by his uncle, Mr. Pratt.[1] After the ceremony they went from Lord Lucan's by themselves to Camden Place for a few days, and from there to Mr. Pratt's at Wilderness, in Kent. Are to be presented at the birthday. Clothes all very superb ; all from Paris. (That I think wrong at an English court.) My brother says they laughed exceedingly at setting out in two post-chaises, to see the bride and bride-groom dressed with the utmost plainness in one carriage, and in the other that followed the lady's maid and valet fine to a degree ; but this is quite the *ton* now. Their establishment is very large ; so numerous I style it uncomfortable—house-steward, man-cook, two gentlemen out of livery, under-butler, Mrs. Pratt's

---

[1] John Pratt, of Bayham Abbey, who bequeathed his estates, in 1798, to the Marquis of Camden.

two footmen, Mr. Pratt's two, upper and under coach-
men, two grooms, helpers, &c., &c. These are men-
servants; female ones, I dare say, in proportion.
They were married the last day of the year 1785.
Everybody told us it would never take place, as
three matches with noblemen had been broken off;
but I've often heard the lady's reason for refusing each.
I always thought our friend Pratt had a better chance
than either of the trio.   The first, she said, never
entertain'd her with anything but politics, but a dry
topic for courtship; the second made a horrid husband
to his first wife; and the third had not sixpence in
the world, from his own extravagance.   She was not
wrong in refusing all three!"

On January 13th, 1786, in a letter to a friend, Mrs.
Powys gives an amusing account of a party of distinguished foreigners visiting unexpectedly her friends
and neighbours, General Conway and his wife, Lady
Ailesbury, at Park Place.

"Of all persons put in agitation by fine folks, I
was more surprised at Lady Ailesbury, as I think,
were I a Duke's[1] daughter, and so constantly in high
life, I should never have trepidations of that kind, but
as her Ladyship was telling us of it when she dined
with us a few days after, I must give her credit for
the alarm, and no doubt it was provoking enough.
As they were sitting at dinner, and nearly finish'd the
first course, a letter was brought to General Conway
from Count Zekany, saying himself and party, according to promise, were coming to wait on the General
and Lady A. 'Who brought the letter?' 'A servant, sir.' 'And when do they come?' 'They are
just here, sir.' This put all into confusion, for, as

[1] Duke of Argyll.

1786 their dinner was half over, they could do nothing more than order the *maitre d'hôtel* to make as elegant a second course as soon as possible, and in they came in a few minutes, Count Zekany and his lady, Count Ravenhully and his lady, and another lady, all strangers to Lady A., but by name knew them to be the principal families of their own countries. However, she had pretty nearly recovered her presence of mind, when she was again struck dumb by one of the Counts begging to introduce the lady who came with them as the Princess of Hesse. 'Then,' says she, 'I thought it was all over with me;' but they all so soon became acquainted, were so free and easy and polite, making so many apologies for not being acquainted with English customs, and having come in the middle of dinner (they only sup, I believe, abroad nearly as early as the English dine), but they sat down and ate very heartily. Luckily, Lady Ailesbury's two daughters were with her, the Duchess of Richmond[1] and Mrs. Damer,[2] and as all spoke French and Italian, the visit passed most agreeably. They admir'd the place, as 'tis impossible to do otherwise, and everything they saw. In short, as her Ladyship said, were so much easier pleased than many English fine people she had had to entertain, that she was really sorry to part with them the next day. Towards the evening another distress popped into her head, viz., that foreign men and their wives seldom occupy the same beds, and, as the house was near full, this was of some consequence ; so she bid her General

---

[1] Mary, wife of the third Duke, daughter of Lady Ailesbury's first marriage.

[2] Anne, married to Hon. John Damer, Lady Ailesbury's daughter by her second marriage. See note at end of book.

whisper his friend, and find out what was to be done,   1786
and in this they complied with the vulgar English
fashion, and Lady Ailesbury sending the Duchess and
Mrs. Damer up in the attics, made room for all their
guests."

In March Mr. and Mrs. Powys set out for Bath,
after waiting a fortnight with their boxes packed, the
roads being quite impassable from snow ; but five out
of the six weeks there she was ill with rheumatism.

In May they went to stay with Mr. and Miss Ewer
in London, in Charlotte Street.

"I was scarcely enough recovered to partake of
the spring diversions of London, as indeed they are
now all so late, it must be a very strong constitution
that can.   My favourite Ranelagh I ventured to but
once, as 'tis not *polite* to enter the Rotunda till eleven
at soonest.   To the play I went, as those are early ;
and I was really glad not to be deprived of again
seeing Mrs. Siddons, and Jordan.   The men actors at
this period do not shine in London.   We took Caroline
(who was too young at eleven for public places), to
see Sir Ashton Lever's museum,[1] the Exhibition, the
late Duchess of Portland's sale of curiosities,[2] and the
British Museum, all which highly entertained her, as
did Astley's[3] and Sadler's Wells.[4]   The music at the
Abbey, so very fine by every one's description, I
thought it most prudent to avoid, as my health was
not equal to being full dressed and there by eight in
the morning, so I postponed the pleasure till the next

[1] At Leicester House, museum of natural history ; contained 26,000
articles.
[2] Took thirty-seven days to dispose of by auction.
[3] Celebrated riding-school and circus, then held at the Royal Grove,
Lambeth.
[4] A theatre.   Grimaldi, the famous clown, acted there.

1786 year, as everybody seem'd to think it will be annual.
We went to a very fine collection of Des Enfans'
pictures, and went with Caroline to see the great fish
balloon [1] at the Pantheon [2] and Kensington Gardens.

June 5th.—Went with the Ewers for a week to
Mr. Creuzé's, Layton Stone, Essex. Phil was this
summer promoted to a lieutenancy in the Guards.

August 29th.—Went to my mother's for the races
at Reading. The first opening of the new town-hall,
a fine room 74 by 36, not including the recesses at
each end for the two judges.

October 29th.—We went to Mr. Powney's, Ives
Place, for a few days; while there we went to see the
stag turn'd out,[3] a pretty sight on a fine day, as there
is generally a large party with his Majesty.

The 10th of October was the first of the subscription assemblies at Henley, which our son Phil had set
on foot. All the neighbourhood there.

November 16th.—Went to Mr. Ewer's, at Clapham,
for a week. We went one morning to town, and saw
the "artificial flower-garden," a pretty invention, worth
seeing once; all kinds of flowers in paper, put into
beds of earth, and box edging, sand walks between.
We breakfasted that morning with Lord Bayham." [4]

1787 In February Mr. and Mrs. Powys, and daughter,
went to Bath for six weeks, their son Phil joining
them there. To Clapham in May, where she says:
Went to see the waxwork at Spring Gardens,
and after, the three figures of the King of Prussia.

[1] The first air balloon ascended at Versailles, September 1783, in the
presence of Louis XVI. and his family.

[2] The Pantheon, built in 1770–71, for concerts, balls, promenades, &c.

[3] The Royal Stag-hounds.

[4] Mr. Pratt, just then made Viscount Bayham, his father becoming
Earl Camden.

The exhibition of pictures this year but indifferent, 1787 and Ranelagh[1] very thin, till the last four or five nights.

May 23rd.—We went to see the famous painted ceiling at Whitehall Chapel, formerly the banqueting house. It was painted by Rubens (and was cleaned by Cipriani[2] in 1786). The room itself, a most noble one, 36 yards long and 24 yards high, and 18 over the windows; under the organ, *now blocked up*, that which Charles I. came out from upon the scaffold.

June 2nd.—Mr. Powys, Miss Ewer, and myself went to the music at the Abbey;[3] got there by half-past eight from Clapham, and the doors were opened by nine; but, though entered with the first group, could only have the second row in the gallery—no doubt all fill'd before the principal doors are open'd. The performance that day "Israel in Egypt." The chorus certainly very noble; but I own, upon the whole, I am disappointed in the *sound*, tho' not the *sight*. Certainly the *coup d'œil* is beyond imagination, taking at one view the royal family, so numerous a company, and the orchestra; but for music, I must say I've been entertained as *well* at the music-room in Oxford, where there is not one pillar to deaden the sound, and a less space than Westminster Abbey for the vocal performers to show the compass of their voices.

N.B.—I forgot, in the year 1785, to set down our having been to see Mr. Walpole's[4] at Strawberry

---

[1] Ranelagh ceasing to draw, was shut in 1803, and pulled down 1805.

[2] John Battista Cipriani, born at Pistoia, Tuscany, circ. 1727, came to England in 1755; died December 1785.

[3] Westminster Abbey.

[4] Horace Walpole bought Strawberry Hill, May 1747, from Mrs. Chenevix.

1787   Hill; but I found a memorandum of many curious pictures I had seen there, and some other things; but I suppose there never was a house which contained so many valuable rarities.   Among the pictures I set down were :—

> Madame de Maintenon.
> Madame de la Vallière.
> Comtesse de Grammont (Miss Hamilton).
> Madame de Sevigné, when young; very beautiful.
> Ditto, small, with that of Madame de Grignan, her daughter.
> An original and only picture of Ninon de l'Enclos.
> Original of Henry VIII., by Hans Holbein.
> Cowley, when a boy, by Sir Peter Lely.
> Numbers of fine miniatures, and other curiosities.

The most beautiful inlaid marble chimney-piece.[1] Fine old delf.   Cardinal Wolsey's red hat.[2]   On a toilet are the combs of Queen Elizabeth, Mary, Queen of Scots, and that King Charles used for his wig.   A small clock in the library which belonged to Ann Boleyn;[3] a curious picture of flowers done in feathers; a chair of a high priest.   Some ebony chairs,[4] six hundred years old, so hard nothing can penetrate them; cane bottoms.   Four drawings of Madame de Grignan's castle in Provence; Johanah's chair, five hundred years old, made of the Glastonbury thorn, and numbers of curiosities in cabinets, that we hardly had time to see one quarter of them.

Henley Bridge,[5] a most beautiful stone one, finished

---

[1] Copied from the tomb of Edward the Confessor; white marble, inlaid with scagliola.

[2] Found by Bishop Burnet, Clerk of the Closet, in the Great Wardrobe.

[3] Given her by Henry VIII.

[4] Walpole mentions these chairs as costing him a handsome sum, and calls ebony "the luxury of our ancestors."

[5] The architect was Mr. William Hayward.   Walpole states General Conway regulated the bend of the arches.

in the year 1786. In each centre arch is a head in
stone, carved by Mrs. Damer, daughter of General
Conway and Lady Ailesbury—one of " Thames," the
other " Isis."

Of this bridge the following lines were written by
the Rev. Thomas Powys :—

> " Through this fair arch henceforth with conscious pride,
>   Let Thames and Isis [1] roll their mingled tides,
>   Hastening to swell old Ocean's watery stores,
>   And sound their triumphs to his farthest shores.
>   Tho' Tiber's classic waves distinguish'd flow,
>   Our English rivers claim superior praise,
>   From Damer's sculpture, and from Denham's lays."

July 23rd, 1787.—The house at Fawley (Court),
was whitened this year.

August 9th.—We were at the musical festival
at St. Laurence's Church, Reading, to hear Mrs.
Billington.[2]

August 27th.—Went to the Reading races. The
last ball a very brilliant one.

September 8th.—My brother went to Lord Camden's, and from thence to Lord Bayham's,[3] Wilderness, Kent.

September 27th.—Thursday, we went to Maidenhead races the middle day. The whole of the royal
family there. We dined at Mrs. Winford's, Thames
Bank.

In November spent a week with Mrs. Winford.

December 1st.—My brother return'd from his London residence as king's chaplain.

December 24th.—A deep snow as usual now on

---

[1] Miss Freeman of Fawley Court sat for the head of Isis.
[2] Celebrated singer, who died in 1818.
[3] Lord Camden's son, once pupil to Rev. T. Powys.

1787   Christmas Eve for some years ; our road blocked up till January 7th.

1788   *January 20th*, 1788.—My brother went to Mr. Annesley's to stand godfather and christen his son Charles.

April 23rd.—Went to London to see a fine collection of pictures, Dr. Newton's, late Bishop of Bristol ; and the next month went to see Mr. Aufrere's collection, which are indeed most capital, as none bad, and one of each fam'd master.   Mr. Aufrere's garden too is laid out in great taste ; a curious collection of plants, a very large room in it of the finest prints, and a temple where the view of the Thames is uncommonly grand, and where the rowing matches, they inform'd us, are seen to the greatest advantage.

May 19th.—Sir Richard Cope was so obliging as to give me two tickets to see the procession of the Knights of the Bath in Westminster Abbey, one of which I gave to my friend Miss Ewer.   We went through the Jerusalem Chamber with great ease to our seats, which were the best in front, the procession passing close to us, and. the box erected for her Majesty and the princesses close to us, so that we had an excellent view of the whole.

May 22nd.—Went to see Osterley Park,[1] Mrs. Child's.   The house is good, well furnish'd, and some fine pictures ; but the situation dreary and unpleasant, and the menagerie, which for years I had heard so much of, fell far short of my expectation ; that of Lady Ailesbury's at Park Place is vastly superior in elegance ; nor were there so many different birds as I have seen at others.   The gallery is 133 feet long ; at the upper end a very capital picture by Vandyke,

<hr>

[1] Now the Earl of Jersey's, formerly Sir Thomas Gresham's.

Charles I. on horseback, the Duke D'Espernon 1788
standing by him.   At the lower end of the gallery
is the Duke of Buckingham on horseback, prime
minister to Charles I., who was stabb'd by Felton,
(a Vandyke). Over the chimney-piece Lord Stafford,
whole length, and a large white dog, likewise by
Vandyke; a beggar boy by Murillo, and many other
fine ones.   The ceiling of the staircase by Rubens.[1]
The room call'd the Etruscan apartment, all the
designs from Herculaneum, executed by Berners.
The Gobelin tapestry room is done in wreaths of
flowers from nature, in the most elegant taste, and
numbers of curious birds, formerly in the menagerie.
One room, call'd the English bed-chamber, as all the
furniture is English; a bed embroider'd on apple-
green satin, a large pier-glass, the first plate made in
England, &c., &c.

May 23rd.—I took Caroline to see Mrs. Siddons
for the first time.   It was the new tragedy of "The
Regent," written by Mr. Greathead, in which Mrs.
Siddons shone with her usual lustre; and her brother,
Mr. Kemble, was very great as the Regent.   Likewise saw "The Romp," in which Mrs. Jordan so
much excels, and the inimitable Miss Farren[2] in the
part of Estafania in "Rule a Wife and have a Wife."

May 26th.—We were at Merlin's exhibition in the
morning and Dillon's exhibition of philosophical fire-
works in the evening.   During the intervals Mr. Cart-
wright performs on the musical glasses, the sounds
on which are most harmonious, whilst Mr. Dillon
lights up an aërostatic branch suspended from the

---

[1] Represents the apotheosis of William III., Prince of Orange, brought
from Holland by Sir Francis Child.

[2] Afterwards Lady Derby.

1788 cupola of the saloon, in which light is produced in an instant of time, which Mr. Dillon carries at will, and extinguishes in an instant; wonderfully pretty. The portable hygæian chair, by which persons may swing themselves with safety, at Merlin's, are very clever, and the physicians say are extremely conducive to health; their motion I found easy and pleasing. The mechanical easy-chairs for the gouty and infirm seem very useful, and are only fourteen or twenty guineas; but the hygæian chairs were £40, too expensive for most people merely for pleasure.

May 23rd.—Mr. Powys and myself were at the play at Richmond House. It was the first night of performing "False Appearances," a piece General Conway translated from the French of *Les Dehors Trompeurs*. The characters were as follows:—

The Baron	Earl of DERBY.
Monsieur de Forlis . .	Captain MERRY.
Champagne	Captain HOWARTH.
The Marquis	Lord HENRY FITZGERALD.
The Countess	Hon. Mrs. DAMER.
Celia	Miss HAMILTON.
Lisette	Mrs. BRUCE.
Locayle	Miss CAMPBELL.

The prologue and epilogue were both very clever; wrote by General Conway, and spoken with great spirit by Lord Derby, and Mrs. Damer. The whole was amazingly well acted. The house filled with all the fine people in town.

June 2nd.—Caroline went with a party to Vauxhall for the first time, but it did not strike her so much as Ranelagh.

June 6th.—We were to have returned home, but as we had many preceding days been disappointed of

hearing Mr. Sheridan's long-expected speech,[1] and I 1788
had a ticket for one of the best seats in the hall, Mr.
Powys was so good as to insist on staying, tho' he did
not choose to go himself, and refused a peer's ticket
for the same day.   I much wished to hear this so
celebrated an orator.   I got in, and sat most commo-
diously in a front row.   Never was anything so
crowded as the hall, every part full and of the highest
rank.   Must I own myself greatly disappointed?   Few,
perhaps, would be so honest as to give their sentiments
so contrary to the multitude ; but indeed Mr. Sheridan
answer'd not my expectation as to oratory, eloquence,
or manner, the latter totally unpleasing, as a continual thumping upon his desk and most vehement
passion never surely can be styled elegance.   He
spoke four hours and a quarter.   We had been once
before that day, when Middleton was examined, who
could not recollect one thing that was ask'd him.   The
hall [2] was then very thin, but on the day of Sheridan's
speech the sight was really magnificently grand.   The
Duchess of Gloucester and her children sat just by us,
likewise the Duchess of Cumberland ; all the ladies in
muslin gowns and undrest caps, as hoops wore at
that time.

The celebrated painter, Mr. Gainsborough, died
soon after we came down this year.   I must not
forget to mention seeing that capital picture, " The
Woodman," a copy from life, whole length.   I think
I never saw a more pleasing portrait, and must now
be sold for an immense sum.   There was a beggar
boy too, a fine piece.   The exhibitions were thought
of but indifferently this year.   That charming picture

---

[1] On the impeachment of Warren Hastings.
[2] Westminster Hall, where the trial took place.

1788 by Copley, "The Death of the Earl of Chatham,"
there are in it fifty-five portraits, all taken from life.
I have a printed description of it, but too long to
write out here. I had seen it before, but was vastly
pleas'd to have a second view of it at the Bishop
of Bristol's exhibition in Spring Gardens. 'Tis now
to be sold; what a pity if Lord Chatham's family do
not purchase it.

August 7th.—Lord Bayham, who came to Fawley
the day before, took my brother with him to Brecknock Priory in Wales, a grouse-shooting.

August 20th.—We went to my mother's at Reading for the race-time. Miss Ewer met us there.

The races not good, the balls tolerably full, considering how many families at this season leave their
seats in the country for the different watering-places
now in vogue. The middle day went to the play,
Thornton's Company being then in the town.

August 29th.—Returned to Fawley, where Mr.
Ewer met us; we went to see the Druid's Temple
that General Conway has just put up at Park Place;[1]
it was brought from Jersey, being a present to the
General from the people of that island. The stones
are hardly of height sufficient to make any figure
at a distance from the beautiful spot 'tis now
placed on.

Went to pay a visit to the Birch's, St. Leonard's
Hill near Windsor, a place they had purchas'd this
summer. An excellent house and pretty situation.
One day dined at Mr. Fisher's, one of the Canons
of Windsor; saw the castle, where are great improvements since I was last there, four or five apartments
newly furnished. Mr. West's fine painting, at which

---

[1] Had been placed there in 1785.

he was then at work; the beautiful embroidery round 1788
the canopy of the queen's throne; the superb bed of
the same work is a good deal faded since I last saw
it; the beautiful altar-piece in St. George's Chapel,
painting by Mr. West, is a capital performance.

The Dean of Bristol[1] and Mrs. Hallam drank
tea there (St. Leonard's Hill).

19th October. — On Friday began our Winter
Henley ball, and was a very full one, the whole
neighbouring families making it a point to attend.
Got home about four, as there is always a supper
and dancing after.

We were very gay this autumn, having a very
tolerable set of strollers at Henley; most of the
ladies bespoke plays, as Lady Ailesbury, Mrs. Damer,
both Mrs. Freemans, Mrs. Fanshawe,[2] Miss Grote,[3]
myself, &c., and as all the families attended each
other's nights, we had very crowded houses, which
lasted all that moon.

November 15th.—Tom, (her second son), went to
keep his term at Oxford.

November 18th.—My brother went into waiting
as King's Chaplain at St. James's, his Majesty then
very ill at Windsor. His unhappy malady just then
become public, thought by most people owing to the
Cheltenham waters being too powerful for one who
has lived so very abstemious as the King ever has
done, and using such vast exercise without drinking
any wine. He was removed to Kew soon after this,
the queen and princesses going there too. Sure never
any one was ever more to be pitied than her Majesty,

---

[1] Father of Hallam the historian, grandfather of Tennyson's friend.
[2] Living at Holmwood, Shiplake.
[3] Living at Badgemore, Henley.

1788 as no couple could be happier than they were before
this greatest of all misfortunes.

N.B.—The King went to Kew 29th November.

November 19th.—We went for one night to Mr.
Lefevre's, Heckfield, Hampshire, returned thro' Reading, took post-horses at Pangbourne and sent our own
back, and from thence went to Mr. James's at Langley
Hall, Berks; got there to dinner; we had never been
there since his new house was finish'd, which is a very
noble one.   Large hall, drawing-room, two eating-
rooms, library, an inner hall, grand staircase, and
some small rooms, many apartments above so spacious
and convenient; out of every bed-chamber a large
dressing-room, and light closets as powdering rooms
to each.   The grounds now laying out.   We were
particularly happy to see Lady Jane so happily married,
to a man so pleasing as Mr. James, as I believe their
first interview was at Reading races some years since,
when she was with us at Hardwick, then Miss Pratt.[1]
. . . She has now four fine little ones. . . . They
have a fine fortune, which they spend elegantly, without any form or ceremony, making every friend partake
of the happiness and good-humour they so eminently
possess themselves.

November 25th. — Left Langley, and met my
mother at Micklem's at Reading, as she had just
parted with her house there.   A severe frost set in
two days before.

December 12th.—Our fourth and last winter assembly (Henley), which ended very brilliantly.

24th.—No more snow, but the frost so intense
as that continued on the ground which fell the 24th
November.   No rain all that time, or for near nine

---

[1] Daughter of Earl Camden.

months to do any good. The 31st December was 1788
the coldest day by the weather-glass of the intense
cold of 1788.

January 6th.—Tenants' annual feast at Fawley 1789
Court. We were there together with other principal
tenants. The young people all as usual danced with
the tenants six or eight dances; then we came up to
cards and supper. The day always passes very agreeably, as it gives pleasure to see so many people all so
happy. Many clever songs were sung by the gentlemen as well as farmers, and droll toasts given after
dinner. Among the toasts were :—

1. May the rich be charitable, and the poor happy.
2. Short shoes and long corns to all the enemies of Great
Britain.
3. May all great men be honest, and all honest men great.
4. Peace and Plenty.

9th.—Our two sons at a ball at Mr. George Vansittart's, at Bisham Abbey, near Marlow. It snowed ;
hard frost continued.

On January 12th snowed very hard, and drifted till
our road was impassable.

On 13th rained amazingly hard all night, so as to
fill the ponds which had long been dry. The two
new ones made last summer ran over, to the great joy
of the farmers and poor, who have been infinitely
distressed for water. Mrs. Freeman forced to send
water-cart to Henley. Three wells fail'd in that
town, and we lived daily in fear for my brother's, as it
goes 123 yards deep.

January 16th.—The snow greatly melted, but still
we were obliged to set men to make a way thro', and
it froze so hard on the 15th that about us was a sheet
of ice.

1789   Heard of the death of Miss Campbell, daughter
of Lord William, and niece to Lady Ailesbury, who
brought her up. She died on the 12th January. Her
Ladyship and General Conway were almost incon-
solable. The General wrote an elegant copy of verses
on this melancholy event.

On 21st, having been twice prevented by the
weather, we set out for Mr. Annesley's, Bletchingdon
Park. We had not been there since the alterations he
has made. I've mention'd being there before, and
then spoke of an amazing grand staircase, which for
its vast extent is described, I think, in Plot's " History
of Oxfordshire" as one of the finest in England ; but
now in the same space it took up, is as large a one
as one generally sees, a fine saloon and drawing-room,
besides a very fine hall, which was the entrance before,
only from that first hall you formerly entered a second,
which was entirely taken up by the vast staircase.
The present eating-room is most elegant, having a
recess at each end taken off with pillars of Sienna
marble. We had a large party there, besides most
days Oxford gentlemen to dine.

The gentlemen were shooting or hunting in different parties each morning, as Mr. Annesley keeps a
pack of harriers, and, with some more of that neighbourhood, a joint pack of fox-hounds. On Wednesday the 28th we returned home. Young Phil went
that evening to a play, ball, and supper given by Lord
Barrymore.[1] We had all tickets, but only went to the
play on the Saturday following.

January 31*st.*—Lord Barrymore had the last

---

[1] Richard, Lord Barrymore, born August 14, 1769, hence in his nineteenth year.

summer (1788) built a very elegant playhouse[1] at 1789
Wargrave, had a Mr. Young from the Opera-House
to paint the scenes, which were extremely pretty.
His Lordship and friends perform'd three nights one
week. We were all there the 31st. It was extremely
full of the neighbouring families. The play was "The
Confederacy" and "The Midnight Hour." The
characters as follows :—

Brass	Lord BARRYMORE.
Gripe	Mr. LOWDER.
Money Trap	Mr. THOMPSON.
Jessamy	Mr. DAVIES.
Clip	Captain DIVE.
Dick	{ Mr. ANGELO, Jun. (friends of Lord B.'s.
Flippanta	Mrs. JACKSON
Corinna	Mrs. BENSON } of Thornton's Company.
Araminta	Miss BRIDENSON
Clarissa	Mrs. THORNTON
Mr. Clogget	A GENTLEMAN.
Mr. Amblet	{ EDWIN, Jun. (a most incomparable actor).

In "The Midnight Hour."

Marquis	Captain DIVE.
General	Mr. ANGELO, Jun.
Sebastian	Lord BARRYMORE.
Ambrose	Mr. BARRY.
Matthew	Mr. DAVIE.
Nicholas	EDWIN, Jun.
Julia	Mrs. BALL.
Flora	Mrs. JACKSON.
Cicely	Mrs. THORNTON.

The cake, negus, and all kinds of wines were
brought between the acts; the cake alone one night
they say cost £20. The ball and supper on the

[1] Total cost of building this theatre from first to last was over
£60,000. First wardrobe 2000 guineas. It stood on what is now the
kitchen-garden of Mr. F. Selous, the present owner of Barrymore House,
Wargrave. It held seven hundred. Managers, John Edwin, and T. W.
Williams, alias "Anthony Pasquin."

1789 Wednesday very elegant, as March[1] had orders to get everything possible. A service of plate was sent from London for the occasion. We hear his Lordship is going to build a ball and supper-room adjoining to his theatre.

March 23*rd.*—We all went to tea at Mr. Cooper's,[2] at Henley, to see the illuminations at Henley town on the King's[3] recovery. Every house was lighted up, and as we walked about for hours in different parties from the neighbourhood, the whole made a very fine sight. Fawley Court looked vastly well from the bridge. On the 25th my brother illuminated the parsonage, which look'd amazingly pretty from the bottom of the lawn, and at many distant spots, being a white house. We had the farmers, their wives, &c., to dinner. Had a large bonfire, and barrel of ale given to the village, and the day was pass'd quite to the satisfaction of all here on so truly joyful an occasion.

April 15*th.*—Dined at Mrs. Grote's,[4] Badgemore.

April 28*th.*—Went to stay some time with Miss Ewer at Clapham. Whilst there went often to Ranelagh, plays, &c., the Shakespeare Gallery of Boydell's exhibition of pictures; the sale of the late Mr. Gainsborough's pictures; his celebrated Woodman, whole length, sold to Lord Gainsborough for £500.

Caroline learn'd to dance of Zuchelli.

June the 8*th.*—Went to Ranelagh the night after

---

[1] Barrett March, owner of the Red Lion Hotel, Henley-on-Thames. Lord B. gave a ball in the Red Lion Hotel, February 1789.

[2] Gislingham Cooper at Phyllis Court, Henley.

[3] From his first attack of insanity, begun the previous year.

[4] Wife of George Grote, father of George Grote, the historian of Greece.

the Spanish ambassador's fête on the recovery of his 1789
Majesty, who had ordered everything to be left in the
same state, that the public might view it, and very
magnificent indeed it must have been.   Four rows of
illuminated lamps round the Rotunda, in many vary-
ing forms, as baskets of flowers, wreaths of roses, &c.
All the boxes were form'd like Turkish tents, with
each a festoon curtain that drew up at once when the
suppers were placed in the inside, which was done by
a gallery being made round the Rotunda behind.
This must have had a wonderful pretty effect, as each
box was well illuminated, a waiter at each in a
Spanish dress, and a gentleman out of livery.   The
Queen and Princess supped in a pavilion made for the
occasion, where the orchestra is on common nights,
that had a festoon curtain of white lute-string, with
a gold fringe four inches broad, the back part hung
with pea-green satin embroidered with colour'd
flowers.   The supper was in a very curious set of
Sevre china, which the next morning was sent as a
present to her Majesty.   Before supper the royal
family were placed in another box, fitted up for them,
opposite to a Spanish stage erected for that night, to
show the Queen some Spanish dancing which children
perform'd in the dress of that nation.   But what was
the most elegant display of magnificence was a lottery
for the ladies, who had each a ticket given them as
they enter'd, wrote on the outside such a number ;
"No blanks."   Miss Sturt had the great prize, worth
150 guineas, a watch and chain.   I must not here
omit to mention the name that young lady went by
at this time.   Being exceedingly pretty and very little,
she was always styl'd "the pocket Venus."   The
Queen's prize was a picture of the King of Spain,

o

1789 set with diamonds, the Princess Royal's a toothpick case, and all the ladies some elegant trifle. We heard the lottery cost £700. Some fine gold cups, dishes, &c., used at the Queen's table were likewise sent to different people as presents. In short, the whole was magnificent, and more so, it is said, than any of the other ambassadors. The mat was taken up from the floor and green baize put down in compartments; for the convenience of many dancing parties the boards were left in spaces for them.

July 7th.—The Dean of Bristol, Dr. Hallam,[1] his lady and daughter, came to spend two days at Fawley.

July 9th.—We dined at Mr. Finch's at Ewelme,[2] in Oxfordshire. In the church of this place is a very fine old monument of the Duchess of Suffolk, granddaughter of the poet Chaucer; her father, Thomas Chaucer, who died 1435, likewise is buried here, under a black marble tomb. Ewelme was the chief place of his residence. By his wife Maud he had one daughter named Alice, who was thrice married, first to Sir John Philips, Knight; after to Thomas Montacute, Earl of Salisbury, who left her very rich; her third husband was the famous William de la Pole, Earl and afterwards Duke of Suffolk. He founded an hospital[3] at Ewelme, call'd God's House, still kept up. The Yorkists seized him in his passage in Dover roads, and cut off his head upon the side of the boat. His body was buried in the Charter House Hall. The Duchess survived him several years, and, after an honourable life, died at Ewelme in 1475. I took

---

[1] Father of the historian, and grandfather of the Hallam of "In Memoriam."

[2] Word derived from "Ea" and "Whelm," meaning outgush of water. A beautiful clear stream rises here.

[3] Twelve almsmen occupy the hospital, who receive 10s. each a week.

the above account from Ogre's "Life of Chaucer." 1789
The monument of her in St. John's Chapel, in
Ewelme Church, has been a very magnificent one.
There are eight figures on the base of the tomb, each
holding a different coat of the family arms. There
are three compartments—in the lower one a skeleton,[1] the ceiling of that very finely inlaid, but difficult
to see. A looking-glass laid down gives a perfect
view. The Duchess's figure is finely executed—a ring
on her finger very like an old one I have of Lady
Twysden's,[2] and much resembles some I've latterly
seen made this year 1789, so generally do fashions
come round in a course of years. The tiles with
which the whole church seems to have been paved
are very curiously inlaid, and I was told by an anti-
quarian each tile is the arms of some one of the
family. Over one of the pillars is a good stone head
of Edward III., like his pictures, and the iron is still
fastened to the pulpit which formerly held the hour-
glass. Mrs. Piozzi,[3] in her tour of 1785, mentions
going to hear a famous preacher at Dresden who
kept an hour-glass by him, finishing with strange
abruptness the moment it expired. This was of use
among our distant provinces as late as Gay's time.
He mentions it in his pastorals, saying, "he preach'd
the hour-glass in her praise quite out." There was
a palace at Ewelme, built, as they suppose, by
Richard II. Now small remains of it, and the whole
monument begins to be defaced, which is a great pity,
as it likewise is that great families are not left rich,

[1] Supposed to represent the Duchess in her shroud. The upper
figure on the tomb is one of the three known examples of females
wearing the Order of the Garter placed round the arm.
[2] Mr. Powys's great-grandmother.
[3] Mrs. Piozzi, formerly Johnson's Mrs. Thrale.

1789 to perpetuate in this pleasing manner the memories of their ancestors.

August 17th.—My brother Powys went to Bristol. That night we all went to Lord Barrymore's theatre at Wargrave; the plays "The Beau's Stratagem" and "The Romp." His Lordship acted "Scrub" amazingly well.

August 20th.—Mr. James, of Langley Hall, came to us to go to the ball at Wargrave on the next day. Lady Jane was prevented coming, as one of their children was ill. On the Friday we went to Wargrave; were not to be there till twelve, on account of the play being later that night, as they began later for the Prince of Wales.[1] A box had been built for his Royal Highness, and a ball-room and elegant supper-room out of it, just finished. After the play the Prince and company entered the ball-room. His Royal Highness began, and they danced two dances before supper. Caroline, who we had given leave to go as in our own neighbourhood, tho' too young (not fifteen), for public assemblies, danc'd with Mr. James. The supper was announced at one. The circular room one of the prettiest for such an occasion I ever saw; the tables round the circle set off the most elegant entertainment that possibly could be, (from London), to the greatest advantage. The dome was lighted with colour'd lamps, and the sideboard, likewise circular, under the dome, at which no more than six of his lordship's own servants[2] attended, and with such uncommon cleverness that no one of the company but had everything wished for

---

[1] Rooms to dress were prepared for the Prince of Wales at Wargrave Hill; not sufficient accommodation at Barrymore House.

[2] They were dressed in scarlet and gold.

in an instant. We fancied there would have been 1789
a separate table for the Prince, but he sat himself
down amongst the rest without the least ceremony,
seem'd quite free, easy, and perfectly good-humoured
the whole evening, talk'd to almost the whole company, took particular care to turn every one by the
hand in going down the dances, which accomplish-
ment, to be sure, he particularly excels in, more than
most others. With such ease and grace he dances
that he was sure to be known by his manner, tho'
without star or any other signature of his birth. He
retired after two more dances, and set off in his post-
chaise for York. What a pity such an accomplish'd
young man, knowing so well how to make himself
admired and beloved, can be wanting in duty to such
parents as his ; but time and his own good sense will
very soon, I've no doubt, make him see the impro-
priety, even to his own future happiness, in this
juvenile conduct. We got home about six, much
indeed pleased with the evening's entertainment.

August 24th.—We all went to Reading for the
race-time. Lord Barrymore[1] was steward. Of course
the sport was good, and assemblies brilliant. We
were at the last only.

November 30th.—Young Phil and Tom went with
General Conway to the Blenheim play. We were all
offer'd tickets, but the weather was then so bad we
declined going.

The Miss Michells and us dined and lay at Mr.
Gardiner's,[2] Hardwick. Returned to Fawley about
four, drank tea at Mr. Horne's, at Wargrave, and at
nine went to Lord Barrymore's, who had invited some

[1] He gave a fifty-guinea cup to be run for.
[2] Mr. Gardiner was then renting Hardwick.

1789 part of our neighbourhood to a "little dance," as he
express'd it on his cards. ·It was a very agreeable
small party, a very elegant supper. Two long tables in
the circular room, as not company sufficient for those
round the room as before, and in the centre was a
stove, which made it charming warm. My lord, and
one of his brothers, and Mrs. Bertie sang some good
catches after supper, which, as all have charming
voices, was very pleasant. Dancing a good deal after
supper, made it between six and seven before we got
home the next morning.

   December 29th.—On Tuesday the 29th our nearest
neighbour, Mrs. Freeman, of the Park (Henley), was
so obliging as to give our son, Phil, a ball on his
approaching nuptials ;[1] all this vicinity and some other
company was invited. The ball-room was hung with
festoons of flowers, and the windows illuminated, the
supper magnificent. They danced again after supper,
and got home about four.

1790   *January 1st.*—Our fourth and last Henley ball for
the season ; they had been kept up with great éclat,
and always attended by the whole agreeable neighbourhood.

   January 5th.—On the Tuesday we were at Lord
Barrymore's play at Wargrave, the last of the three
nights, as they had acted on the Saturday and Monday — the plays, "A Trip to the Jubilee," "The
Citizen," and "Don Juan." My Lord acted in all of
them as well as possible. In the first, "Beau
Clincher," "Philpot" in "The Citizen," "Scara-
mouch" in the last. The theatre was amazingly

---

[1] He was engaged to Miss Louisa Michell, daughter and co-heiress
of Richard Michell, of Culham Court, Berks.

crowded, the Duchess of Bolton,[1] the Cravens, 1790
Poyntzs, Lord Inchiquin, &c., and General Conway,
Lady Ailesbury, &c., &c. Mr. Goddall perform'd
"Sir Harry Wildair" and "Maria" in "The Citizen."
Many of my Lord's friends acted, and others from
Thornton's Company.

On Friday the 8th January his Lordship gave a
masqued ball, to which we declined going, tho' he
obligingly desired we would send for as many tickets
as we chose. Caroline being too young for such an
entertainment, and the two Miss Michells not wishing
to go, the more ancient part of the family would not
go without them. We heard it was very grand. The
Prince of Wales[2] and many of the nobility, in all
about 470.

January 11th.—Mr. Powys, my brother, and young
Phil went to London to settle the writings for his
marriage. Phil took lodgings in Bond Street, and
Mr. Powys and my brother return'd till the lawyers
had finished, for us all to go up. The two Miss
Michells went from Culham Court to their house in
North Audley Street.

February 2nd.—At a very elegant ball and supper
at Mr. Clayton's, Harleyford.

February 18.—Our dear young Phil married to
Miss Louisa Michell, at St. George's Church, Hanover
Square. My brother Powys perform'd the ceremony.
We all, with Miss Ewer, came from Clapham, after-
wards breakfasted in North Audley Street. About
one o'clock the new married pair set off in their post-

---

[1] Second wife of the sixth Duke. She and Lord Barrymore invented
a special language, which was only known to their set, done by arranging
one vowel and one consonant to each word. *Vide* Pasquin.

[2] The Prince remained unmasked the whole evening.

1790 chaise for Culham Court for a week. Miss Michell went to Mr. Lockwood's,[1] in town, till their return.

March 4th.—At Covent Garden Theatre to see "The Dramatist," "Capt. Cook," &c.

March 22nd.—Went to Drury Lane Theatre, "The Belle's Stratagem" and (Mrs. Jordan's) "Spoilt Child," the first performance.

April 12th.—We were at the professional concert, Hanover Square, Marchese Mara and Cramer; and heard them also at the Opera on the 15th.

29th.—Went to the Shakespeare and Macklin's galleries of pictures, and likewise the exhibition at Somerset House.

June 2nd.—Dr. and Miss Cooper came to fetch Caroline, to go with them to the review on the following day. The first time I had ever parted for a night with my dear girl, tho' then fifteen.

23rd.—Caroline was confirmed at Henley Church by the Bishop of Oxford.

13th July.—We went to the Annesleys, Bletchingdon Park. On 17th drove to Blenheim round the park. Annesley drove Mr. Powys in the phaeton and six. Mrs. A. Caroline and I by turns in her pony-chaise, and the dear little Arthur, went with one of us in the post-chaise.

August 21st.—Mrs. Williams' water-party. Tom and Caroline invited to go with their brother from Culham. We went to breakfast at Mrs. Winford's, Marlow, and went in their boat to Sir George Young's,[2] so saw Mr. Williams' barge, and heard the music. They went up to Clifden Spring, danced all

---

[1] The Lockwoods were country friends as well, living at Hambleden, Bucks.

[2] Formosa Place.

the way. After a most elegant dinner on board the
barge, not back till between eleven and twelve at
night.

August 23*rd.*—My brother went to Lord Camden's, and we to my mother's at Reading for the races
and ball,[1] Caroline for the first time.

September 18*th.*—Died the Duke of Cumberland,
brother to his Majesty, George III. We went into
mourning for him Sunday the 26th, black silk with
love ribbons. Changed mourning October 24th, and
went out November 7th.

September 21*st.*—Went to Lord Barrymore's theatre. The first time of opening since so enlarged.
We had been to see the interior parts of it the week
before, and most clever and superbly elegant it was.
It now holds 400.[2] The play, "Figaro" and "Robinson Crusoe," well performed three nights.[3]

September 28*th.*—All of us, excepting my brother
and Caroline, were at Lord Barrymore's masqued
ball; for our neighbours, finding the last year's had
been conducted with such propriety, had all agreed
to go, if we did. Our party consisted of the Park
(Henley), Fawley Court, Culham Court, the Winfords, and our own families. Got there by eleven,
and home between six and seven. I may say we
were very highly entertain'd. The whole beautiful
theatre was laid into a ball-room. The rotunda,
supper-room, and two others all decorated with fes-

---

[1] Lord Barrymore won three races at Reading, and fifty events on
the turf this year; out of 140 engagements.

[2] It held 700 spectators. See *General Magazine* for March 1792,
account by Gabriel Cox, the stage carpenter and designer.

[3] Lord Barrymore was "Antonio" and Mr. Ximenes "Double Fee"
in "Figaro." In "Robinson Crusoe" Lord Barrymore played "Pierrot,"
and Delphini "Crusoe." At the end Delphini (once clown at Covent
Garden) and Lord Barrymore danced the Pas Russe.

1790 toons of flowers in the most elegant taste, and everything on the tables that could, I believe, be thought of. Numbers of fancy dresses and many good masques, and a great many black dominoes; my lord and all his party in these, and unmasqed (except at times when in droll characters); Mr. Powys, myself, and our two sons in black dominoes. The company in general unmasqued in about two hours, and almost all at supper. The Prince and his friends were to have been there, but could not on account of the Duke of Cumberland's death; but he desired it might not be put off.[1] As it was so sudden, it was almost impossible to have given all that were invited notice of its being defer'd.

October 12th.—Our first Henley ball as agreeable as usual.

October 19th.—Second Henley ball.

November 5th.—Walked to see Mr. Cooper's place at Bix before his alterations, which he had just begun. His shrubbery and root-house finish'd last summer; very pretty. In the latter some pretty verses of his own writing.

December 9th.—We were at a private ball at Lord Barrymore's[2] (he gave one the week before, to which we were also invited). It was very pleasant and elegant as usual. His Lordship had added to the rotunda a great length since the Monday to make that the ball-room, as the other was carpeted all over and converted into a card-room.[3] The supper

---

[1] This ball was given by Lord Barrymore to celebrate his majority, attained August 14, 1790. It was at this ball the Margravine of Anspach recited a ballad while masqued.

[2] September 30, this year, Lord Barrymore sent a turtle weighing 150 lbs. for the electors' dinner at Reading.

[3] Lord B. was very fond of quinze, and in one evening lost at it 2800 guineas.

was in two different rooms, after which his Lordship, 1790
&c., sang, and then the young peopled danced; got
home soon after six.

December 20*th.*—Mr. Annesley of Bletchingdon
chosen member for Oxford by a majority of 515.

March 2*nd.*—Mr. Powys, Caroline, and myself 1791
set out for Bath. Our son and daughter and Miss
Michell went about ten days before us. Spent a
very pleasant month there. Our lodgings in the
new part of Bath—Portland Place.

April 5*th.*—My brother went to London to preach
as King's Chaplain.

April 13*th.*—We were all at Lord Barrymore's
theatre at Wargrave; "The Rivals," "Robinson
Crusoe," and "Blue Beard"; at home about four in
the morn. His Lordship perform'd "Acres" as well
as it could be done.

On Saturday, June the 4th, the King's birthnight,
Miss Ewer was married to Mr. Shrimpton at St.
George's, Bloomsbury, by my brother Powys.

June 8*th.*—My brother went to his residence at
Bristol.[1]

June 21*st.*—A large party, thirteen of us, dined
at General Conway's cottage at Park Place. (Either
the "Chinese Cottage" or Boat House.—*Editor.*)

June 25*th.*—A shocking accident. John Heath,
our coachman, who had been at home some days ill
of a fever, got up unknown to his family, came to our
house, and threw himself down into our well in a fit
of frenzy. For a day and a half sent out parties to
search, but at last, knowing he could not have been
able to go any distance, drew the well. He was a

---

[1] Through Earl Camden, the Rev. Thomas Powys was now a Prebend of Bristol, as well as his other benefices.

1791 very young man, and left a wife and three small children.

July 17*th.*—Mr. Slaney[1] died. He was so kind as to leave my three children fifty guineas each, and myself the value of about £2000, if I survived his sister, Mrs. Keeling. As I had not the least reason to expect anything from so distant a relation, I must ever feel myself grateful for this testimony of his regard.

July 21*st.*—Miss Cooper came for a week, and we went on the 22nd, a large party, to Clifden Spring by water, towed there and back in Mr. Freeman's new boat, a very elegant one. We did not dine, as usual, at the Spring, but borrow'd Miss Winford's Temple near Marlow, and there left our hampers of provisions till our return.

July 25*th.*—The Culham Court family went to Oxford, as young Phil was one of the stewards of the races, and Mr. Spencer being the other. The Duke[2] and Duchess of Marlborough would not (as usual) attend the diversion, but endeavour'd to keep company from going; but, to the universal satisfaction, the balls never were so brilliant. How strange that these parents seem ever to act contrary to most others, by giving dissatisfaction instead of pleasure to their children.

August 6*th.*—I went in the morning to Lady Stapleton's[3] to pay the wedding visit to Lady Despencer, who, with his Lordship,[4] was then at his mother's.

---

[1] John Slaney, of Norwich.

[2] Third Duke of Marlborough.

[3] Mary, daughter of H. Fane of Wormsley, Oxon, widow of Sir Thomas Stapleton of Greys Court, Oxon.

[4] Thomas Stapleton, of Greys Court, Oxon, succeeded to the barony in 1788.

October 11*th.*—Went to the Reading county ball, 1791 at the request of Mr. Annesley, their member.

14*th.*—First Henley ball of that season ; very good one.

18*th November.*—My brother went to residence at St. James's ; read private prayers to the royal family ; was at Court on the Thursday, when the Duchess of York [1] made her first public appearance.

November 24*th.*—On this day our dear grandson Henry Philip was born about noon. I was unfortunately so ill I could not be at Culham, as I had promised Louisa.

December 3*rd.*—Went to one of Mr. Walker's lectures on astronomy at Henley, at which all the neighbourhood had attended.

9*th.*—Our Henley assembly.

January 2*nd.*—We all went to Culham early in 1792 the morning ; from thence to Walgrave [2] Church, to the christening of our grandson. His great-grandmother, Mrs. Girle, was godmother, but as it was very bad weather, she was fearful of venturing from home, so I stood for her ; Mr. Powys and our son Tom for themselves.

January 6*th.*—Our last Henley ball for the season, finished with great éclat and very full.

January 20*th.*—On or about this day died my cousin, Mrs. Cooke, daughter of Mrs. Keeling, who is Mr. Slaney's sister.

February 19*th.*—The deepest snow, and by far the coldest weather we had that year.

February 23*rd.*—On this day died the celebrated painter, Sir Joshua Reynolds, aged 69.

---

[1] Princess Royal of Prussia, married 29th September 1791.
[2] Wargrave, often then called Walgrave.

1792 *March* 16th.—At Lord Barrymore's play at War-grave, and the 30th at another, "The Merry Wives of Windsor,"[1] both amazingly well performed.

N.B.—This was the last play acted, as the beautiful theatre was soon after taken down.[2]

April 17th.—Miss Michell (sister of Mrs. Philip Lybbe Powys, junior), was married to Mr. West,[3] brother to Lord Delaware, at St. George's, Hanover Square, by my brother Powys. The bride and bridegroom came down the same day to Culham Court, as Rose Hill was not then ready for them to live at.

May 5th.—On this day our son Philip took possession of our beloved Hardwick,[4] and went with his family to reside there. On the 7th we all went for some days to Hardwick.

May 31st.—A very elegant ball and supper, given at the town-hall, Reading, by Lord Radnor and the other officers of the militia. His Lordship was Lord Lieutenant of Berks.

June 12th.—Mr. and Mrs. Shrimpton[5] came to Fawley. The next day we all went to Ascot races.

June 26th.—Mr. Powys, Caroline, and myself, went to Dr. Cooper's[6] at Sonning, and set off the next morning on our tour to the Isle of Wight.

---

[1] Also that time was performed "The Battle of Hexham," a musical drama, and "Blue Beard."

[2] Lord Barrymore's extravagance told even on his princely fortune. In May 1792 he sold his house in Piccadilly to the Duke of Queensberry, known as "Old Q.," and now the theatre was dismantled and sold, October 15, 1792, by Christie & Co., to satisfy his creditors.

[3] Hon. Frederick West, son of John, second Earl Delaware.

[4] Hardwick had been let, ever since Mr. and Mrs. Powys let it in 1784, to Mr. Gardiner.

[5] *Née* Ewer.

[6] The Rev. Edward Cooper, LL.D., rector of Sonning, son of Gislingham Cooper, and his wife, Anne Whitelock.

JOURNAL OF ISLE OF WIGHT

1792

We had fixed to visit the Lakes, but the Doctor's 1792
health was so indifferent we persuaded him from going
so far, but as he ever found himself better by change
of air, he was very desirous of taking some journey.
The first day we went no farther than Basingstoke,
went through Lord River's Park[1] by Heckfield; 'tis
reckon'd a fine place, but I'm not partial to that part
of Hants; dined and lay at " The Crown "—an excellent inn. Wednesday we proceeded to Winchester
(to " The George "). This city is situated in a valley
through which runs the river Itchen. It was formerly
the residence of the West Saxon kings, one[2] of whom
created it into a bishop's see. Athelstan granted it
the privilege of six mints for the coinage of money.
It has been three times burned down, and about the
year 860 was demolish'd by the Danes. Close by the
west gate stands King Arthur's palace. Egbert was
crown'd here, and afterwards Alfred, and Edward the
Confessor. The unfortunate William Rufus made it
a point of being crown'd here every Christmas, and
Richard Cœur de Lion after his arrival from the
Holy Wars and his long imprisonment, was a second
time crown'd in the Castle. Henry V. held his parliament here before he embark'd for France.

Adjoining to the Chapel, and on the spot where
the castle once stood, Sir Christopher Wren, by
command of Charles the II. form'd a design for a

[1] Strathfieldsaye.
[2] King Kynegil, the convert of Birinus.

1792 palace,[1] in which he meant to entertain his whole
court with various kinds of amusements, and though
the plan was only in part carried into execution,
the building is magnificent. The south side 216 feet
long, the west 328, and notwithstanding it is a shell,
it cost upwards of £25,000. The Grand Duke of
Tuscany presented Charles II. with several marble
pillars of exquisite workmanship, which were to have
supported the roof of the grand staircase; these
George III. gave to the Duke of Bolton. A handsome balustrade runs quite round the top, and the
inside of the court is decorated with a portico; had
not Charles's death put an end to its completion, it
would have been a palace worthy that gay and expensive monarch. The only use it has been put to
since is as a place of confinement for the French and
Spanish prisoners during the late wars; it is now
call'd the King's House. We walk'd for some time
around its environs; 'tis on an eminence pleasantly
situated. We next went to the Cathedral, and after
to the College, founded by William of Wykeham,
May 26th, 1387,[2] for seventy scholars, the wooden
trenchers were all laid and they going to supper,
and we stay'd while the grace was chanted. The
Cathedral is a noble Gothic architecture, and generally allow'd to be equal to the Abbey Church of
St. Alban's; the length 525 feet.[3] Cromwell's army
committed horrible outrages here, destroying all the
beautiful carved work and painted glass, overturn'd
the communion table, and burn'd the rails that sur-

[1] On the plan of Versailles. For two years the works proceeded. In
1810 the completed portion was made into barracks.
[2] The date of the first stone of the chapel laid, but school commenced
in 1386.
[3] This is the largest English cathedral, 560 feet.

rounded it. The west window[1] escaped their depre- 1792
dations, and the magnificent tomb of William of
Wykeham was happily prevented from sharing the
same fate.

In the High Street is the market-cross,[2] 43 feet
in height, some say erected in commemoration of
the introduction of Christianity, some say as late as
Henry VI.

We left Winchester on Thursday morn. About
five miles on the right is Hursley,[3] the seat of Sir
William Heathcote, but so surrounded by venerable
oaks we did not get a sight of the house. Soon
after this, had our first view of the sea. On a very
elevated part of Southampton Common is a summer-
house of Mr. Fleming's,[4] from whence must be a
very fine view. We got to Southampton early, dined
and lay there one night. . . . As we spent a fortnight there on our return, I shall say no more of it
at present. Friday morning, Sir Hyde Parker having
recommended Captain Wassell to convey us to Cowes,
we set off in his thirty-ton vessel, a most commodious
one. The wheels were taken off our carriages, and,
with the horses, put on board another vessel. We all
expected to be affected by the sea, but were most
happily disappointed, and after a most pleasant sail of
two hours in a beautiful morning, were landed at West
Cowes. In our voyage we saw several seats, first
Dummer, that of Mr. Dance (who married the widow
of Mr. Dummer); next that of Captain Parr; third,

---

[1] Was collected from all remains in other windows after, but is
undoubtedly old.

[2] Of fifteenth-century work.

[3] Once the property of Richard Cromwell, ex-Protector. Here Keble
was vicar, who wrote the "Christian Year."

[4] Stoneham Park.

R

1792 Governor Hornby's; fourth, Luttrell's Folly; fifth, Calshot Castle, and, as we approached Cowes, the castle of that name. We were vastly pleased with the civility and orderly behaviour of Captain Wassell and his seamen. We stayed only a short time at Cowes for some refreshments for ourselves and horses, and the wheels to be replaced for travelling. While this was performing, we walked round the castle down to the bathing-machines, &c. West Cowes seems to have many pretty cottage lodging-houses, a pretty view of the sea, and, very convenient for bathing, is become a fashionable place for the last two years,[1] but I've heard not wholesome for invalids on account of its muddy shore.

We set off for Newport intending to lay there, not being certain the house Sir Hyde Parker had taken for us in Upper Ryde was ready for our reception; so when we got to the " Bugle Inn," Mr. Powys and Mr. Cooper, while the dinner was getting ready, rode over and found everything in order for the next day. Newport is one of the pleasantest towns in the island, houses small, streets uniform, well-paved, and a remarkable neatness throughout the place, inhabitants remarkable for civility, all kinds of shops, and everything to be got there, a theatre, and two markets held every week, at which the farmers' daughters appear, we heard, in a high style of beauty and elegance.

In our short journey from this place of about six miles are seen some delightful views of the sea. The oak woods one goes thro' are beautiful, the view from Wootton Bridge particularly striking when the tide is in. . . . We got to Ryde about one on Saturday, and found our house (for we were too numerous

[1] From this, Fashion marked it for her own in 1790!

not to want a whole one), tolerable; the place indeed 1792
may be said to consist merely of cottages, but all
taken up with company, and more daily wishing to
come; indeed, 'tis so charming a country, and from
it the sea appears in its highest beauty, so that in
a few years I make no doubt it will be a very fashionable spot. . . . Neither so reasonable as now, as we
had our little domain for two guineas a week,[1] with
eight bedrooms for ourselves and servants, tho' not
very spacious, very neat, and comfortable.

Sunday, July 1st.—We went to the chapel at
Ryde, service only once a day at half-past three.
Mr. Gill, a very worthy man, curate there, and two
more churches every Sunday. How we wished to
procure him a good living; but neither himself nor
his large family ever repine at their situation in life.
The singing very good, accompanied by several
instruments. We had in the morning driven down
to the beach, from which one sees many pretty
houses; a Mr. Windham's and Dr. Walker's, the
latter supposed to be "Godolphin's Cottage," by
Mrs. Charles Smith in her novel of "Emiline"; no
doubt a sweet spot, but not equal to that of Sir
Archibald Macdonald's, the Attorney-General's, a
most delightful place, with such a command of the
sea. Dr. Walker, Admiral Hotham,[2] Sir Hyde,[3]
and Lady Parker all came that day, and the next
we went to dine at Knighton, the seat of the
latter about six miles from Ryde. Very near them

[1] The price of a single room in the season now!
[2] Sir William, eleventh Baronet and first Baron Hotham, created so
for his naval services.
[3] Sir Hyde, Admiral of the White, knighted for his services in
American war, married Anne Palmer Boteler of Paradise House,
Henley-on-Thames.

1792 in the road is Ashley's Sea-mark,[1] erected in George II.'s reign, 1735. We drove up the hill on which it stands. 'Tis a triangular stone pyramid. Before us was the harbour of Brading, bounded by Bembridge to the right and St. Helens to the left; the view from thence is grand beyond description; the coast of Sussex bounded the distance before us. After this we soon reached Knighton House,[2] situated in a dale surrounded by woods, from the walks of which are views of the sea. The building, tho' very ancient, is not gloomy, and spacious and pleasing in the inside, tho' the windows are latticed and retain their antique pillars of stone. One part of this stone edifice is finely variegated by ivy binding its gable end; on each side the house is a fine range of woods; on one side of the hill is seen St. Catherine's, on the other the downs of St. Boniface. I took a sketch of the old mansion. We were so agreeably entertain'd with Knighton and its hospital owners, that we did not reach Ryde till very late.

On the 4th we took a ride to see the Priory, Sir Nash Grose's, reckon'd one of the most capital situations and sea views near Ryde. . . . We return'd back a different way along the beach, as the tide was not up by Dr. Walker's and Sir Archibald's. The next day it rained. . . . The fleet lay at Spithead just opposite, only three miles distance.

On Saturday, July 7th, we hired another thirty-ton vessel, whose captain kept the "Bugle Inn," Lower Ryde, as civil a captain as our other, and still more reasonable, as he only ask'd half-a-guinea for the day; he had been recommended by Sir Hyde,

[1] Should be Ashey's Sea-mark, 424 feet above sea.
[2] This beautiful old house was pulled down in 1820.

who was gone on board the *Duke*, Lord Hood,[1] 1792
commander, having desired to go volunteer for a
month's cruise with his Lordship. Seven sail of the
line had, as I before mention'd, lain opposite to Ryde
all the time we had been there, viz., the *Duke*,
Brunswick, *Bedford*, *Orion*, *Hannibal*, *Elfreda*, and
the *Assistance*, and we heard the news from India
before most people in London, as we saw the vessel
come in with despatches from Lord Cornwallis,[2]
and Sir Hyde Parker happened to be on board
the *Duke* with Lord Hood at the time. But to
return to Saturday, when our vessel arrived at the
fleet, the Lords of the Admiralty were arrived from
Portsmouth, and just going to survey each ship, to
see if everything was in proper order before they
set sail. Lord Chatham, &c., were on board a ten-
oared barge, the men in the neatest uniform of white
jackets and trousers, and the band of music playing.
Each ship was to be manned, as 'tis termed, as their
Lordships enter it, and so entertaining a ceremony I
never before saw. On a drum beating, 300 men fly
up with such agility, it quite amazes any one not
conversant in sea affairs, and in a few moments are
standing at the yards and ropes in the most exact
order, without any of those fears the lookers-on
cannot help feeling for them. In this manner their
Lordships went from ship to ship, beginning with the
Duke, and when the survey of each was over, the
drum beat, the music play'd, and they boarded the
ten-oar'd barge, and the 300 sailors came down the
ropes as quickly as they had ascended, and as the

---

[1] Admiral Hood, a famous British seaman, born 1724, died 1816.
[2] Then Governor-General in India, engaged in the war against
Tippú Sultán.

1792 barge approach'd the next ship their crew as instantaneously mounted.   We follow'd them to as many
of the seven as we chose, but wishing to go on
board the *Duke* before the above ceremony was
concluded, as Lord Hood was to have a turtle-feast
for the Lords of the Admiralty, we sail'd back to the
Duke. Sir Hyde had been so obliging as to signify
our intention to Captain Brown, who order'd their
barge to come for us, and as we enter'd the ship the
music play'd, and we were received in the highest
style of politeness, and ushered into Sir Hyde's
elegant apartment; but as he was dressing in an
inner cabin for dinner, we insisted on not hindering
him; but Captain Brown took us all over the ship.
'Tis a 98-gun man-of-war, and as it was many years
since I had been on board one, I was nearly as much
astonish'd as our young people and the servants, who
had never seen one. . . . The upper deck a fine promenade of 160 feet in length, and the middle one
airy and convenient, nor seem'd crowded tho' 600
sailors on board, and that morning there were sent
off, as they were to sail so soon, 200 women and
children. We were shown the chaplain's, secretary's,
and doctor's apartments, with a fine medicine-chest
in a closet adjoining.   In one room fifteen midship-
men were set down to a hot dinner; in another store-
room we were shown the bread and cheese cut, and
weigh'd each day's sailor's allowance; in another hung
a quantity of beef; all these apartments were below
water. Then we went upstairs in a pleasant long room
rather low ceil'd, where some of the officers were just
going to an early dinner, on account of the grand one
between five and six. The day before their Lordships
had another turtle, to which they did not get till past

seven.   The officers entreated us to partake of their 1792
early dinner, which we declin'd, but had cakes and
wine and water, as they seem'd quite hurt by a refusal,
tho' we had a cold collation on board our vessel, and
had ordered a late one at Ryde in the evening. . Having seen everything, we took leave of Sir Hyde and
the polite officers, and with their band playing were
conveyed back to our vessel in their barge.

Sunday.—Went at usual hour to church.

Monday.—Mr. Powys and I, Caroline, and Miss
Cooper[1] drove in two whiskys to Newport.   Mr.
Cooper[2] went airing by the sea in the chaise with
the Doctor.   I must not forget to mention how cheap
fish were at Ryde.   Sand-eels, the nicest little things
I ever tasted, like whitebait, one day nine fine mackrel
for 1s., lobsters and crabs 4d. a lb., the best shrimps
I ever tasted, and another day thirteen whiting-cole,
superior to whitings, 9d.—all, they told us, very dear,
as the fleet being at Spithead made such a difference
in the price of every article.

Dr. Cooper had taken his own whisky, and we
had hired one on purpose, as we thought the convey-
ance so agreeable to what a close carriage would be ;
but they were of no use in the island, as not wide
enough for the ruts, and tho' the roads were certainly
much better than I remember them formerly, they
may still be call'd very indifferent.   The inhabitants
brag of their not having one turnpike, but if they had
many, one should not mind paying for so great a convenience.   But there are whiskys to be hired at all the
inns, made for the roads, and they let them out with
a little boy as guide and gate-opener, as there are
numbers of the latter (the former, very difficult to find)

---

[1] Daughter of Dr. Cooper.   [2] Son of Dr. Cooper.

1792 for 4d. a day.   Their post-chaise boys all have a chair
to sit in instead of a coach-box, and never ride the
horses.

'All Tuesday morning we, with numerous other
people, were waiting at the benches at the end of the
village commanding the sea to see the fleet set sail.
It was a pretty sight to see the flashes and hear the
guns firing of each ship, but they did not set out till
Wednesday.   We passed the next morn with Mrs.
Williams, an agreeable old lady, who resides with her
son and daughter at a sweet cottage at Ryde; the
son, Captain Williams of the Royal Navy, a very
agreeable young man, an intimate acquaintance of Sir
Hyde's.   Thursday we all paid a morning visit to
Lady Parker, who we found very dull at his absence;[1]
but as we told her one month was so soon over, we
would not let her give way to melancholy, and made
a party for the Saturday morning to meet at Newport
market, a very fashionable rendezvous, to see the
farmers' daughters, so much talked of for their beauty
and neatness.   When we got to that pretty town,
it seem'd as if all the smarts of the island were assembled.   The beauties afore mentioned came on
horseback with their baskets.   They have a room
where they new dress, and we were told a hairdresser
always attends.   We found them arranged in great
order in the market, appearing indeed very smart and
neat, and many pretty girls, tho' the Beauty of the
island was not there that day.   There are very excellent shops of all kinds in Newport, and every fashionable thing to be bought there.

[1] Her natural fears for his safety might well be increased by the fact
that his father, Sir Hyde, fourth Baronet, after brilliant services in the
West Indies, sailed from Rio Janeiro in 1782, and was never heard of
again.

Sunday.—Church at the usual time, and a large
party to tea, and a long walk in the evening.

Tuesday.—Captain Williams went with us a long
walk, to show us Binstead Parsonage and the ruins
of Quarr Abbey.   Binstead is about a mile and three-
quarters from Ryde, through sweet woods, with often
a sea view.   The Reverend's residence is literally
a cottage, but in the most romantic style possible,
standing in a sweet garden commanding a view of
the ocean, the thatched cottage surrounded by tall
firs and other trees.   Over the door and each window
is the bust of some poet or great man, and under that
which stands over the entrance is written in capitals, "Contentment is wealth."   Myrtles under every
window growing wild.   From thence is Quarr Abbey,[1]
the ruin of an ancient monastery, a charming walk
thro' a wood.   'Tis now only a farmhouse, but you
see the walls of the old abbey, and here and there a
ruined arch.

Wednesday morning we went a longer excursion
to Sandown Fort, about seven miles from Ryde,
through the village of Brading, near which we passed
a very good house of Sir William Oglander's,[2] situated
in a beautiful vale.   When we got to Sandown Fort,[3]
the roaring of the sea and dashing of the waves was
more noble than we had yet seen.   It seems it is the
only place an enemy could land in the island.   We
got out of the carriages as the horses seem'd alarm'd,
and walk'd along the beach about half a mile to
Sandown Cottage, a summer residence of the famous

---

[1] Founded by Baldwin de Redvers, temp. Henry I., 1132, for Cistercians.

[2] Nunwell Park, seat of the Oglanders ever since the Conquest.

[3] Dates from Charles II.

1792 Mr. Wilkes,[1] commands an uncommon view of the sea and surrounding cliffs, very fine garden, in which is a menagerie. Strangers have leave to see the place by setting down their names in a book kept on purpose. The cottage itself has only a very few small rooms; but as Mr. Wilkes often entertains many families, he has erected in the gardens many of the fashionable canvas ones, fitted up in different manners and of large dimensions. One call'd the "Pavilion," another the "Etruscan," a third a dressing-room of Miss Wilkes, others as bedrooms, all very elegantly furnish'd, and very clever for summer (and in the Isle of Wight, where it seems a robbery was never known), but to us who reside so much nearer to the vicinity of the Metropolis, the idea of being abroad in such open apartments strikes one with some rather small apprehensions. Some of the rooms contain very capital prints and very fine china, indeed altogether well worth seeing, tho' the country round it is not near so pleasing as near Ryde, tho' the sea more noble.

Thursday, the 19th July, we set sail in our own vessel, Lady Parker and her party and our own, for Portsmouth, as we had been inform'd we must see the great annual fair kept there, which lasts three weeks. In about an hour and a half we got near Portsmouth. Had a view of the Navy Hospital, and Southsea Castle. We first sailed round and round all the ships lying there, as the *Royal George*, the *Queen Charlotte*, *Princess Royal*, and others. Captain Williams being with us, showed us in each what was particularly worth our observation, and had

---

[1] Who called it the "Villakin." Mr. John Wilkes bought it in 1788, and spent most of his time there till his death in 1797.

before asked the favour of Sir Andrew Douglas, 1792
captain of the *Alcide*, to send his ten-oar'd barge
to land us at the docks; and Lady Parker had sent
her compliments to Mr. White, Master of the Works,
to beg he would show her friends his department.
He came to us immediately, and I'm sure took infinite
trouble in explaining everything to us. The walls
of the dockyard are at least two miles in circumference, and contain about eighty-three acres [1] of ground.
About 3000 men are usually employ'd there, consisting of labourers of every kind. They were then
beginning a new dock, about an acre of ground, and
we saw some of the foundation-stones ramm'd down.
But what most entertain'd me was the construction
of a ship, which Mr. White was so obliging as to
show me, in different parts of the yard, in every state
from its very commencement to the finishing. In
one just begun, we saw about thirty whole trees,
which made the arch, after that on the outside are
fasten'd planks the contrary way to what the trees
go, which are done with wooden pegs, each two feet
long (as no nails are used in a ship). From thence
we went to the store boat-house, 160 feet in length.
It contain'd about three hundred boats of different sorts
and sizes, as many slung up to the ceiling as were on
the floor. After we had gone over all the works, too
numerous to mention, Mr. White insisted on our going
to his house after our fatigue, where we were politely
entertained with cake and sandwiches, and the gentlemen all said the very finest old hock they ever tasted.
His house seems a very good one, and many good
pictures. All the buildings in the dockyard seem as

---

[1] It contains more than 120 acres now.

1792 if quite new built,[1] and have a handsome appearance.
From Mr. White's we had another long walk to the
fair.   The booths were placed regularly down the
middle of a very long street.   Each indeed might be
styl'd a smart shop, furnish'd with every kind of article that could be wanted; shop-bills given at each
to ascertain that they sold the very best assortment
of everything in the newest taste from London ; but
the smart shopmen might have added, "and every
article much dearer than you could have purchased
them in the Metropolis."   But I dare say every lady,
as well as those of our party, had a "fairing" presented
them, and then the extravagance of the price was
not thought of.   It was just then the fashionable rage
for Barcelona handkerchiefs, and such numbers were
sold it quite amazed one.   We dined at "The Crown."
had an elegant dinner, very badly dress'd, at as dirty
an inn as I was ever at.   After coffee we took another
promenade through the fair to get some trifles all of
us seem'd to have forgot.   Then drank tea, and set
off in our vessel for Ryde, with wind and tide both
against us.   But as it was a delightful still evening,
and all fond of the sea, we had no fears, nor got any
colds, tho' not at home till past ten, too late for Lady
Parker to go to Knighton ; so some of their party
slept at Captain Williams', and some at the inn. . . .

On Friday, July 20th, Mr. Cooper, and Mr. Powys
went to Southampton to take lodgings, and returned
in the evening, having succeeded, and inform'd us
quite in the *genteel* part of the town, being above Bar.
On Monday we left the island with regret.   Captain
Williams had asked Sir Andrew Douglas to let Dr.

---

[1] It had been burnt down three times, viz., in 1760 from lightning, in
1770, and in 1776 from an incendiary.

Cooper have his man-of-war barge to take him over, 1792 as going in much less time than our large vessel.   We were becalm'd, and exactly five hours on board, but being fond of the sea and a fine day, we were not tired of our long voyage, but we afterwards heard they were thirteen hours going back; that indeed would have been rather too long for even the gentlemen's patience to have held out; what would have become of the ladies' fortitude I know not.   We got to our lodgings by dinner-time, and met Mr. and Mrs. Horne of Bevis Mount, who desired us to come and break-fast with them the next morning. . . . 'Tis only a mile from the town.   A most elegant breakfast waited our arrival.   I was rather disappointed in the house and grounds.   The house Mr. Horne is greatly im-proving, but they own the Leasowes, (Mr. Shen-stone's), which they had just sold when they purchased Bevis Mount, was far the prettiest spot.

Wednesday it rain'd the whole day.   Thursday we call'd on Lord and Lady Macclesfield,[1] whose family came to Southampton the day after us, and after our visit to them we drove in our whiskys to see Netley Abbey, rather preferring a drive round Southampton Ride than crossing at Itchen Ferry.   'Tis a pleasant round, and one passes many sweet houses.   The first, Belle Vue, a fine prospect . . . now the residence of Sir Richard King.   The next, Bevis Hill, General Hib-bert's, &c.   In a vale farther on, about three miles from Southampton, is Hans Sloane's,[2] Esq., a good brick house. . . . Netley Abbey is, without exception, one of the first objects of its kind in Great Britain.   It at present belongs to a Mr. Dance, who married the widow of Mr. Dummer, his predecessor, who enclosed the

[1] Home neighbours at Shirburn Castle, Oxon.   [2] Paultons.

1792 venerable ruins with a wall. The beautiful woods surrounding it, and prospect from it, command the stranger's attention in a peculiar manner, and the venerable pile is really one of the most picturesque objects I ever saw. The architecture is grand, and the east window of the church must have been uncommonly fine. A small part of the beautiful ceiling still remains, and a spiral stone staircase that went to the gallery is not yet fallen in. . . . Godwin and Leland say that it was founded by Peter de Rupibus, who died 1238, but Tanner attributes it to Henry III., who, A.D. 1239, founded an abbey of Cistercian monks, with whom Dugdale agrees. The chapel is in form of a cross; some remains of a refectory and kitchen appear. The whole is so overgrown with ivy as to inspire the most pleasing melancholy. The present vulgar opinion of what is call'd the Abbot's Kitchen is deem'd a subterranean passage leading to the castle.

Saturday, 28th.—We drove in the whisky to see Broadlands, the seat of Lord Palmerston; they were then gone abroad, which we were sorry for, being acquainted with the family; besides, we could not but be anxious as the troubles had commenced in France,[1] and they had taken their four children with them. . . . The house is undoubtedly good, but not grand. The entrance gives one the best idea, as you ascend a pleasing portico; but the inside, from the Italian taste, strikes me with gloominess, as the height of all the windows is dreadful, and one may judge must be uncomfortably so, as Lady Palmerston has a settee on wheels, which is placed on two or three steps; and on inquiring from the housekeeper what that was for, she

---

[1] This was the year of the National Convention.

replied that her Ladyship might *see* out of the windows. 1792
There is a desk on it to read, write, or draw upon, so
that the machine is clever, only nowadays, when all
windows are down to the ground, one should be more
averse to ascend to have a prospect.   The hall is
adorn'd with very fine statues, and the collection of
pictures all over the house very capital. . . .

Monday, 30*th.*—We set out to see a part of the
Isle of Wight we had not before, and went to Lymington early in the morning.   The first village we passed
was Milbrook, next by the village of Redbridge, which
bridge (as they were building a new stone one), was
rather a tremendous road, but we got safe over it. . . .
Soon after you are through the village and that of
Totton you reach the New Forest, and see your
straight road for many miles, which to me is ever a
disagreeable view ; but the beauty of that forest in
some measure makes amends, as the trees are so
noble, and many grand clumps, through which, in the
most picturesque manner, one sees other woody lanes,
uncommon, and therefore very striking to the eye.
This forest, we were told, is at least forty miles in
circumference.   Lyndhurst, a pleasant village, and
much frequented in the summer season, is ten miles
from Southampton, situated in the heart of the forest,
on the declivity of a hill.   It once boasted of a monarch
for its inhabitant.   The King's House [1] indeed, as a
royal one, makes an indifferent appearance ; 'tis now
the Duke of Gloucester's, who is Ranger.   It commands a fine view of the Southampton river and the
sea.   On the left, soon after you leave the town,
is Foxlease, the seat of Sir Philip Jennings Clerk

[1] The official residence of the Ranger, and where the Forest Courts
are held.

1792 (Lady Jennings now lets it); Burleigh Lodge and Cuffnels, now George Rose's, Esq., secretary to the Chancellor of the Exchequer. The seat of the Compton Willis's merits the notice of people of taste. Proceeding thro' Brockenhurst, three miles from Lyndhurst is the seat of Edward Morant, Esq., a very fine house.[1] In about another five miles, in which is an uninterrupted view of the Isle of Wight, we got to Lymington, a small neat seaport, eighteen miles from Southampton. It is pleasantly situated on an eminence, from which the island is but a short passage by sea, not far from the celebrated rocks called the Needles. Near this place are said to be the most famous saltworks in the kingdom. The quay is spacious. Ships of considerable burthen sail from this place. Hurst Castle is nearly opposite this town. We stayed at Lymington no longer than to have some sandwiches; and leaving our carriages, as we imagined we could hire some vehicle at Yarmouth, we took a vessel, which conveyed us the seven miles in about an hour and a half. When we landed at Yarmouth, to our sorrow, we were inform'd the only post-chaise was gone with another party, and as we were determin'd not to lose the fine view of Freshwater, we had no alternative but to walk part of the way, first taking a boat, which in about an hour row'd us to the church, where we landed, and had then about two miles to walk to the cliff, and when we arrived the view fully answer'd our fatigue. There we rested on a bench, where the waves dash'd just up to us. We then mounted the cliffs, and came on Afton Down, which commands a most noble view of the sea, something like that at Mr. Wilkes', but, the cliff

[1] Brockenhurst Park.

being higher and more broken, renders this more 1792
sublimely beautiful. The fine white sand, the vein
of which runs (as the miners inform'd us), entirely
through from the extremity of the point opposite
Yarmouth to the downs of Afton. It belongs to a
Mr. Urry of Yarmouth; the profit very great indeed.
Vessels lie in Alum Bay to load with it, being the
only sort in these kingdoms fit for making the white
glass, and 'tis likewise used for the china manufacture
at Worcester; nor will any other do for these uses.
We walk'd back to Yarmouth, got there about eight
in the evening, and were not sorry to find our dinner
ready at a very small neat inn (" The Angel"). . . .
About nine the next morning we got into our vessel
and arrived at Lymington; there we breakfasted, and
set off in our whiskys for Southampton. Southampton
is one of the most neat and pleasant towns I ever saw,
twelve miles from Winchester; was once wall'd round,
many large stones of which are still remaining. There
were four gates, only three now. It consists chiefly
of one long fine street of three-quarters of a mile in
length, called the High Street, and in Leland's time
was supposed to be the finest street of any town in
England. The Polygon (not far distant), could the
original plan been completed, 'tis said, would have
been one of the first places in the kingdom, perhaps
in the world, regarded in the view of modern architecture. At the extremity a capital building was
erected, with two detached wings and colonnades. The
centre was an elegant tavern, with assembly, card-
rooms, &c., &c., and at each wing hotels to accommodate the nobility and gentry. The tavern is taken
down, but the wings converted into genteel houses.
On the 3rd August 1792 the first stone of the new

s

1792 church, called All Saints, was laid. We saw it from a stand erected in the High Street just opposite, and the windows of every house were filled with company to see the procession of mayor and aldermen, attended to and from the other church[1] by a vast concourse of people. A very fine sermon was there preach'd by Mr. Scott, and an anthem sung. When divine service was over, about half-past one, they all proceeded to the spot where the inscription, on a glass plate, was read with an audible voice by the town-clerk, signifying "that the first stone of All Saints Church was laid on the 3rd of August 1792 by Mr. Donellen, Grand Freemason"(this gentleman is son to George II., and very like the present royal family). They call'd for silence when he read it, and it was then placed by him between two stones, and let down by pullies; then a prayer was said by Mr. Scott, and the most profound silence was preserv'd till the amen was resounded by the multitude; then three times three, after which the celebrated Mr. Bird sang "Rule Britannia;" and, after he had done, three times three again, when all dispersed, and the gentlemen retired to a grand entertainment.

Our time at Southampton was indeed spent pleasantly. . . . Lady Hyde Parker and Captain Williams breakfasted with us the morning we set out, August 7th. We stopped at Winchester, and lay that night at a most excellent inn at Popham Lane. The next day set off about twelve, passed Kempshot, the Prince of Wales' hunting-box; nothing remarkably pleasing in the view of it; stopped at a neat little inn on Heckfield Heath, just by Lord Rivers' park, and got about

[1] St. Lawrence.

five to dinner at Dr. Cooper's at Sonning;[1] lay there 1792
that night, and got home to Fawley to dinner on
August 9th, after a most pleasant tour, which we
should all have enjoyed in a much greater degree had
we not visibly seen poor Dr. Cooper's health daily
declining, though the journey seem'd to have been of
service as often as we changed the air ; but at last we
thought him too far gone to be at any great distance
from home, and entreated him to return, which he always
seem'd unwilling to do, perhaps thinking it might be
less anxiety to his children if he had died at any other
place, as never were father and children more fond or
attentive to each others' happiness.

August 14th.—We went to stay at Hardwick.
On 15th had a very pleasant day upon the water;
went in a large boat, and dined at Goring Spring,[2]
formerly famous for its water. It belongs to Mr.
Powys.

August 27th.—Died at his living at Sonning, the
Rev. Dr. Cooper[3] very much regretted by all his
friends.

August 28th.—The Reading races. The middle
night we were at the play, " The Child of Nature,"
and " No Song no Supper." We had been at the
races the first day, and were set off for the course on

---

[1] Dr. Cooper was vicar of Sonning, Berks, and rector of Whaddon,
near Bath.

[2] Goring Spring, now little used, was reckoned good for ulcers, sore
eyes, scorbutic affections. Mr. Richard Lybbe, hearing complaints of
water being sold, not from the spring, ordered every vessel to be filled
and sealed with his arms, certain people to supply it, and limited the
charge to 1d. a quart for attendance and sealing. *Reading Mercury* of
February 13th, 1724, gives a long list of persons cured.

[3] Edward Cooper, son of Gislingham Cooper and his wife, Anne
Whitelock, joined his mother in selling Phyllis Court and Henley Manor
to Sambrook Freeman in 1768. His portrait represents a rosy, round-
faced divine, with a most amiable expression.

1792 this too, but unfortunately were overturn'd, or I may say fortunately, as neither my poor mother, Caroline, or myself were the least hurt. Caroline and I at first thought of not attending the theatre after this accident, but in the space of an hour or two we had so many inquiries, and report, as is generally the case, had made us all suffer such a number of misfortunes, that we determined to show ourselves alive and well; so had the glasses of our coach mended, and enter'd the playhouse, to the infinite surprise of all our acquaintances, and received such numerous congratulations as were quite flattering.

September 28th.—Our first winter, Henley ball.

November 14th.—Died Sir Sidney Meadows,[1] aged 92. Had rode that day in his riding-house. We went into mourning for him Sunday 25th.

December 11th.—Miss Cooper married to Captain Williams,[2] of the Navy. They set off for his house in the Isle of Wight.

December 28th.—Last Henley ball for the season.

1793 *January 1st, 1793.*—We went to Hardwick for some days.

March 14th was the day our dear Caroline was married to Mr. Cooper, son of the late Dr. Cooper, of Sonning, Berks, a match that gave all her friends the highest satisfaction, as there cannot be a more worthy young man. We had all intended to have had the ceremony perform'd in London, but found some difficulties about residence, parish, &c., so determin'd to have it at Fawley; so sent to our son Thomas not to come up, but meet us there, with Phil and Louisa. I was so affected with the loss of my dear girl (who till

---

[1] Mr. Powys's grandmother was a daughter of Sir Philip Meadows.
[2] *Vide* Isle of Wight Tour, same year.

latterly I had never parted with for even one night), 1793
that I dreaded how I should behave at the time.
They all persuaded me not to go with her; so her
father, Mr. Cooper, and herself went to Fawley the
day before, and the ceremony was over before any
but our own family knew that it was to be performed
there. And Tom, who had been all the week before
in parties in our large neighbourhood, was afterwards
complimented at keeping a secret even better than a
lady! As soon as it was over, Mr. Powys and Tom
set off for London, and Phil and Louisa for Hardwick,
the bride and bridegroom for Sonning.

September 18*th.*—To stay at Hardwick, and 26th
at Wasing Place.

October 25*th.*—Paid a visit at Mr. Grote's,[1] to the
bride, Mrs. George Grote. Dear little Henry was
inoculated[2] at Hardwick by Mr. Coulson of Henley,
and had the small-pox as favourably as possible.

October 18*th and November* 14*th.*—Two Henley
balls ; another December 20th, very full, and ended the
year with great *éclat.*

Here ends my sort of journal for the year 1793 ; for
though in my annual pocket-book I always set down
the visits of each day, yet here it would take up too
much room ; for in so excellent and agreeable a neighbourhood it would be a constant repetition of dinners
at each mansion within seven or eight miles round.

This was a very mild winter, no snow till February 1794
28th, and that soon went off.

Will Heath, our gardener George's son, kill'd by
a bull at Fawley Court.

---

[1] Badgemore, Oxon. Mrs. G. Grote, a remarkably clever woman,
wife of the historian, and wrote his Memoirs.
[2] Introduced into England by Lady Mary Wortley Montagu in 1721.

1794   *March 12th.*—Mr. Powys and I went to Bath.

March 25th.—Went to Bristol; dined at the Dean's. On 27th went to see Miss Wallace in " The Child of Nature." She left Bath soon after for the London theatre.

April 24th.—My brother went to London to Lord Bayham's, on the death of Lord Camden.[1]

July 23rd.—My mother went to her house at Henley.

August 25th.—Mr. Powys and myself went to Mrs. Micklem's, at Reading, for the races. Lords Radnor, and Craven, stewards. Races tolerable, the second ball very good. Four brides, all pretty women, Mrs. Chute of the Vine, Mrs. Derby, Mrs. Stevens, and Mrs.   . Mr. Annesley, of Blechingdon, had a horse run the first day, and won; another the second, and that won. The play acted, as usual, the middle night. On the 29th, the day after the races, Mr. Dundas, chosen Member for the county in room of Mr. Hartley, made the town very gay. A great procession about one o'clock thro' every street. Mr Dundas, accompanied by many gentlemen on horseback and six or seven carriages followed with the freeholders of Berks.

September 2nd.—I rode my poor black horse for the last time; soon after he went blind, and seem'd so uncomfortable to himself, that we thought it were charitable to put him out of his misery, tho' I believe all the family joined with me in tears on this occasion.

October 27.—Our dear Caroline[2] brought to bed of a son.

December 3rd.—Edward Philip Cooper was chris-

---

[1] Lord Camden died April 18, 1794.
[2] Her daughter, Mrs. Cooper.

tened at Harpsden Church.[1]   My mother, Mr. Powys,
Mrs. Williams, and Mr. Henry Austen, sponsors.   He
had been half-christened before.

December 17th.—The severe frost began.

December 25th, Christmas Day.—It begun to snow
early, and lay very deep.   *N.B.*—The weather was
so bad from the 17th that we never could use the
horses for seven weeks.

On the 9th January they dined at Henley Park,
obliged to walk there, accompanied by the maid with
bundles of clothes, as horses could not be used from
snow and ice.   Mrs. Powys stayed two nights, and
says, "In the evenings we play'd many pools at quadrille: that old game was now become fashionable.
Had to walk back in the style we came."

January 24th.—The coldest day that has been
known for years; the glass down to 8.

January 26th.—Snow'd harder than at all, had
never been off the ground, but thawed by the sun in
the daytime, and always froze hard in the night.

February 2nd.—The gentlemen had to walk to
their club at Henley.   The intense cold all January
was hardly bearable.   I could do nothing but read,
was forced to keep warm gloves on, and never quitted
the fireside when indoors, tho' made it a rule to walk
every day when the snow was not falling.   People
were sadly alarm'd about firing, as the coals at Reading and Henley were just gone, and vessels[2] could
not get up with more.   We thought ourselves particularly fortunate that our London stock lasted till the
last week, when we got half a sack from Henley, of

---

[1] Mr. Cooper, then in holy orders, was curate at Harpsden for the
Rev. Thomas Leigh, rector, who was non-resident.

[2] This shows the coals were conveyed in barges.

1795 such terrible sweepings up that they were really of little use, and no wood to be got.

On the 8th February the thaw began; on the 9th a fog and rain, most of the snow gone, but the ice very thick, and such floods all round Henley, even at Fawley, which on such a hill appear'd quite a phenomenon; but the ponds being full of ice, and the ground so hard that rain could not penetrate either, the water ran down the yard and avenue in torrents. On the 11th, managed to drive to Harpsden to see my Caroline, as we had never met since the 23rd December. On the 12th, Phil, Louisa, and Henry came to Fawley, as we had not seen them for the same length of time, but, at the distance of Hardwick, was less surprising; but the weather had not done with us, for at eleven that night it began again to snow.

On the 18th, the hardest frost, and the coldest night, we have had at all. The three following days it snowed all day.

February 25th, the Fast.—My brother being in residence at Bristol, our son, Mr. Cooper, preach'd. The frost had lasted eleven weeks on the fast-day.

March 1st.—Snow as deep on the ground as ever.

March 13th.—Snow not all gone; had been on the ground thirteen weeks.

March 24th.—Went to Hardwick; fine weather.

April 14th.—Mr. Powys and myself went to London. Much ill-health after the severe weather. London and Bath worse than the country.

April 16th.—In the morning went to Mrs. Dawson's, the famous milliner in Pall Mall, to see the new Princess of Wales [1] go for the first time to

---

[1] The unfortunate Caroline of Brunswick, who had been married to the Prince of Wales on April 8, 1795.

the drawing-room in her new state coach.   The 1795
crowd, as one might suppose, was immense ; no carriages allowed to go up or down Pall Mall ; but as
it was a fine day, the companies who could not get
into the houses walk'd for some hours up and down,
and when the Prince's carriages came, made a lane
for them to pass.   It certainly was a fine sight, tho'
almost too gaudy to be pleasing.   On Saturday, we
being out in the carriages, were stopped by another
procession of eighteen carriages, the Lord Mayor
and Sheriffs going with the address on the Prince's
marriage.

April 23rd, First day of Term.—The Lord Chancellor and Judges, attended by forty carriages, went
by Mr. Shrimpton's.[1]

April 29th.—We went to see the panorama views [2]
of the cities of London and Bath.   The latter so very
pleasing and exact, altogether a most wonderful performance.

April 30th.—At the play of " The Country Girl."
Mrs. Jordan excellent as usual.

May 5th.—At the play " Wheel of Fortune."

May 9th.—At the exhibition of pictures of Lord
Howe's [3] victory.   Vastly well worth seeing ; and
another, an exhibition of the House of Commons, in
a large picture on one side of the room, all the portraits in that painted in a large size ; and hung up
on the other side the same apartment, the likenesses
of all the gentlemen I know, so exact they must give
pleasure.

---

[1] Where they were staying ; Mr. Shrimpton had married their friend
Miss Ewer.

[2] At the Colosseum, Regent's Park.

[3] On 1st June 1794 against the French off Ushant.

1795　　The 10th May, the weather again very cold;
fires begun again. The last day of our stay in town
with our kind friends. . . . London life now is every
evening from card-party to card-party, where the heat
of the room is hardly bearable, which, with the terrible
late hours of the present time, makes one not the
least wonder that most people are complaining of bad
health.

Mr. Powys and myself return'd to Fawley, I cannot say (tho' in the country), to still life, for except in
the most important point of late hours, our most agreeable and sociable neighbourhood never suffer their
friends to pass a day solo.

June 9th.—At the course at Ascot Races. The
Royal family there, but being but indifferent weather,
did not get out of their carriages.

June 11th, Thursday.—Again at the races, and
being a fine day, all the Royal family there. They
first drove about in their coaches; the Princess Royal
in a very low phaeton and six Shetland ponies. The
Princess of Wales got out of her coach, and went into
a sort of summer-house built for the family. We saw
her kneel down and kiss the Queen. After that everybody had a near view of her Highness, as the Queen
and about sixteen of them came down and walk'd
with the King, Prince, &c., for two hours within the
railing. The company whose carriages were not near
enough, got out and leant on the railing, and immense
was the crowd; but the Royal family walked round
and round in a group, that every one might see their
new Princess, who seem'd very lively, beautiful complexion, fine hair, and altogether a pretty little figure,
tho' not handsome; dressed (perhaps on purpose),
rather particular, as the other fifteen ladies were in

the dress of the times, all clear muslins; so had her 1795
Highness, but under it a pink petticoat, which look'd
remarkable. She had a purple sash and hat, and a
black lace cloak. There was a cover'd tent within
these rails, where the Royal family all dined, and then
walk'd about again. The King without his hat,
looking so happy and good-humour'd. Before they
went away they all drove about in their carriages
again, and left the numerous spectators all expressing
their satisfaction at the day's diversions, as there had
been besides very great sport on the turf.

June 13th.—Poor Mrs. West[1] died at Rose Hill,
to the great grief of all who knew her. 'Twas a sad
task upon us to break the event to our Louisa, her
sister (Mrs. P. Lybbe Powys, junior), who was then
very near lying-in. Mrs. West was buried on Wednesday 17th, at Walgrave Church, by my brother
Powys, who half-christened the child, who was vastly
well, and a lovely baby.

June 21st.—The longest day; had fires from the
morning, which was a very white frost!

Went to Mrs. Scott's in the morning (Danesfield);
met Lady Skinner and Mrs. Law, who had walk'd
from Culham Court.[2] We all went to see Medmenham Abbey, formerly a famous spot much frequented
by Lord Le Despencer, Wilkes, &c.

June 26th.—A vast deal of rain, and so cold we
still *had fires!*

July 3rd.—Louisa Powys brought to bed of a girl
(Caroline Louisa), at Hardwick House at three in the
morning.

---

[1] *Née* Charlotte Michell.

[2] Culham Court was then let to Mr. and Mrs. Law. Rose Hill was
built by General Hart in Chinese style; had spiral turrets, bells, and
dragons.

On Thursday, 9th July, to the infinite regret of every one who knew him, died at Park Place, Marshal Conway,[1] one of the most worthy of men.   My brother and Mr. Powys had that morning walk'd with him over his delightful grounds, yet one cannot say we were surpris'd at so sudden a seizure at his age, and with his complaints.   It was what we had long been apprehensive of; and that they might not live to enjoy the alterations they were making, which were now nearly completed, having made the house equal to the spot it stands upon. . . . Whoever are the next possessors of it, the present inhabitants of the country must ever remember the kindness and affability of the Marshal and Lady Ailesbury.

July 13*th.*—My brother Powys set out for Ireland on a visit to Lord Camden.   He was appointed first chaplain to the Lord Lieutenant on his going there. Soon after my Lord wrote him word the bishopric of Killala was vacant and at his service, worth about £3000 a year.   My brother sent my Lord word, tho' he must ever feel infinitely obliged by his kind intention, yet at his time of life, to leave family, friends, and country were three things to give up that more than balanced the *three thousand* a year.

July 29*th.*—We had a water-party with the Freemans of Fawley Court, who have a delightful boat, with awning, and every convenience of curtains, &c., to secure one from bad weather.   We set off for Clifden Spring.   Took up Mr. and Mrs. Law from

---

[1] Conway's picture, by Sir Joshua Reynolds, represents him as a good figure, a high, slightly retreating forehead, dark eyes, aquiline nose, well-formed mouth and chin, and amiable expression.   Conway had a slight paralytic stroke in July 1776, but he died of cramp in the stomach, brought on by over-fatigue, and exposure to weather.

Culham Court. It was too cold to dine as usual on 1795
the turf, so got out and walk'd while everything in
the boat was got ready for dinner.

We had all a curiosity to see the ruins of the once
magnificent Clifden House, so we set off, and mounted
a very steep hill; the whole fabric, except one wing,
a scene of ruin—the flight of stone steps all fallen in
pieces; but what seem'd the most unaccountable was,
that the hall, which had fell in, and was a mass of
stone pillars and bricks all in pieces, but two deal
folding-doors not the least hurt, looking as if just
fresh painted! They were the entrance into the inner
hall; an archway over them had fallen in. Poor
Lady Orkney[1] was then residing in the remaining
wing. It seems she was much affected by a will that
was deposited in a place where the flames were too
fierce for anyone to venture, tho' she tried herself, and
a man offer'd to venture too. The contents were not
known, as it was not to be opened till her second son
came of age. The fire at Clifden was on May 20th. We
din'd at Mrs. Freeman's at Henley Park that night,
and about 9.30 the servants came and told us Windsor
Castle was on fire. On returning to Fawley Rectory,
we saw the roof fall in—a tremendous sight; but on
reaching the rectory, from my dressing-room window
I saw it could not be Windsor Castle. The fire was
caused by the carelessness of a servant turning down
a bed. Very few articles of value were saved. The
loss is estimated at £50,000.

August 5th.—Went to Mr. Fane's at Wormsley,
to pay them and the Dowager Lady Macclesfield[2] a

[1] Mary, third Countess of Orkney, daughter of the Countess of
Orkney, and Murrough, first Marquis of Thomond.
[2] Mary, widow of third Earl Macclesfield.

1795 visit. Her Ladyship went next day to her house at Shirburn Woods.

August 23rd.—Fawley Church opened after being repaired.

August 25th.—My brother return'd that day from Ireland, very much entertain'd by his visits to the Lord Lietunant,[1] and admiring many parts of that country, tho' not regretting having refused being a bishop there. He told us 'tis amazing the style of living at the Castle, Dublin, and Phœnix Park. His King *there*, he said, lived with infinitely more state than his King in *England!* Lord Camden sent Caroline and me each an Irish stuff.[2]

August 28th.—A fishing-party with the Coopers. Took a cold dinner to Mr. Freeman's island. I caught two dozen and three.

September 2nd.—Had our annual buck from Blenheim.

September 9th.—Fishing-party and cold dinner at Medmenham Abbey.

September 15th.—To Hardwick.

September 16th.—Phil's little daughter christened at Whitchurch by the name of Caroline Louisa—Mr. West, Caroline, and myself godparents.

September 22nd.—A fishing-party with the Laws, Culham Court. The Goldings with them; caught thirty-two dozen gudgeon. I caught six dozen and four that day.

November 26th.—Another fishing-party with the Fawley Court family, &c. We had a very elegant dinner at their island.

November 29th.—Our dear Caroline[3] brought to bed of a daughter, Isabella Mary.

---

[1] His old pupil, first Marquis Camden.   [2] Poplins.
[3] Mrs. Cooper, of Harpsden Rectory.

December 14*th.*—Mr. Powys and myself dined at 1795
Park Place.[1] Lady Ailesbury insisted on our going.
It was a visit we much wished to avoid, as her
Ladyship was going to quit that sweet place for ever
the next day but one, and, of course, everything
bore so melancholy an appearance that it was hardly
possible to keep up one's spirits on the thoughts of
losing so kind a neighbour. Mrs. S. Hervey, Mrs.
Jennings,[2] &c., were there.

January 1*st*, 1796.—At the christening of Isabella 1796
Mary (Cooper), at Harpsden, myself and Mrs. Leigh
godmothers, Dr. Powys godfather. Stayed to dinner
and supper; not home till two in the morning.
Weather very different from last year; quite mild,
had no frosts, but high winds and rain.

I paid my first visit to Mrs. Atkyns,[3] Crouchley
Park.

January 7*th.*—The Princess of Wales brought to
bed of a daughter.[4] *N.B.*—On my birthday!

February 18*th.*—The Gentlemen's Club at March's,
" Red Lion," (Henley-on-Thames).

February 22*nd.*—The same. Louisa and I dined
with the Coopers, who were return'd from the Isle
of Wight, and who were fortunate to see Captain
Williams, who came to refit his ship, and *was detain'd a whole month for want* of an east wind.

Thursday, February 25*th.*—Mr. Powys and myself
to Bath. Mr. P.'s health had long wanted the waters,

---

[1] Amongst other gifts Lady Ailesbury gave Mrs. Powys when leaving
Park Place, were fourteen quires of paper containing plants, sea-weeds,
roses, &c., she had collected.

[2] Of Shiplake Court.

[3] Crowsley Park, Oxon. Mr. Atkyns was heir to his aunt, Mrs.
Wright, and after her death assumed the name of Atkyns Wright.

[4] Princess Charlotte.

1796 but I was too ill to go sooner. Lay that night at Mrs. Micklem's, Reading. Set off next morning at 7.30 A.M.; got to the "White Lion," Bath, by six. Next morning into lodgings, No. 9 George Street.

March 9th.—Had the pleasure of hearing Dr. Randolph preach, and on fast-day my brother, Mr. Powys, came from Bristol to preach at the Octagon, whose sermon was so generally admir'd, he was much desir'd to print it. I had the pleasure of seeing Mr. Powys' health mend daily, my own was very indifferent the whole time I was there. Only went to two plays and one dress-ball, but card-parties impossible to escape, both at Bath and London. One evening was much entertain'd by Breslaus,[1] whom we had not seen for years. At one time he made five or six of us think of the same card, desired from different gentlemen each to take a piece of money from their own pockets, mark them as they liked, lay each down on the table under a card. He never came near the table, but in a few minutes desired them to look for their own pieces under some lids of boxes on another table, and see if their marks were what they made. Wonderful how he could deceive one. The elegant new pump-room is finish'd since we were last at Bath, which renders the crowd in meeting there, much more commodious than it used to be.

April 4th.—Left Bath for home.

April 14th.—Dined at West's, Rose Hill. The christening of his little girl.

June 21st.—We dined at Mrs. Winford's, Thames Bank, and went before dinner to see Mr. Williams' new house, called Temple,[2] near Marlow. It's certainly

---

[1] A conjurer.   [2] The seat of General Owen P. Williams.

a very good one, but fitted up and furnish'd in so 1796
odd and superb a style, that one cannot help fancy-
ing oneself in one of those palaces mention'd in the
Arabian Nights' Entertainments ; but what surprised
us, there is not a picture, but that of Mr. Williams
himself. Statues of every kind, and at the farther
end of a most magnificent greenhouse is an aviary
full of all kinds of birds, flying loose in a large octagon
of gilt wire, in which is a fountain in the centre, and
in the evening 'tis illuminated by wax-lights, while
the water falls down some rock-work in form of a
cascade. This has a pretty effect, but seems to alarm
its beautiful inhabitants, and must be cold for them,
I should imagine. . . . We came away amazingly
pleased with having seen so extraordinary a place as
Temple must be justly esteem'd.

July 2nd.—Our daughter, Louisa Powys, brought
to bed of a girl.

July 6th.—Stayed with Caroline, Mr. Cooper being
gone to London to meet his brother,[1] Captain Williams,
who soon after had the honour of being knighted by
his Majesty for his gallant behaviour at sea.

July 16th.—My brother received a letter from his
Excellency Lord Camden, saying that Lord Rawdon,
a few days before, had offer'd him a living in Essex
to give to any one he chose, and if it was agreeable
to our son Thomas,[2] it was at his service. So very
unexpected a kindness from his Lordship, through
whose interest my brother Dr. Powys had only the
week before received the promise of being made a
Canon of Windsor, was almost too much for our gratitude to express by thanks.

---

[1] Brother-in-law.
[2] Mrs. Powys's second son. It was High Rhoding, in Essex.

1796   *July 23rd.*—We all dined at the Speaker's, Mr. Addington,[1] at Woodley Lodge,[2] near Reading.

July 26th.—My brother the Doctor went to London to kiss hands on being made Canon of Windsor.

It is impossible to quote all Mrs. Powys's diary, and only the most generally interesting portions are selected, but to those who are interested in the neighbourhood of Fawley, I give the following list of people living in the different houses with whom a ceaseless round of hospitality was given and exchanged.   Her *most intimate friends* were her own relations the Coopers of Harpsden, and Bix ; Mr. West of Culham and Rose Hill, brother-in-law of Mrs. Lybbe Powys, junior ; the Freemans of Henley Park and Fawley Court ; Winfords of Thames Bank ; Grotes of Badgemoor ; Stonors of Stonor, (afterwards Lord Camoys) ; Atkyns Wrights of Crowsley ; Laws, then renting Culham Court ; Botelers of "Paradise House," Henley ; Macclesfields of Shirburn Castle ; the Fanes of Wormsley, and Stapletons of Greys ; Hall of Harpsden Court ; Fanshawes, Jennings, and Howmans of Shiplake.   The Rev. Arthur Howman was vicar of Shiplake fifty years ; he was also a Canon of Windsor, &c.

August 4th.—Dr. Powys went to his month's residence at Windsor, and on 14th September dined at Mr. West's,[3] Culham Court.

October 7th.—Lady Williams sent for from Harps-

---

[1] Afterwards Prime Minister, and in 1805 created Viscount Sidmouth. Married only daughter of Lord Stowell.

[2] Now called Earley Court.

[3] Mr. West from thenceforth lived at Culham Court. The Laws, his late tenants, continued to live in the neighbourhood.

den to Portsmouth, to meet Sir Thomas there, who
had taken five more frigates.

October 18th.—The Coopers, Mr. Coulson, and all
of us to Hardwick. Sophia Charlotte's christening
at Whitchurch. Dr. Powys godfather. Tom performed the ceremony.

October 22nd.—All our gentlemen dined with Mr.
Cooper of Bix, on a turtle.

November 7th.—I paid my first visit to Lady
Malmesbury,[1] as that family were just come to Park
Place, which they had purchased on the death of our
ever-to-be-regretted neighbour, Marshal Conway.

November 22nd.—Went from Hardwick, where we
had been staying, to Bath.

November 26th.—The Duke[2] and Duchess of York
came to their house in the Crescent, the centre one,
which they have just purchased, and the next day the
Prince of Wales came to them. We were that Sunday
at Queen's Square Chapel. The Duchess had taken
a seat there, and was handed in by one of the gentlemen, her attendants, and the beautiful Mrs. Bunbury[3]
was with her Royal Highness.

November 30th.—At the concert new rooms to
hear Signora Storacé.

December 3rd.—At the play, "The Dramatist,"
and "Agreeable Surprise." The Duchess there, who
was at all the public amusements.

December 15th.—Mr. Shrimpton and Mr. Powys
dined at the Marquis of Lansdowne's.[4] Among many

---

[1] Lord Malmesbury, a diplomatist of the first rank, son of James
Harris, Secretary and Controller of Household to Queen Charlotte.

[2] Second son of George III.

[3] Lady Sarah Bunbury, *née* Lennox, daughter of second Duke of
Richmond, much admired by George III. in his youth.

[4] William, second Marquis.

1796 other gentlemen the Archbishop of Bordeaux, a very agreeable man. He could not talk English. He now lives on a pension from our Government, tho' formerly in such state and magnificence at Bordeaux, as to have treated two regiments in his courtyard.

December 22nd.—At the play to see Miss Wallace as " Beatrice," in " With the Lock and Key."

December 28th.—To see Miss Wallace act " The Jealous Wife," which she performed incomparably.

1797 *January 2nd,* 1797.—Monday, January 2, was Mr. Tyson's ball at the Upper Rooms,[1] and I fancy never any master of the ceremonies had a fuller, or one more magnificent, from the number of persons of quality then at Bath, of whom I will set down a list of those I can recollect seeing there. We were obliged to go an hour before it began to get a tolerable place, but by that means were fortunate to get very good ones near the throne (sofa, so called), placed there for the Royal Family. When they enter'd, the whole company got up, and continued standing while "God Save the King" and "The Duke of York's[2] March" was played. The Duchess of York, and Princess of Orange were first led up the room and seated on the throne, the ladies of quality on benches on each side. The gentlemen none of them sat down, but the Prince of Wales, Duke of York, the Stadtholder, Prince of Orange, and many noblemen stood and talk'd to the ladies till the ball began, when they mixed with the crowd, which was immense, above 1400.[3] I will now put down the

---

[1] Built by Wood in 1771, not the same rooms Beau Nash ruled over till his death in 1761.

[2] The Duke was Commander-in-Chief of the Forces.

[3] The ball-room of the Upper Assembly Rooms was 1c6 feet long.

names of the nobility I remember to have been there, 1797 tho' I've no doubt I shall omit many.

Prince of Wales.
Duke and Duchess of York.
The Stadtholder and Princess of Orange.
The Prince of Orange.
Lord and Lady Harcourt.
The Chancellor [1] and Lady Loughborough.
Lady Mary Howe, and her sister.
Lord and Lady Clifden.
Earl of Sussex.
Earl of Galloway.
Earl of Miltown.
Earl of Strafford.
Lord Molesworth.
Viscountess Downe.
Earl of Peterborough
Lord Ashbrook.
Lady de Clifford.
Marquis and Marchioness of Blandford.
Duke and Duchess of Beaufort.
Duchess of Rutland.
Marquis of Bute.
Earl and Countess Inchiquin.
Right Hon. Lord Caledon.
Lady Mary Knox.
Earl and Countess of Altamont.
Countess of Ormonde.
Lady E. Butler.
Lady G. Sutton.
Earl Milton.
Lord Thynne.
Marquis of Worcester.
Lord Malden.
Lady Elizabeth Chaplin, Lady C. Johnstone.
Count Travinville.
Earl and Countess of Cork.
Duke and Duchess of Newcastle and two daughters.
Earl of Peterborough.

[1] Then Lord High Chancellor.

Earl of Plymouth.
Lord and Lady Hood.
Lord Coleraine.
Marquis of Lansdowne.
Countess of Ely.
Lady Malmesbury.
Lords George and J. Beresford.
Besides Baronets and their wives, innumerable.

January 3rd.—At the play "The Deuce is in Him." The Royal Family there, and when Signora Storacé sang "God Save the King," I do believe half the audience shed tears, as her manner, voice, and action was beyond anything one could imagine.

January 6th.—King's ball; the master of the ceremonies of lower rooms; a very full one, but nothing like Tyson's. Indeed, many of the nobility had gone, and the Prince, Duke, and Stadtholder's family; very disagreeably crowded; rooms smaller. The Duchess of York left early.

Mrs. Norman had her post-chaise weighed, and it was thirteen and a half cwt. and five pounds, without the coach-box, trunk, chaise seat, or imperial. We none of us imagin'd it would have been so much. The pump-woman gives £1000 a year for the place. To mend the road two miles the London way costs £22 a week.

January 11th.—We walked about the whole morning to take leave of our favourite place. The pump-room very full of company, many emigrants, and one with large gold earrings; to us in England this appear'd extraordinary, but is, I believe, common in France.

January 14th.—Returned to Fawley.

January 23rd.—At a very elegant ball at Mr. West's, Culham Court. About fifty were met about

eight, and came home by six. His sister, Lady Matilda 1797
Wynyard, and the Colonel were there to stay.   Little
Miss West[1] came into the ball-room just before she
went to bed, and seemed quite pleased with the music
and dancing.

February 7th.—Had a letter of the death of Mrs.
Hill of Court of Hill, Shropshire.   We all went into
mourning.

February 15th.—Doctor Powys kissed hands on
being appointed Dean of Canterbury.[2] When he
went to the Queen's drawing-room her Majesty said
she supposed she ought to congratulate him, but
hardly could, as they should so feel his loss as Canon
of Windsor, and desired she might have wrote out
the four sermons he had preached to them there,
which, as soon as he returned to Fawley, he did, and
sent them with the following lines to her Majesty :—

"To Her Majesty.

"Madam,

"By your command (which who can disobey?)
These humble pages at your feet I lay,
Which in the plainest language of the heart,
The preacher's unaffected zeal impart :
Not that the truths I teach, the rules I give,
Can make you better think, or better live ;
But when on Britain's throne the Royal pair
Is known to make religion's cause their care,
And their example a support affords,
To Truth and Virtue, (past the power of words),
In strongest language taught, their subjects see,
From what they are, what others ought to be."

---

[1] Charlotte Louisa, only child of Mr. West by his first marriage. She
died in 1869 unmarried.
[2] Mr. Pitt was instrumental in this.

1797 *March 8th, Fast-day.*—The Dean preached before the House of Commons from 2 Chron. xv. 2.[1]

March 15th.—I rode out most days on horseback, as I had now got a little Welsh pony to carry me vastly well, which, after losing my black, I hardly expected.

March 27th.—Caroline and Cooper went to London to Sir Thomas Williams, to see his new ship, the *Endymion,* launched.

April 22nd.—The Dean went to Windsor, from thence to London and Canterbury.

May 18th.—The Dean returned from Canterbury.

May 24th.—Caroline (Cooper), brought to bed of a girl (Cassandra).

June 19th.—Died Mr. Vanderstegen at Cannon's End, near Hardwick, Oxfordshire.

July 7th. — Cassandra Louisa's christening at Harpsden Church. Mrs. Austen and my daughter Louisa godmothers, Dr. Isham godfather.

July 21st.—Went to stay with Mrs. Winford at Thames Bank. We all went to a play at Marlow, bespoke by Major Goodenough, "My Grandmother" and "The Chapter of Accidents," very well acted indeed for a strolling company, and in a barn, that had not a stage to show the performers to advantage.

August 21st.—The Dean went to Windsor.

September 4th.—Poor Mrs. Micklem died at her house at Reading, the greatest loss to all who knew her.

October 10th.—First Henley ball.

November 6th.—Henley ball.

---

[1] This sermon was printed by desire, and the thanks of the House formally tendered. The Dean was Chaplain-in-Or inary to the King.

November 20th.—The Dean went to Canterbury. 1797
We had intended going with him, but afterwards
thought it better to defer our first visit to the large
old Deanery till summer.

December 19th.—I went to Harpsden. Mr. Powys
and Tom went to Bletchingdon Park to shoot, and
were robbed by a highwayman only four miles from
Henley, on the Oxford road, just at three o'clock.
We hear the poor man was drowned the week after,
by trying to escape, (after having robbed a carriage),
through some water which was very deep. He
behaved civilly, and seemed, as he said, greatly distress'd.

December 23rd.—Edward drove Caroline and myself to Reading in the tandem.

January 29th, 1798.—The Gentlemen's Club. Caro- 1798
line and I met the Fawley Court family at the Henley play. All the gentlemen came to the farce ; a
very full house, and better performers than one would
have imagined. "The Jew" and "The Poor Soldier." The company put £100 into the Henley Bank
to answer any demands upon them, and as a surety
of their good behaviour. Rather unusual for strollers in general.

February 8th.—We all went to the Henley play,
bespoke by the Freemans. A very full house, and
to add to its brilliancy, the beautiful Miss Jennings [1]
was there.

March 1st.—Set off for Bath. Went in the Dean's
chaise to Newbury. From thence took a post-chaise
and lay at Marlborough. Reached Bath about three

[1] The daughter of the virtuoso Henry Constantine Jennings, of
Shiplake Court, by his second wife, Miss Nowell. Miss Jennings
afterwards became Mrs. Lock.

1798 on the 2nd. Friends were very angry with us, but we told them the truth, that we really wish to live a rather quieter life than theirs, but would certainly see them every day as long as they stay'd, but begged to be excused so many dinners and parties, as Mr. Powys riding, and I constantly walking all the mornings, we were so old-fashioned a couple as to enjoy ourselves (by ourselves), sometimes of evenings, rather than be always in such immense crowded rooms.

March 24*th.*—At a party at Miss Cresswell's. Met Miss Sally More, sister to Mrs. Hannah More.

March 30*th.*—In the morning we went to see the exhibition of ivory-work, most exceedingly curious ; Windsor Castle, Greenwich Hospital, Eddystone Lighthouse, &c., most ingeniously carved from solid pieces of ivory. Likenesses of their Majesties astonishing well done. Any device carved for lockets, bracelets, rings, or toothpick cases in as small pieces as I did the cherry-stone baskets, and done with something like the same knives ; and must be equally trying to the eyes. 'Tis done by Stephany and Dresch, the only artists in this line.

April 3*rd.*—Went to Mrs. Lutwyche's party (always at home on Tuesdays). We thought there were numbers of people, but Mrs. Lutwyche express'd herself quite hurt two or three times that Mr. Powys and I should be there the first time when she had hardly any company, "only seven tables,[1] and that is so very few, you know, Ma'am." I really am very ignorant, for I did not know it, and thought it a squeeze ; but how unfashionable I am in disliking these immense parties I kept secret.

April 8*th.*—Went to the Octagon Chapel with

---

[1] Card-tables.

the Badderleys, to hear the famous Dr. Randolph. 1798
Indeed he is a very good preacher, not quite so
pompous as his predecessor.

April 11th.—Went in the evening to the Fantoc-
cini. The whole in French, entertaining for once.
Our daughter, Louisa Powys, was this day brought to
bed of a son, Richard Thomas Powys.

April 14th.—Returned to Fawley.

May 26th.—This week we heard of my cousin
Wheatley's eldest son, Captain Wheatley of the Guards,
being taken by the French at Ostend.

May 20th.—Dined at the Bishop of Durham's,
Mongewell.

June 14th.—The Hon. Frederick West [1] married
to Miss Maria Middleton, of Chirk Castle.

June 23rd.—I went to Brown's, the famous gardener at Slow (Slough), and purchased a number of
plants.

July 12th.—We all went to pay the bridal visit at
Culham Court, and found Mr. and Mrs. West at home.
Were most highly entertain'd by her playing on the
pianoforte, accompanied by him on the tambourine.

On Thursday, the 26th July, Mr. Powys and myself
set off to pay the Dean our first visit at Canterbury.

CANTERBURY JOURNAL

1798

We left Fawley about ten, and got to Mr. Shrimpton's in London by three. We stayed in town all the
next day, as we wish'd to see Miss Linwood's worsted
work, then exhibiting at Hanover Square Concert

---

[1] Of Culham Court. His second marriage.

1798 Rooms,[1] and tho' we had heard so much in its praise, it fully answered every expectation ; indeed it is beyond description.   They are chiefly taken from the most celebrated artists, as Raphael, Guido, Rubens, Sir Joshua Reynolds, Stubbs, Opie, &c., thirty-four pieces, besides the cave with a lion and tigress, which being at the upper part of the room, had a very fine effect. In the inner apartment is a fine whole-length Salvator Mundi, by Carlo Dolci.[2]   We observed several Catholic gentlemen take off their hats as they stood admiring this fine portrait.   Many people, I'm certain, must take many of them for real paintings, instead of needlework.   It happened to be a pleasant day, and not too hot for walking, and as in London there are so many shops to dispose of one's money in articles one is apt to think cannot be got in the country, we traversed the streets from eleven to three, and again in the evening, but the Metropolis seem'd totally deserted, even in Bond Street hardly a coach to be seen.   However, we had the unexpected pleasure of meeting Lord Camden, whom we had not seen since his return from Ireland, and he made us quite happy in telling us he intended to pay a visit at Canterbury the next week.

We were not sorry to quit the dull town [3] the next morning.

Saturday, July 28th.—We got to Mr. Wheatley's about half-past two, and were received with the greatest cordiality by our relations at Lefney House,

---

[1] Miss Linwood continued to exhibit till her death in 1845.   In all, she worked sixty-five pictures in crewels on fine linen, exquisitely worked and shaded.   A picture of Napoleon is in the South Kensington Museum.

[2] She refused 2000 guineas for this, and bequeathed it to the Queen. Lord Spencer has several of her pictures.

[3] When is London dull now?

which they built some few years since, a fine situation 1798
about four miles from Dartford in Kent. A beautiful
view of the river, and long reach just opposite Par-
fleet, where the *Dragon, Ajax,* and some frigates lay,
with so many vessels constantly passing and repassing,
make a most pleasing scene. Not so at the time
of the Mutiny,[1] as the *Lancaster* lay just against
Lefney, and caused so much alarm that Mr. Wheatley[2]
sent to the Admiralty for assistance. Major Wheatley, their eldest son, is now among the Guards that
were taken prisoners at Ostend. They have often
letters from him that they are all well treated and
in good health. The latter is certainly a comfort to
his family ; but as to the first, as the letters are seen,
and sent open, it may or may not be true. His lady
had just lain-in of a son at the time he went ; how
great must her anxiety have been in such a situation.

Mr. John Wheatley and Mr. Keeling (related to
them, and to my mother by the Mitfords), were staying
at Lefney. Miss Wheatley, and the most beautiful
boy of three years old, little Leonard, quite the darling
of his parents as well as the whole family, and one
could not help laughing when one thought of the
dear little soul in the character of an uncle !

Sunday we had prayers and sermon at home, as
no morning service that day at their parish church.

Monday, July 30th.—Went to see our old acquaintance, Lady Hardy, who when we lived at Hardwick
House, Sir Charles and her Ladyship then resided
about four miles from us at Woodcot Clump, Oxon.
From thence we went to Lady Fermough's at May

---

[1] General mutiny in the Royal Navy, 1797.
[2] Mrs. Wheatley was a daughter of Mrs. Hussey (*née* Slaney), so
first cousin to Mrs. Powys.

1798 Place. We had the pleasure of meeting there besides the family our Bath acquaintances, Mr. and Mrs. Lutwyche, and the two Miss Mayos. After this we call'd at Mr. Harance, Foots Cray Place, a house built after the model of Lord Le Despencer's—of course a magnificent one, many fine pictures.

Tuesday, July 31st.—We left my cousin Wheatley's after a most agreeable visit. As we passed through Dartford we had been desired to notice a very particular circumstance when you are up the hill at the end of the town, viz., the churchyard being higher than the steeple of the church, and it really is literally so, as we saw the tombstones above the spire! The road is beautiful the whole way. From Gravel Hill you've a fine view of Greenhithe Water, where at that time was a fleet of colliers; at the 18th milestone you see Mr. Roebuck's; at the 20th, Northfleet; at the 22nd you have a view of Gravesend, with the several men-of-war and East India ships lying there; on the right, about the 26th milestone, is Lord Darnley's[1] and Mr. Day's, called the Hermitage; at the 27th, 28 miles from London, is Rochester, which seems but an indifferent town. After you are through it, you see Chatham across the river Medway, and the Marine Barracks. The *Temeraire*, man-of-war lay there. Then we got up Rochester Hill, had a view of the Nore at the 31st milestone, and three men-of-war, the *Pallas*, *Scorpion*, and *Isis*. Changed horses at Sittingbourne, 39 miles from London; after through the town, had a view of that of Feversham. Broughton Hill we at last arriv'd at, which we had been shown by our postboy 14 miles off as being to ascend. Indeed,

[1] Cobham Hall.

if it were not for the many beautiful views, and all 1798
being new, the road is so hilly and sandy it must
have appeared tiresome, as in one distance of 15
miles you go up sixteen hills, and, indeed, having
calculated our time by other roads, we sent the
Dean word we should certainly be with him to
dinner by half-past four, and at last he began to be
alarmed, as it was past seven before we reach'd
Canterbury.

In driving up to the Deanery[1] through the Green
Court, as 'tis called, of fine elms, we were much
struck by its appearance, as instead of the forlorn
old brick mansion we had expected, we saw a good-
looking white stone house, nine sash windows in
front besides the staircase, a venetian one, and on
entering found the inside contain'd many capital
rooms, modernly furnished, but as we were rather
fatigued we did not go over the apartments till after
dinner. On one side the hall is now a very good
eating-room, on the other the library; an excellent
staircase which leads to two very noble drawing-
rooms. In the first, which is 35 feet by 22, are the
pictures of seventeen deans; some (as now bishops in
lawn sleeves), of these portraits have really a pleasing
effect. Out of the first drawing-room is another
large one, and out of each excellent bed-chambers.
In the first drawing-room are seventeen of the Deans'
pictures, two very good ones in the eating-room,
the present Archbishop of Canterbury, Dr. Moore,
and Worth, Bishop of Winchester. The four last
Deans have not yet given theirs, which I think is
not right, as they are certainly very ornamental in
such a house, and there is room for twenty more

[1] Once the Priory. Built by Prior Goldstone in 1494.

1798 at least, tho' the best room is fill'd.[1] In another part of the house is that styled the Archbishop's bedchamber and dressing-room, and many more, tho' not so large, and in the back part of the house numbers of small ones and spiral staircases, dark passages, &c., &c., which put one in mind of the haunted castles in our present novels, and in that antique style I had formed my idea of the whole house; but, as I before said, it has been greatly modernised by one of the late Deans.

Wednesday, August 1st.—I had numbers of ladies to visit me on my arrival, thirty-four, as I see by the list on the first three mornings in and around Canterbury; and Mr. Powys nearly as many gentlemen. I'm sure the whole circle were uncommonly polite in their attentions to us. We that evening drank tea at Dr. Wolsby's. one of the prebends; they have an excellent house in the Green Court, close to the Deanery; in their drawing-room a very fine picture of Prince William of Gloucester[2] when young. Dr. Wolsby was tutor to his Royal Highness. We met at Mr. Wolsby's Mr. Hallett, his sister, and two nieces, Miss Hayes and Mrs. Cotton. We had seen Mr. Hallett some years back at Culham Court. After tea we all walked to "The Oaks," another Green so-called, to see the regiments of the York, Hereford, West Kent, and supplementary militia perform their exercise, and a very pretty sight it was; the music

---

.[1] Mrs. Powys would be satisfied now, as thirty portraits of deans hang in the house, and Dean Farrar, the thirty-first, has had them all cleaned. The following are the pictures in Mrs. Powys' time : Wotton, Goldstone, Rogers, Nevil, Fotherly, Boys, Bargrave, Eglionby, Turner, Tillotson, Sharp, Hooper, Stanhope, Lydall, Lynch, Friend, Pelter, North, Moore.

[2] Duke of Gloucester, and brother of George III.

of some of the bands very fine.   Colonel Cotterel 1798
(a relation of Mrs. Freeman of the Park [1]), was so
obliging as to have his band entertaining the ladies
(of whom numbers attend every evening), till half-
past nine, always ending with "God save the King."
After that was concluded we all walk'd home.

Thursday, August 2nd.—My Lord Camden, who
had fixed for coming to see my brother that week,
came to dinner, and brought with him the Bishop of
Clogher, the gentleman to whom his Lordship had
given the Bishopric of Killala when my brother
refused it.   The Bishop is a most agreeable man,
and we were all happy that he was removed from
Killala,[2] though the poor man seem'd quite melancholy
at the thought of returning to Ireland, now my Lord
Camden [3] was come to England.   Most happy were
we all to see his Lordship again, and express our
gratitude for the obligations he has conferr'd on our
family.   He look'd vastly well, and, as ever, a most
agreeable, sensible man.   Mr. Wilson, one of the
Canons of Windsor, who was tutor to Mr. Pitt, came
to us that day for dinner, and as we had no lack
of bedrooms, as at Fawley, he lay at the Deanery,
as he was going to Walmer Castle (Mr. Pitt's [4]), the
next day.   We had a great deal of company that
morning, and Dr. and Mrs. Wolsby to dinner.

Friday, August 3rd.—Lord Pembroke and Lord
Malmesbury in the morning.

Saturday, August 4th.—Lord Camden left us to

[1] Henley Park, Oxon.
[2] This was the year of the Irish Rebellion.
[3] On account of the Rebellion, Lord Camden was recalled by the
Government, and a Viceroy who possessed military experience appointed
in the Marquis Cornwallis.
[4] Pitt was then Warden of the Cinque Ports.

1798 pay a visit to Mr. Pitt. The Bishop stayed with
us a few days, and was so obliging as to attend me
that morning to see the Cathedral, which I think
is one of the finest pieces of Gothic architecture I
ever saw.

August 5th, Sunday. — The anniversary of our
36th wedding-day! I had that morning at Canterbury a most formal ceremony to go through, tho' not
quite equal to the above-mentioned in 1762!   At
half-past ten we went to the Cathedral ; my gentlemen,
who were to sit in stalls by the Dean's, proceeded to
another door, and I was conducted solo by the Verger
in a black gown and cap, holding a long staff, all up
the choir, through such a concourse of officers, soldiers,
ladies, gentlemen, and inhabitants, that I began to
think I never should reach the Dean's lady's pew, as
it is styled, quite at the upper end, where, when arrived,
I was locked in by myself, and, as I supposed, every
soul observing me, being in full view of the whole
congregation (but one soon finds use reconcile one to
most things, as the next Sunday I did not feel near
so much at the same entrée).   The Archdeacon, Dr.
Lynch, preached about twenty-five minutes, a most
worthy, good, kind man. As to cathedral-worship, I
daresay I may be wrong, but the chanting one's
prayers does not to me seem devotion properly expressed, and in general the clergymen who read them,
and the boys who repeat, seem so evidently endeavouring to excel each other in vociferous exclamation, that
it gives their characters too frivolous an appearance.
As to anthems or sacred music in that style, it must
ever be most awfully pleasing. After the service was
over, at which numbers of regiments attended (as there
was then in Canterbury four or five thousand militia),

the rest are assembled in the Cathedral churchyard, 1798
and walk two by two into the outward part of the
Cathedral, as a pulpit has been there erected, and
divine service constantly performed to all those who
had not been before. Mrs. Bridges desired me to
come to her house to see the procession, as she has
a beau-window just near to the great door. . . . We
din'd on Sundays at three, the evening service beginning at five.

Monday 6th.—After returning many visits, we took
a long walk to what is call'd the Dungeon, but properly Dain John, a sort of terrace above the city.
On our return, Mrs. Wolsby conducted me through
all the streets, but I must own I was disappointed
in the appearance of Canterbury, though the inhabitants say 'tis amazingly improved lately. What it must
have been I can hardly guess, as now 'tis certainly
a melancholy, dirty town, streets all so narrow, and
hardly any smart shops, whereas now in most country
towns there are many capital ones.

Tuesday 7th.—The Bishop of Clogher left us to
meet Lord Camden at Mr. Pitt's at Walmer Castle.
Mr. Pitt had sent to desire the Dean would come
with him and lay there, which he did. Mr. Powys and
myself dined that day at Mr. Hallett's at Higham, a
sweet place four miles from Canterbury on Barham
Downs; fine prospect, very good house, and a distant
view of Ramsgate Cliff. Our party at dinner twelve.
. . . They wished us to stay cards, but as no moon
and the days getting short, most of the company
begg'd to be excused, and we got home by nine,
just in time to hear "God save the King," play'd
by the band arranged before Dr. Wolsby's house in
the Green Court, where Prince William had dined

1798 with a large party. We were all invited, but had
been engaged some days before to Mr. Hallett. . . .

Thursday, August 9th. — The Dean and Mr.
Powys dined at the Archdeacon's, a large party of
gentlemen.   I went in the evening to a card-party
at Mrs. Bridges; only three tables, about thirty-six
of us; several ladies from the country.   As winter and
summer seem quite equal for routs [1] at Canterbury,
every evening the card-tables are set out.   Friday,
Mr. and Mrs. Shrimpton and Mr. Ewer came to stay
with us.

Sunday, 12th.—At the Cathedral, dined at Dr.
Wolsby's, went at three to evening service, drank
tea at the Doctor's, and after, we all walked to Mrs.
Milnes' at The Oaks, who had desir'd us to come to
her house to see the soldiers exercise, and hear the
band play.   Mrs. Milnes' house in The Oaks is an
ancient mansion, extremely large; indeed, there are a
great number of good ones belonging to the church,
within the precincts.

Monday 13th.—We all set off to Barham Downs
by ten A.M. to see the troops reviewed.   Twenty
cannons fired a *feu-de-joie* in honour of the Prince
of Wales' birthday (then thirty-six years of age).
The whole garrison of the city paraded on the ground
in front of the Royal Cavalry Barracks, and made
a most brilliant appearance, forming a square consisting of artillery, the Prince of Wales', and the
17th Dragoons, the West Kent, and Hereford Militia,
with the supplementary men attached to each battalion,
forming a body of near 5000 men.   At eleven Sir
Charles Grey came into the field, where he was met
by Prince William of Gloucester, the Earl of Pem-

---

[1] Old-fashioned name for this class of entertainment.

broke,[1] &c. The concourse of people, as one may 1798
suppose, was very great; in general the horses were
taken from the carriages, and the company either
remain'd sitting in them, or walk'd in parties on the
Downs. The review over, the music ended with
"God save the King." On our way back we paid
a visit to the Milnes. We were not at home till three,
then dressed and went to dinner at Mrs. Peiray's, a
large party of thirteen, and in the evening a great
deal more company to tea and cards.

August 14th.—We that morning received a letter
from our son Thomas, with the most melancholy
intelligence of the death of Lady Williams by a most
unfortunate accident. As she was driving herself in
a whisky, a dray-horse ran away and drove against
the chaise, by which she was thrown out and killed
on the spot;[2] never spoke after. We were so alarm'd
for our dear Mr. Cooper,[3] whose health had been so
bad for some time, and who was one of the most
affectionate of brothers, that we were quite miserable,
and wrote immediately to Caroline that, if they the
least wished it, we would return immediately after
we received her next letter, and, as that must be
some days coming, we were greatly distress'd, and
hardly knew how to manage, as the very next day
had been some time fixed on for us all to set out for
our intended tour through the Isle of Thanet; but
when we came to consult about what was best to
be done, we all thought, as our journey was to be
only three days, we should really be much quieter
and more alone than we could be at Canterbury, and

---

[1] George Augustus, eleventh Earl.
[2] This happened at Newport, Isle of Wight.
[3] Their son-in-law, and brother to Lady Williams.

1798 should be returned before the letter from home could arrive; so on Wednesday, August 15th, Mr. and Mrs. Shrimpton, Mr. Ewer, Mr. Powys, and myself set off a little after nine for Margate. On the right we passed Hystreath, a Mr. Dean's, and Renlow Church and ruins on the left, and one mile from Margate the famous inn call'd "Dandelion," where are breakfastings in the season at 1s. 6d. each; sometimes 700 people there, balls, masquerades, &c.; for the latter there were then printed advertisements posted up for the week following. We got to Margate a little before one,[1] seventeen miles from Canterbury, It is now become one of the first watering-places in the kingdom; the town well pav'd and lighted, many new buildings; Harley Square very fine; the assembly-rooms remarkably elegant, near 100 feet by 40. There are three public libraries, but Hall's claims the pre-eminence. In the centre a beautiful chandelier; in the piazza round the library, seats are fixed for the accommodation of the company; trinkets and toys of every description, which are raffled for, from one shilling to five guineas every evening. We din'd and lay at Mitchener's Hotel, from whence is a most noble view of the sea. Two English men-of-war, the *Alchmeer* and *Iris*, Swedish frigates, and thirteen merchant ships of that nation detained there. It was not known what their lading consisted of, but the largest supposed to be bomb-shells. As the hotel is on the Parade, numbers of these ships were close under our windows. 'Tis very unfortunate that few if any of the lodging-houses have a view of the sea, which makes most families prefer Ramsgate. We walked about till dinner-time, and again in the

[1] Four hours doing seventeen miles shows the state of the roads then.

evening on the pier, for rebuilding of which an Act 1798
of Parliament was obtained in 1787, and is now
finished, and is the fashionable promenade of the
place. A fine large shop is opened there, where the
company may have fruit, cakes, ices, jellies, &c.
Seven yachts go to, and from London every day, from
70 to 100 tons burden, furnish'd with good beds and
every accommodation. At the time of going out and
coming in of a packet, the pier is so crowded that
'tis not uncommon to see upwards of a thousand
people of all descriptions making their remarks, and
laughing at the sick passengers, after a disagreeable
voyage. The morning amusements after bathing, are
riding and walking, in the evening going to the different libraries to raffle, which makes the theatre and
assembly rooms less frequented than might be expected. The most public walk is on the fort, on
an eminence, from which is an extensive view of
the sea ; the walks near the cliffs, with fields and
meadows on one side, and the wide extended ocean
on the other, all beautiful.

Thursday 16th.—We set off about half-past nine
for Ramsgate. About two miles from Margate is
seen the beautiful Church of St. Peter's, a well-known
sea-mark. We went the road to Broadstairs thro'
Kingsgate, two miles from Margate. It received
that name by order of Charles II. at the time he
landed there, in his passage with the Duke of York
from Dover to London in 1659. Holland House
fronts the sea, nearly opposite to which is a small
fortification with port-holes for cannons. At a small
distance is a commodious house for accommodation,
and affords good entertainment for visitors, of which
large parties dine, and drink tea during the season.

1798 When the tide is out, the sands afford a most pleasant ride or walk. We pass'd a fine lighthouse, and the Goodwin Sands, at which a ship without a mast always lays at quarantine.[1] At Broadstairs, about three miles from Margate, we only stopped to take a view of the place. 'Tis a very pleasing one. The pier was destroyed by a storm, January 1767, but the harbour being of great utility, it was rebuilt by voluntary subscription in 1772. It commands a most extensive view of the coast of France to the southward. . . .

We soon got to Ramsgate—a large, pleasant town, well paved and lighted, the lodging-houses much more agreeable than those at Margate, as most have a view of the sea from Sion Hill, and Albion Place. The former fronts the pier, which was begun in 1750, and is a great attraction to strangers, though not yet finished. From thence you see Dover. The harbour is commodious, and used for a place of refuge for the shipping in bad weather, and will contain upwards of 300 sail of vessels at one time. The assembly-rooms front the harbour, and are much attended; balls once a week during the season, at which Le Bas, master of the ceremonies, attends from Margate. After having viewed everything, we proceeded on our tour.

About a mile from this town we saw Pegwell Bay. We then went thro' Sandwich. Richborough,[2] situated between Ramsgate and Sandwich, is said to have remained in a respectable state above a thousand years, when both town,[3] and castle were

---

[1] Mrs. Powys must mean the lightship
[2] The Roman castle, Rutupium.
[3] Town of Stonar.

destroyed by the Danes about the year A.D. 1000. 1798
Not the least trace of this city is now to be found,
and the ground has become an open cornfield. The
walls in some places are 12 feet thick, composed of
flints and Roman bricks. The whole eastern side
of the castle is destroyed, the remainder ruinous and
overgrown with ivy, and stands a monument of its
former greatness, in its present melancholy state.
We pass'd the Earl of Guildford's, and went by the
saltpans, where they make salt. We reach'd Deal
to dinner at 3.30. We went to the " Three Kings,"
a very bad, dirty inn indeed, but were in some degree
compensated by our eating-room opening into a
balcony the length of the house, commanding a most
beautiful view of the sea. We counted seventy-two
sail. Some very large ships lay there—the *Ardent,*
Superb, Severn, Ariadne, Fairy, and *Eugenie* sloops,
a Swedish sloop of war, with twenty-three sail of
detain'd Swedish vessels remaining in the Downs.
It was very entertaining to see the boats putting off,
or coming on shore, at the beach under the windows.
After dinner we proceeded on our journey, and very
near Walmer Castle (Mr. Pitt's), then passed Dover
Castle, from which we descended the hill into the
town. Dover Castle is just seven leagues to Calais,
The cliffs there, now appear'd to us very plain ; could
distinguish a ship laying there, and the different
colours of their cornfields.

We went to the York Hotel, Mr. Payner's, an
excellent inn, and most civil people ; there we drank
tea, supp'd, and lay. Mr. Pitt, and the Chancellor, had
been there in the morning to read the French newspapers just come in, but they contained nothing of
consequence. This hotel must have suffer'd amazingly

1798 since the war with France, as the travellers to, and from both kingdoms, usually frequented it, and in many different parts was wrote up in capitals, "Chaise de la poste," &c., &c. After breakfast, we went up to the castle; we had been informed we could not now, as in time of peace,[1] see hardly any of the interior part, which undoubtedly is quite right; no one is admitted, as there have been great improvements, and a subterranean passage from the castle to the city, all under the hill. Over that gate we entered, are the governor's apartments. There is an old tower, built by Claudius Cæsar, at a distance from the present castle; the latter, our conductor told us, was by Queen Elizabeth. From thence we saw Calais and some spires of its churches; and had it been evening, we should have had a much clearer view of it. The soldiers since the war have erected small thatched cottages about the castle for themselves and families. We, of course, went to view Queen Elizabeth's *pocket-pistol*, (the cannon so called), and Shakespeare's Cliff, which indeed seems a most tremendous height. It is supposed that any one standing on one of the highest turrets of Dover Castle is as much above the valley below, as the highest Egyptian pyramid is from the ground on which it stands—the measure taken is 499 feet. A French general that was lately taken, and brought to Dover, behav'd very ill, and was most exceedingly angry at not being suffer'd to walk about in this garrison town, which, if he had the least consider'd, was not the least likely he should have had leave. We dined at our inn, and about three set off for our return to Canterbury. . . .

Sunday, August 19*th.*—The Dean preached. After

[1] Nelson had just won the battle of the Nile, against the French.

evening service to tea at Mrs. Milnes' at The Oaks. 1798
To see the troops in the evening.

August 20th.—Went to return our visit to Sir
Harry and Lady Oxenden, who reside about eight
miles from Canterbury; a fine place,[1] a noble old
mansion standing in a park. There are eight rooms
a floor. You enter a fine hall. Sir Harry has a most
capital collection of pictures, for which he built a fine
room, 40 feet by 28, and 20 in height, in which are
thirty-one pictures, all by the best masters. For one
he was the other day offered seven hundred guineas,
and not a large one. Returned to dinner; in the
evening had a card-party — only five tables — the
seventeen Deans in that drawing-room looking down
upon us as if smiling at the difference of the times,
some of them most likely never having seen a card-
table. However, I hope they approved. The early
hours of Canterbury, so different from those of the
metropolis, as company had all left the poor Dean solo
before ten o'clock. I forgot to mention the library
belonging to the church of Canterbury, reckoned a
very fine one, containing many valuable books, which
are annually added to, and a great many curiosities,
which Mr. Weston was so obliging as to show us.

Tuesday, August 21st, began the diversions of the
race-week. Mrs. Shrimpton and myself, before our
tour, had each of us bought a summer white Canterbury muslin[2] of the famous Mr. Calloway, as all
the ladies, in compliment to his manufactory, intended
to appear in them at the balls. As to going to the
assemblies myself, I had given up all thoughts of, after
I heard of the death of poor Lady Williams. I had

---

[1] Broome Park.
[2] Several hundred persons were then employed in this manufactory.

1798 received a letter from Caroline to insist on our not
shortening the time of our return, as his (Cooper's),
health was tolerable, and it was time alone, could
restore peace of mind; but I insisted on my friend
Mrs. Shrimpton attending all the gaieties of the week.
We dined that day at two, and at half-past four went
to the race-ground. I stayed in the carriage for the
reasons afore mentioned. The ladies in general went
into the stand, which we were told is an excellent one,
one room enclosed, and an open balcony for those
who choose to stand out. So pretty a course I never
saw; 'tis on Barham Downs; the view pretty, and
many gentlemen's seats around there. The race was
rather better than most are at this period; but the
vast number of the military, carriages, &c., made the
most gay appearance possible. Mrs. Shrimpton went
with Mrs. Wolsby, and other ladies, to the ball in the
evening, which was very brilliant. Prince William
was staying at Dr. Wolsby's for the whole week, and
made it a point to attend everything; and everybody
was charmed with his affability and good-humour.
There was a public breakfast each morning at twelve.

August 22nd.—It was very crowded this day, and
dancing after the breakfast. Dined again at two,
went to the course at four, started at five. The company seemed as numerous as the day before.

Thursday, August 23rd.—A charity sermon was
preached by the Dean at the Cathedral for the benefit
of the hospital; indeed I must say an excellent one;
and as I walked down the choir I was continually
complimented by numbers of the audience in my
brother's name on the pleasure they had received.
The Dean was much gratified that there had not been
known so large a collection, £129, 9s., besides the

box.   Prince William gave £10.   This was all mentioned in many newspapers, and the discourse on the
occasion much praised.   Mrs. Shrimpton went again
to the ball, equally brilliant with the former one.

August 24th.—We dined again early, as some of
our gentlemen went to the course.   Our friends Mr.
and Mrs. Shrimpton, and Mr. Ewer, were obliged to
leave us that evening, as they could not get any
lodging at Ramsgate or Margate, and it was got so
late in the season.   As they always go to the sea in
the autumn, they were rather in haste, as they wish'd
to return home before they proceeded on their other
excursion.

Saturday, August 25th.—The races being now
over, and Prince William having been so engaged
each day that he had it not in his power to accept the
Dean's invitation to dine with him till now, and he
hoped it would be no inconvenience to us to dine
at four; for as there was always a play to end the
week's diversions, he had been requested to bespeak
one for that evening.   Dr. Wolsby had before hinted
to us that the Prince did not like only a gentlemen's
entertainment, so we desir'd Dr. and Mrs. Wolsby
to bring with them Miss Letitia Sands and Miss
Burt, two very pretty young ladies she had been
chaperone to at the balls, and with whom the Prince
had danced both nights.   We had fourteen in all,
besides Prince William, and the four above mentioned; his two aides-de-camp, Major Ellerton and
Captain Hambleton; Lord Pembroke, and his aide-
de-camp, Captain D'Urbin; Major Fellows, Major
Gore, and ourselves.   In the morning, not having
been used to the company of princes, I rather wished
the day over; but we had not been in the drawing-

1798 room ten minutes before his agreeable easy manner
made one so perfectly acquainted, that I found I could
talk to him with the same nonchalance as to any other
officer in the room.   When dinner was announced,
he took my hand and led me down to the eating-
room, which was rather a long promenade, but we
had room sufficient to show how we perform'd, as the
staircase, and approach to it is spacious.   He placed
himself next to me, and tho' the two beautiful young
ladies were very near us, politeness, no doubt, made
him address most of his conversation to the Dean's
sister, tho' an old grandmother!   And indeed (like
his Majesty), I do think he was never a moment
silent; but it gave me pleasure to see, despite his
volubility, that he perform'd well on most of the
dishes, particularly on a fine haunch of venison sent
us by Lord Pembroke.   While at dinner, he told
me I must go to his play.   " I should certainly," I
said, " wait upon his Royal Highness."   " And will
you oblige me with tea and coffee soon?"   " Undoubtedly."   After that the carriages were ordered,
and he conducted us to the theatre, and led me into
his box.   " God save the King" was immediately
played, and then the curtain drew up.   The comedy
was " The Castle Spectre," and " Spoil'd Child."   Performance tolerable ; but what seem'd to give the
Prince the highest satisfaction, the house was immensely crowded.   During the play (for he there
talked almost as much as during dinner), he told me
he was to sup at Dr. Wolsby's, and then leave Canterbury and set off for Ashford.   I said I feared his
Royal Highness would be tired to death from his
obliging attention.   " Oh, not the least, for when
tired I can sleep full as well in my coach as a bed."

There I envied him, for I never can, if ever so much 1798 fatigued. The play over, his Royal Highness wished us a good night, conducted us ladies to the carriage. The Prince left Canterbury that night, or rather, I suppose, the next morning.

August 25*th.*—Dinner for Prince William of Gloucester.

Salmon Trout.

Soles.

Fricando of Veal.   Rais'd Giblet Pie.

Vegetable Pudding.

Chickens.   Ham.

Muffin Pudding.

Curry of Rabbits.   Preserve of Olives.

Soup.   Haunch of Venison.

Open Tart Syllabub.   Rais'd Jelly.

Three Sweetbreads, larded.

Maccaroni.   Buttered Lobster.

Peas.

Potatoes.

Baskets of Pastry.   Custards.

Goose.

Sunday, August 26*th.*—On Sunday the boys at the King's School, all passed thro' the Green Court to the Cathedral, which was a pretty sight from our chamber windows.

I forget to mention a sad catastrophe which happened in the garden of the Deanery to one of the finest and by far the largest mulberry-tree [1] I ever saw. It was supposed to be from a thunderstorm which happened one night, as on the next morning we found about half of the immense bough lying on the ground, and yet not quite broken off. My

[1] There are several mulberry-trees now, said to have been planted by the monks.

1798 brother sent for a famous gardener, who propped
them up, as he said to saw them off would be injuring the main trunk.   How it may be another year
one cannot say ; but the broken branches that season
produced as many mulberries as usual, to the great
joy of the young ladies and gentlemen of the schools,
whom the Dean invited daily to amuse themselves in
gathering them.

August 28th.—Mr. Powys and myself set off from
the Deanery about one in the Dean's chaise.   We
chang'd horses at Sittingbourne, and then went to the
" Bull Inn," Rochester, the landlord, Mr. Paternoster,
an uncommon as well as odd name, where we lay, and
found it a noisy, disagreeable house, as it happened
unfortunately to be fair-day.

August 29th.—After breakfast we walk'd about
Rochester to view the town, Deanery, &c.   'Tis
eighteen miles from hence to Dartford.   At Dartford
we changed horses and took some egg-wine, and
proceeded on our journey to Clapham.   We got to
the Shrimptons by four.

August 31st.—In the morning we went to London
a-shopping, and at Wedgwood's, as usual, were highly
entertain'd, as I think no shop affords so great a
variety.   I there, among other things, purchas'd one
of the new invented *petit soupée* trays, which I think
equally clever, elegant, and convenient when alone or
a small party, as so much less trouble to ourselves and
servants.

Sunday, September 2nd.—At Clapham Church,
heard a very Methodistical sermon.

September 4th.—Mr. Powys and myself left our
kind friends at Clapham, setting off about 9.30.   Our
own horses met us at Crawford Bridge.   We dined

at the "Bull Inn," Maidenhead. Got home to Fawley 1798
about six that night.

November 13*th.* — Lady Malmesbury gave the
colours to the "Loyal Henley Association,"[1] in a field
just opposite Park Place. A tent was erected for her
Ladyship and the company she invited, where the
carriages set us down, and the ladies were handed into
the tent by Lord Malmesbury, who had desired us to
be there by half-past eleven. A sermon was preached
by Mr. Jeston,[2] after which her Ladyship presented
the colours, and made a speech to the Association ;
after which Major Jackson thanked her Ladyship in
the name of the whole corps in a very manly oration ;
and when the officers and soldiers had finished all their
manœuvres, the carriages were call'd up, and those
who had before been invited to the cold collation
drove on to Park Place, where in the eating-room,
everything for the most elegant breakfast was set
out. . . . A dinner for all the gentlemen was at the
town-hall at three. The weather was intensely cold,
but it happened most luckily to be a very fine
day.

November 14*th.*—I was terribly alarmed by an
express from my mother's servant, who, on going into
the parlour about two o'clock, had found her fallen
back in her chair, quite insensible, and all over blood.
We went immediately to her, and sent for Doctor
Taylor,[3] but fortunately our apothecary, Coulson, lived
next door, and by blisters, bleeding, and leeches, she
was then greatly recovered before the doctor came.

---

[1] Henley-on-Thames.

[2] The Rev. Humphrey Jeston, then in sole charge of Henley parish,
and Master of the Royal Grammar School there.

[3] Of Wargrave.

X

1798   He suppos'd she had broke a blood vessel, but tho' so
much better, he told me not to be alarmed if, at her
great age of eighty-six, she should be again seized
in the same manner. I stayed with her a week,
when, as she was so much better, and Mr. Powys
confin'd at home by the rheumatism, I returned to
Fawley.

November 26th.—Gentlemen's dinner at Henley.

November 29th.—Thanksgiving-day.[1]

December 22nd.—Tom went to his living in Essex.

1799   *January 3rd,* 1799. — On this evening, Lady
Malmesbury gave a ball at Park Place. The company was to be there at nine. There were seventy-
five of us, about seventeen couple of dancers;
twenty-one in the house, Lord Grantham and his
mother, Lord and Lady Lavington, &c.; cards in
one room, and the dancing in the library; tea,
orgeat, lemonade, cakes, &c., brought round every
half-hour. At one, supper was announced in the room
out of the library, two tables the length of the eating-
room, forming a crescent at the upper end in a beau-
window. On this, every elegance was display'd, and
set off to the greatest advantage by gilt-plate, glass
lustres, and other ornaments. By each plate was laid
for the fruit, a small gold knife and fork, and two
dessert spoons. About half-past two we return'd to
the library, and the dancing recommenced; at three,
coffee was carri'd round, and after cakes, &c., as
before, the company began to disperse; every one
seem'd to have been highly entertain'd. The house
is most superbly furnished with every elegance from
Italy, France, and, in short, every country — fine
pictures, pier - glasses, paintings, of the Vatican

---

[1] For Nelson's victories over the French.

Library, some curious tables, &c., that belonged to the 1799
unfortunate Louis XVI., and many other curiosities
too numerous to name, with the finest collection of
books anywhere to be met with.[1]   But what gave us
a real satisfaction, so intimate had we been with
Marshal Conway and Lady Ailesbury, that it was
really a painful sensation the idea of visiting again at
Park Place; but now the whole house is so totally
alter'd, one cannot have an idea of its being the same.
The noble library[2] the Marshal had just completed,
we used to go up the staircase to.   Those stairs are
taken away, so that you now go through two elegant
rooms, which were Lady Ailesbury's dressing-room
and bedroom, making a suit of apartments to the
library which has a very good effect, and renders the
whole appearance totally different to those who were
before perfectly acquainted with it.

January 30th.—Went from Hardwick, to stay
with Caroline, while Cooper went into Staffordshire
to see his living at Hamstall Ridware, that Mrs.
Leigh[3] had just been so kind as to present him to.
The roads were so bad with snow and frost, we
were obliged to go round by Caversham, but got
safe to Harpsden to dinner.

February 1st.—It continued snowing, and was so
deep we were much alarmed for Cooper on his journey,
as he had promised to write; but the Oxford mail
had been stopped that day, a circumstance that had
not happened for thirteen years.

February 3rd.—Snow continued, but we were

[1] Collected by James Harris, the great literati, father of Lord
Malmesbury.
[2] This was pulled down by Mr. Easton in 1867.
[3] The Leighs of Addlestrop, Gloucestershire, and Stoneleigh, Warwickshire. Cooper's mother was a Miss Leigh.

1799 happy in having a letter from Cooper to say he was got safe back to Oxford, having been forced to walk many miles, and hoped by the same method[1] he might be able to get home the next evening. There was no church on the Sunday at Harpsden or Fawley, as no one could get to either. The icicles on the trees hanging down was a most beautiful sight, when the sun shone on them.

February 4th.—A hard frost. Cooper came by the Oxford stage. It continued to be snow and frost till February 15th, when it thawed. On the 19th the floods on the Thames, and Loddon, from our windows, was quite astonishing.

March 28th.—Mr. Powys and I went to Hardwick on our way to Bath. Reached Bath on the 29th.

March 31st.—Arrived the first news of the Austrians having beat the French.[2]

April 9th.—At Mrs. Lutwyche's party in the evening. Ten tables, six to each, and numbers who, like us, did not play.

April 11th.—At the play, "Laugh while you can,' and "Blue Beard."

Sunday, April 14th.—Mr. Clark preached. I went to church at half-past ten. Mr. Powys was just then taken with a bleeding at the nose, but, as much used to it, he desired I'd go, and he would follow me. But having stayed out the service in great anxiety, I return'd home and found it still bleeding, and had never ceased. I sent to the apothecary, who gave him something without effect. I then sent for Mr. Grant, the surgeon, who advised me to send to Dr. Mappleton as acquainted with his constitution. The doctor being out, it was between four

---

[1] A contrast to travelling in 1898.   [2] At Montenotte.

and five in the afternoon before he came. Poor
Mr. Powys was near fainting, and I from my fears
could hardly support it. But the doctor begg'd me
not to be alarmed, as he was almost certain he
could stop it by *Ruspini's Styptic*, which was directly
sent for, and as soon as applied stopped the bleeding,
and most thankful was I, as he was really nearly
exhausted, and the loss of blood must have been
immense. The doctor told us he knew not what it
is, but though a quack medicine, it was wonderful
the cures he had known by it in wounds, inward
bruises, or bleeding at the nose, and he advises every
one to keep some in their house, which I certainly
shall.

April 15th.—Tyson's, the Master of the Ceremonies' ball at the Upper Rooms. We were to have
been there, but after the fatigue and anxiety of the
day before, we did not think of it. Mr. P. was better
than could be expected, tho' extremely weak for a
long while.

April 19th.—Having been very indifferent ever
since Mr. Powy's illness, and too low and nervous to
be blooded, I was, by Dr. Mapleton's advice, cupped [1]
by Mr. Grant.

April 26th.—At a party at Mr. Purvis's ; six tables.
Went from thence to a party at Mr. Leigh Perrot's ; [2]
eight tables, ninety people. The Prince of Wales was
at Bath when we were. He was not very popular,
from the company he brought with him—Mr. Sheridan's son, and Mr. Day. The latter's great merit

---

[1] Truly a *Sangrado* system. This, and Mr. Powys's case, are
examples of " survivals of the fittest."

[2] Of the Leighs of Addlestrop ; took the name of Perrot, on succeed-
ing to a portion of the Perrot estates at North Leigh.

1799 seem'd to be that he could drink at a sitting two bottles more than any one. The Prince once said to him, "You are a jolly fellow, Day. When I am king, I'll make you a peer by the title of my Lord *Cinque Port.*" Not a bad pun of his Royal Highness! A Miss Fox, a very beautiful girl, was of the party, but kept quite invisible. His Royal Highness was almost constantly at Mrs. Carr's, attracted by the beauty of her two daughters, the Misses Gubbins, though it was said the most beautiful, Miss Honor, was not the Prince's favourite, but both play'd and sang to him every evening, and he generally supped there. The poor girls are really to be pitied, as 'tis not their's, but their mother's fault, to be in such a constant round of dissipation, and playing very deep at cards, from the same bad example. I think the Prince looked in better health than the year before, but they said he was not, and though he came to drink the waters, from his manner of living they certainly could not be of much service. Bath always abounds in droll anecdotes, and on its being thought the Prince looked very dull, it was given as a reason that a few days before he left London he had had his fortune told. The manner of it is, the person puts in his hand to a person that is invisible, who having observ'd it a little while said, "You'll not live long." The Prince not liking, I suppose, this observation, came again the next day in quite a different dress. When on again putting in his hand, the voice said, "You'll not die a natural death." This still more discompos'd him. Indeed it was no wonder, and we all could not help wishing it might be a warning for him to behave more proper to his high station. The Duke of York was fearful he might not be graciously received, and sent to the

Mayor before he came, that he might.   However, 1799 the lower class cannot always be led, and as he got out of his carriage, call'd out very vehemently, "Where's your wife? Why did you not bring your wife, as your brother does?" He did not stay long, and carried Mrs. Carr and her daughters to London, where it is said the former was to set up a faro table.

The famous Mrs. Macartney left Bath this spring, and is gone to a house, her nephew, Mr. Greville, lent her in London. She says she "must come to Bath for her health sometimes, but had rather live in hell than on the Queen's Parade, where the families were so shockingly impolite as not one to visit her." She offer'd her hand lately to Colonel Mackenzie, who refused it, and kindly gave notice to her nephew, Greville, to look after his curious aunt.

The once celebrated beauty, Miss Wroughton, still keeps up her consequence by her large parties, and fine concerts every Sunday evening, where Ranzini, and many amateurs sing and play. The Prince always attended to hear Miss Mayo (Mrs. Lutwyche's niece), sing and play, and indeed I never heard any one so charming. Not that I attended Miss Wroughton's Sunday concerts, as I quite agreed with the two amiable Duchesses of Newcastle, and Hamilton, who never would appear there on those evenings. The amiable Lady Nelson, who as usual was at Bath with her father-in-law,[1] had some music sent her from Russia endeavouring to be expressive of her lord's victories. She sent it to Ranzini, and some of the opera musicians came from London to perform it. The great ball-room was the place fixed upon, and there were about

[1] The Rev. Edmund Nelson.

1799 one thousand three hundred people, but the amateurs
were disappointed, as the "Battle of the Nile,"[1] as
one might suppose, was only a monstrous continued
noise.   But, however, every one was grateful to her
Ladyship.   I think I never saw any one more altered
in the course of one year than Lord Nelson's father,
a most worthy old man with long grey hair, but seems
now so broke at his son's victories, which he says is
literally being overcome with joy, so much so that
he can hardly bear it.   Dr. Randolph, the celebrated
preacher, had the living of Bradford given him, but
does not reside there, which the King, when he heard
that he was constantly at Bath, said the chapel there
was no cure of souls.   Coals in April 1799 were only
10d. a bushel at Bath, when 5s. in London, viz., £9
a chaldron.

May 4th.—We left Bath.   We wished to return
home, as we had receiv'd a letter lately from our son
Thomas to inform us he was going to add another
daughter to our family.   We got to Hardwick for
dinner about half-past four, and on the 5th returned
to Fawley.

May 7th.—The weather amazing cold, and tho' I
began to ride as usual in summer before breakfast,
I could hardly bear it.

May 23rd.—Phil went to London to kiss hands
on his being appointed Clerk of the 'Chequer.

Lord Bayham's (the present Earl of Camden),
first son was christened on the 6th June 1799 by
the Bishop of Clogher.   My brother, the Dean of
Canterbury, was to have performed the ceremony,
but as his Majesty was godfather, it's always then a
bishop.

[1] Fought on August 1st, 1798.

July 15th.—Mr. Powys and myself set off by eight 1799
in the morning to Mrs. Powney's, Ives Place, to meet
our cousin, the Marchioness de la Peire,[1] as they have
at last arrived in England after numerous distresses
they had met with during the war. The Marquis was
not at all well; she looks amazingly so, for all that
she has gone through. We had not seen her for
nineteen years. Of course, she was not the very
beautiful woman we remembered her on leaving England, but still a fine countenance. The eldest of their
four daughters, Clementina, was with them.

July 18th.—The review on Bulmarsh Heath.[2]

July 29th.—The Shrimptons, and Miss Palgrave,
came from Hardwick to stay at Fawley, and we had
the pleasing satisfaction of finding our future daughter-
in-law [3] as amiable as she had been represented to us.

August 26th.—Dined at Fawley Court, to hear
the two famous musicians, the Leanders, play on the
French horn, who Mrs. Freeman had down for a
week, and invited the neighbouring families round, in
different parties every day. It certainly was a very
high entertainment.

August 27th.—On this day was buried Mrs. Amy-
and,[4] widow to the clergyman, my brother, the Dean,
succeeded to, in the living of Fawley; they have a
vault in the chancel. The hearse and six coaches

---

[1] She was the daughter of Mrs. Flowyer, half-sister to Mrs. Girle,
Mrs. Powys's mother.

[2] George III., the Queen, Dukes of York and Cumberland, the
Speaker, and Prime Minister, Mr. Pitt, present. The Margravine of
Anspach gave the Newbury troop colours.

[3] Miss Elizabeth Palgrave, eldest daughter of W. Palgrave, of Cottishall, Norfolk, was then engaged to the Rev. Thomas Powys, second son
of Mrs. Lybbe Powys.

[4] Widow of the Rev. Thos. Amyand, rector of Fawley from 1758
to 1762.

1799 of four, with servants, and her son and son-in-law in their own carriage. The ceremony was perform'd by my brother about twelve.

September 9th.—Mr. Powys, and myself went to the Shrimptons' at Clapham to meet Mr. Palgrave, who had just come from Norfolk. Tom went a day or so before us.

September 10th.—Went to London. Saw the Panorama, which I think one of the cleverest inventions that can be, and this view of it was particularly interesting, as it was the view of Lord Nelson's victory, which must give the highest satisfaction to all lovers of their country.

September 16th.—Mr. and Miss Palgrave set out for Norfolk, and Mrs. Powys and myself for Fawley.

September 23rd.—Caroline and Cooper went to his new living[1] in Staffordshire for a few days to furnish the house ; the four children and two maids came to us. They had been staying a week at the Hall's,[2] Harpsden Court, previously.

Sunday, September 13th, was to me one of the most melancholy days I ever experienced, as it was to part me and my dearest Caroline, who was to set off the next day for Staffordshire ; and as Mr. Cooper was to do duty at Henley Church that day for Mr. Townsend, he thought it best they should all lay at Henley, to make the separation less dismal. They would not stay to breakfast, but set off as soon as they got up. The dear little children stay'd till after morning church, and not knowing or feeling any of the anxiety that we did, seem'd perfectly astonished

---

[1] Hamstall, Ridware.
[2] For convenience of the removal from Harpsden Rectory, in which they lived.

to see us shed tears, and that we did not feel equal 1799 pleasure with themselves at the idea of their journey.

October 28*th.*—Mr. Powys and I went to Mr. Annesley's, Blechingdon Park. On 31st, Mrs. Annesley drove with her sister Grace in her phaeton, and Lady Hardy and I went in the post-chaise to Blenheim, to see the new china-rooms. They are not in the house, but built just after you enter the park, four little rooms fill'd with all sorts of old china fix'd to the walls by three screws, one of which takes out to let them be removed, others are placed on pedestals or shelves. The whole has a pretty effect, but to others might be more amusing than to Lady Hardy and myself, as each of us has most of the same sort.

November 5*th.*—Our dear son Thomas, was married at her father's at Cottishall, Norfolk, to Miss Elizabeth Palgrave.[1] They set off the same morning for London.

November 9*th.*—The bride and bridegroom came to us to dinner from Mr. Shrimpton's, and most happy were we to see them again, and told them we should not let them go to reside at their cottage [2] till after Christmas. Tom was now curate at Harpsden.

November 11*th.* — The Gentlemen's Club, at Dixon's, Henley. (First meeting of the year.)

January 7*th*, 1800.—Tom went to London, the 1800 next day, to his living [3] at Essex.

January 15*th.*—Tom and Elizabeth, to our great regret, left us this day to reside at their cottage at Remenham, Berks.

---

[1] They were married by the celebrated Dr. Parr.

[2] Remenham Lodge.

[3] Though curate at Harpsden, he was vicar of High Rhoding, a living in Essex.

1800   *January 27th.*—The Dean went to London to preach a charity sermon for the *Welsh clergy.*

March 7th.—We set out from Hardwick for Bath, to Mr. Shrimpton's lodgings, 36 Milsom Street, as they were so kind as to insist on our going to them till we could get lodgings to our mind. Bath very full.

March 11th.—At the play (Diamond's benefit), " The Stranger," and " Shipwreck."

March 15th.—At last got lodgings, No. 34 Gay Street.

March 27th.—Went with Mrs. Shrimpton to Charlton's benefit—" The School for Scandal," [1] and " The Chimney-Corner."

April 4th.—The Rev. Mr. Berners, of Hambleden, died in London, to the great regret of all our Fawley neighbourhood.

April 25th.—Returned from Bath.

May 20th.—The Dean went to London to the *levée*, to congratulate his Majesty on his escape from the horrid assassin [2] at Drury Lane Theatre, and Phil from Hardwick, went with his uncle.

May 29th.—The Dean went to London to present the Canterbury address to his Majesty, with the Archbishop.

June 24th.—Mr. Powys and myself went to stay with Tom at Remenham. That evening we cross'd the water to Fawley Court to see the night-blooming *Cerus*,[3] a very curious plant.

---

[1] First produced in 1777.
[2] Hadfield's attempt to shoot the King, took place May 15th.
[3] *Cereus grandiflorus*, of Jamaica, introduced in 1700 to England.

STAFFORDSHIRE JOURNAL

1800

Mr. Powys and myself set out in our own chaise 1800
from Fawley, on Monday the 7th of July, about half-
past six, took our own horses to Benson, where we
breakfasted at Shrub's, and from thence had post-
horses to our own carriage the whole journey. From
Benson to Woodstock, and Oxford. At the latter we
called on Dr. Isham and the Vice-Chancellor, Dr.
Marlow; dined at Chapel House, changed horses at
Shipston, and Stratford-upon-Avon. We lay at Hock-
ley, as wishing to avoid the noise of such an immense
town as Birmingham, where we got to breakfast on
Tuesday by ten, to Lloyd's Hotel, which inn quite
answered the favourable description Mr. and Mrs.
Atkyns Wright gave us of it. We set out to walk,
upon the very worst pavement I ever saw, to see Mr.
Bolton's manufactory, but very unfortunately we could
not, as the very day before it had been advertised in
the newspaper that it would not be shown any more,
owing to some French emigrants having the week before behaved very unhandsome when admitted there.
However, we went to see the japan manufactory,
which is certainly worth going to, but nothing equal
to the button manufactory, the process of which is
certainly one of the most entertaining I ever saw. I
was presented with a most curious specimen (now in
my fossil case), of one we saw made from beginning
to end, of the most curious workmanship, with a purple
stone in the centre. We after this walked a long time
about this immense place, curious certainly to see,
tho' its vast extent, crowds of dirty inhabitants, and

1800 bad pavement, made the whole not so pleasing.   From
hence we went to dinner at Lichfield, where Mr.
Cooper sent a servant to meet us, with the key of a
gentleman's grounds, going through which shortened
our way to Hamstall Ridware,[1] where we got to tea.
Cooper had walked about a mile from their house on
our arrival, at which our dearest Caroline ran out to
meet us ; but after so many months' absence, she and
myself were so overcome, that strangers might have
supposed it a parting scene, instead of a most joyful
meeting ; but my sorrow was soon turned to its
contrast, to find them all so well, and pleasantly
situated.

July 9th.—In the evening we went a trout-fishing
on the Blythe, a river running at the bottom of a
meadow before their house.

Thursday.—Walk'd up the village to Smith's the
weaver, to see the manner of that work, and 'tis really
curious to see with what astonishing velocity they
threw the shuttle.[2]

Hamstall Ridware Church is a rectory dedicated
to St. Michael, a very neat old spire building of stone,
having two side aisles, chancel, &c., and makes a magnificent appearance as a village church. . . .

Monday 21st.—That evening we all walk'd up to
Farmer Cox's, a very fine high situation, and most
extensive views ; indeed the prospect all round Hamstall is delightful.   This place is a mile north of
King's Bromley across the Trent, near Needwood
Forest, about two miles west of Yoxall.   The Blythe
runs through the centre of the parish, and falls into

---

[1] The living of her son-in-law, the Rev. Edward Cooper.

[2] Power-looms were not introduced till 1807 ; the shuttle was then
thrown, and batten worked by hand.

the Trent. The present Mrs. Leigh gave Mr. Cooper 1800
the living in 1799. The ancestors of this noble family
assumed their name from the town of High Leigh,
Cheshire, where they were seated before the Conquest.
Before Charles I. set up his standard at Nottingham,
he march'd to Coventry, but finding the gates shut
against him, he went the same night to Stone Leigh,
the house of Sir Thomas Leigh,[1] where, as Lord
Clarendon says, he was well received. Edward, Lord
Leigh, took his seat in the House of Peers, March
15th, 1764, and, dying unmarried, his sister, the
Honourable Mary Leigh,[2] the present lady of the
manor, succeeded to his estates here, and at Stoneleigh, (supposed to be about £1600 a year), now her
principal seat, is about fifteen miles from Hamstall
Ridware.

Yoxall is a pleasant rural village,[3] situated in a
valley on the south-west borders of Needwood Forest,
seven miles from Lichfield and four miles from Burton-
on-Trent. Good roads to both, and a turnpike across
the Forest to Uttoxeter and Ashbourne.

July 22nd.—We took a long hot walk to the
village of Murry, to see a tape manufactory, of which
seven gentlemen of that neighbourhood are proprie-
tors. The noise of the machinery is hardly to be
borne, tho' the workpeople told us they themselves
hardly heard the noise! Such is use! The calender-
ing part is worth observation, as the tapes all go
through the floor of an upper room, and when you

[1] The King made him a baron in 1643. He lived to see the monarchy restored.
[2] This lady dying without issue, the property passed to their relations the Leighs of Addlestrop.
[3] Yoxall was in 1809 added to the Rev. Edward Cooper's livings by presentation of Mr. Leigh of Stoneleigh.

1800 go down to the apartment under it, you see them all coming through the ceiling, perfectly smooth and glossy, where the women take them, and roll them in the pieces as we buy them at the haberdasher's, whereas in the upper room they all look tumbled and dirty.

July the 26th had been a day long fixed upon by Mr. and Mrs. Bailey for a large party of the neighbourhood to dine in the Forest of Needwood. They had invited about forty of their acquaintance, who were all requested to meet at the great oak called Swilaar, famous for its immense size. The fête was to have been given in 1798, but that summer most of their friends were gone to different watering-places, and the next was such incessant rains, they were obliged to give up this rural entertainment, which most fortunately for us was postponed to the 26th July 1800, a day for fine weather none could exceed. It seems Mr. Bailey had promised his friends a dinner in the Forest, if Mr. Erskine[1] succeeded in gaining a cause for the relatives of David Garrick, of which Mr. Bailey was one. I think it was Mr. Peter Garrick who left about £30,coo to be divided according to a will he made, but at the time of his death, his faculties were so deranged by age and illness, being then eighty-five, that the apothecary who attended him contrived to make him sign another will, in which he left everything to himself. Of course the family had recourse to the law, and by Erskine's abilities was restored to their property, and the medical gentleman forced to quit the kingdom to save his life. Mr. and Mrs. Bailey had drove early in the morning to the Forest, to see all the dining-

[1] Afterwards, in 1806, Lord Chancellor.

tables placed under the shade of the trees;[1] and a 1800
most elegant cold collation indeed it was, or at least
I may say intended to be so, but we none of us could
help laughing with the donors themselves, who told
us, in placing the tables in the most shady parts, they
had literally forgotten the sun was drawing on to that
spot, as well as their visitors, so that the intense heat
of the weather made the hams, tongues, chickens,
pies, &c., &c., literally all lukewarm. After our
repast the ladies made walking parties to different
places in the forest; some of us went to take a more
correct view of the great oak, where we met in the
morning. "'Tis styl'd Swilaar Oak, or the Father
of the Forest, girts at 5 feet height 21 feet, the
lower stem 10 feet clear, the whole height 65 feet,
the extent of the arms 45 feet. 'Tis supposed to
be 600 years old, stands singly upon a beautiful lawn
surrounded with extensive woods; no elms or beech
trees are met with in Needwood Forest; hazels, thorns,
and maples, very few ash, and two very fine ancient
limes of vast size." (From Shawe's "Staffordshire.")

N.B.—A copy of verses wrote by Dr. Darwin[2]
on this oak, reckoned very fine, I shall write at the
end of this journal. Shawe states: "The Forest of
Needwood, the most beautiful part of the Honour of
Tutbury, is situate in the northern extremity of the
hundred of Offlow, and in the four parishes of Tutbury,
Henbury, Tatenhill and Yoxall, between the rivers
Dove, Trent, and Blythe. In the reign of Elizabeth
the Forest of Needwood was in compact by extenua-

---

[1] Horace Walpole said there was a particular breed of bloodhounds
in Needwood Forest, the size of a mastiff, blackish back, belly reddish-
brown.

[2] Dr. Erasmus Darwin, author of "The Botanic Garden," &c., grandfather of Charles R. Darwin.

1800 tion 23½ miles ; in it 7869 acres, now said to amount
to 9400, thinly set with oak and timber trees, well
replenished with covers of underwood, thorns, and
hollies ; the berries of the latter in winter are most
beautiful.   In the forest were ten parks."

When the gentlemen retir'd from the dinner-tables
they were placed in a more shady situation for tea and
coffee, against the return of the ladies from their walks,
after which we again took a very long promenade to
view the most picturesque scenes.   From some parts we
saw Dovedale, and other parts of Derbyshire.   The
company separated at different hours in the evening,
according to their distances from home.

Monday, 28th.—We all set out early in the morn
to see Shuckborough,[1] Mr. Anson's, and Hagley, Lord
Curzon's.   We went through Blythberry and Coulton,
the latter a village rather remarkable for many of its
cottages being built in a marl-pit with woods over it,
the roots of its trees growing and hanging loosely
over their little gardens, which are deck'd with all
manner of flowers, and kept with the greatest neatness.
We pass'd a Lady Blount's, a white house, a Catholic
family, related to that of Maple-Durham, near Hardwick.   Shuckborough is a remarkable good house, finely
furnished, and lately enlarged.   There are numbers of
valuable statues, busts, &c.   Mrs. Anson. who was
Miss Coke, daughter of Mr. Coke of Holkham in
Norfolk, and married a Mr. Anson[2] in 1794, is, I
think, one of the most capital painters, and excels in
every kind of drawing.   Every room is ornamented
with some of her performances.   Three of their children, full-length portraits, at the upper end of a large

---

[1] Shugborough.
[2] Thomas Anson, father of first Earl of Lichfield.

room, is, I think, equal to any artist; also several 1800 copies from Titian, and other famed masters. . . . We gave up going over the gardens, as we knew we should have a long walk at Hagley. On our way there, we passed the houses of two families much talk'd of in that part of the country in the year 1757, when a novel was wrote on the subject call'd "The Widow of the Wood." The real name of the heroine, . . . the hero, Sir William Wolsley. Their houses very near each other; both pretty places. We pass'd, too, the College Church, where the marriage was perform'd late in an evening; but 'tis a droll history altogether. It was contrary to the clergyman's desire, but she begg'd it might be kept a secret the time of their marriage, and it was afterwards discover'd she had another husband.[1] We din'd at Wolsley Bridge, a very good inn. . . . We sent in our names for leave to walk round Lord Curzon's grounds,[2] and he desired we would go into any part of it we chose, without being attended by his gardener. The house seems a comfortable old mansion, with some new rooms, and more to be added. The grounds are delightful, the river running thro' them, and many beautiful cascades. After having gone a long tour we proceeded to mount the famous Cannock Hills, of a vast height, and having reach'd the top were quite repaid by the most beautiful scenes. I picked up some remarkable stones on the Cannock Hills.

Thursday, 31st.—We dined at Mr. Carey's, minister of Abbot's, Bromley. Before dinner we went to see Lord Bagot's park. The number and size of the oaks here are quite astonishing; nor had any of us

---

[1] Sir William re-married.
[2] Hagley is the property of Lord Lyttleton.

1800 the least idea to what a size oaks would grow. His Lordship has been offered for them an hundred thousand pounds.

Thursday, August 7th.—We set out for Lichfield, which, having only seen as we came through it, we now determined to spend a long morning there in viewing the Cathedral, &c. We breakfasted by seven, and got there, as we intended, before the service began. The Cathedral[1] is indeed a very fine one, not so large and unlike that of Canterbury, quite modernised by Mr. Wyatt; a fine window over the communion-table, painted by Egginton of Birmingham, a Carlo Dolce, the same as that we had just seen by the same hand put up at Mr. Stonor's chapel,[2] at Stonor in our neighbourhood, a present from Mrs. Stonor's father. The Dean (Proby) and Mr. Nares, the reviewer, were in residence and at church, the former a very old man. After service, Mr. Nares was so obliging as to walk over it with us, and as Mr. Shaw's account of the whole will be much more accurate than I could give, I shall set it down here :—" Its dimensions in length, from east to west of the whole fabric, 411 feet, whereof from the west door to the great cross aile or transept, 179 feet ; to the entrance in the choir, 34 feet ; length of choir, 110 feet ; height of the great steeple in the middle, 246 feet. In the front 183 feet ; in the south of which are a peal of ten bells. Anno Dom. 1433, Heyward sat Bishop of Coventry and Lichfield, the Cathedral was beautified in the ornaments thereof." Indeed, "the west front," says Fuller, "is a stately fabrick, adorn'd with excellent imagerie, which I suspect our age is far from being

---

[1] Commenced building in 1129. Dedicated to St. Chad.
[2] Stonor Park, Oxon, seat of Lord Camoys.

able to imitate ; but alas!" says he, "'tis now a political 1800
case indeed, almost beaten down to the ground in our
civil wars." Plot says, "Three such lofty spires no
church in England can boast the like, being adorn'd
with studs and carved work. The glazing and tracery
in stone-work of the west window were the gifts
of James I. ; a curious piece of art." Till then, the
Cathedral remain'd in its pristine beauty, when it
suffer'd greatly by three sieges,[1] in one of which Lord
Brook,[2] of fanatic principles, lost his life. He drew
up his army, pray'd a blessing upon his intended work,
earnestly desiring that God would by some special
token manifest unto them His approbation of their
desire, then planted their great guns by the south-east
side of the close, when, by some accident, this Lord
was shot in one of his eyes, as he lifted up his beaver
that he might the more clearly see the execution done ;
but though completely harness'd with plate-armour
cap-à-pie, he suddenly fell down dead. Nor is it less
remarkable that this accident was on the 2nd March,
the festival of the famous Bishop St. Chad, to whose
memory Offa, king of the Mercians, first erected this
stately church ; but notwithstanding this Lord lost his
life, the army of Cromwell exercised the like barbarisms
as were done at Worcester, demolishing all the monuments, pulling down the cornices, carved work, batten-
ing in pieces the costly windows, and destroying the
records belonging to the church, stabled their horses
in the body of it, kept courts of guard in the cross
aisles, broke up the pavement, polluted the choir with

---

[1] The first in 1643, when it was fortified for royalty.
[2] He expressed the impious desire that he might behold the day
when no cathedral should be left standing. He was shot by "dumb
Dyott" from the middle tower.

1800 excrement, hunted a cat with hounds through the church, and, to add to their wickedness, brought a calf wrapped up in linen, carried it to the font, sprinkled it with water, and gave it a name, in scorn and derision of that holy sacrament baptism; and when Prince Rupert recovered the church by force, Russel, the governor, carried away the communion plate, &c.

In September 1651, a canonier dwelling in Stafford, who had been one of those that shot down the steeple at Lichfield Cathedral in the siege of 1646, as he was charging his piece (upon the arrival of Major Harrison), to be fired in triumph, was shot in the arm with that cannon, which suddenly took fire, his chin and arm lay shot off; he only survived a few days.

Colonel Dawson, governor of Stafford, by authority from Parliament, employed workmen to strip off the lead from this stately cathedral, October 1651, and one Picton, July 26, 1653, knocked in pieces the fair bell call'd "Jesus." About the bell was this inscription :—

> "*I am the bell of Jesus, and Edward is our king,*
> *Sir Thomas Haywood, first caus̀ed me to ring.*"

Bells were esteem'd sacred ever since they were first used in the year 604.[1]

The vestry at last was the only place that had a roof to shelter them during divine service; the great steeple was laid down below the bottom of the great spire, the west front shattered, and all the doors and windows—2000 shots of great ordnance and 1500 hand-grenadoes having been discharged against it. Dr. John Hacket was appointed Bishop in 1661.

[1] The first peal of bells in England were at Croyland Abbey, Lincolnshire.

When he came down, he found his cathedral in a 1800 state better to be conceived than described ; the honour of restoring it to its former splendour was reserved for this worthy prelate. The very morning after his arrival, he roused his servants by break of day, set his own coach-horses, with teams, and hired labourers to remove the rubbish, and laid the first hand to the work he meditated.

From the Cathedral we went to the Rev. Mr. Saville's garden, who is a great botanist, and has a large collection of curious plants. We then went a mile and a half from Lichfield to a Mr. Glover's, whose paintings are in very high repute, more particularly landscapes. After walking back to Lichfield, we amused ourselves going from shop to shop ; there are a variety of good ones in this city, particularly of the Wedgwood manufactory.

N.B.—I forgot to mention among many new monuments in the cathedral is a very fine one to Lady Mary Wortley Montagu.[1]

August 12th.—All our party went a trout-fishing, but the heat was so intense it was hardly bearable.

August 13th.—Mr. Cooper, and Mr. Powys, went to the assizes at Stafford. On their return they entertain'd us with a droll copy of verses on Lord Stafford's picture being hung up in the town-hall in 1800 :—

> " With happy contrivance to honour his chief,
> Jack [2] treats his old friend as he treats an old sheep ;
> But with proper respect to the Garter and Star,
> Instead of the gallows he's hung at the bar.
> To remove from this county so foul a disgrace,
> Take down the old Peer, and hang Jack in his place."

---

[1] She died in 1762. The monument is by Westmacott.
[2] Mr. Sparrow.

1800 *Thursday 14th.* — I walked down to the river Blyth by seven in the morn to see Caroline and the three eldest children bathe, which they did most mornings, having put up a dressing-house on the bank. . . .

Monday, August 18th.—We all pass'd a dull, gloomy day, the following one being upon fixed for leaving our dear relatives.

We reached Fawley on Wednesday the 20th by seven o'clock.

August 26th. — Tom's daughter, Louisa Mary Powys, born.

August 27th.—We went to see Elizabeth and my new grand-daughter ; both pure well.

October 7th.—Louisa Mary Powys christened at Remenham.

October 27th.—Tom's little girl inoculated.

October 28th.—We went to stay at Mr. Fane's, Wormsley.

October 29th. — This morning Lady Elizabeth, (Fane), and all the ladies went in their coaches, attended by the gentlemen on horseback, to West Wycombe Park, to see the furniture, china, &c., of Lord Donegal, which were to be sold the next week. He had taken the house of Sir John Dashwood for seven years, but by gaming, racing, and every extravagance he was obliged to have an auction and sell everything—very unpleasant to Sir John Dashwood who had a very fine collection of pictures and some furniture in the house.

December 1st.—My poor mother was again seiz'd with a second fit of apoplexy. I went to her most days, and by the seventh Mr. Coulson thought her near as well as before her seizure.

January 2nd, 1801.—My poor mother continued 1801 very low and weak, and knew none of us for some time past.

January 7th.—Caroline Cooper was brought to bed of a boy (on my birthday). He was christened Frederick Leigh Cooper.

On the 8th of January, it pleased God to relieve my dear mother from that state of miserable insensibility she had so long been in, without suffering the least pain. She was eighty-nine years of age, having outlived my father near forty years, whose inexpressible loss I experienced 5th of July 1761. My mother was buried by him in Beenham Church, Berks.

March 1st.—Mr. Powys and myself set out for Bath. . . .

March 4th.—At Mrs. Lutwyche's party. Sixteen card-tables, fifty-six people.

April 3rd, Good Friday.—Mr. Sibley, and two other clergymen gave the sacrament.

April 6th.—Went to see the model of Rome. At Tyson's ball in the evening. The Duke and Duchess of York at it.

April 20th.—Left Bath.

May 3rd, Sunday.—Our son Cooper preached, as Caroline, himself, and family came to stay with us the week before.

May 27th. — The Coopers, to our inexpressible grief, set out with their five dear children to Staffordshire.

July 14th.—We went to see Mrs. Stonor of Stonor, who was so obliging as to show us their new [1] chapel,

---

[1] This is a mistake; the chapel had been *restored.* Stonor Chapel, together with East Hendred, Berkshire, and Hazlewood, Yorkshire, are the only three chapels in England that have never passed from the Church of Rome.

1801 a most elegant one, and a very fine painting on glass done by Egginton, a present from Mr. Blundell, her father. The altar fine marble, brought from France since the Revolution.

July 17th.—Mr. Powys and Tom went to see the Annesleys at Coley,[1] near Reading, which place they had taken to remove most of their family, as the scarlet fever was very bad in their village near Bletchingdon Park. I was glad to see Coley again, as 'tis many years since our friends the Misses Thompson have been dead; but we were rather surprised that one of the sisters, Lady Jennings, now living, and who sold the place, should have left all the family pictures just in the same places we remember them.

July 23rd.—Mr. Powys and myself set off for Canterbury, but first went to Mr. Shrimpton's in London.

July 25th.—Went to see the panorama, a view of Constantinople well worth seeing, and after to see an original portrait of Bonaparte at the battle of Marengo, taken from life by Barrois. He is represented giving orders to General Berthier at the moment of victory; their two horses, natural size, in the background held by a hussar. There was another full-length picture of him in London at that time, but thought not so good as this.

Monday, July 27th.—Set off for Canterbury. . . .

July 31st.—Went to Leigh Abbey, Mr. Barret's. The house, place, and owner all extremely well worth seeing.

August 3rd.—Mr. Powys and myself set off for Ramsgate. Dr. Wolsby had been so kind as to take

[1] Coley Park, now seat of Berkeley Monck, Esq.

lodgings for us, the place was very full, and now much 1801
more fashionable than Margate. Our lodgings were
diminutive after the spacious rooms in the Deanery,
the largest ten feet square only, for which we gave
three guineas a week. Mr. Anson, for a house with
a view of the sea, the largest in Ramsgate, gave
eighteen guineas a week, and only five windows in
the front. . . .

August 7th.—I went with Miss Page in their
landaulet to Margate, Kingsgate, and Broad Stairs.
Opposite Margate was the ship[1] in which Lord Nelson
had just come in from Boulogne, where he had destroyed ten gunboats, but not burnt the town, as had
been reported, his Lordship saying it was never his
intention to fight against women and children. The
firing off Boulogne we heard very plain at Ramsgate
that evening. He was said to be going from thence
to do the same at Flushing, and took a great many
men from Ramsgate and Margate to show them, as
he had told them, some service. His Lordship did
not come on shore, and sail'd the next day.

Saturday, August 8th.—From the pier this evening we saw the fleet returning from the Baltic, about
nine men-of-war. They did not stop in the Downs.

August 22nd.—Went with Miss Page, and Miss
Harrison, to Margate. We observed a hoy coming in
so crowded that we really fear'd many of the passengers must have tumbled out or the vessel upset
as they were getting out; sometimes 200 people in
one. The pier was full of people looking, and laughing at the oddity of their disembarking.

August 24th.—Returned to the Deanery, Canterbury, for the race-week.

[1] The *Medusa.*

1801   *August 25th.*—Went to the Cathedral at ten.
Lord Camden, and the Bishop of Clogher, came to
my brother's. Lord Darnley was steward of the races.
A great deal of company ; public breakfasting every
morning at twelve ; ordinaries for the gentlemen at
two, as the race was after dinner, from which the
company returned to dress for the balls, which began
about seven. A play on the last day. Saturday no
ball.

August 26th.—I attended Lord Camden, and a
large party to the breakfast-rooms, and I am sure a
very cheap elegance, as only one shilling each person.
We dined at two, and I went in his Lordship's carriage
to the race-ground. . . .

August 27th.—In the evening Lord Camden, Mr.
Powys, and myself went to the ball, which was very
brilliant indeed. So many jewels I've not seen for
a great while, and the ladies mostly dress'd in silver
Canterbury muslins, which it seems are now in London called the Chambery, to sound, I suppose, more
fashionable, though all manufactured by Callaway in
this city. I think one hardly ever saw so many pretty
women, Lady Darnley [1] one of the most beautiful. . . .
Lord Camden danced the whole evening (as he told
us on the Tuesday), with Lady Darnley, and vastly
well indeed did both perform.

Monday, August 31st.—We left Canterbury, lay at
Rochester. We were surprised to see so many fields
of canary-seed, but it seems Kent is the only county
where it is sown.

September 16th.—We dined at Mr. Howman's, [2]

[1] Elizabeth, wife of the fourth Earl, third daughter of Right Hon.
William Brownlow.

[2] The Rev. Arthur E. Howman, for fifty years Vicar of Shiplake, from
1799 to 1848.

minister of Shiplake, Mrs. Atkyns Wright, and Mrs. 1801
Fanshawe there.

October 10*th.*—We dined at Lord Malmesbury's,
Park Place. Invited to a turtle, sent them by Lord
Lavington. We set down twenty-two. Lady Minto[1]
had just come from Vienna with her six children.
After tea and coffee in one room cards, in the other
dancing, Lady Minto's children had all learn'd at
Vienna, and I never saw any dance equal to them in
reels, waltzes, corsars, &c., &c.

Sunday, November 29*th.*—The snow so deep no
woman could get to church ; the Oxford mail stopped.
The snow lasted till December 3rd, succeeded by
great floods.

November 10*th.*—Elizabeth (Mrs. Tom Powys),
brought to bed of a son.[2]

January 2*nd.*—Snowed all day. The snow and 1802
frost continued on and till January 19th, having begun
on 23rd November.

On January 23rd the little boy at Remenham
christened, named Thomas Arthur.

January 30*th.*—Went to Fawley Court, and saw
Mrs. Freeman[3] for the first time since her fall, then
two years ago.

February 3*rd.*—Set off for Bath.

February 23*rd.*—At the Upper Rooms, reopened
this season on Tuesday, twenty-five tables.

Tuesday, February 2*nd.*—At the Upper Rooms,
twenty-seven tables.[4]

[1] Wife of first Earl Minto.
[2] Thomas Arthur, afterwards Vicar of Medmenham, Berks.
[3] This was Mrs. Strickland Freeman, not the dowager, Mrs. Freeman, who lived at Henley Park.
[4] This shows the prevalence of cards then. *Vide* Anstey's "New
Bath Guide," for the universal mania for gambling.

Returned home March 25th.

April 25th.—My dear Caroline (Cooper), brought to bed of her third son, Henry Gisborne. . . .

August 10th.—Mr. Powys and myself set out on our second journey into Staffordshire. Set out from Fawley at eight, got to Benson by ten, where we breakfasted, to Oxford at one, changed horses at Woodstock, and got to Chapel House by four, and to Stafford Bridge by nine, where we dined and lay, an excellent house for accommodations, tho' small, and the most reasonable in their charges I ever knew. Next morning set out early for Warwick, where we met Colonel Gregory, who had insisted that we should stay at least one night with them on our journey. We intended to see Warwick Castle. We were taken in at the porter's lodge, who inform'd us he was alway ordered by his Lordship to desire a note wrote by one of the company to request seeing the Castle. While this was taken to the house, the porter, a most respectable old servant in the family livery, showed us into a room hung round with armour, &c., of Guy, Earl of Warwick. In the centre stands the famous porridge pot belonging to that hero. It's made of brass, and contains 102 gallons, and the porter inform'd us was three times filled with punch at the present Earl's[1] coming of age. Warwick Castle I think a place as much worth seeing as any I ever was at. The family being there, could only see the ground-floor, on which are nine fine rooms. You go from the first to the last in a straight line, which measures 333 feet, and has a fine effect to the eye. The house is grandly furnish'd, many fine pictures, and numbers of ancient curiosities, a vast deal of old armour, &c., &c. Colonel

[1] George, second Earl of Warwick.

Gregory wish'd us to go to Kenilworth Castle, five 1802
miles from Warwick, to see the inside of that famous
ruin ; but as we knew this must make us late for Mrs.
Gregory's dinner, we only stopped to take an outside
view of the venerable pile, and then proceeded to the
Colonel's seat called Stivishall Hall. . . .

August 12*th*.—After breakfast we set out thro'
Coventry, by Kenilworth to Lichfield, where we
dined, and reached Hamstall by tea-time, finding all
the family (Coopers), perfectly well. . . . We returned
to Fawley on September 9th. . . .

September 21*st*.—We all went to Reading to see
the cheese fair, and were much entertain'd by the
sight of such quantities of that useful commodity, and
afterwards saw Astley's horses perform their wonders
round a circus. We were in what was called the
boxes, 2s. a seat ; there was a vast number of the
neighbouring families there.

December 31*st*.—No frost or snow hardly this
winter, but constant fogs, and rain almost daily.

February 1*st*.—Mr. Powys and myself set off for 1803
our annual Bath tour.

February 8*th*.—At the Tuesday card assembly ;
twenty-three tables.

12*th*.—We were at the cotillon, or fancy ball.

February 24*th*.—Saw the panorama of London.

25*th*.—Went to see the " Invisible lady made
visible," (a very foolish thing).

In March, Mr. Dutton, brother to Lord Sher-
bourne, married at Bath the celebrated beauty,
Miss Honoria Gubbins. Settled on her in case
of no children £5000, and £300 pin-money, and
£15,000 on younger children, if any. We were then
at Bath.

1803   Colonel Cotterel drove four cream-colour'd horses
this year at Bath, which he had bought of the King,
who met him one day, when his Majesty told him he
was quite happy they were in such good hands.

When the influenza was so violent this spring at
Bath, Dr. Parry visited 120 patients in two days ;
and Mr. Crook, the apothecary, only wish'd he could
have a lease of this same influenza for eight years—
he should not desire a better fortune.

Oberne, the Bishop of Meath, preach'd an excellent sermon at this season at Bath against card-parties,
and concerts on Sunday evenings. His wife, Mrs.
Oberne, went the day after to pay a morning visit to
an old lady, who told her she was very angry with her
husband, as she had just received twenty-eight cards
of refusals to her next Sunday's party. " Oh, how
glad I am," says Mrs. Oberne, " to hear this." The
lady bridled up, and replied, " However, it shall not
hinder my parties." Miss Wroughton declared she
would always have her Sunday concerts, for all the
bishops. This latter lady, formerly one of the first
of the Bath beauties, was lately styled by a wit at
that place, " A proof print of former times." Mr.
Whaley, a fine travelled young clergyman, a widower,
who has spent already two good fortunes, a great
taste for virtu, was married this year, after a three
weeks' courtship, to a Miss Heathcote, aged sixty,
with a fortune of fourscore thousand pounds in her
own power. She had the finest dresses made for the
occasion I ever heard of, her gowns laced to the
highest expense of fashion, and all jewels that was
possible. She wore round her neck a necklace with
medallions of the twelve Cæsars, on which the following lines were made :—

" No longer at thy virgin state repine,
  Twelve Cæsars now upon thy breast recline.
      O happy she ! "

She has an elegant house in the Crescent, and he
has one in St. James' Square, Bath, which, tho' most
elegantly furnished, after he returned from Paris, finding paper-hangings were there call'd vulgar, immediately took all down and hung all with satins.

We returned to Fawley, April 20th.

June 13th.—The christening of Tom's little Catherine Jane. We dined at Remenham.

August 2nd.—Mr. Powys and I set out for our
son Cooper's in Staffordshire, and reached Hamstall
on the 3rd about six. Had the inexpressible joy to
see Cooper, Caroline, and their six dear children in
perfect health.

August 5th.—Our wedding-day. We had been
married now forty-one years, and I believe I may
most sincerely say, as perfectly happy as 'tis possible
to be.

August 10th.—A party of eight we started, some
driving, some riding, at 7.30 A.M., to Derby. We
got to Tutbury, where we breakfasted ; 'tis five miles
from Bourton on the south bank of the river Dove.
We walk'd up to the fine old ruin of the castle, where
Mary, Queen of Scots, had formerly been a prisoner.
The views from thence are remarkably picturesque.
The castle is about seven hundred years old. The
Saxon arch gateway into the church [1] is very fine.
In 1568, during the time of the Duke of Norfolk's
intrigue in the reign of Elizabeth, Mary, Queen of
Scots, was removed hither from Bolton Castle, a
house of Lord Scrope's, on the borders of Yorkshire.

[1] Once the Priory Church.

z

1803 She was seventeen years in different confinements. From the walls of Tutbury Castle, which has so long echoed the sighs of the unfortunate queen, she was removed in 1586 to Chartley, and from thence in September 1586 to Fotheringay Castle in Northamptonshire. The west end of Tutbury Church, notwithstanding the ravages that have been made in this fine old fabric, still exhibits a specimen of Saxon architecture more rich and beautiful than any of the kind in this island.

We set off for Derby about ten, got there to dinner, walked about the town, which may be called a good one. Next morning we went to the celebrated china manufactory, where we all purchas'd many articles; from thence to view the silk-mills, which seems the most curious invention that can be. Mr. John Lombe had a patent to bring this contrivance to England from Italy. Before you enter the manufactory you pass an immense wheel;[1] by that one 99,947 other wheels are all turn'd. There are three sorts of silk from China and Italy. Near three hundred little girls are employ'd in tying knots as the silk breaks, and numbers of boys. From thence we went to the Derbyshire spar manufactory. There, we all made many purchases. We return'd to the "George" inn, and took some refreshment before setting out for Burton. This town is a tolerable one, a bridge there very remarkable for its length. We were much disappointed with the famous Burton ale, and all of us agreed we had never tasted worse.

August 25th.—We went to see Beau Desert, the Earl of Uxbridge's, a large old white house, situated

---

[1] This wheel, twenty-three feet in circumference, was turned by water from the river Derwent.

on a vast eminence, commanding a most beautiful 1803
prospect. 'Tis a great pity that now none of the
family reside there; 'tis now almost unfurnished, and
looks desolate. In one fine room they had put the
present fashionable large window - frames, and the
largest panes of plate-glass I had ever seen, which
cost five guineas a pane.

August 31*st.*—Returned to Fawley. . . .

November 4*th.*—We were much alarm'd by fire at
Fawley Court, which broke out in the morn in the
carpenter's shops erected for the repairs now doing
there. Four fine horses were smother'd, three or
four burnt, stables, and the shop, many of the new
mahogany window-frames, and the plate-glass of them
broke. The family were away. Fortunately it did
not reach the house, though it did considerable
damage. . . .

December 30*th.*—A ball and supper at Lord Malmesbury's, Park Place. The company about sixty-four.
There by half-past seven. Supped at twelve. Got
home before four in the morning.

January 1*st,* 1804.—The first day for three weeks 1804
without rain.

January 12*th.*—Mr. Powys and myself set out on
our annual Bath excursion.

January 27*th.*—I was at the ladies' Catch Club.
Mrs. Badderley was so obliging as to get me a ticket,
a difficult thing to get. About three hundred and
seventy-two, mostly ladies. No supper, but cake, ices,
and jellies carried round between the acts.

February 6*th.*—At the dress-ball, Upper Rooms.
Took my god-daughter, Charlotte Powney. The
Duke and Duchess of Devonshire and family, and
the French General Boger, who dined at her Grace's

1804 most days. He was permitted to come to Bath, but
not London. We wondered he had been allowed to
come to such a public place as that, but he pleaded
his health. Major and Mrs. Plunket there. His lady,
the famous novel-writer, Miss Cumming, an extremely
plain woman. . . .

March 16th.—Home to Fawley.

November 2nd.—The Dean, Mr. Powys, and
myself went to Mr. King's at Wycombe. Mr. King
took us to see Lord Carrington's,[1] a fine old place,
just out of the town. It is now being fitted up by
Wyatt in the ancient style, as such places should be,
and not modernised. Nothing can be more magnificent, and 'tis supposed it will cost at least £50,000.
Nothing could be more polite than my Lord, and her
Ladyship. Their family consists of girls, and only
one son, who is the youngest.

November 10th.—I went to Mr. West's, but they
were gone to London to thank the King for his visit
to Culham Court the week before.

November 26th.—Louisa (Powys), and myself went
to Mr. West's, and they gave us a full account of the
late royal visit—the King, Queen, some of the princesses, five gentlemen, thirty-two horses, and numbers
of servants; but they were prepar'd for all by Lady
Matilda Wynyard, who was staying at Culham Court;
indeed, they had fix'd the week before, but put it off,
which was rather inconvenient; but they had a dinner
ready at one, at which hour his Majesty generally
dines. They seemed much pleased with the place
and their reception; would have all the children[2] in the

---

[1] Wycombe Abbey.
[2] The late Miss West remembered the good-natured King playing
with her half-brothers, with his riding-whip, on the door-steps.

room with them the whole time ; and when they went 1804
over the apartments, the King, who always goes into
every room, popped into one where the maid was
dressing out the flowers, &c. She started up, and
was greatly alarmed, but his Majesty laughed, and
said to her, " Don't be frightened ; I won't steal any
one thing." [1]

January 12th, 1805.—Mr. Powys and myself went 1805
to Bath.

January 24th.—The cotillon ball.

January 28th. — The dress ball, Upper Rooms,
immensely crowded at ten ; but the number of card-
parties quite spoil the balls, as 'tis fashionaable to
attend five or six before you go to the room. It was
endeavoured to alter these hours, but fortunately for the
old people, and those who drink the waters, it was not
permitted, and at eleven,[2] if in the middle of a dance,
the music stops. But as I suppose 'tis reckon'd vulgar
to come early, one sees nothing of the dancing or
company for the crowds. The rooms are not half so
agreeable as they were some years ago, when the late
London hours were not thought of ; and how prejudicial must they be to the health of all, is very visible
in the young as well as in the old. Formerly youth
was seldom ill ; now, from thin clothing and late hours,
you hardly see a young lady in good health, or not
complaining of rheumatism, as much as us old ones !

---

[1] Mr. West had hot rolls brought from Gunter, wrapped in flannel,
by relays of horsemen ! The King said, "Ah ! Gunter, Gunter ! I am
glad you deal with Gunter, West : nobody like Gunter !"   The King
wiped his shoes carefully on entering, and on Mr. West telling him not
to mind, said, " No, West, I am not going to carry dirt into any man's
house."

[2] This was introduced by " Beau Nash," when the inexorable master
of the ceremonies at Bath.

1805 Sixteen thousand strangers at Bath in the season 1805!

March 5th.—Our grandson, Warren Cooper, born, 1805.

March 29th.—Returned from Bath.

May 29th.—Mr. Powys and myself set out for London. Got to Mrs. Shrimpton's, Bedford Square, at half-past four.

June 9th.—I have seen the panoramas, the Rock of Gibraltar, the Bay of Naples, and the view of Edinburgh, all particularly pleasing.

June 10th.—Mr. and Mrs. Cox came to dinner. He is the author of "Miscellaneous Poetry," a very entertaining book. I copied the following from it :—

> "From their coasts by the gales should our navy be toss'd,
> And in spite of our tars should our Channel be cross'd,
> Frenchmen never our dear native land shall explore,
> If not sunk in the sea they shall die on the shore.
> Then let Nelson and Sydney [1] new triumphs prepare
> And the Corsican tyrant may come if he dare!"

June 14th was the first day of Term, when all the judges, counsellors, &c., &c., came to breakfast with the Chancellor in Bedford Square, a few doors from Mrs. Shrimpton's. There were fifty-one carriages, and on their return the Chancellor's (Lord Eldon's [2]), state-coach, with long-tailed horses, and two more of his own coaches followed the state one, in which he went to Westminster Hall. Unfortunately it was a very wet day. The seventeenth carriage was the state one.

June 17th.—The Dean came from Windsor to breakfast with us. We all went to Laurence's, the painter.

---

[1] Sir William Sidney Smith, a distinguished admiral.
[2] Lord Eldon became Lord Chancellor in 1801.

June 18*th.*—The Dean went to the Archbishop 1805
of Canterbury's at Lambeth to stay one night on his
way to Canterbury. Mr. Powys and myself set out
for Fawley.

August 1*st.*—I rode my donkey for the first time,
which Mr. Powys had just bought me. It cost three
guineas and a half.

August 12*th.*—Mr. Powys and myself set off for
our son Cooper's, in Staffordshire. We hired a post-
chaise for the time at a guinea a week, of Hicks,
coachmaker in the Fair Mile.[1]

August 14*th.*—We went out most mornings and
evenings in the two donkey-chaises—very clever
vehicles indeed. Caroline drove one, and little Edward was so pleased at being postillion to grand-
mamma, that, though I sometimes drove myself, he
most days rode my donkey, the carriages only holding
one person each.

 · Monday the 26th had been for some time fixed
on for us to go to Matlock and Dove Dale. We
set out a party of seven ; we went through Blithbury
and Abbots Bromley. We got to the Rev. Mr.
Stubbs' at Uttoxeter by half-past one, who asked us
to dine with him. We went to see the church, rather
an extraordinary one, very ancient, and the pews so
oddly managed[2] as three or four to go through each
other, and so very narrow that, if those belonging to
the outward ones happen to come first, without they
are the most slender persons, it's impossible to pass
each other. Caroline and myself, who are not so,

---

[1] At Henley-on-Thames.
[2] This was the case at Shiplake Church, Oxon, before the restoration
of 1870. The seats in the first pews in the chancel had to be *lifted up*,
to admit persons to the seats behind.

1805 could not help laughing, and saying it was lucky *we* did not belong to this church. . . . We set out from Mr. Stubbs' after dinner. We got to Ashbourne early enough to walk about before supper. 'Tis a very pretty town. We lay there, and set out for Dove Dale early on Tuesday, and went through the most romantic and beautiful road, call'd the " Via Gellia," lately made through his own grounds by a Mr. Gell. In the midst of this woody scenery at a distance rises a grand solitary rock, the characteristic feature of this vale, known by the name of Dove Dale *Church*. It consists of a large face of rock, with two or three spiry heads, and one very large one. The valley of Dove Dale is very narrow at the bottom, consisting of little more than the channel of the Dove, which is a considerable stream, and a footpath along the banks. I mentioned having gone through " Via Gellia," but I made a mistake ; it was *after* we left Dove Dale, on our way back to Ashbourne, where we dined, and got to Matlock in the evening, to the Old Bath Hotel, still reckoned the best. When I was there in 1757, breakfast was at eight, dinner at two ; now dinner at four and supper at half-past nine ; and what is pleasanter, you have your tea and breakfast with your own party *only*, at what time you like. There is generally dancing after supper, the ball and dinner rooms both very handsome and large. The view from the front of the hotel is quite beyond description. . . . Matlock, like all other water-ing-places at this period, is expensive living ; they charge so much each person for *breakfast, dinner, tea, and supper*. The bed-chambers small, but very neat ; each door labelled 8s. a week, and numbered. Ours was 34.

Wednesday, 28th.—We set off to walk all round the 1805
environs of Matlock; ascended the rock call'd Matlock, 120 yards high; on each side a row of lofty elms,
call'd the "Lover's Walk." We crossed the river
Derwent in a boat kept for that purpose, and ascended
by a winding path up the rocks to the finest natural
terrace, call'd the Hay Rock, from whence you have
a perpendicular view down a vast precipice to the
river. . . .

August 29th.—We set out at seven o'clock from
Matlock to breakfast at Derby. Within three miles
of that town we passed Kedleston, Lord Scarsdale's.
We walk'd about the town, purchasing spar, china,
&c.; re-started to Hamstall, which we reached by nine.

September.—Mr. Powys and myself left Hamstall,
to return to Fawley. A dismal parting as usual.

October 18th.—Tom,[1] who was now the Dean's
curate, did the whole duty.

October 23rd.—Our daughter, Louisa Powys of
Hardwick, was brought to bed of a girl. Our seventeenth grandchild.

December 7th.—Mr. Powys and myself went to
the play at Henley, bespoke by Lady Elizabeth Fane.
A very full house. Sheridan's play of "The Rivals,"
an excellent one, and vastly well perform'd. One of
their actors, Mr. William Penley, is as capital a performer as any I've seen in London or Bath. The
theatre, a new one, a very nice one indeed.

December 12th.—It snow'd in the night, and continued all day. Mrs. Atkyns Wright had bespoke a
play, and we were engaged to dine at Mr. Coventry's.
We had great difficulty in getting down our hill. How-

---

[1] Tom succeeded his uncle, Dean Powys, as Rector of Fawley in 1810,
presented by Strickland Freeman, Esq.

1805 ever, got safe to Henley; dined at Mr. Coventry's. We all went to the theatre at half-past six, and, despite of the weather, Mrs. Atkyns Wright had a full house. The plays, "The Way to get Married," and "Of Age, To-morrow."

1806 *January 3rd, 1806.*—First Henley assembly. A very good one—twenty couples.

Thursday, January 16th.—Mr. Powys and myself set off for Bath about nine; took our coach to the "Black Bear," Reading, from thence in post-chaise.

January 23rd.—Thursday, to the inexpressible loss of the nation, died Mr. Pitt, only forty-seven years of age. 'Tis impossible to say how much he seemed to be regretted by every one we met.

January 27th.—At the dress ball, Mr. King was now master of the ceremonies at the Upper Room, as Tyson had given it up.

February 3rd.—Cotillon ball.

February 22nd.—At the play, "The School for Friends." The first time I had seen the new theatre; a very fine one.

March 6th.—At the play (Mrs. Didier's benefit), "To Marry or not to Marry," and the farce "A Tale of Mystery."

March 29th.—At the play, to see Cooke perform Sir Pertinax MacSycophant in "The Man of the World," written by the late Charles Macklin, and the pantomime of "Harlequin Æsop, or Hymen's Gift."

April 1st.—We left Bath. The illness now everywhere term'd "the influenza" very prevalent. Mr. Powys very ill, with such a lowness and debility.

April 16th.—The christening [1] of little Emily at

---

[1] Two grandchildren, Emily, Philip Powys's child, and Augusta, Thomas Powys's.

Hardwick. I was unluckily too ill to go, as I was 1806
one of the godmothers.

April 30th.—We all went to Remenham, to the
christening of little Augusta Powys. . . .

June 17th.—We went to the town-hall, Henley,
to hear Mr. Scobel, the schoolmaster's, scholars re-
hearse, which they did vastly well. The hall was
immensely crowded by all the neighbourhood, and
was very elegantly ornamented all round with wreaths
of roses, &c. . . .

October 24th.—Our dear old friend, Mrs. Freeman,
of Henley Park, died, after a most lingering illness.

October 30th.—On this day our ever to be la-
mented friend, Mrs. Freeman, was buried in the family
mausoleum, Fawley Church. The Dean perform'd
the ceremony ; a great concourse of people.

January 12th.—Mr. Powys and myself set out for 1807
Bath.

January 17th.—Master Betty[1] acted for his last
night at Bath, and though we had no very great desire
to see him, thought it would be foolish to lose the opportunity. He acted in the play of "Mahomet," and was
just the thing we had expected ; for tho' he certainly acts
well, yet his youth and manner could never make one
suppose him the character he represents, and his voice
now is quite horrid. The company at Bath did not
seem the least sorry at his departure, and the actors,
as one may suppose, were much rejoiced. Some years
hence I dare say he will be an excellent performer.

February 2nd.—A morning subscription concert,
for the benefit of Miss Randal, at the New Room,

---

[1] Called the "Young Roscius." A portrait of him exists in the students'
room, Reading Free Library ; died young. His real name was W. R.
Grossmith ; born in Reading, Berks.

1807 York Hotel. She is only six years old, and is indeed
a most wonderful little creature; plays on the piano
in a most wonderful manner, and has a sweet voice;
she is accompanied on the harp by her blind father,
and by her uncle, Mr. Parry, on the flageolet. It was
a pleasing sight to see the little performer lifted on
the platform by her uncle, and as she walk'd up the
room she was spoken to by all she pass'd near, and
met with great applause. Before she was three years
old she could play three tunes.

February 3rd.—Was at the procession of Mr.
Walter Long's burial, which went from his house in
Gay Street to be buried at his estate at Wrexham,[1]
Wiltshire. The cavalcade was very magnificent. First,
seven men on horseback, then men with plumes of
feathers, his own mourning chaise and four, the hearse
and six, Lord Hood's coach and six, and post-chaise
and six, six chaises and pair, and the concourse of
people that follow'd were not to be numbered. He
was ninety-six years of age, and died worth £800,000,
which he left to his sister, then ninety-one, at her
death to his nephew, John Long, and at John's death
to a brother of Mr. John's, and at his death to a Mr.
Jones. He left above fifty hundred pounds legacies.

February 14th.—I went to the play "Adrian and
Orilla," and the "Forty Thieves."

March 15th.—The Bishop of Ferne preach'd at
Queen's Square, a most excellent sermon; indeed he
is a most amiable man, and his lady equally so. We
could not help feeling for what they suffered in Ireland—their house torn down, their furniture taken,

---

[1] Should be Wraxall Manor, once an abbey; has been in the Long
family since 1426. Mr. Long was a great admirer of Miss Linley, but
she married R. B. Sheridan instead.

and every place ransack'd, his loss above £10,000, by 1807
the Irish rebels; and what must have caus'd them infinite distress, most of their own servants were concern'd in the whole. Poor Mrs. Clever's health was
so much hurt, and she still feels it so much, that she
fears she shall never have fortitude to return to his
bishopric in Ireland.

April 2nd.—Set out for Fawley; weather intensely
cold.

July 14th.—Cooper, Caroline, their eight children,
Miss Morse the governess, and two servants came
from Staffordshire to Hardwick.

July 31st.—Mr. Powys and myself went to Hardwick to see the Coopers; the children in high spirits
with their five Hardwick cousins, so only saw thirteen[1] together, as Tom's were not there. The Coopers
came to us afterwards.

August 15th.—I drove to Mrs. Innes's[2] in my
donkey-chaise, and its being quite a new carriage in
this part of the world, I gain'd the attention of every
one, and children follow'd me all over the town.

September 16th.—We all went to Tom's at Remenham to dinner, and to the christening of their last
child, Bransby William Powys.

October 1st.—Our dear Caroline Cooper and children set off for Staffordshire.

December 2nd.—Staying at Hardwick; the gentlemen went a shooting, and had great sport,[3] killed six
woodcocks, four rabbits, one hare, but missed a shot
at a fine cock-pheasant.

---

[1] Mr. and Mrs. Powys had eighteen grandchildren at that period.
[2] Mrs. Innes lived at "Paradise House," Henley.
[3] What would the battue-shooter of the present day think of this bag
for a party of four men?

1807   *December 17th.*—To a play at Henley, bespoke by Lady Stapleton, " Laugh when you can," and the " Devil to Pay." A very full house; all the neighbouring families there.

December 22nd.—The play at Henley bespoke by Mrs. Atkyns Wright, " Town and Country," by Morton, and " Blue Beard." A very full house, tho' a great fog and *no moon.*

December 31st.—Another play, bespoke by Miss Grote (of Badgemore), " How to Grow Rich," and " Mother Goose."

1808   *January 13th,* 1808.—Mr. Powys and myself set off for Bath. . . .

March 9th.—I went to Ranzini's concert to hear Madame Catalani,[1] but was disappointed with numbers, as she came from the opera in London all night, caught a violent cold and sore throat ; above a thousand had been in the concert-room hours, some they said by three o'clock ; we did not go till six, and had not a very good seat. At eight, when it was to begin, Ranzini came on the platform to say how shock'd Madame Catalani was at disappointing the company, but she was really too ill to sing the songs given out, but she would try some others. We began to fear a riot, as some hisses began. However, Madame came, and I daresay did what she was able, but was quite unable to sing, and retired with many apologies. The next morning handbills were given out that she could not sing that night as she had intended, as there was to have been two, but that she would come down next Wednesday to Ranzini's concert, and to those who had been on the evening before she would sing on

[1] Angelica Catalani, born 1782, made her *début* on the stage 1802, came to England in 1806.

the next Thursday morning, so every one seem'd 1808 satisfied, till the Tuesday morning following, when bills were again circulated that she was too ill to come down ; so here it finally ended, except to poor Ranzini, who behaved uncommonly generous, desiring every one who was at the first concert, or those who had tickets for the second, to call at the rooms, where each would be return'd their half-guinea.

March 10th.—At the cotillon ball, the Lower Rooms, a remarkably good one. A French emigrant who was permitted to be at Bath was reckon'd a remarkable good dancer, and certainly was so. He had not been latterly, as some gentleman had said one night, " No wonder he dances fine, when he was a dancing-master," but they say that was only a joke.

April 7th.—The Coopers, Mr. Powys, and myself went by nine o'clock to see Mr. Freeman[1] ride in his riding-house, and very entertaining it was. He rode six different horses, and Miss Caroline Strickland rode two of them.

August 2nd.—We set out for Hamstall, Staffordshire.

August 5th.—Our wedding-day, the *forty-sixth;* married 1762.

October 29th.—The Dean was taken with a fit of the gout.

December 31st.—Mr. Scobel[2] did duty. I was too ill to venture out.

And here, alas! the facile, agreeable pen of Mrs. Powys ceased, or, at any rate, none of her great-

---

[1] Strickland Freeman of Fawley Court, Bucks, was a great horseman ; he wrote a book upon training and breaking horses. Caroline Strickland was his niece.

[2] Master of the Royal Grammar School, Henley-on-Thames.

grandchildren possess any further diaries. The abruptness seems almost painful to the reader, the last entry, as we see, refers to her being ill ; possibly that prevented her resuming her able pen for a while, but if she did write any more daily entries, they are lost. Hitherto her life may be said to have been free from much trouble, but a frightful loss was in store for her, for on April 12, 1809, her husband died suddenly and most unexpectedly. What that blow must have been to her tender heart, those who have read her words as to her nearly forty-six years of wedded happiness can understand. Mr. Powys was laid to rest on April 20 in the family burial-place at Whitchurch, Oxon. His age was seventy-five.

This was not the end of her misfortunes, for the Dean, "her brother," as she always affectionately named him, died on October 7, whilst in residence at Canterbury, and was buried there. Presumably Mrs. Powys was with him till then. She now retired to Henley to live in a house in New Street, on the north side next the river, now occupied by Miss Latter. Very possibly it was the same house as her mother, Mrs. Girle, had lived in for some years till she died in 1801, probably having a lease of it, but this is not certain. The house is a large solid red brick mansion with gabled roof, of the style of Queen Anne, but a portion appears to be of older date. Many of the rooms are or have been panelled ; the drawing-room at the back, from its greater loftiness and more modern style, was built more recently, possibly for herself or her mother.

At the back is a charming old walled garden, in the centre of which stands a magnificent Ailanthus Glandulosa, or "Tree of the Gods." Before the

modern boat-houses were built by the river, all the
bedroom windows at the back commanded a fine
view of the entire regatta course, now unfortunately
blocked out. From the street front of the house a
view of the river to the bridge is obtained. As in
old days the broad-wheeled waggons stood, and the
cheese fair was held, at the wharf at the bottom
of the street, we can fancy Mrs. Powys's lively interest
in it all.

The whole house is very quaint, with little steps
up and down, uneven floors in some rooms, and hosts
of delightful old cupboards ; several very large bedrooms.

In this same house Bishop Woodford, of Ely, was
born in 1820. His mother was an Appleton, whose
family lived there after Mrs. Powys left. New Street
is *new* only in name, as it is at least 500 years old !

Mr. Strickland Freeman presented the living of
Fawley, now vacant, tô the Rev. Thomas Powys,
son of our Mrs. Powys, and nephew of the Dean,
and he was inducted April 6, 1810. As has been
stated, he married in 1799 Miss Elizabeth Palgrave.
At this time he was the father of six children, to
which three more were added at a birth in the following May ! One trusts the birth of the triplets
may have made a fresh interest in Mrs. Powys's now
saddened life.

The only letter of her writing existent, is the
following, addressed to her daughter-in-law, Mrs.
Philip Lybbe Powys of Hardwick :—

"HENLEY,
17th April 1812.

"MY DEAR LOUISA,—Give me leave most sincerely
to congratulate you on your late legacy, and believe

me no one feels more pleasure in it than myself. I fear I shall hardly be able to write legible, as I've had such a fall I can hardly use my right arm, as unfortunately I fell on that shoulder, and 'tis now in constant pain, and I suppose the rheumatism is settled there. I hope to hear you are all well, to whom joyn in love, and believe me.—Your ever affectionate

"CAROLINE POWYS."

Yet one more peep at her before the veil drops, in an extract from a letter from Mrs. Elizabeth Powney to her.

Mrs. Girle, Mrs. Powys's mother, had a half-sister, who married first a Mr. Phelp, by whom she had a daughter, married to the Marquis de la Peire. After the death of Mr. Phelp, Mrs. Phelp remarried a Mr. Floyer. A daughter by this second marriage married Pennystone Powney, of Ives Place, Berks, on December 20, 1776. This lady writes the following, and sends it by her son :—

"IVES LODGE,
CHELTENHAM,
November 1, 1815.

"MY DEAREST CAROLINE,—I cannot let the opportunity slip of my dear Richard's going into Berkshire without sending you a few lines to know how you are, as Charlotte and myself frequently write but can get no answer, tho' I do sometimes hear of you from Madame de la Peire—however, not that lately. My son has promised if he possibly can, to leave this himself on his way through Henley, and see you. He is going to Maidenhead on business with Mr. Payne. . . . I hope you will be able to see my dear Richard. He is truly a most affectionate child, like

all yours, who I hope are well? Pray my kindest
regards to all of them. Mr. Henry Powys,[1] your
grandson, called on me one day at Bath. I was
extremely sorry when I came home to find his card
only. . . . If it is irksome to you to write, tell him
[her son], all you wish to say, and he will write to
me from Maidenhead. . . .

"ELIZABETH POWNEY."

On August 17, 1817, the Rev. Thomas Powys
died at Fawley Rectory, leaving a widow and eleven
children, the eldest not quite seventeen. Our Mrs.
Powys appears to have gone to comfort and help her
daughter-in-law in her affliction, and she did not long
survive this fresh blow, but died at Fawley Rectory,
and was buried at Whitchurch by the Rev. G. Hunt,
in her husband's grave, on November 7th in the same
year, 1817, aged seventy-nine years.

Mrs. Powys from her parents had been a considerable heiress, owning property at Beenham,[2]
Berks, from her father (Mr. Girle); a house in Lincoln's Inn Fields which he built, and which we find
in her note-books they took up residence in on
September 14, 1754; from her mother she owned
one-third of an estate at Lulsley, Worcestershire,
besides considerable sums in the public funds inherited from both parents. That she was an excellent wife and mother, an affectionate friend, and
excellent mistress, is easily perceived by her diaries.
Many are the notices of old servants, too numerous
to insert here, with this exception :—" Sarah Lovejoy,

---

[1] Henry Philip, eldest son of Philip Lybbe Powys of Hardwick.
[2] Beenham tithes were purchased by Sir Charles Rich, of Mr. Powys
of Hardwick in 1802.

died May 1778, after a long illness; nursed all my four children; a most diligent, faithful servant."

A word or two must be recorded of the career of Dean Powys, her beloved brother-in-law, at whose house the last twenty-five years of her life had been spent. Thomas Powys was born at Hardwick, September 25, 1736; he was christened on St. Luke's day; godfathers, Thomas Powys of Lilford and his uncle Ambrose Powys; godmother, his aunt Anne Powys. What school he went to is unknown. It is possible he had a tutor at home. In 1753, when he was in his seventeenth year, he matriculated at St. John's College, Oxford, took his B.A. degree in 1757, M.A. 1760. He took orders, and was ordained priest, February 15, 1761, and in May following his relation Thomas Powys, of Berwick, gave him the living of Munslow, Salop. He also became chaplain to John, Lord Montagu. October 30, 1762, he was made Rector of Fawley, Bucks, by presentation of Sambrook Freeman, Esq. of Fawley Court. On May 18, 1769, made Rector of Silchester, Hants, by presentation of Lord Camden, then Lord Chancellor, the living having lapsed to the Crown by Dr. Shipley's (the former Rector's), promotion to the Bishopric of Llandaff. Lord Camden procured Mr. Powys a prebendal stall at Hereford on December 5, 1769, vacant by promotion of Dr. Bazzington to a bishopric. On April 24, 1779, Lord Thurlow, then Chancellor, made him a Prebendary of Bristol. In November 1781 Mr. Powys became Chaplain to the King. March 1795 he was appointed first Chaplain to Lord Camden, then Lord Lieutenant of Ireland; in December of same year he became Doctor of Divinity, and Lord Camden offered him the Bishopric of Killala,

which he refused. August 25, 1796, on the death of
Dr. Sheppard, he was installed Canon of Windsor.
May 26, 1797, through Mr. Pitt he was made Dean
of Canterbury, his predecessor, Dr. Cornwall, going to
the See of Bristol. Dean Powys died at Canterbury,
October 7, 1809, aged seventy-three, and was buried
there. He was a most genial, able man, a great
favourite in society, and had a remarkable talent for
rhyming. Many of his poems are existent in the
family ; amongst them two odes to his favourite
friend, General Conway, of Park Place. Berks.

NOTES

NOTES

NOTE I.—(Page 103.)

List of plate, &c., piteously described by Mr. Richard Lybbe as "taken awaie," by the Parliamentary troops during the Civil War from Hardwick House, Oxon.

	£	s.	d.
On great basin and ewer, worth . . .	29	o	o
On deep bason	9	o	o
A pair of great flagons	28	o	o
Two double gilt salts with covers, at . .	24	o	o
On chafing dish, at	8	o	o
On cream bole, at	6	o	o
Three thick boles, parcel gilt with a couver .	26	o	o
On great gilt bole	7	10	o
A little gilt bole with couver . . .	3	10	o
On gilt fruit dish	4	o	o
On little sugar dish	2	10	o
A gilt bole with mother of pearle . . .	3	o	o
On silver tankard	7	o	o
On little gilt salt	o	12	o
Two dozen silver spoons, and four gilt spoons, and two silver forks	24	o	o

Beside this, money, and a bed with velvet hangings is mentioned as taken, the whole valued about £800 then, which, with the depreciation of coin in these days, would now be worth much more.

NOTE II.—(Page 106.)

Elizabeth Lybbe, who married J. Merrick, M.D., of Reading, and was mother of James Merrick, poet and author, left an interesting note about Dame Alice Lisle, of Moyles Court, Hants, who was condemned to death by the infamous Judge Jeffreys for sheltering and hiding two fugitives, a divine and a lawyer, from the field of Sedgemoor on the evening of July 28, 1685.

Lady Lisle was the widow of John Lisle, who sat in the Long Parliament and in the High Court of Justice, was made a peer by Cromwell in 1658, therefore not in favour with the Stuart line. Dame Alice, of a kindly heart, is said to have sheltered Royalists, as well as Roundheads, in their need. She was three times acquitted by the jury, yet condemned, and executed on September 2, 1685, at Winchester, and lies buried at Ellingham, near her home, Moyles Court.

This is the note of Elizabeth Lybbe, whose mother was Sophia Tipping, daughter of Sir Thomas Tipping, married to Richard Lybbe, of Hardwick House, Oxon :—

" Lady Tipping, my grandfather's wife, was sister and co-heiress with Alice, wife of Lord de Lisle ; her title I think the Government acknowledge. The severe sentence of taking off her head was pronounced on account of her suffering Hix, a traitor, to take shelter in her house, which her woman discovered. My aunt Lisle was much older than my grandmother, and from age and a quiet conscience, slept at her trial, as she did the night before she suffered, when my pious aunt Tipping slept with her.

"The day of her execution was September 2, 1685. She had many daughters, but one son, John, who left his estate to L'Isle, Esquire, of Crooks Eason, Hants.

"My grandmother (Lady Tipping), was a most remarkable woman for strict piety, sedateness of temper, and good conduct ; my grandfather leaving it much to her care to manage the family. They had sixteen children, six sons only."

Dame Lisle was over seventy years of age when she was executed. Her mother was Lady Beckonshaw, daughter of William Bond, of a well-known Dorset family of the Isle of Purbeck.

NOTE III.—(Page 117.)

"CHRYSAL," REAL CHARACTERS.

In an old note-book of Mrs. Powys's is a list of the characters depicted in "Chrysal, or the Adventures of a Guinea," which was published in 1771. Of late days it has been sometimes denied that the description of "The Monastery" in volume iii. page 231. of "Chrysal," was an account of the pranks of the latter - day

Franciscans, of Medmenham Abbey; by this list it will be seen
that it was known to be, by a member of society who lived in the
actual days of the existence of the sham monks, and other characters described, and who knew personally some of the people in
this list.

Real Characters in " Chrysal."

Volume I., Page 79.—Lord Anson.
„ „ 85.—Sir Edward Faulkner.
„ „ 98.—Mr. Pitt (afterwards Lord Chatham),
     discovers cock's horns to be sham.
„ „ 100.—Lord Chesterfield.
„ „ 104.—Lord Howe.
„ „ 116, 117.—Dr. Hill.
„ „ 141.—Mother Douglas.
„ „ 211.—Wilkes.
Volume II., Page 24.—Duchess of Newcastle.
„ „ 38.—Aminadab Gideon, the Jew.
„ „ 57.—" Dr. Hunchback," Mr. Whitefield.
„ „ 58.—Ballad Singer, Fook.
„ „ 63.—Mother Douglas.
„ „ 165.—King of Prussia.
„ „ 215.—Prince Ferdinand.
„ „ 215.—Lord March.
„ „ 238.—Lord Sandwich.
Volume III., Page 9.—Admiral Keppel.
„ „ 17.—The General, Lord Albemarle.
„ „ 231.—*The Monastery, Medmenham Abbey,
     Bucks.*
Volume IV., Page 134.—Churchill, the Poet.
„ „ 202.—Kidgell.
„ „ 211.—Wilkes, his " Essay on Woman."
„ „ 215.—Lord March.
„ „ 217.—Lord Sandwich.

There is little doubt in the editress's mind that the virtuoso in
volume i. page 91, was Henry Constantine Jennings, of Shiplake
Court, Oxon, who collected every description of curiosity, from
statuary and pictures to shells and other objects of natural history.
No doubt Mrs. Powys, being on very friendly terms with his second
wife, omitted his name in the list, either out of respect to her, or
as a fact patent to herself.

NOTE IV.—(Page 118.)

WEST WYCOMBE CHURCH.

The final break up of the sham Franciscan Monks of Medmen-ham Abbey took place in 1762. One reason for the dissolution of the "Hell Fire Club," as it was called, doubtless was the growing scandal of their mysterious rites in the neighbourhood, culminating with the adventure and escape of the monkey, dressed as the Devil, described in volume iii. of "Chrysal."

But this same year, Sir Francis Dashwood was made Chancellor of the Exchequer; he also succeeded to the title of Lord Le De-spencer—probably the feeling of *noblesse oblige* would press more heavily upon him. He had commenced the restoration of the church tower of West Wycombe Church in the previous year, and on October 25, 1761, the peal of six bells announced its completion. This tower is surmounted by a low spire, on the top of which is a hollow ball, with seats round the interior to hold twelve persons; the only access to this is from a ladder outside. A portion of the tower, and chancel, of the church is old. To join these, Sir Francis Dashwood built a nave, which resembles more closely a ballroom than a church; the pulpit and reading-desk are arm-chairs, with book-stands in front, mounted on simulated low chests of drawers which draw out, forming steps. The font, the size of a basin, has three doves perched on it, whilst a serpent is represented climbing the pillared stem. The wooden seats or forms were mov-able, and in each window the sills were formed into cupboards. Outside, on the north wall of the church, was painted a fresco of St. Lawrence, the church's patron saint, grilling on a gridiron, with these words, "Though I give my body to be burned and have not charity, it profiteth me nothing." Also, to the south stood a sun-dial with this text, "Keep thy tongue from evil-speaking, lying, and slandering." And it is quite possible these texts were placed there to rebuke those who may have exaggerated the dissipations carried on at Medmenham. The church was finished in 1763. The mausoleum, described by Mrs. Powys, witnessed a curious scene on August 16, 1775, when the heart of Paul Whitehead, which he had left to Lord Le Despencer, was deposited there. Whitehead died December 30, 1774. Why the heart was not buried before, is a mystery. Anyhow, a comic funeral was held. The Bucks militia, with a band of flutes, French horns, bassoons, &c., attended in procession. The heart, placed in a marble urn covered with crape, was placed in a niche of the mausoleum, three volleys were fired, and a merry time of feasting held afterwards.

Lipscomb says in his "History of Buckinghamshire," the heart was stolen from the urn in 1839, despite the inscription on the urn :—

> " Unhallowed hands this gem forbear,
> No gems or orient spoil,
> Lie here conceal'd, but what's more rare,
> A heart that knew no guile."

In Chambers's "Book of Days" it states, under the church at West Wycombe, half-way down the hill, is a door leading to a long subterranean passage, uniting a series of caves, divided into several parts by columns left in the chalk. These are said to have been excavated by Lord Le Despencer. In the middle is a pool of water, called the Styx, said formerly to have been deeper, and only to be crossed by a boat ; now it is bridged by stepping-stones, leading to a large, lofty, circular cave, from the roof of which is a hook for hanging a lamp. In these caves it is asserted the club held their meetings after the break up at Medmenham.

The principal members of the community at Medmenham were—

President, Sir Francis Dashwood, afterwards Lord Le Despencer.
Sir John Dashwood King, Lord Le Despencer's half-brother, the last survivor of the Club.
Earl of Sandwich.
Hon. Bubb Doddington.
Selwyn.
John Wilkes.
Lord Melcombe Regis.
Sir William Stanhope.
Charles Churchill, poet.
Paul Whitehead, poet, and secretary.
Robert Lloyd, poet.
Henry Lovibond Collins.
Dr. Ben Bates,
Sir John d'Aubrey, only present a few times at meetings, as too young.

The cradle that Wilkes is said always to have slept in at Medmenham was still in existence there when Miss Berry visited Mrs. Scott, of Danesfield, in 1811.

NOTE V.—(Page 130.)

In Bitterley Church, Salop, the parish Henley Hall is situated in, are the tablets of Thomas Powys of Snitton, who died on November 19, 1639, and his wife Elizabeth, daughter of Richard Smyth of Credenhill, in the county of Hereford, who died July 1, 1645, placed to their memory by their son, Thomas Powys of Henley Hall, together with his own, and his two wives.

Thomas of Henley Hall died April 21, 1671, his first wife, Anne Littleton, daughter of Sir Adam Littleton, of Stoke Milborough, Salop, died June 30, 1655, and his second wife, Mary Cotes, died June 7, 1668.

Sir Littleton Powys, Thomas's illustrious eldest son, is also buried at Bitterley, together with his wife Agnes, née Carter. She died November 28, 1720, ætat 66; he survived her till March 13, 1731, ætat 85.

Sir Thomas Powys and his second wife, Elizabeth Meadowes, were originally buried at Lilford Church, Northamptonshire, but the first Baron Lilford, pulled Lilford Church down in 1778, and removed the bodies of his great-grandfather and his second wife, together with the monument, to Thorpe Achard Church, Oundle, a joint parish to Lilford. Sir Thomas's first wife, Sarah Holbeach, dying before he bought Lilford of the Elmes family, was buried at Mollington, Warwickshire, her maiden home. The monument to Sir Thomas is in white marble in classic style, representing him by a semi-recumbent figure, clad in the robes of a judge of the Queen's Bench. On either side of him are two upright female figures; at the head, one symbolical of religion; at the feet, another intended to represent eloquence. The sculptor's name was Robert Handstow; the elaborate inscription is from the pen of Matthew Prior, as follows:—

"Here lies interred Sir Thomas Powys, Knt., second son of Thomas Powys of Henley, in the Co. of Salop, Sergeant at Law, and Anne, daughter of Sir Adam Littleton of Stoke, Milborough, in the said Co. By his first wife, Sarah, daughter of Ambrose Holbeach of Mollington in the Co. of Warwick, he had 3 sons, Thomas, Edward, and Ambrose; and 3 daughters, Sarah, Anne, and Jane. By his second wife, Elizabeth, daughter of Sir Philip Meadowes, Knt., he had two sons, both named Philip. He was appointed Solicitor General in 1686, Attorney General 1687, Premier Sergeant at Law 1702, one of the Judges of the Queen's Bench 1713. He died the 4th of April 1719, aged 70.

" As to his profession :

" In accusing, cautious; in defending, vehement; in all his pleadings, sedate, clear, and strong; in all his decisions, unprejudiced and equitable. He studied, practised, and governed the law in such a manner that nothing equalled his knowledge, except his eloquence; nothing excelled both, except his justice; and whether he was greater as an advocate, or a judge, is the only cause he left undecided.

" As to his life :

" He possessed by a natural happiness all those civil virtues which form the Perfect Gentleman. And to those by Divine goodness were added that fervent zeal, and extensive charity, which distinguished the Perfect Christian.

" The tree is known by its fruits : He was a loving husband and indulgent father, a constant friend, and a charitable patron, frequenting the devotions of the Church, pleading the cause, and relieving the necessities of the poor. What by his example he taught throughout his life, at his death, he recommended to his family and his friends.

> " To fear God and live uprightly,
> Let whosoever reads this stone
> Be wise and be instructed."

Dame Elizabeth Powys died at Lilford, December 4, 1728, and was buried by the side of Sir Thomas on December 12, 1728.

NOTE VI.—(Page 214.)

NOTES ON THE ALTERATIONS MADE AT HARDWICK

After the cessation of the Civil War, Anthony Lybbe, as mentioned before, rebuilt the river front of the house facing south, called in a deed, dated September 11, 1672, "The New Building," also he made " the garden called the lower garden joining the rest of the New Building, and of the Mote going to the said lower garden, and of all the orchards called the New Orchards, lying between the ancient east wall of the capital messuage, and nye the field there called Culverfield, and of the new erected summer-house, and banqueting house there, lately built at the north-west corner of the said new orchard, and of all the stables and haylofts, lately also erected by the said Anthony Lybbe, in the yard house a back court out of the said messuage, and called by the names of the 'New Stables' there."

The next alterations are from a book of memorandums of Mrs. Richard Lybbe (*née* Twysden):—

"1718.—The two south windows by the great parlour sashed, gates and palisades at the lower end of the walk to the river made.

"1719.—A turret built over the cloister passage with a clock.

"1720.—A new walk made down the middle of the great orchard ; a garden plat made at the end of the summer-house.

In 1755 Mr. Powys, father-in-law of our Mrs. Philip Lybbe Powys, put up a billiard-table "in the room next the old drawing-room."

In Mrs. Philip Lybbe Powys's Diary occurs : "Alterations made at Hardwick from 1765."

"As 'tis most likely no further improvements will be made by us at present at Hardwick, I shall set down from a little book what trifling things were done there, as I always made memorandums of them, as my father Powys used to do, as I find it pleasing by such notes to recollect how things were formerly :—

"In 1766 my brother, Captain Richard Powys, and myself began the Menagerie ; 'twas where before was called the Wilderness Walk.

"1767.—The cut laurel hedge, parallel to the gravel terrace, we let grow up rude, taking away every other tree, and planted the ever-greens now there, as there were no evergreens in the pleasure garden, but the above straight laurel hedge, and old yew arbour, and high yew hedge from that to the bird-house, or place for canary birds.

"1768.—Cut down the above yew hedge, opened arches in the yew arbour, which before was entirely close, except a small arch at each end, and as it stood by itself was called 'the hearse' ; but as 'twas a favourite place of my father's, we would not cut it down, but by opening, and planting about[1] it, made it look tolerable. Made that year my flower-garden, just by the Menagerie.

"1769.—Planted the weeping willows by the canal, made the rusticated stone-work, and planted to hide the ditches, laid the lower part of the pleasure-ground down in grass, and planted single trees. It was before a vineyard, currants and gooseberries, &c.

"1771.—Took down paling that inclosed the woods in circles on the lawn, in front of the house, put the fences, and Dutch stiles, farther back out of sight, cleared the underwood to show the stems of the

---

[1] This is now a long tunnelled arbour, with seats each side.

beech-trees, which before were not seen from the windows, as the paling and underwood came down on each side, even with the old hawthorn now standing. The grove gate which was down there, removed to the chalk-pit; by these alterations the fine natural clump shows itself, under which is a root bench.

" 1772.—Laid the green slope before the breakfast parlour window into the pleasure garden by taking down a wall, and high yew hedge which divided them. The single yew-tree now standing, was the uppermost one of the hedge, which with the wall went down from that to the canal, where a necessary house, answering to the chicken-house now stands behind the shrubs on the opposite side, which were that year planted against the wall by the farm-yard, and a water-closet made amongst those trees.

" The white Chinese railing all taken away, and a green rail run across the avenue.

" 1774.—Built part of a new high wall in the kitchen-garden by the melon ground. It is to be returned up the hill, to meet the upper wall. (*N.B.* — Was done June 1788.) Forty-six walnut trees were cut down that year in the approach to the house, and by grubbing up a hedge on the other side laid the two fields together, the road only between them. New fancy gates at each end, a clump planted at the farther one, and a grass walk made round Culmar Field. Planted shrubs and evergreens on the outside of the garden wall, from the Ha-ha to the garden, close by the bird-house, and a sand walk thro' the shrubberies. The wall from the Ha-ha to the canal, intended to be pulled down.

" 1775.—In September planted round the outside of the lower wall in the kitchen-garden in Gittam Field, to hide the outhouses, barns, &c., from the Whitchurch road. Filled up a very deep hole by the housekeeper's room window, in the pleasure ground, and turf'd it.

" 1776.—Put up new white gates at each end of Gittam; planted off the road by short white posts; planted a clump of evergreens at the farther gate, and at the lower corner a clump of Lombardy poplars. The latter were all stolen, and the former eat by cattle.

" 1778.—Planted a clump of those poplars on our sandhills, Goring Heath, by the clump of firs. These firs are now seen from Shotover Hill, near Oxford, and look well from the Bath road just beyond Reading, where is a pretty view of Hardwick woods. If the poplars grow there, they will be seen to great advantage very soon, as I measured some I've planted which grew about six feet in one year.

2 B

"1778.—This year, by my mother's generosity, we made some alterations in the house—viz. lower'd the large bow-window in the brown wainscot drawing-room, new framed and glazed it, and the same in the room under it, which was then Mr. Powys's study ; but by taking in two closets, which makes a recess for the sideboard, and putting up a new chimney-piece, it now makes a useful eating-room. (*N.B.*—The above only cost £100.)

"1779.—New painted the stucco parlour, and great staircase.

"1783.—Pulled down that part of the pleasure garden wall before mentioned, opposite my dressing-room window, from the bottom of the gravel walk to the canal, continued on the Ha-ha to the clump at bottom, and put up the white pillar which was one of those at the old Ha-ha, formerly belonged to iron gates there, as I've heard my father Powys say, though never was the approach to the house. Could it be made so, and the stucco parlour as the hall, 'twould be much more eligible than at present, as the entrance is the worst part of the house.

"1782.—Pulled down the old summer-house, or canary bird house as 'twas called, and built on the same spot a greenhouse, 27 feet long, 12 wide, 10 high. Put no windows till the next year, as we waited for the old sashes from the breakfast parlour. We this year made a doorway thro' a closet in our bed-chamber into the small room adjoining, which we now paper'd, and put up a new bed, fitting it up for Caroline, and that year new painted the front bed-chamber, paper'd the closet within it, new papered the billiard-room and the mahogany bedroom and closet.

"1783.—Put new sashes, and lower'd the windows of the break-fast parlour, and to make it uniform in the front to the river, lower'd and new sash'd the passage windows, and one in the study.

"1784.—The underwood of Vachel's Walk cut down, as it always is every seven years. If we had stayed at Hardwick. we talk'd of grubbing it up, and lay it in a grass slope from Straw Hall, instead of the present close walk from the Dutch Stile, leaving single trees and clumps on the hill, as the present straight walk between the cut hedge to Straw Hall looks too formal. New fenced round the Menagerie this year."

Mrs. Powys adds a little note later to say the Menagerie was destroyed. It seems to have contained choice trees, as she had chairs made for Hardwick from wood of the trees "in the Menagerie," which cost four guineas and a half each to make.

Why the poplars were stolen, was because they were then almost unknown in this country. The first Lombardy poplar was brought by Lord Rochford in his carriage from Italy to General Conway, and planted by him at Park Place, Berks. This was only a few years before, and it is probable the Powys, obtained their plants from General Conway, their intimate friend.

In 1838 and 1839 Mr. Henry Philip Powys, grandson of our Mrs. Powys, on coming into possession of Hardwick at his father's decease, had the walls scraped of the whitening, which the bad taste of a preceding generation had placed over the grand old red bricks. The Elizabethan grand staircase also freed from a disfigurement of white paint ; a colonnade on north side of the house removed, and many other alterations, taking out what French windows had been placed in lieu of mullioned ones, restoring the mullions, and placing sashes between them.

Since the long tenancy of Mr. W. Day Rose a wing with a fine billiard-room, and bedrooms over, stables, tennis-house, lodges, &c., have been built by him ; but all these improvements belong to a far later date than our narrative, therefore for space' sake, must be only glanced at here.

NOTE VII.—(Page 229.)

HON. MRS. DAMER.

Anne Conway, the only child, and heiress of General Conway by his marriage with Lady Ailesbury, was born in 1748.

Horace Walpole, cousin of her father, stood as her godfather, and from infancy she was his pet and plaything. She early showed remarkable quickness of intelligence.

When quite a child, laughing at a model of an Italian street artist, she was reproved by David Hume, he telling her she could not make a similar. She immediately set to work to model a head in wax, which she afterwards reproduced in stone. She had lessons from Ceracchi, and Bacon ; she also studied anatomy under Cruikshank. On June 14, 1767, she married John Damer, eldest son of Joseph Damer, Lord Milton, afterwards Earl of Dorchester. The marriage turned out a very unhappy one. Mr. Damer was a wild, dissolute spendthrift. He, and his brothers contracted a debt of £70,000, and on their father refusing to pay, Mr. Damer shot himself on August 15, 1776, at the "Bedford Arms," in Covent Garden, after a riotous supper with boon companions. He was only thirty-two, and heir to £22,000 a year. Horace Walpole remarks of this affair : " £5000 a year in present, and £22,000 in reversion, are not, it would seem, sufficient for happiness, and cannot check a pistol."

Mrs. Damer was left with a jointure of £2500; she now devoted herself to her favourite art of sculpture.

In 1779 she was taken prisoner by a privateer, as she was on her way to Jersey, to her father, General Conway, then Governor of the island, but was allowed eventually to proceed to him. The two heads of "Thamesis and "Isis" on Henley Bridge, the latter a portrait of her friend, Miss Freeman of Fawley Court, were executed in 1785. To these were added a dog, for which she was highly honoured by the Academy of Florence. An osprey eagle which stood in the gallery at Strawberry Hill, and under which Horace Walpole fondly inscribed, "Non me Praxiteles pinxit, sed Anna Damer." Three busts of Nelson; one she presented to William IV., now at Windsor; one is in the Council Chamber of the Guildhall, London. A bust of Charles James Fox (her intimate friend), which she gave to Napoleon; he in return gave her a snuff-box with his portrait set in diamonds. Besides these she executed a statue of George III., busts of Queen Caroline, Lady E. Foster, Lady Melbourne, Lady Ailesbury (her mother), Miss Farren, Miss Berry, &c., &c. In the journal of Miss Berry will be found a number of letters from Mrs. Damer, and to her.

Horace Walpole left her Strawberry Hill with all its contents. On the death of Lady Ailesbury, her mother, who resided with her, Mrs. Damer, finding it lonely, in 1812 resigned the house and property, together with £2000 per annum left to keep it up, to the next heir, Lord Waldegrave, and in 1818 bought York House, Twickenham. On May 28, 1828, she died, and was buried at Sundridge, Kent. She desired her working tools, apron, and the ashes of her favourite little dog "Fidèle," to be buried with her. "Combe Bank," in the parish, had long been in possession of the Argyll family. Her mother was buried at Sundridge, in a tomb designed by Mrs. Damer. Her own tablet is in the chancel of the church, and bears this inscription—

Hic propre jacet
Uno chara cum matre loco,
ANNA SEYMOUR DAMER,
Sculptrix et Statuaria, Illustris Femina,
Henrici Seymour Conway, et Carolina Campbell, Filia.

NOTE VIII.—(Page 254.)

LORD BARRYMORE.

Richard Barry, Viscount Buttevant, was the son of Richard Barry, sixth Earl of Barrymore, by his wife, Lady Emilia Stanhope, third daughter of William, Earl Harrington. He was born August 14, 1769. His father dying when he was four years old, he succeeded to the title and family estates of Castle Lyons, Rath Cormack, Ireland, &c. He had a sister, Caroline, a year older than himself, afterwards Comtesse de Melfort, and two younger brothers, Henry and Augustus. When old enough for a tutor, his mother placed him with the Rev. John Tickell (afterwards rector of Gawsthorpe, Cheshire, and East Mersey, Kent), at Wargrave-on-Thames, under whose tutelage he remained till his fourteenth year. His attachment to his old tutor and his wife, who remained living at Wargrave, probably led him in after life to frequent that village, where he lived in what is still called "Barrymore House," now the property of the famous traveller, Frederick Selous, Esq. Mrs. Tickell was the sister of Mrs. Hill, wife to Joseph Hill, owner of Wargrave Hill, the beloved friend of the poet Cowper, who in his poetical epistle addressed to him, describes him as—

> "An honest man, close-buttoned to the chin,
> Broad cloth without, and a kind heart within."

Lady Barrymore died in 1780, when her son was only eleven. At fourteen he went to Eton. On going there, his grandmother, the Countess of Harrington, presented him with a cheque for £1000 for pocket-money, a most injudicious gift, which probably laid the seeds of his future extravagance, as from his former tutor and his amiable, simple-minded wife, it is not likely he could have acquired extravagant habits. His grandmother dying soon after, he was henceforth master of his own destiny. In Anthony Pasquin's "Life of Lord Barrymore," is a portrait of him; an elegant-looking young man, with regular, agreeable features, an aquiline nose, a high intellectual-looking forehead, his hair brushed straight back, and with a generally amiable expression. Doubtless had he lived longer, the extravagance of youth, and follies induced by the roistering company he frequented, would have been toned down, and he would have eventually settled into a useful, perhaps intellectual, member of society. The freaks he now entered on were more the follies of a boy than a man ; such as he, and his brothers changing the different inn signs at night, so that the landlord of the " Red Dragon," say, would wake some morning to see the sign of the " Black Bull " from miles off, dangling as his sign-board ! They would lash the windows with their whips in the night, so as to break them. One favourite freak was to offer to send friends to London, or elsewhere, by one of his own carriages, he, and a brother slyly substituting themselves for the postillions, and then needlessly bump and charge the banks *en route*, when the inside passengers would cry for mercy. Lord Barrymore would sometimes place himself in his carriage, and imitate the cries of a female in distress, to the curiosity, and amazement of the people on the way. On the islands near Wargrave, and in the woods, he and his merry companions would have wine, &c., buried, and then make picnics to some spot where a *cache* existed, dig up the " Falernian." and make a feast. Barrymore House consisted mainly then of two long rooms, called the " Upper," and " Lower Barracks." Anthony Pasquin tells us, along these, hammocks were slung, as many as twenty guests at a time in the house, and no good inn then in Wargrave. Woe betide the man who sought his hammock before the conventional late morning hour, before the rest ; he was condemned to condign punishment, administered by a mock court of justice.

From early youth Lord Barrymore had showed an aptitude for music, and improvisation, and a great partiality for the stage. At eighteen he began theatricals at Wargrave in a barn, and subsequently erected the theatre mentioned in these pages. He now proceeded to every extravagance, money could be spent on ; following his injudicious friend, Sir John Lade's foolish conduct in raising money by help of the Jews, &c., on a fortune of £4000 per annum, with £100,000 ready money on his attaining his majority. His favourite sentence was " D—— the expense ! "

He bought from Henry Constantine Jennings, the celebrated virtuoso of Shiplake Court, Oxon, a pack of hounds ; purchased some stags for hunting. Hounds and horses, together with his carriages, were kept at Twyford, no adequate stables being at Wargrave. Four negroes in scarlet and silver, proficient on the French horn, accompanied the pack. His strings of horses, and splendid equipages rivalled the stable establishment of Chantilly. He, and " Pasquin," alias his friend J. W. Williams, delighted in painting the harness, and coach-panels with crests, coats of arms, and other devices.

In 1787 he commenced his turf career, in which he showed great discrimination as to horse-flesh, and won numerous races,

riding himself. His racehorses were kept at Newmarket, under
Perren. A list of them, and their achievements, would take too long
here. He was an eminent whip, and would often drive a coach-and-
four from Wargrave to Newmarket, or the reverse, starting in the
middle of the night; but, like many Jehus, he disliked trusting another
man with the "ribbons," and having once been upset with Captain
Taylor in Wargrave in a post-chaise, he ever after had a horror
of being driven.

Unfortunately addicted to quinze, loo, &c., he frequently lost
large sums at the tables. He had also a passion for the pugilistic
art, and enlisted in his service a tinman, called Hooper, who, though
a small man, not much over 11 stone weight, beat men of much
larger proportions. At one time Lord Barrymore had six pugilists
put up at his expense at the "George and Dragon," Wargrave.
He was a splendid swordsman, taking lessons from Angelo.

His stage expenses must have been enormous, as besides the
actors enumerated in these pages, many other professional celebri-
ties acted for him. Delphini, the famous clown of Covent Garden,
became his stage-manager, living at what is now called "The Croft,"
Wargrave. So liberal was he, that every bargeman who passed, was
treated to unlimited Burgundy. Good-natured, too, for in some
curious old letters found many years ago in the roof of Wargrave
Hill (in possession of the editress), from Mrs. Tickell to her sister,
Mrs. Hill, when in London, frequent mention is made of his con-
veying fish, parcels, &c., to and fro between the sisters by his coach.
Through Mrs. Hill, he was one of the earliest subscribers to Cowper's
poems.

Nothing seemed to upset his good-humour. His ridiculous pet
chorus of "Chip chow, cherry chow, fol de riddleido," seems to
have been at any moment on his lips, even at the end of a duel,
where his opponent,[1] appearing in a ridiculous costume, excited his
laughter. Harmless shots were fired, and the belligerents left the field
arm in arm, he singing the above! His entertainments were most
costly—thirty shillings a head for a supper by D'Aubigné; £1500
a night at Wargrave at times; two entertainments at Ascot races in
1791 cost 1700 guineas, given for the Prince of Wales, who eventually did not come!

A forest Catch Club, instituted by him, met the first Friday in
the month at the "Rose Inn," Wokingham.

In 1791 he contested the election at Reading, against Mr.
Neville of Billingbear, but lost it. His pecuniary difficulties in-

[1] Mr. Howarth.

creased, so his property was sequestrated, the last two years Mr. Hammersley, the banker, making him an allowance of £2500 out of it. In the spring of 1792 his house in Piccadilly, was sold to the Duke of Queensberry, better known as "Old Q."; his theatre at Wargrave, in October the same year; yet we find him playing within a few days of the latter in a cricket match of Wargrave and Twyford gentlemen, against Wokingham, for 100 guineas.

He, and his brother Augustus, both entered the Berkshire Militia, and in March 1793 Lord Barrymore was marching at the head of a party of French prisoners from Rye to Dover, pausing for refreshment at a little public-house at Folkestone. He called to his servant, to give him a lift in his curricle, which had been following. He gave the servant his gun, loaded with swan-shot, with which he had been shooting seagulls : this was placed in a careless way between his legs; it discharged, shooting Lord Barrymore in the head. He lived for only forty minutes after, and was buried at Wargrave on March 17, 1793, thus ending his short career in his twenty-fourth year.

Augustus Barry immediately resigned his commission in the Berks Militia. Henry Barry succeeded to his brother's title. He married, but died without children in 1823. With him the title was extinct, Augustus having predeceased him.

For more particulars of Lord Barrymore's life, see his Life by Anthony Pasquin, alias J. D. Williams, written in 1793, and "Last of the Earls of Barrymore," by John R. Robinson.

INDEX

Abbots Bromley, 359
Ailesbury, Lady, 112, 182, 223-225, 229, 235, 284, 323
Aldith, 100
Alexander, Bishop of Lincoln, 16
Alfred's Tower, 170, 171
All Souls' College, 41
Alum Bay, 273
Amesbury Hill, 49, 173, 174
Andover, 61
Annesley, 195, 196, 216, 238, 251, 253, 278
Ascot, 282
Ashburton, 70, 77
Assembly Rooms, York, 17
Atkyns, 287
Atkyns, Wright, 290, 349, 361, 366
Axminster, 65, 78

Badgemore, 240
Bailey, Mr., 336
Baker, Mr., 93
Baldock, 14
Baltimore, Lord, 151
Bamfield, Mr., 161
Bank Paper, 164
Barham Downs, 307
Barleborough Hall, 27
Barrymore, Earl of, 188, 238, 239, 244, 246-250, 254
Barton Mills, 2
Bateman, Lord, 130
Bath, 50, 214, 225, 288, 291-293, 299, 324-328, 332, 349, 351-353, 357, 362, 363
Bayham, Lord, 226, 229, 234
Beaconsfield, 121
Beckford, Alderman, 166
Beckford, Mr., 166, 167
Bedford, Duke of, 9
Bedford, General, 113

Beenham, 8-10, 60
Belchier, Mr., 34
Bell Inn, Henley, 179
Belton House, 16
Belvidere, 150
Bensington, 35
Berins Hill, 35
Berthier, General, 346
" Betty, Master," 363
Bevis, Mount, 269
Birches, 234
Birt, Mr., 20, 123
Bisham Abbey, 237
Blandford, 63
Blandy, Miss, 38
Blenheim Palace, 43-45, 124, 197
Bletchingdon, 194-196, 198, 200, 216, 238, 321
Blickling, 211, 212
Blount's Court, 153
Blount, Sir Walter, 132, 140, 338
Blundell, Mr., 346
Blythe River, 334, 327
Bolney Court, 179
Bolton, Duchess of, 247
Bolton, Duke of, 80
Bonaparte, Napoleon, 346
Boston, Lord, 113, 202
Bowles, Mr., 137, 138, 141
Brading, 265
Brand, 2, 3
Bramshill, 115
Bridport, 65
Bristol, 49, 152, 251
Bristol, Dean of, 235, 242
British Museum, 57
Broadstairs, 311
Broadway Hill, 46
Brook, Lord, 341
Brown, " Capability," 145, 148, 195, 299

Brunswick, Princess of, 150
Bryanston Park, 64
Buckingham, 154
Buckingham Palace, 116, 117
Bucklebury, 8
Bulmarsh Heath, 329
Bulstrode, 120, 121
Burford, 141
Burleigh, 14, 15
Byng, Admiral, 13

CADOGAN, Lord, 60, 155, 213, 216
Camden, Lord, 120, 122, 179, 185, 187, 188, 190, 191, 201, 222, 249, 284, 286, 289, 305, 348
Cannock Hills, 339
Canterbury, 229-320, 346, 347, 368
Canterbury, Dean of, 295, 296, 297, 303, 316, 320, 332, 368
Carlisle, Earl of, 19
Carrington, Lord, 356
Carr, Mrs., 326, 327
Castle Howard, 18, 19
Catalani, Angelica, 366, 367
Catherine, Empress, 6, 212
Caversham Park, 60, 161, 162
Charles I., 102-105
Charles II., 66, 176, 256
Charlotte, Queen, 90, 92, 159
Chatham, Lord, 261
Chatsworth, 28, 29
Chaucer, 45, 242, 243
Cheltenham, 48
Cherbourg Cannon, 33
Chesterfield, 25, 26
Chesterfield, Earl of, 13
Chesterford, 2, 12
Child, Mrs., 230
Chilterns, 215
Christchurch College, 35, 36
Chute, Chaloner, 203, 204
Chute, Mr., 203, 204, 213
Clarendon Printing House, 40, 41
Clayton, Lady Louisa, 217-219
Clayton, Mr., 118
Clifden, 285
Coke, Lord, 11
Coleraine, Lord, 161
Coley, 246
Conway, General, 111, 112, 173, 214, 223, 232, 238, 245, 247, 251, 284, 334

Conyngham, Mrs., 128-143
Cooper, Gislingham, 240
Cooper, Miss, 248, 252, 263, 266, 269
Cooper, Rev. Dr., 248, 263, 275
Cooper, Rev. Edward, 250, 270 et seq.
Cope, Sir John, 115, 116
Cope, Sir Richard, 230
Cornwallis, Lord, 261
Coronation of George III., 87-93
Corsham, 202
Court, at, 151
Court of Hill, 127-144
Cowes, 257, 258
Creuzé, Mr., 205, 206
Crowsley Park, 287
Culham Court, 123, 247-249, 252-253, 254, 283, 356
Culham House, 153
Cumberland, Duke of, 9, 114, 249
Cumford, 31
Curzon, Lord, 339
Cust, Lady, 16

DAMER, Mrs., 224, 225, 232
Dance, Mr., 257
Darnley, Lady, 348
Darwin, Dr., 337
Dashwood, Sir James, 198, 200
Derby, 353, 354, 361
Derbyshire, 24-32
Despencer, Lord Le, 117, 118, 155, 156
Devonshire, 65-79
Dillon, Mr., 231
Dillon, Viscount, 199
Ditchley, 198, 199
Donellan, Mr., 274
Dorchester, 64
Doughty, Mr., 208
Dove Dale, 359, 360
Druid's Temple, 234
Dummer, Mr., 257
Dundas, Mr., 278
Dunstable, 33
Dutton, Mr., 351

EASTBURY, 62, 63
Edgecumbe, Lord, 70, 71
Edgecumbe, Mount, 71-73
Egginton, 340
Elizabeth, Room of Queen, 109, 110

Elmes Family, 95
Englefield, Sir Henry, 182, 189
Erskine, Lord Chancellor, 336
Evesham, Vale of, 46, 47, 125
Ewelme, 242, 243
Ewer, Miss, 194
Ewer, Mr., 310, 317 *et seq.*
Exeter, 66-69

FAIRMILE, 359
Fane, Lady Elizabeth, 344
Farrar, Dean, 304
Farren, Miss, 231
Fawley Court, 97, 145-148, 177, 185-188, 216, 229, 237, 240, 284, 329
Fawley Rectory, 123, 214-216, 240, 371
Ferne, Bishop of, 364
Ferrers, Earl, 56
Fitzclarence, Lord Augustus, 105
Fleming, Mr., 257
Fonthill, 166, 167
Freeman, Mrs. Sambrook, 145, 147, 148, 182, 185, 216-220, 235, 237, 246, 363
Freeman, Sambrook, 145-149, 182, 185-187, 221
Freeman, Strickland, 367, 369
French Prisoners, 74
Frost, Severe, 156-158, 280

GAINSBOROUGH, 233, 240
Galloway, Lady, 198
Garrick, 183, 336
Gay, 243
George II., death of, 57
George III., 58, 59, 152
George III., coronation of, 87-92
"George, Royal," 73
Giardini, 161
Girle, Miss, 33, 93
Girle, Mr., 80, 371
Girle, Mrs., 46, 122, 214, 344, 345, 368, 370
Gibbons, Grinling, 37
Glasshampton, 126
Gloucester, 48
Gloucester, Prince William of, 304, 307, 316-319.
Goring Spring, 275
Gosport, 81, 82, 84

Grandison, Lady, 178, 180, 181, 188
Grandison, Sir Charles, 128
Gregory, Colonel, 350
Grose, Sir Nash, 200
Grote, Mr., 277
Guerre, La, 44
Guildford, 84, 85

HAGLEY, 338
Hallam, Dr., 242
Halls of Harpsden Court, 290, 330, 331
Hammond, Dr., 8
Hamstall Ridware, 330, 334, 335, 343, 344, 353, 359, 360, 361, 367
Hanger, Mr., 161
Hardwick Hall, 26, 27
Hardwick House, 97-111, 214, 215
Hare, Sir Thomas, 11
Harleyford, 118, 119
Harpsden, 297, 330, 331
Hatfield, 14
Heathcote, Miss, 352
Heathcote, Sir William, 257
Heckfield, 61, 163, 236
Hedsor, 113
Hendon, 167
Henley, 187, 188, 228, 229, 240, 250, 253 277, 279, 321, 330
Henley Hall, 130, 131
Henley Park, 217-220
Heythrop, 199, 200
High Tor, 31, 32
Hill, Mr., 127, 129, 132, 135, 139, 141
Hill, Mrs., 128, 131, 132, 136, 138, 142, 143, 295
Hoare, Mr., 168-73
Hodges, Miss, 182-184
Hodges, Mr., 179, 181, 190
Holkham, 5, 9, 10, 11, 212
Holly Copse, 105
Honiton, 60, 77, 78
Houghton Hall, 6, 7, 212, 213
Hoveden, 208
Howman, Rev. Arthur, 290, 348, 349
Hundred House, 126
Hurley Priory, 175-177
Hursley, 257
Hurstbourne, 164
Hussey, Mr., 202

INNES, Mrs., 365
Ives, Mr., 211
Ivy Bridge, 70, 77

JACKSON, Major, 321
Jackson, Mr., 1-8, 10-12
James, Mr., 236, 244
Jeffreys, John, 120
Jennings, 164, 290, 346
Jennings, Miss, 297
Jerningham, Mr., 208
Jersey, Lady, 197
Jersey, Lord, 197
Jesse, Mr., 105
Jeston, Rev. Humphrey, 321
Jordan, Mrs., 248

KAUFFMAN, Angelica, 173
Kedleston, 361
Keeling, Mrs., 252, 253, 301
Kent, Mr., 205
Killala, Bishop of, 305
King, Mr., 356
King's Gate, 311
Knighton House, 260
Knole, 148-150

LANSDOWNE, Marquis of, 291
Laurence, the Painter, 358
Lavender Drops, 156, 159
Law Family, 283, 284, 286
Leatherhead, 84, 85
Leeds, 23
Lefevre, Mr., 236
Lefney House, 300, 301
Leicester, Lord, 8
Leigh Family, 287, 335
Lever, Sir Ashton, 225
Lichfield Cathedral, &c., 340-353
Lichfield, Lord, 199
Linley, Miss, 152, 153, 161
Linwood, Miss, 290, 300
Lloyd, Mrs, 208
Lombe, Mr. John, 354
Long, Mr. Walter, 364
Lovelace, Lord, 175-177
Lowestoffe, 211
Ludlow, 133-137
Lulsley, 371
Lutwyche, Mrs., 298, 302, 324, 327, 345
Lybbe Family, 95, 101-107, 109, 110

Lymington, 272, 273
Lynch, Dr., 306

MACARTNEY, Mrs., 327
Macclesfield, Lord, 181, 220, 269, 290
Magdalen College, 42
Maidenhead, 59
Malden, Lord, 183, 189, 191, 193
Malmesbury, Lady, 321-323
Malmesbury, Lord, 321, 349, 355
Malton, 18
Manchester, Duke of, 211
Mapledurham, 338
Margate, 310-312
Marlborough, Duke of, 43-45, 142, 143, 163, 252
Mary, Queen of Scots, 27, 353, 351
Matlock, 30-32, 359-361
Mawley, 139-141
Mayo, Miss, 327
Meadowes, Sir Philip, 107, 110
Meadowes, Sir Sidney, 276
Meath, Bishop of, 352
Mecklenburg, Princess Charlotte of, 87
Melcomb, Lord, 156
Mereworth, 151
Michell, Misses, 245, 247, 248, 254
Michell, Mr., 123
Micklem, Mrs., 288
Middleton Park, 197, 198
Mills, Mr., 192
Milnes, 19, 23, 308, 309
Milnes, Mr. Pem, 19, 23, 24
Mitford, 301
Molesworth, Miss, 222
Monkey Island, 113, 114
Montagu House, 57
Montagu, Lady Mary Wortley, 343
Montagu, Sir Charles, 178, 180
Mount Edgecumbe, 71-73
Mount, Mr., 34, 203
Morant, Edward, 272
Moravians, 20-23
Morten Henmarsh, 45
Museum, British, 57, 225
Museum, Oxford, 37, 38

NEEDWOOD FOREST, 336-338
Nelson, Lady, 327, 328
Nelson, Lord, 328, 330, 347
Newark, 16

New College, Oxford, 39, 40
New Forest, 271, 272
Newport, 258, 263, 264
Newport Pagnel, 33
Newton, Dr., 230
Nicholas, Isle of St., 73, 75
Norfolk Journal (first), 1-12
Norfolk Journal (second), 205-214
Norman, Mrs., 294

OBERNE, Bishop of Meath, 352
Oglander, Sir William, 265
Orkney, Lady, 115, 285
Osterley Park, 230, 231
Oxenden, Sir Harry, 315
Oxford, 35-42, 145
Oxford, Lord, 5-7, 212, 213, 350

PALGRAVE, Mr., 329-331
—— Miss, 329-331
Palmerston, Lady, 271, 272, 274
Palmerston, Lord, 270
Panes Hill, 194
Pantheon, 152
Pardoe Family, 133, 134, 143
Parker, Lady, 259, 264, 266
Parker, Sir Hyde, 257-263
Park Place, 111-113, 223-226, 234, 284, 287, 291, 321-323, 349
Peire, Marchioness de la, 329
Pembroke Family, 53, 54, 165, 166
Pembroke, Lady, 38, 89
Percy Family, 81-84
Phillips, Mr., 153
Piozzi, Mrs., 243
Pitt, Mr. George, 61, 93
Pitt, Mr. William, 64, 305, 307, 313
Pleydell, Mr., 64
Plymouth Journal, 59-85
Polygon, Southampton, 273
Pope, Sir Thomas, 37
Pope Sixtus, 172
Poore, Bishop, 62
Portsdown Hills, 84
Powney, Mrs., 226
Powys Family, 94-99, 107, 108, 110, 119, 120, 130, 131, 201, 220, 221, 223, 251, 367-373
Pratt, Mrs., 160, 185, 215, 222, 223
Price, Sir Charles, 153
Pump-room, Bath, 288, 294

QUAKERS, 144
Quarr Abbey, 265
Queen Charlotte, 87, 90, 92, 116, 117, 151, 152, 159, 217-220, 235, 241, 242, 295
Quin, 74, 75, 90

RADCLIFFIAN Library, 41, 42
Rainham Hall, 5
Ramsgate, 311-313, 347
Randolph, Dr., 328
Ranelagh, 240-242
Ranzini, 327
Reading, 35, 59-61, 157, 229, 234, 236, 245, 247, 249, 275
Remenham, 332, 363, 365
Rhodes, Mr., 27
Richmond, Duchess of, 224
Rivers, Lord, 93
Rochester, 320
Rock Family, 131
Rosehill, 123
Rougemont Castle, 69
Royal Academy, 122
Ryde, 257, 259, 260, 263, 264, 265, 268

SADLER'S Wells, 225
Saffron, 12
Salisbury, 61, 62
Salt Hill, 34
Saville, Rev. Mr., 343
Scarborough, 18, 19
Scarsdale, Lord, 360
Schutz, Mr., 121, 153
Scobel, Mr., 367
Seymour Portman, Mr., 64
Shaftesbury, 79
Shawe, Mr., 337, 338
Shelbourne, Lord, 155, 351
Sheridan, Mr., 233
Sheridan, Mrs., 161
Shiplake, 290, 287, 297, 348, 349, 359
Shire Stone, 46
Shotover, 121, 122
Shottesbrook, 119
Shottesbrook Park, 119
Shrewsbury, Earl of, 124, 199
Shrimpton, Mr., 251, 254, 291, 299, 308, 310, 320, 329, 331, 332, 346

Shrimpton, Mrs., 251, 315-317, 358
Shropshire Journal, 124-145
Shugborough, 338
Siddons, Mrs., 225, 231
Sidney, Sir Philip, 54
Simpson, Miss, 25
Simpson, Mr., 25
Slaney, Mr., 205, 207-209, 211, 213, 252
Slater, Miss, 19, 23, 31, 32
Slater, Mr., 23, 24, 38, 32
Slatter, Canon, 100
Sonning, 275, 276
Southampton, 257, 268, 269, 273-275
Spanish Ambassador's Fête, 241, 242
Spilman, Mr., 5, 7, 8
Staffordshire Journal, 333-344, 330, 351, 353
Stanford Court, 127
Stanhope, Sir William, 155
Stapleton, Bishop, 68
Stapletons of Greys, 252, 290
Stokes Bay, 82
Stonehenge, 51-53, 173, 174
Stonor Chapel, 340, 345, 346
Storace, Signora, 294
Stourhead, 163, 168-173
Stowe, 153, 154, 155
Strahen, Miss, 138
Strathfieldsaye, 93
Strawberryhill, 227, 228
"Straw Hall," 108, 115, 174
Strickland, Miss Caroline, 307
Stubbs, Rev. Mr., 359, 360
Stukeley, Dr., 51-53
Sturt, Miss, 241
Suffolk, Duchess of, 242, 243
Swaffham, 3
Swilaar Oak, 336, 337

Tallard, Marshal, 29, 45
Taplow, 115
Taylor, Dr., 321
Tessier, Mons., 183, 184, 189, 191
Thorley Hall, 2
Townsend, Lord, 3
Trinity College, Oxford, 37
Turner, Sir William, 7
Twysden, Lady, 110
Twysden, Miss, 177
Tyson, 292, 293, 325, 345

Urry, Mr., 273
Uttoxeter, 335, 359, 360

Vanderstegen, Mr., 296, 299
Vansittart, Colonel, 119
Vansittart, Mr. George, 237
Vaux Hall, 232
Villiers, Lady, 182, 187, 189, 190
Villiers, Lord, 178, 179, 181 183, 185-187, 189-192, 278
Vincent, St. Rock, 49
Vine, The, 203, 204

Wakefield, Town of, 19, 24
Wales, Dowager Princess of, 152
Wales, Prince of, 244, 245, 247, 250, 281, 282, 308
Wales, Princess of, 280-283
Walker, Dr., 259, 260
Waller, Mr., 121
Walpole, Horace, 74, 204, 227
Walpole, Lord, 8, 102
Walsingham Abbey, 5, 212
Walton Hall, 27
Wanstead House, 205
Wargrave, 244-247, 249, 250, 253
Warner, Lee, 5, 212
Wasing Place, 203, 230
Wenvo Castle, 20
Wesenham Hall, 3-6, 8, 11, 12
Westerton, 20
Westminster Abbey, 230
Westmoreland, Lord, 151, 156
West, Mr., 254, 288, 290, 299, 356, 357
West, Mrs., 254, 283
Weston, King's, 152
West Wycombe Church, 117, 118, 155, 156
Wheatley, Mr., 137, 148, 151, 301, 302
Whitchurch, 157
White, Mr., 269
"White Horse" Inn, Ipswich, 206
Whitelock, Mr. William, 177
Whitelock, Sir Bulstrode, 177
Wickham, 81
Wight, Journal of Isle of, 255-269, 271-273
Wilcox, Bishop, 175
Wilcox, Mr., 175
Wilkes, John, 266, 283

Wilkes, Miss, 266
Williams, Capt., 264, 265
Williams, Lady, 309
Williams, Mr., 248
Williams, Mrs., 175
Williams, Mr. Peers, 289   165, 166
Wilton House, 53, 54, 105, 106
Winchester, 80, 81, 255-257, 274
Windsor Castle, 115, 215, 234, 235, 285
Winford, Mrs., 202, 229, 248
Woburn, 33
Wolsby, Dr., 304, 305, 307, 308, 316, 317
Woodstock, 43, 100
Woolton Bridge, 258

Worcester, 46, 144
Wormsley, 285
Wright, Mrs., 153
Wroughton, Miss, 327, 352
Wykeham, William of, 256, 257

XIMENES, Mr., 249

YARMOUTH, 209-211
York, 16, 17
York, Duchess of, 292-294
York, Duke of, 291-294
Yorkshire Journal, 13-33

ZUCHELLI, 240

THE END

Lightning Source UK Ltd.
Milton Keynes UK
UKOW051438230712

196440UK00001B/107/P